PLATO REDISCOVERED

D1605562

Studies in Social, Political, and Legal Philosophy
General Editor: James P. Sterba, University of Notre Dame

This series analyzes and evaluates critically the major political, social, and legal ideals, institutions, and practices of our time. The analysis may be historical or problem-centered; the evaluation may focus on theoretical underpinnings or practical implications. Among the recent titles in the series are:

Moral Rights and Political Freedom
   by Tara Smith, University of Texas at Austin
Democracy and Social Injustice
   by Thomas Simon, Illinois State University
Morality and Social Justice: Point/Counterpoint
   by James P. Sterba, University of Notre Dame; Tibor Machan, Auburn University; Alison Jaggar, University of Colorado, Boulder; William Galston, White House Domestic Policy Council; Carol C. Gould, Stevens Institute of Technology; Milton Fisk, Indiana University; and Robert C. Solomon, University of Texas
Faces of Environmental Racism: Confronting Issues of Global Justice
   edited by Laura Westra, University of Windsor, and Peter S. Wenz, Sangamon State University
Plato Rediscovered: Human Value and Social Order
   by T. K. Seung, University of Texas at Austin
Punishment as Societal-Defense
   by Phillip Montague, Western Washington University
Liberty for the Twenty-First Century: Contemporary Libertarian Thought
   edited by Tibor R. Machan, Auburn University, and Douglas B. Rasmussen, St. John's University
Capitalism with a Human Face: The Quest for a Middle Road in Russian Politics
   by William Gay, University of North Carolina at Charlotte, and T. A. Alekseeva, Institute of Philosophy and Moscow State University

PLATO REDISCOVERED

Human Value and Social Order

T. K. Seung

ROWMAN & LITTLEFIELD PUBLISHERS, INC.

ROWMAN & LITTLEFIELD PUBLISHERS, INC.

Published in the United States of America
by Rowman & Littlefield Publishers, Inc.
4720 Boston Way, Lanham, Maryland 20706

3 Henrietta Street
London WC2E 8LU, England

British Cataloging in Publication Information Available

Library of Congress Cataloging-in-Publication Data
Seung, T. K.
Plato rediscovered : human value and social order / T.K.
Seung.
p. cm.
Includes bibliographical references and index.
1. Plato. 2. Philosophy, Ancient. 3. Political science—
Philosophy. I. Title.
B395.S38 1996 184—dc20 95-30781 CIP

ISBN 0–8476–8111–4 (cloth: alk. paper)
ISBN 0–8476–8112–2 (pbk.: alk. paper)

Printed in the United States of America

∞ TM The paper used in this publication meets the minimum requirements of
American National Standard for Information Sciences—Permanence of
Paper for Printed Library Materials, ANSI Z39.48–1984.

For

PONG SHIK KANG

My Mentor
and
My Friend for Life

Contents

Preface

Political philosophy is one of the great inventions by Plato's genius. Before this invention, there was nothing remotely resembling it. But ever since it has served preeminently as the paradigm for all political philosophers—from Aristotle and Cicero to Rousseau and Rawls. There is always a great story behind a great invention, but no one has yet told the story of how Plato came to make his invention. All we know is that it could not have been a simple affair. Plato formulates his political philosophy not once, but twice: first in the *Republic* and then in the *Laws*. Between these two long dialogues, he writes a much shorter work, the *Statesman*, which is an inquiry into the nature of statesmanship. These three works, known as Plato's political dialogues, have generated a series of tough questions. Why has he given us two versions of his political philosophy? What is the relationship between these two versions? Is the knowledge of Forms equally important for both versions? Where does the *Statesman* stand in relation to these two versions?

Although these questions have proven to be intractable, they may be only on the surface of the complicated story behind Plato's great invention. They have been raised and discussed, in general, on the natural but naive assumption that the construction of his political philosophy is restricted to the three political dialogues. That is, all his other dialogues are addressed to nonpolitical topics such as the immortality of the soul, the nature of love, and the theory of knowledge and Forms. This naive assumption has led to the firmly fixed practice of segregating political and nonpolitical dialogues in Plato scholarship. In this book, I contest this long-standing practice of segregation. I show that Plato introduces the nonpolitical topics for discussion not for their own sake, but as important steps in his relentless search for political art. The invention of political philosophy thus becomes his ultimate aim for writing both the political and the nonpolitical dialogues. We cannot truly understand the nature of his invention until we know the relevance of nonpolitical to political works.

Plato's invention takes place in two stages. The first stage opens with the *Gorgias* and leads to the birth of the *Republic*; the second stage begins with his critical review of the *Republic* and ends with its eventual revision in the *Laws*. In the *Gorgias*, Plato sets forth all the basic issues that will occupy his attention for the rest of his life. At the center of these issues stands the challenge of Callicles and his philosophy of power politics. To meet this challenge, Plato writes a series of dialogues that culminates in the *Republic*. The thematic connection of this dialogue to the *Gorgias* is indicated by Thrasymachus's outburst in the first book of the *Republic*. He aggressively restates Callicles' view of justice as the advantage of the stronger, which is further amplified by Glaucon and Adeimantus, and Socrates invites them to construct an ideal state to meet the Calliclean challenge in this amplified form.

The path from the *Gorgias* to the *Republic*, however, is neither direct nor straight; it goes through two sets of three dialogues each: (1) the *Lysis*, the *Phaedo*, and the *Symposium*, and (2) the *Protagoras*, the *Meno*, and the *Euthydemus*. The first set advocates the way of love, especially the love of wisdom (*philosophia*), which can be fulfilled only by fleeing from the world of phenomena to the world of Forms. This is the ascent to Platonic Heaven, which is celebrated in the *Phaedo* and the *Symposium*. In these dialogues, political philosophy is not even mentioned, because it is not necessary for the blessed life in the world of Forms. The ascent to Platonic Heaven, however, is not a proper way of meeting the challenge of Callicles. On the contrary, it is only an escape in disguise.

Realizing that the only proper response to the Calliclean challenge is to establish a just social order in the world of phenomena, Plato under-

takes the journey of descent from the world of Forms to the world of
phenomena. This journey is executed in the second set of three dialogues, in which the problem of civic virtue and political art becomes
his primary concern. For many readers, the central issue for the *Protagoras* and the *Meno* is supposed to be the question of whether virtue
can be taught. But the virtue in question is not any ordinary virtue but
civic virtue, which is identified as political art in the *Protagoras*, and
then defined as the master art that employs all other arts in the *Euthydemus*. This is the art of constructing and governing a just state, and Plato
presents his first exposition of this art in the *Republic*, which is his
initial formulation of political philosophy.

What happens after the *Republic* in Plato's thought? This is by far
the toughest question in Plato scholarship. It is widely believed that he
became highly critical of the metaphysical premise for the construction
of an ideal city in the *Republic*, especially his theory of Forms and
knowledge. In the *Parmenides* and the *Theaetetus*, he subjects it to careful scrutiny and rigorously exposes its deficiencies. Though many
scholars agree on this point, there is little agreement on what Plato has
allegedly done to improve his deficient theory, because his late dialogues are exceedingly difficult to interpret. In this volume, I interpret
those dialogues as a series of attempts to construct a new theory of
Forms and knowledge. In this new theory, Plato lays the foundation for
the composition of the *Laws*, which is his second formulation of political philosophy.

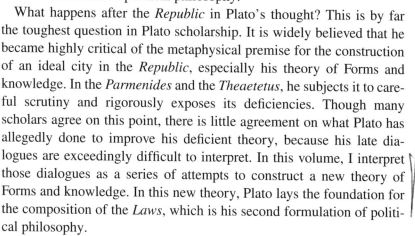

Plato's journey from the *Republic* to the *Laws* involves all the dialogues written between those two. Hence, it is an even more complicated maneuver than his journey from the *Gorgias* to the *Republic*.
These two journeys produce two different versions of Platonism, which
may be called the skyscraper and the bedrock versions. The skyscraper
version is given in the middle dialogues, and the bedrock version in the
late dialogues. The skyscraper version represents the Forms as concrete
paradigms. In the bedrock version, they are presented as no more than
abstract universals.

The skyscraper version paints a lavish picture of Platonic Heaven: it
is adorned with a complete system of normative rules and principles.
The bedrock version does not paint such a lavish picture, but makes the

modest claim that Platonic Heaven provides the basic normative ideals
and principles. The difference between these two versions may perhaps
be better explained in terms of modern mathematical Platonism. The
skyscraper version claims that Platonic Heaven contains the complete
edifice of mathematics from arithmetic and geometry to calculus and
topology. The bedrock version, on the other hand, holds that it contains
only the basic mathematical ideas, and that mathematical systems have
to be constructed from those ideas.

The skyscraper version of Platonism is clearly implausible; it has
long been an object of disbelief and derision. Felix Cohen called it
transcendental nonsense. This implausible theory of Forms has been
taken as the essence of Plato's philosophy, and Platonism in general
has been dismissed from the contemporary world of normative discourse. The skyscraper version, however, was not Plato's final position,
but only a way station to the bedrock version, which is far more plausible and resourceful than the earlier one. But this version has not been
clearly identified, largely because Plato does not present it as a distinct
doctrine opposed to the skyscraper version. Instead, he formulates the
bedrock version by a subtle transformation of the skyscraper version,
and never spells out their distinction. Since he formally presents only
the skyscraper version, it has been received as his official doctrine.

The identification of the skyscraper version as Plato's official doctrine has gone hand in hand with the admiration of the *Republic* as his
greatest work. For its literary merit, this work may indeed rank higher
than any other dialogue. It glistens with beautiful metaphors and vi-
brates with dramatic actions. Even so, Plato regarded it as relatively
immature in philosophical content, and dedicated the rest of his life to
restating the positions he had taken in the *Republic* and making up
for their deficiencies. The bedrock version of Platonism is delivered
progressively in this series of restatements, which are given in his late
dialogues.

In this volume, I explicate the bedrock version in its entirety for the
first time, that is, its logic and semantics, its physics and metaphysics,
its ethics and politics. I develop the thesis that the bedrock version provides our basic normative intuition. It is called Platonic intuition because it is the intuition of Platonic Forms. I further show that Platonic

intuition alone can provide the necessary basis for constructing and justifying positive norms. In Kantian language, Platonic intuition is not only transcendent but also transcendental for our normative life. This is the heart of normative Platonism, which I present as a union of intuition and construction.

In the final chapter of this book, I show why the bedrock version of Platonism alone can effectively surmount the challenge of normative relativism and positivism. Although relativism is out of fashion, it still retains one enduring attraction. It seems to explain and respect the immense diversity of human culture. Some scholars have advocated normative pluralism as a way of appropriating this feature of relativism without succumbing to its evil. However, pluralism cannot avoid the fate of being reduced to relativism unless it accepts the bedrock version of Platonism as the universal basis for the construction of different cultures. Such a universal basis is also the semantic and epistemic condition for overcoming cultural subjectivism and imperialism in cross-cultural comparison and communication. Since the bedrock version of Platonism is such a universal basis, it can provide a new semantic and epistemic foundation for normative discourse and inquiry.

Now I must mention a few things about my method of interpretation. Plato's dialogues can be compared to an archipelago, a long chain of islands. Though each of the islands, large or small, may look like an independent entity, they may be geologically connected. There are two ways of surveying those islands: the monadic approach and the connectionist approach. The monadic approach is to study each of Plato's dialogues as a monad or a self-contained whole; the connectionist approach is to explore their interlocking relations. The monadic approach has been the standard method for Plato scholarship, because it is simpler and easier than the connectionist approach. However, the simpler method cannot deliver a synoptic view of the Platonic corpus; such a comprehensive understanding requires the connectionist approach.

There are two modes for working out Platonic connectionism: static and dynamic. The static mode recognizes no dynamics of development in Plato's thought. For example, Paul Shorey tries to establish the unity of Plato's thought by claiming that all his dialogues, regardless of their chronology, display basically the same ideas. Such a static account, however, cannot do justice to the amazing variety and complexity of ideas contained in the Platonic corpus. This obvious weakness in the static mode of Platonic connectionism is meant to be remedied by its dynamic mode. Perhaps we should read his dialogues as we read the three plays in Aeschylus' trilogy, the *Oresteia*. Though each of them can be read as a self-contained work, they can reveal a far greater significance when they are taken as a continuous development of one basic theme, the divine curse over the house of Atreus. Such a dynamic approach has been popular with German scholars, who have studied the development of Plato's positions on such various topics as love, Forms, and knowledge. In this country, it has been espoused by a few enterprising scholars such as Charles Kahn, Kenneth Sayre, and Mitchell Miller. As a general rule, their efforts have only provoked the ever skeptical response from the mainstream Plato scholars.

The dynamic connectionists have presented many different programs of interpretation. But all of them share one grievous deficiency: none has provided a thematic account that can cover the entire Platonic corpus. For example, Charles Kahn takes many of the early and middle dialogues as a series of proleptic operations for the culmination of Plato's philosophy in the *Republic*. However, he says little for illuminating the thematic connection of the later dialogues. In the meantime, some of the later dialogues have severally engaged the attention of Kenneth Sayre and Mitchell Miller, but their thematic accounts leave out most of the earlier dialogues and even some of the later ones, especially the *Laws* and the *Timaeus*. Thus, none of the connectionists have proposed a unifying theme that can connect all the islands in the Platonic Archipelago. Hence, their thematic projects still remain local and partial.

My thematic project is global and total. I assemble twenty-two dialogues altogether, most of Plato's important works, like the pieces of one big puzzle by weaving them together around the central theme: Plato's invention of political philosophy. This is not to say that the other themes have to be ignored for the sake of this one; on the contrary, it is essential to understand their roles in supporting and supplementing the central theme. I observe the distinction between the primary and the secondary themes. In my view, such familiar themes in Plato's dialogues as virtue and vice, love and beauty, soul and body, being and becoming, are secondary. To be sure, there are a few other important secondary themes, but there is only one primary theme. That the primary theme is indeed the invention of political philosophy is tangibly reflected in the massive size of the *Republic* and the *Laws*. There are ten books in the *Republic*, and twelve books in the *Laws*. No other dialogue is large or long enough to be divided into more than one book. If there were a cartography of the Platonic corpus, the *Republic* and the *Laws* should stand out like two huge landmasses in a vast ocean of many smaller islands.

In today's compartmentalized university, it is a common practice to distribute Plato's secondary themes to many different areas of independent inquiry, such as ethics, aesthetics, mathematics, natural and social sciences. The separation of these disciplines by departments is an Aristotelian legacy. In Plato's dominion, however, all of them are subordinated to political philosophy. Because of its comprehensiveness, Plato called political art the royal art, which was later renamed as the master science by Aristotle. Plato's conception of royal art is even more comprehensive than Aristotle's conception of master science. Whereas the latter is the master of all practical knowledge, the former supremely reigns over the entire domain of human knowledge, practical as well as theoretical. The royal art is meant to rule over the totality of human life insofar as it can be governed by art and science. Such a comprehensive art or science is political philosophy as Plato understands it, and its realization is the ultimate theme that runs through all his dialogues.

In my account, Plato's primary theme is not assumed to be some philosophical system in its germinal form to be developed and elaborated in a series of dialogues. It belongs to a much deeper level of his thought. If I am not mistaken, his primary theme is linked to his existential resolve to meet the challenge of Callicles. What is the ultimate character of this challenge? As we will see in this volume, Callicles stands as a spokesman not only for the ethos of Athenian imperialism and power politics, but also for the conception of the phenomenal world as a theater of aggression and predation. In such a beastly world, the unrestrained gratification of desire is claimed to be the ultimate human value. In the *Gorgias*, Plato tried to argue against this view of human life only to find that rational arguments were useless and powerless against it. In the *Phaedo* and the *Symposium*, he even entertained the pessimistic thought that the flight to the beautiful world of Forms was the only sensible response to this world of power and greed, injustice and suffering.

How can Plato come to terms with the world of phenomena instead of fleeing from it? This is his existential problem. He can resolve it only by devising the art of building a social order decent enough to overcome the arrogance of power and the impudence of greed. This is the art of political wisdom or philosophy. Whereas the art of power politics reduces human existence to the beastly level, Plato holds, the art of political philosophy elevates it to the divine level. These two are radically different ways of realizing human value and fulfilling the destiny of our love (*eros*). For Plato, there is no question so important as the question of *eros* because it is the basic force of not only human life, but all living beings.

In its Platonic sense, *eros* includes all our desires and longings. Its presence and absence constitute the ultimate difference between the living and the dead. Hence the question of life (How should we live?) turns out to be the question of *eros* (What is the best way to fulfill our *eros*?). The challenge of Callicles takes on its critical significance because it is in truth the challenge of *eros*. Brushing aside conventional morality as an ideological yoke imposed on the strong by the weak, he flaunts the art of power politics as the best way of fulfilling *eros*. Plato cannot meet this challenge by simply reaffirming the value of conventional morality. He must show that there is a better way to realize our *eros* than the way of power and greed. To this end, he devises his art of politics. Hence, his political art is his art of *eros*, which emerges as the final product of *philosophia* (love of wisdom). For these reasons, his journey in search of political art is the journey of *philosophia* for the sake of *eros*.

This is not to say that Plato charted his entire journey from the beginning. On the contrary, he takes one step at a time and devises his itinerary as he moves along. Although his thematic journey has one definite goal, his dialogues are written for many different reasons, each of which is occasioned by the progression of his journey. He writes some dialogues to propose new theories, some to revise old ones, others to reassess his accomplishments, and still others to reorient his entire project. Hence his thematic journey is highly unpredictable. In that case, how can we discover the thematic connection of his dialogues? Fortunately, Plato the author carefully provides many clues in various forms such as the frame stories, the dramatic settings, and other literary devices. These thematic indicators are internal; they are deliberately planted in the texts. On a couple of occasions, I use some external materials, for example, Thucydides and a few other historians, in locating the ethos of Athenian imperialism at the center of the thematic setting for the *Gorgias*. Those external materials are not my primary evidence; they only supplement the internal evidence from Plato's own works.

Some readers may assume that my Platonic thematics is based on Platonic chronology, the highly controversial art of determining the chronological sequence of Plato's compositions. But their thematic connection need not be linked to the chronological order of their composition. In chapter 3 of this volume, for example, I bring forth a number of thematic pointers and connectors in support of my view that the *Protagoras* thematically follows the *Symposium*. This thematic sequence, however, need not imply that the *Protagoras* was written after the *Symposium*. No doubt, it is plausible that the thematic sequence of the two dialogues may coincide with their compositional sequence. In whatever sequence the two dialogues were initially composed, Plato still could have revised them later and added the thematic pointers and connectors as we find them in his texts. That is, he might have decided their thematic relationship well after their initial composition.

At any rate, Plato says nothing about the compositional sequence of the *Symposium* and the *Protagoras*, but he takes special pains to indicate their thematic relationship. Evidently he regards it as essential for understanding those two works. If so, there is no reason for us to be overly concerned with the question of Platonic chronology. Instead, we should concentrate our attention on the question of Platonic thematics. So I have designed a thematic project that can deliver a truly synoptic account of the Platonic Archipelago. As we all know, a synoptic vision is a Platonic vision par excellence, but it has been sorely missing from the world of Plato scholarship.

In the course of writing this volume, I talked endlessly with many friends and colleagues about Plato. It was my singular fortune to have frequent discussions with three ardent Platonists, Paul Woodruff, J. M. Balkin, and Rob Koons. I am grateful for the advice of Alexander Mourelatos and Jim Hankinson in deciphering difficult passages of Plato's texts. Erwin Cook and Jack Kroll kindly served as my guides to the world of ancient Greek history and literature. My manuscript was reviewed in part or whole by Christopher Colvin, Thomas Bole, Kyung Hee Nam, Mitchell Miller, and Sharon Vaughan. I am grateful for their comments and criticisms, which have left clear imprints on the book. Thomas Denton was a fountain of wisdom on delicate questions of style and usage. Chul Bum Lee gave me his unflagging support and encouragement from the beginning to the end of this project. Finally, I reverently recall my tender memory of the late Robert S. Brumbaugh, who bravely initiated me into the enchanting but perplexing world of the Platonic Archipelago a long time ago in my youth.

July 15, 1995
Austin, Texas

CHAPTER ONE

The World of Power and Greed

The *Gorgias* and the Early Dialogues

The *Gorgias* occupies a unique position in the Platonic Archipelago. Artistically, it may mark the lowest point in Plato's career; most readers get irritated by its ungraceful construction. Emotionally, however, it may stand on the highest peak; no other dialogue shows the same intensity of passion as this one does. The *Gorgias* pulsates with Plato's heart rather than with his mind. What is it that exercises his soul so intensely? It is the compounding of two great evils, the ethos of power politics and the new political weapon of rhetoric. Callicles is the monster representing the combination of these two evils, and the *Gorgias* is a duel between this monster and Socrates, which is described as a contest between two ways of living, the life of power and greed and the life of justice and piety. Let us consider the nature of this contest.

Athenian Power Politics

The most baffling feature of the *Gorgias* is Socrates' harsh condemnation of Themistocles, Cimon, Miltiades, and Pericles, who have been called the four great leaders of classical Athens. The condemnation is not only harsh, but relentless. The four leaders are brought up for cen-

1

sure three times in the dialogue, once in the Socrates-Gorgias debate (455e–456a) and twice in the Socrates-Callicles debate (503cd, 515d–519a). In the last two occasions, they are branded as the flatterers of the Athenians and their pastry cooks, who were skilled only in the gratification of appetites. This blanket condemnation has sounded simply excessive and groundless even for the most sympathetic commentators. Terence Irwin says that Socrates' account of the four Athenian leaders is "a perversion of the historical conditions, as far as we know them."[1]

What were the historical conditions? Miltiades and Themistocles are remembered as the architects of the two renowned battles of Marathon and Salamis. In 490 B.C.E., when the invading forces of Darius landed on the plains of Marathon and made ready to assault the city of Athens, it was Miltiades who led the vastly outnumbered armies of Athens and Plataea and routed the Persians. Ten years later, the Persians tried again under the leadership of Xerxes and came very close to victory on land, ravaging Attica, forcing the evacuation of Athens, capturing the Acropolis, and burning its sacred relics. This time it was Themistocles who saved Athens by defeating the mighty Persian navy at the battle of Salamis. Even far more important than the victory at Salamis was his astute foresight in building up the Athenian naval powers in anticipation of Persia's renewed attempt at the conquest of Hellas.[2]

A few years after the battle of Marathon, a newly discovered silver mine at Maronea brought a large sum of money to the treasury of Athens. Against the proposal to distribute the money among the citizens, Themistocles persuaded the Assembly to use it for building new ships. He was indeed behind the policy of not only building ships and dockyards as stated in the *Gorgias*, but also of moving the Athenian naval base from the wide, exposed strand of Phaleron and relocating it behind the fortified peninsula of Piraeus.[3] By virtue of his policy, the Piraeus became the hub of Athenian maritime forces. His dream of Athenian naval supremacy was finally fulfilled by Cimon, son of Miltiades, who crushed the Persian navy at the battle of the Eurymedon River in 466 B.C.E. Cimon subsequently played a vital role in transforming the Greek confederacy against Persia into an Athenian empire.[4] Pericles led the empire on this foundation to her power and glory not only by increasing her wealth but also by promoting her culture. He masterminded the

great building program for the Acropolis, and proudly called the city of
Athens a lesson for all of Greece.

The first three of these four heroes were instrumental in saving Athens and the rest of Hellas from the Persians, and the last in elevating her to the supreme position of power and glory. Given these historical achievements, Socrates' condemnation clearly appears to be an act of lunacy and indecency. He does not even mention these achievements, but cavalierly compares them to confectioners and slanders them as mere flatterers of the ignorant multitude. I. F. Stone says, ''The attack on the four reaches a ridiculous climax when Socrates accuses Pericles, the greatest of the four, of having made the Athenians 'idle, cowardly, talkative, and avaricious.' ''[5] The attack is so embarrassing for Plato scholars that it is a customary practice among them to pass it over in silence. Some scholars have tried to brush it aside as an expression of Plato's political bias against the Athenian democracy. But the four Athenian heroes did not all belong to the democratic party; two of them, Miltiades and his son Cimon, came from an aristocratic lineage.

We can make better sense of Socrates' condemnation by taking it as his critique of Athenian imperialism. The four heroes can be viewed historically as four landmarks of Athenian imperialism from its birth to its death. Miltiades' victory at Marathon marked the beginning of a new epoch for Athens. It gave her new confidence and ambition to impose her supremacy over all of Hellas.[6] In the Piraeus, literally and symbolically, Themistocles built the base for Athenian naval supremacy. After Themistocles's ostracism, Cimon completed his maritime project by making her the undisputed naval power. By exploiting her naval supremacy, Pericles finally brought the empire-building program to its completion.

What was the consequence of this imperial project? It eventually ended in the Peloponnesian War and the disastrous defeat of Athens by Sparta. Although this war is never directly mentioned in the *Gorgias*, Seth Benardete says, ''No other Platonic dialogue is as saturated with allusions to events that span the Peloponnesian War (431–404 B.C.E.) as the *Gorgias*.''[7]

Though Pericles has been known as the greatest of the four, he is the one who led Athens into the Peloponnesian War and her eventual defeat.

Socrates' charge that he was good only for the gratification of appetites
is not a ridiculous claim as Stone says, but a well-founded truth. Ambition and greed for wealth and power were the chief motives for the
Periclean war policies. Under his leadership, even the great construction
program for the Acropolis was conceived not as an expression of piety
and devotion, but as an enterprise of greed and ambition. It was a costly
public-work project to give lucrative jobs to many artisans, who had
been laid off by the cessation of hostilities against the Persians. It involved large sums of money, beginning with the initial allocation of
30,000,000 drachmas (almost eleven tons of pure gold), which was followed by an additional allocation of 18,000,000 drachmas. For the construction of Athena Parthenos, they had to use over 2,500 pounds of
gold, which was worth more than 3,500,000 drachmas, and spend another 1,386,000 drachmas on ivory and other items.[8] The golden statue
was the Golden Calf of imperial Athens, and Pericles' chief opponent,
Thucydides (not to be confused with the historian), compared Athena
Parthenos to a bedizened whore.[9]

These huge sums of money for adorning the bedizened whore had
been extracted from the subject states of the Athenian Empire. By the
time the treasury of the Delian League was moved from Delos to Athens
in 454, it had an accumulated reserve of 30,000,000 drachmas. Though
it was a godsend for Pericles' immediate purposes, it was far from sufficient for supporting his many expensive projects. So he reinstated the
tribute system more than once, and the subject states became virtual
slaves who were allowed no voice in this matter. His conservative opponents denounced his grandiose and expensive projects as a wanton
waste of public funds, but they were powerless to block his democratic
politics. In the meantime, his expensive public-works and construction
projects enriched many of Pericles' friends and relatives, and immea-
surably contributed to the general prosperity of the city.[10] Socrates has
every reason to say that Pericles made the Athenians ''idle, cowardly,
talkative, and avaricious.''

Terence Irwin endorses Socrates' critique of Pericles. Always conscious of popular demands, he says, Pericles sought to give the people
what they wanted and took his political aims and values from their
desires instead of trying to make the people better. But he adds that the

cheap charge of gratification and flattery cannot easily be made against Themistocles. After all, he had the foresight to use the windfall from the Maronean silver mines for building up the Athenian navy and eventually defeating the Persians at the battle of Salamis. For the success of this long range policy, Themistocles had to fight against the policy of immediate gratification, namely, the proposal to distribute the newly acquired wealth to the citizens of Athens. Hence Socrates' charge that Themistocles was a leader for the politics of gratification is, to Irwin, "a gross over-simplification—typical of Socrates' political comments."[11]

Although Themistocles' policy was against immediate gratification, it was a policy of long-range gratification. It supported the expansion of power, which was to be used not only for the defense and security of the city, but also for the gratification of her ambition and greed. Gratification is gratification, whether it is immediate or delayed. Moreover, Themistocles' role was not limited to the tactical operation of deploying battleships. He was in charge of spending large sums of money for the construction of ships and dockyards. The politics of wars is always the politics of military-industrial complexes, which inevitably involves big money and power and breeds greed and fraud. It is highly probable that Themistocles may have succumbed to greed, as Socrates suggests in the *Gorgias*. It has been said that he took bribes and became a rich man. Power and wealth also brought him vanity. He built near his home a shrine to "Artemis wisest in Council" on the ground that his own counsels had been wiser than all others.[12]

On the basis of this overview, we may conclude that Socrates' ultimate opponent in the *Gorgias* is none of his three interlocutors, but the ethos of Athenian power politics or rather the moral principle that shaped the imperialism and expansionism of Athens. Socrates is referring to this ethos of acquisitive gratification by calling Themistocles, Cimon, Miltiades, and Pericles the pastry cooks and flatterers of Athens. Athenian imperialism emerged from the Persian Wars. Athens did not call herself an empire, but became the leader of the Delian League, a federation of island and coastal cities. Although these cities originally joined the federation as Athens' allies, they eventually became her slaves. Her imperial rule was highly repressive.[13] She meddled in the internal politics of her subject states, exterminating the uncooperative elements and installing the cooperative elements as her puppets. She was also highly exploitive, imposing heavy taxes on the subject states to support her military forces and fatten her treasury.

The Athenian imperialists used brutal power in dealing with recalcitrant neighbors. For example, when the inhabitants of Melos, a neutral island, refused to surrender to the invading Athenian forces, they were starved into submission. After the surrender of the island, all its male adults were executed, and all women and children were enslaved. The Athenians told the Melians that they had the right to do whatever they wanted to do with the vanquished, because nature always compels gods and men alike to rule over those they can control.[14] This is what Callicles calls the law of nature (483e). It is the principle of power politics; it can justify anything, especially ambition and greed. In his view, it operates as a universal law. His conception of nature is similar to Darwin's: Nature is the domain of the struggle for survival, and the theater of universal predation. This principle of power and greed became the living ethos of imperial Athens. In the *Gorgias*, rhetoric stands as the dutiful handmaid to this living ethos, and Callicles is its chief spokesman.

The ethos of power and greed is best exemplified in the life of a tyrant, as described and admired by Polus and Callicles in the *Gorgias* (470d–473e, 479a–e, 525d), and the Athenian empire was called a tyranny not only by its foes but by its leader, Pericles himself.[15] The new imperial ethos came as a great menace and challenge to the ethos of temperance or moderation (*sophrosyne*), the cornerstone of traditional Athenian values. When Callicles says that a temperate person (*sophron*) is a fool (491e), he is expressing the Periclean ethos of ambition and greed (*pleonexia*), which has flouted the old ideal of temperance. The word *sophrosyne* is conspicuously missing from Pericles' funeral oration; of the two great virtues of Athens, temperance and wisdom, he mentions only wisdom. Even Thucydides avoids using the word *sophrosyne* in his depiction of Pericles. To be sure, he dutifully praises the statesmanship of Pericles and blames his successors and their ambition for leading the state to disaster.[16] In this regard, the Socrates of the *Gorgias* is far more forthright and astute; he says that the seed of disaster had been sown by Pericles and his predecessors.

The ethos of Athenian imperialism has turned the entire Hellas into a merciless theater of mutual aggression and subjugation. The horror of this transformation was most tragically displayed in the civil war of Corcyra. For seven days while the Athenian admiral Eurymedon was watching with his sixty ships, the Corcyreans engaged in a massive form of mutual massacre. The democrats killed the aristocrats; the debtors killed the creditors; the fathers killed the sons. Similar internal killings and fighting broke out virtually in all other parts of Greece.[17] This is a scene of ambition and greed gone wild and savage. The ethos of the Peloponnesian War has bestialized not only the relation of the city-states, but also the internal politics of each state.

Thucydides describes the Peloponnesian War as the triumph of greed and ambition over temperance and prudence. The ethos of unbridled greed turned upside down the ethos of self-control and self-restraint, the foundation of traditional values in all ancient Greece. The Calliclean ethos is the transvaluation of traditional values. Callicles says that the law of nature he advocates governs the world of beasts as well as of human beings and gods. His ethics of power and greed brings down both gods and humans to the same level of beastly existence, and poses a serious challenge to the very idea of civilized human existence. Socrates responds to this challenge by appealing to philosophy and virtue (482a, 507b). But the nature of virtue had been drastically changed, by the time of Socrates' debate with Callicles, especially by the power of philosophy. Let us now look into this drastic change.

From Theonomy to Anthroponomy

In the *Euthyphro*, Socrates examines the nature of piety, the oldest of all virtues. Euthyphro initially defines piety as what is pleasing to the gods and impiety as what is not pleasing to them (7a). This definition captures the traditional concept of piety. But Socrates objects to it on the ground that there are quarrels and disagreements among the gods. What is pleasing to some gods may be displeasing to other gods. Euthyphro's prosecution of his own father may be pleasing to Zeus, but hateful to Cronus and Uranus (8b). If so, the same thing can be pious and impious. This is surely an unacceptable consequence, and Socrates proposes to amend Euthyphro's definition of piety as follows. Whatever all the gods love is pious; whatever all the gods hate is impious. And what is loved by some of them and hated by others is either both or neither. This amendment leads to the central question of the dialogue: "Do the gods love piety because it is pious, or is it pious because they love it?"

In his reply to this question, Euthyphro says that the gods love piety because it is pious (10d). In that case, Socrates points out, it is not pious because it is loved by the gods. Then, piety is not what is pleasing to the gods, as Euthyphro claimed in his definition. What is pious and what is pleasing to the gods are two different things. Euthyphro has been confused between the essence and the effect of piety. In its essence, Socrates and Euthyphro come to agree, piety is a part of justice. But which part? Euthyphro says that piety is that part of justice that attends to the gods, while the other part is concerned with the attendance to human beings (12e). But what is it to attend to the gods?

Socrates and Euthyphro reach a provisional agreement that the art of attending to the gods is an art of exchange between gods and humans. By prayer and sacrifice, the humans offer honor and praise to the gods, and they in turn grant human beings many benefits for their family and state. Now Socrates points out that what the humans do in this exchange cannot be beneficial to the gods, because the gods are in no need of any benefit. Hence, it must be simply pleasing to the gods. If so, piety again turns out to be what is pleasing to the gods (15b). Thus, the whole discussion is brought back to Euthyphro's initial definition of piety, and the dialogue comes to an end without answering the original question.

Although the *Euthyphro* has been known as one of the aporetic dialogues, it clearly establishes one assertion, namely, that piety is not what is pleasing to the gods. This assertion is significant because it rejects the conventional notion of piety. For a better appreciation of this point, let us introduce the distinction between theonomy and anthroponomy. This distinction concerns the origin of *nomos* (normative standards and rules), that is, the question of whether they are given by the gods or made by human beings. Theonomy is the view that they are given by the gods; anthroponomy is the view that they are made by human beings. Anthroponomy is the standard view in modern Europe and America and the rest of the world; we all believe that we make our own laws. In the ancient world, however, theonomy was the standard view. The ancient Jews believed that their God gave them the law. This is the story of Moses and the Ten Commandments. Though not many ancient societies had such a grandiose story as that of Moses' two tablets, most of them believed in the divine origin of their laws and customs.

In a theonomic culture, the laws are believed to be special gifts from the gods; in an anthroponomic culture, human beings make their own laws. These two views were reflected in the two conceptions of a lawgiver (*nomothetes*) in ancient Greece. Lycurgus, the legendary lawgiver for Sparta, is said to have received the law from Apollo of Delphi. It was also believed that Minos had received the law for Crete from Zeus, and that Zaleucus was given the law of Locri by Athena in a dream.[18] These legendary lawgivers did not give the laws of their own making. Because they were the lawgivers of a theonomic age, they received their laws from the immortals. However, the lawgiver of an anthroponomic age is different; he makes the law when he gives it. Protagoras was the lawgiver for Thurii; he was commissioned to draft the constitution for the new Hellenic city. His celebrated doctrine of *homomensura* ("Man is the measure of all things") marks the advent of anthroponomy. In the theonomic world, the god was the measure of all things.

The concept of measure (*metron*) is the concept of normative standard. Theonomy locates it in the immortals; anthroponomy assigns it to human beings. The sophists were instrumental in this radical transformation in the conception of normative standard. With the advent of anthroponomy, the celebrated distinction between *physis* (nature) and *nomos* (law) gained its significance. This distinction was not introduced by the sophists; the notion of *nomos* was much older than the sophists. In the theonomic age, however, the distinction between *physis* and *nomos* was not important. As long as *nomos* was believed to be given by the gods, it was regarded as durable as *physis*. But *nomos* lost its durability and stability with the advent of an anthroponomic ethos, and its difference from *physis* became the central concern for the sophists.

They stressed the variability and mutability of *nomos* in contrast to the permanence and immutability of *physis*.

The theonomic view of law could not withstand the sophists' critique of traditional religion. They were the critical rationalists, who could not tolerate the childish and scandalous stories told about the Olympians, for example, the stories of Zeus's castration of his father and his amorous affairs. They also questioned the epistemic grounds for even talking about the divine beings. For example, Protagoras was famous for asserting that he had no way of knowing whether the gods existed or not, or what they were like if they did exist. Some sophists, such as Prodicus and Critias, denied the existence of gods altogether. Agnosticism and atheism led to the view that the gods were not the entities of real existence, but only objects of human contrivance. They exist only by *nomos* or convention. As convention varies from country to country, so does the nature of deities.

The idea that the existence of gods is dictated by *nomos* turns the theonomic view of law on its head. The gods do not create the laws; the laws create the gods. This reversal of the old belief in the divine origin of *nomos* introduced serious difficulties for the problem of legitimacy and compliance. As long as people believed in theonomy, they did not have to question the authority and legitimacy of their laws. They took it for granted that the mortals had the duty to obey whatever the immortals commanded, and that such obedience was piety, their highest virtue. They also believed in the certainty of divine sanction for disobedience, because they thought that they could not escape divine surveillance and detection. Moreover, divine sanction was not restricted to the wrongdoer; the entire city or tribe could be punished by pollution (*miasma*). For example, Oedipus's guilt brought plagues and other disasters to the entire city of Thebes.

When the theonomic belief in divine sanction was dissolved by the advent of anthroponomy, surveillance and compliance became a much more difficult problem in the administration of laws than they had been in the age of theonomy. Most human beings believe that they can elude the mechanism of human surveillance and escape its sanction. The fear of the gods is much more effective for the enforcement of laws than the fear of the police. The former works internally and the latter externally.

This difference can be stated in the Socratic language of appetites. In theonomy, appetites are internally constrained by the fear of the gods, but this internal constraint is dissolved by the advent of anthroponomy.

Once the appetites are freed from their internal constraints, they become the chief engine for the ethos of appetitive and acquisitive culture, which powers the competition for acquisition, which in turn leads to the war of aggression. Hence the difference between theonomy and anthroponomy can be described as the culture of restrained (by the fear of the gods) appetites and the culture of released (from the fear of the gods) appetites. The latter is the culture of impiety and hybris in the extreme; it experiences no scruples whatsoever against the gods in the gratification of its ambition and greed. And that is the way of Callicles' life.

The Advancement of Technical Arts

The transition from theonomy to anthroponomy is usually accompanied by a rapid development of technical arts or crafts (*technai*) such as medicine, metallurgy, and navigation. This is not to say that these arts were not known in the age of theonomy. They were regarded as divine gifts. According to the myth of Prometheus, human beings did not have the intelligence to invent their arts. In most theonomic societies, the art of making ritual sacrifices and the art of medicine carry a far greater prestige and magical power than any other arts. These two arts are often wielded by the same person, namely, the shaman or medicine man, who receives them as his special calling from the spirits. In the anthroponomic age, art is regarded no longer as a divine gift, but as a human invention. For this reason, Socrates takes for granted that art is the most salient manifestation of human wisdom and intelligence.

In most ancient societies, technical arts in general remain in a stable condition for a long time, and their improvement comes only gradually and incrementally. But this general trend is often broken by trade and war, both of which can stimulate the development of arts and their productive activities. When the growth and spread of arts become noticeable, they can surely give their practitioners the idea that they are human creations rather than divine gifts. On the other hand, when they are secretively passed on with little change from one generation to another, they are more likely to be believed to be divine gifts. The conscious attempt to create and develop the various technical arts gives human beings perhaps the most tangible sense of their mastery over themselves and their environments. This sense of mastery is the central force for the transition from theonomy to anthroponomy.

The Acropolis marks this transition more vividly than any other historical monument. As we noted, the great construction project for the Acropolis was conceived not as a religious expression of piety and devotion, but as a civic enterprise of greed and ambition. Above all, it was meant to be the showcase for a dazzling display of technical arts from sculpture to architecture, that is, the display of human power and mastery. Just imagine the technical feat of moving twenty-two thousand tons of pure white marble down the steep and rocky slopes of Mount Pentelicus about two to three thousand feet and then across the ten miles of plain to the Acropolis, by using only ropes and tackles, sleds and rollers. Though awesome, this feat only provided the materials for the much more awesome task of cutting up and putting together countless blocks of marble used in the construction of the Parthenon.[19]

By the old religious standard, construction of the Parthenon was an undertaking of daunting arrogance and impiety. Though its sculpture depicts Olympian themes such as Theseus victorious over the invading Amazons and Athena besting Poseidon, Peter Green says, its ultimate message is human triumph as exemplified in the power and glory of Athens.[20] Even in the great frieze, the civic procession is far more important than the goddess it is supposed to honor. Green says, "the Parthenon was essentially a monument to civic pride."[21] As far as Pericles was concerned, the entire construction was never meant to honor the goddess. He was only exploiting the state cult as one more instrument in his imperial politics. For this reason, the pious conservatives looked upon the whole project with intense suspicion, and impiety became a frequent charge brought against him and his associates. The Periclean Athens was a city of impiety.

In an age of anthroponomy, war and art tend to form a special partnership. On one hand, war is the best stimulus to the development of art, as has been attested to by the vast technological development during

the great wars of our century. On the other hand, only the vast development of technical arts makes it possible to wage a great war. It takes a
number of highly developed technical arts to equip huge armies, to keep
them fed and clothed, to move them around, and to control them. To be
sure, the highly developed arts make great wars possible but not necessary. But the combination of developed arts and released appetites
makes war inevitable. War is essentially a battle of appetites, as Socrates says in the *Gorgias*. Consequently, the trio of art, appetite, and war
constitute the common syndrome of anthroponomy. In theonomic cultures, arts are far less developed, appetites are far more restrained, and
wars are far less frequent and devastating.

The triadic syndrome of anthroponomy—art, war, and appetite—was
highly pronounced in ancient Greece of fifth century B.C.E. She waged
the Persian Wars and the Peloponnesian War, built her empire for the
gratification of appetites, and witnessed the flowering of technical arts.
She was going through the transition from theonomy to anthroponomy.
About the same time, ancient China went through a similar transition.
The watershed was the Era of the Warring States, almost two centuries
of perpetual wars among the feudal lords from the end of the fifth century to the imperial unification of China in 221 B.C.E. These two centuries of wars witnessed the rapid growth of arts and letters, technology
and industry. The two magic words that captivated the Warring States
were *wealth* and *power* just as in the case of imperial Athens. The ancient Chinese were putting an end to their age of theonomy at about the
time the ancient Greeks were doing it.

Prior to the Era of the Warring States, ancient Chinese life had been
governed by one central text, the *Li Ki* (Book of Rituals).[22] This book
gives a series of elaborate rules for the performance of ritual sacrifices,
but it is much more than a manual of rituals. It also gives all the rules
and precepts for governing the entire spectrum of human behavior. The
central theme of all these rules and precepts is the idea of reverence for
the spiritual beings. The *Book of Rituals* is the Chinese text of theonomy. It records all the normative rules and standards given by spiritual
beings. To abide by all those rules and principles was the virtue of
rituals, usually translated as the *virtue of propriety*, because those rules
and principles defined proper behavior for everybody. It is the Chinese

counterpart of the ancient Greek virtue of piety. Confucius, who lived about a century before the Era of the Warring States, regarded this virtue as the basis for all his ethical and political teachings. After the Era of the Warring States, the *Book of Rituals* yielded its central authority to the writings of Confucius and Mencius, which became the foundation for anthrocentric ethics and politics.

Let us get back to the *Euthyphro* and see how the dialogue is situated in a theonomic culture. In the Hall of the King, Socrates runs into Euthyphro, who had arrived there to prosecute his own father for impiety. When one of his father's laborers got angry with a slave and killed him, his father bound the man hand and foot, and threw him into a ditch. He then sent to Athens to ask the priest how he should handle this murder case. In the meantime, the murderer died in the ditch from neglect before the messenger got back from Athens. Thus, his father killed a man, and Euthyphro feels the duty to prosecute him for impiety (4bc). That his father was seeking instruction from a priest rather than from a civil authority for the administration of criminal law is typical of theonomy. Even more interesting is Euthyphro's reason for prosecuting his own father; it is to avoid the pollution that will come to him and to his house if his father's impiety is not punished. He says that his indictment of his own father is an act of purification. The fear of pollution was an essential feature of theonomy, and purification was believed to be its best remedy.

In the last definition of the dialogue, piety is described as that part of justice that attends to the gods, and this definition presumably excludes from the scope of piety that part of justice that attends to human beings. In a theonomic culture, however, the justice of human beings toward one another is usually included in the province of piety. The notion of attending to the gods should be construed in a much broader sense. The Greek concept of piety was expressed by two words, *eusebes*, which means being fearful of and reverential toward the gods, and *hosios*, which means being hallowed or sanctioned by divine prescriptions and prohibitions.[23] Even the justice and injustice of one human being to another are matters of piety, if they concern divine prescriptions and prohibitions.[24] Euthyphro is indicting his father for impiety, although his conduct involved only a human being.

In the last part of the dialogue, Socrates and Euthyphro try to figure out what is meant by the phrase "attending to the gods" in their final definition of piety. Euthyphro says that it means to offer honor and praise to the gods. Since honor and praise are pleasing to the gods, Socrates says, piety is to do what is pleasing to them. Thus the final definition has come back to the initial definition that has already been rejected. This is the so-called aporetic ending of the dialogue. But this negative ending should not blind us to the important achievement made in the dialogue. We have already noted that Euthyphro's first definition of piety is a perfectly acceptable view of piety in a theonomic culture. His last definition is equally so because it only restates the substance of the first definition. The rejection of these definitions is the rejection of theonomy, and the *Euthyphro* records the end of theonomy in ancient Greece.

The end of theonomy is further elaborated by the *Ion*. The central topic of this dialogue is the power of rhapsodes and poets: "From what source do they derive the marvelous power to compose and recite poetry?" Socrates demonstrates that their power is a divine gift. They are inspired and possessed by supernatural powers (534bc). Throughout the discussion, Socrates stresses the difference between poetry and art, and this is a strange way of looking at poetry for us because poetry is taken for granted to be an art in our age. Socrates wants to know whether the poet and the rhapsode have the same kind of knowledge as the technical experts have in talking about matters of technical expertise. When Ion replies that they do have the same kind of knowledge, Socrates says that a good rhapsode should also be a good general. Since Ion is the best Hellenic rhapsode, he should be the best general in Hellas. A good rhapsode should also be a physician, a lyre player, a horseman, and all other technical experts whose activities he can recite in a poem.

A technical art is a matter of knowledge; poetry is a gift of divine inspiration. This contrast is the central theme of this dialogue. In the domain of knowledge, our intellect (*nous*) is in control of our activities (534b). But our intellect surrenders its control in moments of inspiration and possession. Poets and rhapsodes do not really *know* what they are saying, if *knowing* means the intellectual control and understanding of their utterances. Instead, they become mindless mouthpieces for the divine voice. The sense of control that is associated with knowledge can best be elucidated with the concept of *tyche* (chance), which means the chance events over which human beings have no control. A chance event can be good or bad, but one has no control over it. It takes its own course. Even if it takes place by the necessity of divine or physical law, it is still regarded as a matter of chance because human beings have no control over it. By this standard, the poetic inspiration or possession is a matter of chance, because the poet has no control over it.

The role of *techne* (art) is to overcome the world of *tyche* (chance). In fact, the progress of human civilization can be described as the conquest of *tyche* by the power of *techne*, and its motto can be phrased as "where *tyche* rules, *techne* shall control." For this reason, the *techne/tyche* antithesis was an important polarity in ancient Greece.[25] By the power of technical arts, human beings can gain control over their lives, and this control comes by knowledge. In this technical conception, knowledge is not merely cognitive or theoretical, but chiefly technical and practical. It is the power of intelligence for making and doing things, and this power is exemplified by the technical experts. On the other hand, the power of chance is exemplified by the poets and rhapsodes. For this reason, they are the best representatives for the age of theonomy, while the technical experts are the best representatives for the age of anthroponomy. The *Ion* and the *Euthyphro* jointly mark the transition from theonomy to anthroponomy, the succession of poets and rhapsodes by the technical experts as the culture heroes of ancient Greece.

In a theonomic culture, poetry occupies an exalted position. Poets and seers, priests and shamans, who are the standard media for the transmission of divine messages, are the repositories of divine wisdom. Hence, the Homeric epics carried an authority similar to that of the Bible for Jews and the Christians. In Homer and other poets, the ancient Greeks sought wisdom and guidance for their lives as some Jews and Christians do in their Bibles. Homeric epics and other poems were the standard texts for the education of the young. When Protagoras came to Athens as a harbinger of the sophistic education, he said that the sophists were the successors to the poets (*Protagoras* 316d). In ancient China, the *Book of Poetry* was the most revered text next to the *Book of*

Rituals. These two were inseparable companions in the age of theonomy.

The age of theonomy is the age of poets and seers; the age of anthroponomy is the age of artisans and craftsmen. As long as human beings receive their wisdom from the gods, they are not their own masters. They can gain their sense of mastery only in the domain of technical arts because it is the domain of knowledge. To be engaged in the domain of knowledge is to know the why and the how of one's own undertaking. This was the critical stance of the sophists; their critical rationalism was the extension of technical stance to the domain of ethics and politics. They can no longer justify human behavior simply by citing the divine authority of normative rules and standards as given by the poets and the seers. They feel that they have to give a rational account of those rules and standards. This rational and critical stance would have been an act of impiety in the age of theonomy. It was the virtue of piety to accept those rules and standards as divine pronouncements and obey them reverently. This attitude of pious reverence was replaced by the critical stance of the sophists with the advent of anthroponomy.

Convention and Definition

The end of theonomy inevitably generates a normative crisis, because it brings about the erosion of all theonomic standards. At the outset of the *Euthyphro*, Socrates highlights the difficulty of settling normative questions. They are uniquely different from empirical or mathematical questions. Whereas there are definite methods for resolving empirical or mathematical disputes, he says, there is no reliable method to settle normative disputes. This difficulty does not arise in the age of theonomy, in which the god-given rules and precepts have the undisputed authority for settling all normative questions. If normative rules and standards are not given by the gods, but made by human beings, what is the right way to resolve normative issues? Protagoras and many other sophists advocated normative positivism or conventionalism. This is the

view that normative rules and standards are given in the positive law of
each state.

Against the prevailing positivism, Socrates appeals to transcendent
standards, which transcend all conventions. It is the existence of transcendent standards that is secured in the *Euthyphro*. Socrates and Euthyphro agree that the standard of piety transcends even the pleasure
and displeasure of the gods. Although they cannot agree on the definition of piety, they do not question its existence. The dialogue could
have ended with a different outcome. From the fact that they cannot
define piety, they could have concluded that there was no such thing as
piety, or rather it was only a product of human convention. Instead, they
firmly agree that its existence cannot be affected even by disagreements
among the gods. Though the *Euthyphro* marks the end of theonomy, it
emphatically affirms the existence of transcendent normative standards.
But how can we know such standards? What kind of account can be
given for them? These questions lead to the Socratic questions: "What
is virtue?," "What is courage?," "What is justice?."

There are two ways to answer the Socratic questions. One way is to
appeal to the established convention—for example, justice is so and so
because that is the meaning of justice as established by the present
linguistic convention. This was the way of Prodicus, who was mainly
interested in clarifying the meaning of a term to be defined. His method
was consistent with normative positivism. The other way is to appeal to
transcendent standards, and this is the way of Socrates. His method
goes well beyond the study of positive norms. Typically, the Socratic
definition begins with the examination of established conventions as
they are found in ordinary beliefs and embodied in exemplary instances.[26] These instances provide the basis for what Aristotle calls the
inductive arguments in the Socratic definition (*Metaphysics* 1078b27).
The Socratic enterprise does not stop there but moves on to inquire into
the nature of transcendent standards. Hence, there are two stages in the
Socratic definition: conventional and transcendent. These two stages
correspond to the two types of normative standards and principles: positive and transcendent. The conventional stage is an inquiry into the
nature of positive norms; the transcendent stage is an inquiry into the
nature of transcendent norms.

The *Euthyphro* can illustrate the two stages of Socratic definition. The first definition of piety belongs to the conventional stage; it simply states the conventional understanding of piety as what is pleasing to the gods. But the discussion moves on to the transcendent stage by the time Euthyphro answers Socrates' question of whether piety is pleasing to the gods because it is pious, or whether it is pious because it is pleasing to the gods. If piety is pleasing to the gods because it is pious, as Euthyphro says, the standard of piety is transcendent, and the existence of this transcendent standard cannot be affected even by the aporetic ending of the dialogue. Hence the dialogue can be divided into two stages. The first stage is conventional; the second stage is transcendent. We can detect the same binary structure in the *Laches* and the *Charmides*.

In the *Laches*, Socrates tries to define the nature of courage. In his first definition, Laches gives the most familiar conventional view by characterizing it as the virtue of someone who can hold his ground against the enemy in battle (190e). But this conventional view is too narrow: it is restricted to military affairs. Socrates points out that courage can be shown against other dangers and difficulties such as coping with disease and poverty and withstanding the pressure of desires and pleasures. Laches accepts this extended scope of courage, and amends his initial definition. In his second definition, he describes courage as a sort of endurance. This is again a conventional view, and Socrates points out that endurance can be accompanied by wisdom or folly (192d). Since endurance can produce harm and injury if it is accompanied by folly, it cannot be courage because courage is a good thing.

At this impasse, Nicias joins the discussion and defines courage as the knowledge of what is to be feared and to be hoped for in war and other situations (195a). This definition is clearly unconventional, and the conventional Laches regards it as sheer nonsense. If courage is a kind of knowledge, he says, it is best exemplified by doctors, farmers, and other technical experts because they know the dangers and hopes inherent in their fields of specialty. But he would not call them courageous. Nicias does not dispute this point, but says that the knowledge of what is to be feared and hoped for should be distinguished from technical knowledge such as the physician's knowledge of health and disease. Although a physician may know all about health and disease, he may not know what is truly fearful and dangerous. Nicias says that it is more dangerous for some people to be healthy than to be ill, and that it is sometimes better to die than to recover from illness. Hence to know what is truly fearful and hopeful belongs not to any technical experts but to the brave.

What is this special knowledge of the brave? Laches offers to identify it with the knowledge of prophets because they know whether it is better for a person to live or die. But Nicias rejects this proposal because he believes that prophets do not have that sort of knowledge. Laches begins to wonder who can have it unless it is some god. Now Socrates points out the difficulty that arises from the incompatibility of Nicias's definition with the commonsense view. If he wants to retain his definition of courage as a special type of knowledge, he has either to deny the ordinary view that wild animals such as lions and boars are brave as commonly understood, or to make the absurd claim that they know what is most difficult even for human beings to know. The ordinary view is the conventional view, which Nicias is prepared to reject in holding that wild animals are not really brave but only fearless or foolhardy (197a). But the knowledge of the fearful and the hopeful cannot be had without knowing the future good and evil, which in turn cannot be known without knowing what is good and evil in general. If so, courage turns out to be the knowledge of good and evil in general. This is the final definition of courage.

The final definition produces an unacceptable consequence. If one has the knowledge of good and evil in general, Socrates points out, one should have not only courage but all other virtues (199d). The final definition is the definition of virtue as a whole rather than one of its parts, whereas they have been seeking the definition of courage as a part of virtue. In spite of this aporetic ending, the dialogue clearly presents the definition in two stages, which are respectively represented by Laches and Nicias. Laches presents the conventional stage, and Nicias the transcendent stage. In these two stages, Socrates does not play the same role. In the conventional stage, his role is mainly critical; in the transcendent stage, his role is not only critical but also constructive. He makes positive proposals to improve Nicias's definition; hence his definition is a joint enterprise between him and Socrates. The displeasure and irritation Laches feels toward Nicias's definition should be taken as the typical response of a conventionalist to an unconventional assertion.

It is indeed unconventional to see virtue as knowledge. Here lies the basic difference between normative positivism and transcendentism. In the world of positive norms, the nature of virtue is determined by convention, which dictates for any given society what is virtuous and what is not. To be virtuous, one only has to do what is required by convention. Since positive norms can be bad, they should be subject to critical evaluation. But we cannot take such a critical stance without recourse to transcendent normative standards. Virtue is none other than the knowledge of such standards that can take us beyond the world of convention. The *Laches* does not introduce Platonic Forms as transcendent standards, but assumes that what is truly good can function as such a standard. The virtuous have the ability not only to know but to do what is dictated by this rational standard, just as technical experts know their arts. This is the *techne*-analogy of virtue. In its technical conception, virtue as knowledge means the ability to do things by the power of intelligence rather than blindly follow what is prescribed by convention.

The *techne*-analogy is also a product of anthroponomy. In the world of theonomy, virtue does not require the knowledge of the good and its transcendent standards, because it is the simple obedience to the laws given by the gods. Since these laws are usually inscribed in positive norms, the world of theonomy is a world of convention. In the world of anthroponomy, however, human beings have to make their own positive norms. They cannot discharge this function well without knowing transcendent standards for what is truly good. To be sure, anthroponomy is also compatible with conventionalism; it can refuse to admit nothing other than positive norms. In that case, human beings will be enslaved to their own positive norms. They can free themselves from the yoke of conventionalism only by appealing to transcendent norms and to their knowledge of what is truly good.

The Supreme Virtue of Self-Knowledge

The *Charmides* makes a tandem with the *Laches*. These two dialogues define the two prominent Homeric virtues, courage and temperance. One of them is exemplified by the *Iliad*, and the other by the *Odyssey*. Courage is the virtue of Achilles; temperance is the virtue of Odysseus. The definition of temperance in the *Charmides* also goes through two stages, conventional and transcendent. Just as the two stages in the *Laches* are represented by two interlocutors, Laches and Nicias, so the two stages in the *Charmides* are represented by Charmides and Critias. All the definitions offered by Charmides belong to the conventional understanding of temperance. He initially defines temperance as an orderly and quiet behavior. When Socrates shows its inadequacy, he gives his second definition of temperance as modesty. These two definitions are clearly conventional views of temperance.[27]

When Socrates says that temperance requires much more than modesty can give, he offers his third definition of it as doing one's own, which is much more sophisticated than the previous definitions. So Socrates teases him for having picked it up from his guardian Critias or some other wise man. Socrates has been faulted for making this definition look ridiculous by reading "doing one's own" literally. But it may be his way of showing that the young Charmides does not really understands this sophisticated definition. In fact, Charmides feels at a loss and gives up, and Critias takes over and gives the definition of temperance as the doing of good things (163e). This fourth definition is unconventional; its scope is too broad to be conventional. It marks the end of the conventional stage in the definition of temperance.

Socrates tells Critias that the doing of good things cannot be temperance unless it is accompanied by the agent's knowledge of what he is doing, because one may do something good accidentally. To cope with this inadequacy in the fourth definition, Critias gives the fifth definition: temperance is knowledge of oneself. This is again a conventional view; Critias traces its origin to Delphi (164d). This conventional view, however, becomes the basis for the transition from the conventional to the transcendent stage in definition, when Critias proposes to define knowledge of oneself with the following two formulas:

(1) One knows what one knows and what one does not know.

(2) One knows that one knows and that one does not know.

Of these two, Socrates maintains that (1) is useful but impossible, while (2) is possible but useless. But Socrates and Critias share the belief that the virtue of temperance is not only possible but also useful. Hence, neither (1) nor (2) is an acceptable definition of temperance. This is the outcome of the final definition of temperance.

Let us now try to understand the highly complicated arguments that are given in this final stage of the dialogue. At the outset, I should warn my readers that this is one of the most complicated passages in Plato's entire corpus, and that even the most astute commentators offer little help for unraveling its tangled arguments.though there is nothing objectionable in the identification of temperance with self-knowledge, the next step has been highly controversial. This is the identification of *knowledge of oneself* with *knowledge of itself*, which requires the substitution of *oneself* by *itself*. This substitution has been the object of many commentators' complaints; in their views, it is illegitimate. It is a logical fallacy because *itself* in this case means *knowledge,* which is clearly different from *oneself.*[28]

Gerasimos Santas says, "knowledge of oneself may include a thousand and one things." It may include the knowledge of one's own body, feelings, intelligence, capabilities, and whatever else belongs to oneself. On the other hand, knowledge of itself means knowledge of knowledge, that is, knowing what one knows and what one does not know. The domain of the latter is much narrower than that of the former.[29] Technically speaking, knowledge of itself is only one of the countless items that make up knowledge of oneself. The fallacy, Santas concludes, is obvious and blatant. There is, however, one mystery about this logical fallacy, if it indeed is a fallacy. When the fallacious equivalence of *knowledge of oneself* to *knowledge of itself* is proposed by Critias, Socrates voices no objections or reservations against it. Instead he accepts it as the basis for their discussion. Is he just too careless to recognize this fallacy? We may be able to clear up this mysterious feature of the dialogue by examining the Socratic conception of the self and knowledge.

For Socrates, knowledge is inseparably connected with desire, because it is the knowledge of what is good and what is bad for oneself. One always seeks what one knows to be good for oneself and avoids what one knows to be bad for oneself. Thus knowledge shapes desire, and they together define the state of the soul. In this regard, ignorance is equally important. However, ignorance is not simply the privation of knowledge; it is often a false or mistaken belief. Mistaken beliefs determine the state of the soul as much as knowledge does. When one mistakenly believes that something is good for oneself, one will seek it as much as when he knows it to be good for himself (*Protagoras* 358cd). The mistaken beliefs concern not only true and false values, but also their priority ranking. If one mistakenly believes that wealth is more important than virtue, one will seek wealth rather than virtue. Mistaken beliefs pave the way of vice, just as knowledge paves the way of virtue. If virtue is knowledge, as Socrates says, vice should be ignorance. And mistaken beliefs constitute ignorance.

What one knows and what one does not know jointly determine the state of the soul, its virtue and vice, its value scheme, and its way of life. Since the state of the soul is none other than the nature of oneself, one's knowledge and ignorance jointly determine the nature of oneself. This is the Socratic conception of the self or the soul, and it seems to ignore those features of oneself that lie outside the domain of knowledge and belief. For example, the biological functions of one's body are not controlled by knowledge or affected by belief. But these features do not belong to what can be properly called the human self, which should be distinguished from a mere biological or physical self. The Socratic self is the human self, and it alone is defined by knowledge and ignorance—what one knows and what one does not know.

Socrates next considers the usefulness of temperance. If temperance is defined as (1), its usefulness is obvious. If one knows what one knows and what one does not know, one will always be governed by knowledge, and never by ignorance. The benefit of temperance is not limited to knowledge of one's own knowledge and ignorance. Since a temperate person also knows what others know and what they do not know, that person can make use of others' knowledge and avoid their ignorance, too. By means of temperance, Socrates says, every household and every city will be well governed, because it roots out all errors and governs our life in accordance with knowledge (171e–172a). Temperance as defined in (1) can secure all the benefits of knowledge and avoid all the evils of ignorance by ruling over all technical sciences. This glorious picture of temperance, however, does not satisfy Socrates, for the following reason. Though there is no problem in asserting that one knows what one knows, it makes no sense to say that one knows what one does not know. Let us suppose that what one does not know is medicine. In that case, the assertion that one knows what (medicine) one does not know amounts to the contradictory assertion that one knows and does not know medicine (170cd). The concept of temperance as defined by (1) is self-contradictory and impossible.

Socrates now turns to the usefulness of temperance as defined by (2): a temperate person knows only that he does not know, but he does not know what he is ignorant of. This is a highly limited form of self-knowledge. As defined by (2), one's knowledge of others is equally limited. If another person claims to know something, our temperate person cannot know *what* that something is. He knows only *that* this person knows something. With such limited knowledge, the temperate person cannot distinguish a person who pretends to be a doctor from the one who is really a doctor, because he knows nothing about what these two claim to know, namely, medicine (170e). The temperance of (2) cannot obtain the benefits of knowledge and avoid the evils of ignorance in the way the temperance of (1) can. Unlike the latter, the former cannot rule over the technical sciences. The temperance of (2) is useless for the governing of households and cities.

As many commentators have pointed out, the two modes of self-knowledge appear to be the two modes of Socratic *elenchus*, or interrogation, formal and substantive. The substantive *elenchus* is conducted by someone who knows the subject matter of cross-examination; the formal *elenchus* is conducted by someone without such knowledge. Since the latter lacks the substantive knowledge, it has to rely on the formal criteria of knowledge. The substantive *elenchus* belongs to self-knowledge of (1), and the formal *elenchus* to self-knowledge of (2). Which of these two is the right way to understand the Socratic *elenchus*? Socrates professes to know nothing. If his profession of ignorance is not ironical but sincere, his cross-examination cannot belong to (1). It should be the formal *elenchus*. What kind of formal criterion of knowledge does Socrates employs in his formal *elenchus*? Gerasimos Santas suggests that a formal definition of knowledge can be used.[30] But Socrates never appeals to such a definition in his cross-examination.

He often appeals to the formal criterion of consistency. For example, Socrates says that Euthyphro's definition of piety is self-contradictory because it can make the same act pious (pleasing to the gods) and impious (not pleasing to the gods) at the same time. This is the method of exposing self-contradiction contained in a single proposition or belief. When he argues against Polus that to suffer injustice is better than to do injustice, he uses a different method of consistency (*Gorgias* 472e–479c). He shows that the rejection of this thesis is inconsistent with another belief held by Polus, namely, that it is more shameful to do injustice than to suffer it. This formal method exposes the inconsistency between different beliefs held by the same person. He employs this method in rejecting some definitions of temperance, for example, by showing that they are incompatible with the general belief that every virtue is something good and beautiful.

Though these two formal methods of inquiry are important for Socratic *elenchus,* they are not the most important ones. In the *Euthyphro,* as we noted, Socrates does not end his discussion by exposing the self-contradiction in the first definition of piety. Instead, he makes positive proposals for further discussion. In the *Laches* and the *Charmides*, Socrates rarely appeals only to the criterion of consistency in his arguments. Most of the time he appeals to the criterion of adequacy; he rejects most of the proposed definitions by showing their inadequacy. In the *Laches*, for example, the definition of courage as the ability to hold one's ground against the enemy in combat is rejected because its scope is too narrow to account for the range of courage that can be displayed in noncombat situations. To be sure, even this case of inadequacy can be characterized as one of inconsistency between two beliefs: (1) courage is restricted to combat situations, and (2) it is not so restricted. However, their formal inconsistency alone cannot tell which of these two beliefs is correct and which is incorrect.

The criterion of adequacy is richer than that of formal consistency. It is not a formal but substantive criterion. It is impossible to recognize the inadequacy of a proposed definition for courage without having some substantive knowledge of that virtue. Hence, the Socratic profession of ignorance can only be ironical. If it were sincere, the Socratic definition could not even get started, for it presupposes sufficient knowledge to identify the instances and the scope of the virtue under definition. Just imagine that Socrates and his interlocutors cannot agree on the instances of the virtue to be defined. That will make it impossible to conduct a Socratic definition. But Socrates and his interlocutors seldom disagree on what sort of things are the legitimate instances of courage or temperance. Without such a shared understanding, they could not even initiate the inquiry, and such a shared understanding is not formal but substantive. At the initial stage of Socratic definition, the substantive notion of virtue is indeed derived from conventional wisdom. But the Socratic inquiry always moves beyond conventional wisdom, and this move cannot be made without substantive knowledge of some transcendent standard.

If Socratic *elenchus* is a purely formal method, it can do nothing more than to expose the logical inconsistency in the conventional understanding of positive norms. Such a formal method can achieve the type of self-knowledge as defined in (2). On the other hand, if the Socratic method is substantive, it can make the move from the conventional to the transcendent stage. The substantive method can achieve the type of self-knowledge as defined in (1). This is none other than Socrates' idea of temperance as the power to govern households and cities with knowledge, and thereby make them happy (172d). He asks what kind of knowledge it would take to perform this marvelous function. Critias says that it should be the knowledge of good and evil (174b). This is the final definition of temperance in this dialogue; temperance is self-knowledge, the knowledge of what is good and evil for oneself.

Socrates' Divine Mission

In his debate with Callicles, we noted, Socrates appeals to both the traditional virtues and philosophy at the same time. But he is not appealing to two independent entities; the two become one in his philosophical understanding of conventional virtues. Because virtue is wisdom, love of virtue is love of wisdom, which is *philosophia*. The philosophical understanding of conventional virtues goes through two stages in the *Laches* and the *Charmides*. In the *Laches*, virtue is defined as the wisdom or knowledge of what is good; in the *Charmides*, its definition is further refined as the wisdom or knowledge of what is good for oneself. The definition of virtue becomes self-reflexive; virtue is not simply knowledge, but the knowledge of itself. On the surface, the two dialogues appear to be addressed to two different virtues, courage and temperance, but they really constitute one progressive definition for the Socratic virtue of self-knowledge.

To mark the importance of self-knowledge for the *Charmides*, Plato installs Chaerephon as the first one to greet Socrates when he appears on the opening scene of the dialogue (153b). The presence of Chaerephon thematically connects the dialogues backward to the *Apology* and forward to the *Gorgias*. In the *Apology*, Socrates defends himself against the charge of impiety by appealing to the divine command. Whatever he may have done to provoke the anger of his fellow Athenians, he has done it only to carry out the divine mission. He explains how his mission began. An impetuous friend of his youth, Chaerephon, had once gone to Delphi and asked the oracle whether there was anyone wiser than Socrates, and the priestess of Apollo gave the negative answer to this question. This response was so incredible that Socrates thought it must be a riddle. To decipher the riddle, he started testing those Athenians with a reputation for wisdom only to find that none of them knew anything important. They really did not know what was truly good or bad for themselves. Their ignorance was the ultimate source of their misconduct and misery; hence he had every reason to regard wisdom as the ultimate virtue, especially the wisdom and knowledge of oneself, as he equated it with the virtue of temperance in the *Charmides*.

In the *Gorgias*, Socrates chiefly relies on the virtue of temperance in his confrontation with Callicles. Against his beastly virtue of power and greed, Socrates not only advocates the virtue of temperance, but also derives all other virtues from it (507bc). To indicate that temperance as self-knowledge is the chief weapon against Callicles, Plato deploys Chaerephon as the spearhead of Socrates' entrance into his house. On their arrival, Callicles refers to the display of Gorgian rhetoric with the phrase "war and battle." Socrates' encounter with Gorgias and his company is going to be a bitter war, and Chaerephon fires the first shot for this war. Socrates asks him to put the first question to Gorgias, but Chaerephon does not know what to ask, and seeks Socrates' instruction. Socrates tells him to ask Gorgias *who he is* (447d). This is a strange suggestion because Chaerephon already knows who Gorgias is; in fact, he has just told Socrates that Gorgias is a friend of his. The suggestion is so strange that Chaerephon asks Socrates to clarify what he means by it, and Socrates replies that if Gorgias were a maker of shoes, his answer would be that he was a cobbler (447d). If that is what Socrates had in mind, he should have told Chaerephon to ask Gorgias what he was rather than who he was.

This strange incident at the opening of the *Gorgias* has special significance for the theme of self-knowledge. The question "who is he?" is only a question of personal identity under normal circumstances, but this question in the Socratic formula cannot be answered simply by giving his name. For the Socratic identity can be given only by discovering the state of his soul, which is determined by its self-knowledge. The entire dialogue should be understood as a series of tests for the self-knowledge of all the participants, that is, their temperance. This sovereign role of temperance is prepared by the *Charmides*, where temperance as self-knowledge is claimed to rule over itself and all other knowledge.

If temperance occupies such an exalted position, as Socrates says, it should be able to dictate the just way of behaving toward other human beings, too. But now suppose that the other human beings are not our friends but our enemies, and that we are locked with them in a battle for survival. Would the sovereign virtue of temperance still dictate that we should treat them with justice rather than attack them as our enemies? Could the Athenians show any justice toward the Persian armed forces, when they were about to invade and ravage the city of Athens? What is the scope of justice? Does it include our enemies as well as our friends? These are the questions of justice that immensely distress Callicles and Thucydides alike. The imperial Athenians came to believe that a theater of war was no place for justice, and that everybody had the natural right to do everything within one's power for one's survival.

This is what Callicles calls the law of nature or justice revealed by nature (483c–e). Because the Athenians believed they had been thrown into a theater of perpetual war, Thucydides writes, they claimed to have the right to take advantage of other states and exploit the weak ones.[31]

The world of Callicles is the world of Thucydides; it is the world of power and greed, aggression and predation. In such a world, even the Socratic virtue of temperance may not dictate justice, because justice may not be a matter of wisdom. Callicles may have the right to brand a temperate person as a fool and a coward (*Gorgias* 489e–492b). In ancient Greece, to be sure, the virtue of temperance had been regarded as the basis of all civic virtues, and a temperate person was supposed to be a just one. But it was also taken for granted that the connection between temperance and justice holds only within a community of friends. In such a community, it is obviously fitting to be just toward others, because the others are one's friends and a friend is an extension of oneself. Even Gorgias says that a competitive skill should not be used against one's friends and parents (*Gorgias* 456cd). Aristotle says that friendship is the true basis for the formation of a state (*Politics* 1280b35–40). In antiquity, friendship was based on kinship, and a tribal state was a community of kinship and friendship. But those days of primitive states were gone by the time of imperial Athens.

In the days of Callicles and Thucydides, the ethos of power and greed governed not only the relations of city-states, but also the internal politics of Athens. The city of Athens had become too large and too heterogeneous to be bound by the bond of kinship and friendship, and her internal politics had turned into an internecine war, wherein the politicians fought against one another with the new political weapon of Gorgian rhetoric. If Callicles is a warrior in such a war, how can Socrates convince him that he should seek justice rather than advantage, and that justice is the greatest good? Socrates' argument appears to be contextually misplaced; he appears to advocate for a theater of war what is appropriate for a community of peace and friendship. Hence, many commentators have said that Socrates' position against Callicles is notably ineffectual.

Some scholars, however, have thought that Socrates' arguments in the *Gorgias* are forceful and successful, or at least such is Socrates' own view because he says that his claims are secured and bound fast with arguments of adamant and iron (*Gorgias* 508e–509a). Gregory Vlastos makes this point especially for Socrates' argument against Polus to the effect that it is better to suffer injustice than to do it.[32] To be sure, Socrates gives an adamantine argument from the premise to the conclusion, and we cannot find any fault with his deductive inference. But that does not guarantee the truth of his premise. His argument stands on the premise that it is more shameful to do injustice than to suffer it. As Callicles points out, this premise can easily be rejected because it is derived from conventional wisdom. Since his premise is not proven, Socrates has given only a conditional argument, however adamantine its deductive logic may be. It is true only on the condition that the premise is true.

In his argument against Callicles, Socrates stands on a far more controversial premise, that is, justice is the greatest good of the agent's soul. This premise is by no means an axiomatic truth. Though it is obvious that one can benefit from the justice of others, it is by no means obvious that one can benefit from one's own justice. It may well be the case that my own justice benefits only others. When the others are not my friends but my enemies bent on taking advantage of me, why should I be just toward them? Socrates never takes up this question. Instead he situates his talk of justice not in the Calliclean world of perpetual war, but in the Pythagorean world of universal order and harmony, friendship and partnership (*Gorgias* 506d–508a). In such a world of harmony and friendship, there is no need to argue for the value of justice. In the Calliclean world of mutual aggression, on the other hand, there is no way to vindicate the virtue of justice.

The entire debate between Socrates and Callicles is conducted in two entirely different universes of discourse. Socrates advocates the life of virtue from the Pythagorean world of friendship and harmony, and Callicles responds to it from the Athenian world of aggression and predation. Because the two protagonists are exchanging their arguments from two diametrically opposed universes of discourse, they never succeed in joining their arguments. That is, they just talk past each other. For this reason, even Socrates feels unsure of his position. With his unusual modesty, he admits that he does not himself really *know* what he is talking about, and that he is only engaged in an inquiry with the hope of finding out the truth (*Gorgias* 506a, 509a). Some commentators have said that Socrates is not equipped with adequate resources for handling the momentous questions raised in the *Gorgias*. But what sort of resources does he need?

In the *Gorgias*, Socrates presents the Pythagorean friendship not merely as a beautiful ideal, but as the principle that governs the entire universe. In that case, our universe should be not a theater of war, but a community of love. Only by situating human life in such an orderly and friendly world, can Socrates meaningfully advocate the life of virtue. Hence, the Pythagorean friendship is the most important premise for Socrates' positive argument against the Calliclean ethics of greed and aggression. This important premise, which is introduced only as the claim of some wise men, is yet to be fully incorporated into Socrates' position. To that extent, his response to Callicles' challenge remains deficient and incomplete. In the remainder of this volume, we will see how Plato is going to make up for this deficiency in his other dialogues.

Notes

1. Plato, *Gorgias*, trans. T. Irwin (Oxford: University Press, 1979), 235.
2. Thucydides, *The History of the Peloponnesian War* 1.89–93.
3. J. M. Bury and Russell Meiggs, *A History of Greece*, 4th ed. (New York: St. Martin's Press, 1975), 165–66.
4. Thucydides, *History* 1.98–102.
5. Stone, *The Trial of Socrates* (New York: Doubleday, 1989), 85.
6. Bury and Meiggs, *A History of Greece*, 162.
7. *The Rhetoric of Morality and Philosophy* (Chicago: University of Chicago Press, 1991), 7–8.
8. Peter Green, *The Parthenon* (New York: *Newsweek*, 1973), 70, 82.
9. Peter Green, *A Concise History of Ancient Greece* (London: Thames and Hudson, 1973), 129.
10. Green, *A Concise History*, 117–31.
11. Plato, *Gorgias*, trans. T. Irwin, 237.
12. Bury and Meiggs, *A History of Greece*, 206.

13. Jacqueline de Romilly, *Thucydides and Athenian Imperialism*, trans. Philip Thody (Oxford: Blackwell, 1963), 86–97.

14. Thucydides, *History* 5.105.

15. Thucydides, *History* 1.124.2–3; 2.63.2.

16. Thucydides, *History* 2.65.

17. Thucydides, *History* 3.81.

18. Andrew Szegedy-Maszak, "Legends of the Greek Lawgivers," *Greek, Roman, and Byzantine Studies* 19 (1978):205. The legendary origin of the Spartan and the Cretan laws respectively from Apollo and Zeus is mentioned in the opening passage of the *Laws*.

19. For the story of its construction, see Peter Green, *The Parthenon* (New York, 1973), 76–83.

20. Green, *The Parthenon*, 76.

21. Green, *A Concise History*, 127.

22. An English translation of this text is given in Max Mueller, ed., *The Sacred Books of the East*, vols. 27 and 28, trans. James Legge (Delhi: Motilal Banarsidass, 1885).

23. For a further explanation of their distinction, see K. J. Dover, *Greek Popular Morality in the time of Plato and Aristotle* (Oxford: Blackwell, 1974), 247–54.

24. The broad scope of Roman piety was much more clearly stated than that of Greek piety. The Roman concept of piety begins with a proper attitude of reverence toward the gods and ends with respect for divine law concerning actions toward the state and other human beings. For a fuller account of Roman *pietas*, see Timothy Moore, *Artistry and Ideology: Livy's Vocabulary of Virtue* (Frankfurt am Main: Athenaum, 1989), 56–61.

25. For an instructive account, see Martha Nussbaum, *The Fragility of Goodness* (Cambridge: University Press, 1986), 94–121.

26. Terence Irwin, *Plato's Moral Theory* (Oxford: University Press, 1977), 18.

27. For the conventional character of these views, see W. K. C. Guthrie, *A History of Greek Philosophy* (Cambridge: University Press, 1975), 4:165.

28. This point has been made by many critics. See Max Pohlenz, *Aus Platos Werdezeit* (Berlin: Weidmannsche Buchhandlung, 1913), 53; Hans von Arnim, *Platos Jugenddialogue und die Entstehungszeit des Phaidros* (Leipzig: Teubner, 1914), 111, 117; Julius Stenzel, *Studien zur Entwicklung der platonischen Dialectik von Sokrates zu Aristoteles*, 2d ed. (Leipzig: Teubner, 1931), 11; T. G. Tuckey, *Plato's Charmides* (Cambridge: University Press, 1951), 33–37.

29. Santas, "Socrates at Work on Virtue and Knowledge in Plato's *Char-*

mides,'' in E. N. Lee et al., ed., *Exegesis and Argument* (New York: Humanities Press, 1973), 119.

30. Santas, ''Socrates at Work,'' 125–26.

31. *History* 1.76; 3.44; 5.89–91.

32. Vlastos, ''The Socratic Elenchus,'' *Oxford Studies in Ancient Philosophy* 1 (1983):27–58. His view is criticized by Richard Kraut, in the same issue of the journal, 58–74. My own critique is along the same line.

CHAPTER TWO

The Bond of Love and Friendship

The *Lysis*, the *Phaedo*, and the *Symposium*

In his encounter with Callicles, Socrates appeals to Pythagorean teaching as well as to the traditional virtues and values of Athens, and in this appeal he stresses the ideals of order and geometry, harmony and friendship. However, the Pythagorean ideals do not display their full force because he does not expound their nature. To make up for this deficiency, he needs to give a philosophical account of the Pythagorean ideals. He undertakes this task in the *Lysis*; its topic is the nature of friendship, the central Pythagorean ideal. This dialogue is highly Pythagorean in its content and in its form; its structure is governed by the art of combinatorics, a special branch of mathematics.

The *Lysis*

This is one of the shortest dialogues, but its complexity is staggering. In fact, it is one of Plato's most intricate constructions. Some of Socrates' arguments in the *Lysis* are so confusing and so slippery that they have been branded as eristic by a number of commentators. The ambiguity and complexity of his arguments are largely due to the semantic ambiguity and complexity of the term *philia*. This Greek word can be translated as love or friendship; it can easily be confused with another Greek word *eros*, which also means love, but with an erotic connotation. The word *philia* can be taken either as an active (to love someone or something) or as a passive (to be loved) verb. The object of *philia* can be a person, an animal, or a thing; hence *philia* can be either a one-way relation between a person and a thing (love of a horse), or a two-way reciprocal relation between two persons. In the *Lysis*, Socrates tries to unravel all these tangled semantic relations and confusions to explicate the dynamics of love.

As a general framework for this exploration, three kinds of love are presented in the following sequence: (1) Hippothales' love of Lysis, (2) the love of Lysis by his parents, and (3) the love between Lysis and Menexenus. Though all of these three can be called love, they are quite different. (1) is erotic love, which is based on sexual drives. (2) is parental love, which is based on blood-ties. It is the love of kinship. The relation of Ctesippus to his cousin Menexenus belongs to this love. (3) is the love of two young boys, which is based neither on sexual drives nor on kinship. In one important regard, (3) is different from both (1) and (2). Whereas the latter two may be a one-way relation of loving without being loved, (3) is a two-way relation of loving and being loved at the same time. (1) and (2) may be unilateral, but (3) is bilateral or reciprocal. Socrates introduces (2) and (3) as his way of starting the discussions with Lysis and Menexenus. Thus, (1) is not mentioned as a part of any discussion; Socrates hears about it from Ctesippus. But Hippothales' love of the young Lysis remains as a backdrop for the entire dialogue from the beginning to the end.

The dialogue goes through three rounds of discussion. In the first round, Socrates talks with Lysis about why someone is loved. In the second round, he talks with Menexenus about whether love should be reciprocal. In the third round, he talks with both boys about what sort of people become friends with each other. In this round, he presents a few combinatorial schemata for friendship:

(A) The like is a friend to the like.

(B) The unlike is a friend to the unlike.

Both of them are derived from conventional wisdom. (A) has been advocated by poets and natural philosophers, but they have not explained it. The fact that two things are alike appears to be no reason for their mutual attraction. So Socrates restates (A) in the following two schemata:

(A–1) The bad is a friend to the bad.

(A–2) The good is a friend to the good.

Being good and being bad appear to be good reasons for liking and disliking someone. Schema (A–1) is easily rejected. When two bad people come together, they can only hate each other. Schema (A–2) is also rejected. There can be no friendship between two good people, because they are self-sufficient and do not need each other's help (215a). The rejection of these two schemata is the rejection of (A).

Schema (B) may fare better than (A); it appears to explain the friendship between the rich and the poor, the doctor and the patient. In many cases, opposites attract each other. But Schema (B) is also rejected because of the cases where opposites cannot be friends, for example, there can be no friendship between a friend and an enemy, the just and the unjust, or the temperate and the intemperate (216b). Having exhausted (A) and (B), Socrates introduces another schema:

(C) What is neither good nor bad is a friend of the good.

For example, a sick body, which is neither totally good nor totally bad, is a friend of medicine, which is good. In Schema (C), the good is the object of love or friendship. But there are two kinds of good: intrinsic and instrumental. Medicine is an instrumental good; it is loved not for its own sake but as an instrument. On the other hand, health is an intrinsic good; it is loved for its own sake. The bad (e.g., disease) is the cause of the love of instrumental goods (e.g., medicine). Were it not for disease, we would not love medicine.

What love would still be left in a world totally devoid of the bad? What reason should we have to love anything in such a world? Socrates says that it is desire (*epithymia*) that is neither good nor bad. Desire is the cause of friendship, and the object of desire is what one is deficient in (221d). Desire is the longing for what should properly belong to oneself, though one has been deprived of it. What should properly belong to oneself is what is akin to oneself (*oikeion*), and the latter is the object of love (*eros*), friendship (*philia*), and desire (*epithymia*). From this naturally follows the final schema of friendship:

(D) One is a friend to what is akin to oneself.

However, this Schema cannot avoid the difficulties encountered in Schema (A), because what is akin appears to be a special case of what is like. So Socrates proposes to assume that what is akin is different from what is like. On this supposition, he tries to clarify the relation of what is akin to the good and the bad, and suggests the following three schemata:

(D–1) The bad is akin to the bad.

(D–2) The good is akin to the good.

(D–3) What is neither good nor bad is akin to what is neither good nor bad.

Though Lysis and Menexenus endorse these three schemata, Socrates points out that all of them are variants of Schema (A). Hence none of them can be accepted, but they cannot think of any other possibilities. He can only recapitulate all the schemata they have examined and rejected. Just then the two boys are taken away by their tutors, and the dialogue comes to an end. This aporetic ending hides some positive accomplishments. Though Socrates and his interlocutors have failed in articulating what is meant by "what is akin," they have established Schema (D) as the formula for friendship. To say that they cannot fully explain its meaning is not the same thing as to say that they reject it altogether. In fact, its acceptance is conspicuously stressed by the behavior of all the interlocutors. When Socrates says to Lysis and Menexenus, "If you two are friends to each other, you are akin (or belong to) each other by nature," the two boys positively assent in unison (221e).

The concept of what is akin or what belongs to oneself is as complex as the concept of *philia*. Socrates points out the many different senses of what is akin in terms of the soul, disposition, demeanor, and so on. The concept of what is akin (*oikeion*) is derived from the concept of family or household (*oikos*), which Aristotle regards as the first natural human bonding (*Politics* 1252b10–20). The parental love as represented by Lysis's parents and the sexual love as represented by Hippothales are the two basic elements for constituting a family. The family is made of husband and wife, whose bond is based on sexual attraction. When the family expands by producing children, the relation of parents to children is based on parental love. Hence, the parental and the sexual love are two salient examples of the natural bond between human beings. The love between Lysis and Menexenus is quite different; it is not based on the natural bond of sexual attraction or of parental care. Yet their friendship is also based on something akin to each other, as they emphatically assent to Socrates' suggestion to that effect.

Whatever binds the two boys together in a friendship only adds to the complexity of what it means for someone to be akin to another. It is the richness and variety of *akinness* as the basis of friendship that has been explored in the *Lysis*. As soon as friendship is conceived in terms of *akinness*, the love of a friend turns out to be the extension of the love of oneself because what belongs to oneself is the extension of oneself. This is the ultimate implication of the *Lysis*. It is instructive to compare this conception of love with the one that was examined in the first two rounds of discussion. In the first round, Socrates talked with Lysis on the nature of love in the context of usefulness (207d–210d). One loves a horse because it is useful for riding; one loves a quail because it is useful for cooking. If love is conceived in such an instrumental context, it is difficult to understand why it should be reciprocated. In the second round, this difficulty becomes the topic of discussion between Socrates and Menexenus, and they have no way of resolving this problem (211a–213d).

The third round of discussion introduces a new conception of love, which is diametrically opposed to the instrumental conception. The love of another person is now conceived as the extension of self-love. In Plato's world, Gregory Vlastos says, a human being is never loved as an individual, and Plato does not have the remotest conception of unconditional love for another human being. He regards this as the cardinal flaw in Plato's theory of love.[1] But this is not a complete account of Plato's theory of love. For him, another human being can be regarded either as an extension of or as totally alien to oneself. As long as other human beings are understood as totally alien to oneself, one's love of others is simply unintelligible. On the other hand, if they are conceived as the extension of oneself, one's love of others is the extension of one's self-love. In that case, it has only to be explained why the others should be understood as the extension of oneself. Christians have claimed their God as the common bond of all human beings or at least all Christians, and Buddhists have appealed to the universal selfhood that underlies the individuation of all sentient beings. In the *Lysis*, Plato elevates the ground of akinness between different individuals from their natural and emotional bond to their intellectual bond. This is his intellectual conception of love, which will be further elaborated in the *Phaedo* and the *Symposium*.

The Pythagorean Fellowship

Both in its form and content, as we have already noted, the *Lysis* is highly Pythagorean. We have noted the extensive use of elementary combinatorics in the construction of the dialogue. It is Plato's first use. He will use it again in the *Republic* (in his account of the deterioration of the ideal state), the *Theaetetus* (in his account of perceptual errors), and the *Parmenides* (in his examination of the eight hypotheses). Though I have no proof, I assume that Plato's elementary combinatorics is a Pythagorean legacy. There may appear to be nothing uniquely Pythagorean about the thematic content of the *Lysis*. For the love (*philia*) of friends is as universal a phenomenon as anything can be; parental love and the love of kinship are its basic manifestations. However, the Pythagoreans gave it a unique form by adopting it as the basic ideal for instituting their brotherhood. The Pythagorean Society was a community of *philia*, and their notion of *philia* was revolutionary.

In ancient or primitive societies, the love of kinship or an extended family served as the basis for social solidarity. This kinship-based love was *philia*; the concept of a friend was interchangeable with the concept of a relative. All those who belonged to the same kin were friends to one another, and those who did not were the strangers or enemies. The distinction between a friend (*philos*) and a stranger (*xenos*) was the most important one for the close-knit tribal community. The oldest civic virtue in ancient Greece, *aidos* (mutual respect), was closely related to *philos*. The virtue of *aidos* required not only the respect for each other's rights, but also the duty of defending the other members of the tribe when they were attacked by outsiders.[2] *Aidos* was the virtue of caring for the *philos* against the *xenos*; conversely, friends owed the duty of mutual care and respect to one another.

Though the love of kinship was the most natural basis for a tribal state, it started to show its obvious shortcomings when members of different tribal states were brought into contact by the developing means of communication and transportation. The love of kinship had no resources to cope with the interaction of different tribal communities. The Homeric world tried to deal with this problem by extending the care of the *philos* to the *xenos*. For example, the host had the duty of treating the guest like a friend, though he was a stranger, and the guest had the duty of responding in the same spirit. The famous case for the violation of this host-guest relation was Paris's abduction of Helen, when he came as a guest to Menelaus's house in Sparta. When the extension of *philia* failed in the relation of tribal states, it resulted in a state of war, which in turn led to power politics.

The politics of power rules in the world of strangers, whereas the politics of love governs the community of friends. Power politics begins where the bond of friendship and kinship ends. The ancient Greek city-states were becoming too big to be held together by the bond of friendship and kinship. Though many Greeks down to Aristotle's day did not abandon the ideal that the state was not an assembly of strangers for the sake of convenience but a community of mutually caring friends, this old ideal was no longer operative. The state came to include too many people, who were just strangers by the old standard of friendship. Hence the new ideal of power and *pleonexia* came to replace the old ideal of brotherly love and mutual care, and Callicles stands as the advocate for this new ideal. Since the extension of *philia* could not cope with the expansion of the political communities, the Pythagoreans came up with a new idea of *philia*, the brotherhood based on intellectual kinship. This was their idea of *philosophia*. Pythagoreanism was not merely a school of philosophy, but a new political program that founded a number of cities in southern Italy and Greece.

It has been said that the word *philosophia* was a Pythagorean invention.[3] But what meaning did it have for the Pythagoreans? Though the word is generally translated as love of wisdom, it literally means the lover or friend (*philos*) of wisdom (*sophia*). The expression "the lover of wisdom'' makes sense, but the expression ''the friend of wisdom'' does not if we assume that friendship is a reciprocal relation between two or more persons. In its place, let us try another expression ''the friend or friendship in wisdom''. Love of wisdom and friendship in wisdom are the two dimensions of Pythagorean *philosophia*, both of which are represented in the *Lysis*. Each of the two boys gets passionately involved in philosophy (213d), and their joint involvement constitutes their friendship in wisdom. In search of wisdom, each of them finds the other as someone akin to himself, because they are in love with the same object.

If the relationship of Lysis and Menexenus is taken as an incipient friendship in wisdom, it makes an important contrast with two other forms of *philia* introduced as the backdrop of the *Lysis*. They are the parental love of Lysis's parents, and the sexual love of Hippothales. One is based on blood-ties, and the other on sexual impulses; both of them are physically based and highly emotional. By contrast, the incipient friendship in wisdom between the two young boys is intellectually based. Its intellectual basis is not their own making, but introduced by Socratic inquiry. Before this inquiry, their relation could not have been any more intellectual or any less emotional than the other two forms of love, because theirs was the most natural friendship of two innocent boys. But Socrates knows how to arouse their intellectual curiosity and engage them in a philosophical inquiry, and the two young boys respond by developing their love of wisdom and forming an intellectual partnership.

The *Lysis* demonstrates how the natural bond of two boys is transformed into an intellectual one, the bond of *philosophia*, and this transformation was perhaps the pedagogical ideal Plato had for setting up his Academy. In fact, I suspect, that the *Lysis* was written as a memorial for the founding of Plato's own school at the Academy. In support of this thesis, I will offer the following textual evidence. At the opening of the dialogue, Socrates walks along the outside of the walls from the Academy to the Lyceum, and meets a group of boys at the gate. This event is generally treated as a routine in Socrates' life, because a palaestra is a familiar setting for a Socratic dialogue. But his entrance into the palaestra is never so meticulously described in any other dialogue as it is in the *Lysis*.

On seeing Socrates, one of the older boys, Hippothales, asks, "Whither and whence?" Socrates replies, "From the Academy, straight to the Lyceum." The older boy invites him to join them: "Straight to us. Won't you turn in? It will be worth your while." Puzzled by this remark, Socrates asks, "Turn in where? And whom do you mean by us?" In reply, Hippothales points to an enclosure with an open door, and says that by "us" he means a great number of fine boys passing their time. With his curiosity aroused, Socrates now asks, "What is this place? And how are you passing your time?" Hippothales explains that it is a palaestra recently erected, and that they are passing their time mainly having discussions (203a–204a).

A palaestra chiefly devoted to discussions! That is quite unusual. Moreover, this unusual establishment is situated between the Academy and the Lyceum, the two gymnasia closely affiliated with the traditional education of Athenian youth. In his narration, Socrates mentions the open door and the little gate, and associates the little gate with the source of the Panops. This palaestra is said to have been recently erected. Do these remarks not refer to the recent *opening* of Plato's Academy? There is a further significance in associating the gate with the source of the Panops, which means seeing all things, the synoptic (*synopsis*) vision that Socrates presents as the ultimate end of education in the *Republic*. To open the gate to education is to open the field of vision to see all things.

Lest his readers miss the significance of these allusions and associations, Plato has Socrates put a surprise question to the boys, "Who is your teacher there?" Why should he assume that a bunch of boys should have a teacher for merely talking and passing their time unless Plato wants to depict it as an academic institution. The surprise question does not ruffle Hippothales. He says that their teacher is "a friend and admirer of yours, Mikkos." Socrates replies, "and no ordinary man either, a most competent sophist." A resident sophist for a palaestra! That is another unusual feature of this establishment. I do not believe that there was a sophist named Mikkos. In all likelihood, Mikkos is a fictitious character invented for the occasion. Hippothales says that the sophist is a friend and admirer of Socrates. This is a fair description of Plato himself; Mikkos may be another pseudonym for Plato, invented for this special occasion.[4] He may be big and broad (Plato), but small and short (Mikkos) in comparison with Socrates.

The ensuing conversation takes place in the atmosphere of a typical schoolroom. I cannot recall any other dialogue that is conducted in such an atmosphere. In the early dialogues, moreover, Socrates rarely talks with young school children except for two occasions. In the *Charmides*, he talks with the young Charmides, but he is soon replaced by an adult, Critias. In the *Euthydemus*, he talks with the young Cleinias. As we will see later, however, this dialogue is also closely associated with the problem of teaching. Hence, there is a close connection between the *Euthydemus* and the *Lysis*, which is indicated by the presence of Ctesippus in both dialogues. For these reasons, I am tempted to see the *Lysis* as Plato's work not only for demonstrating the possibility of *philosophia* as an intellectual bond of love, but also for commemorating the establishment of his Academy dedicated to this Pythagorean ideal.

The *Phaedo*

The *Phaedo* is even more Pythagorean than the *Lysis*. It is narrated by one Pythagorean (Phaedo) to another (Echecrates). The chief interlocutors for Socrates are Cebes and Simmias, who are identified as followers of the eminent Pythagorean Philolaus (61d). The central theme of the dialogue is Socrates' conception of *philosophia*, the Pythagorean ideal. He articulates the nature of philosophy as the art of dying or the training for death, and death is the liberation of the soul from the body (64a–c, 67e). The body is a perpetual hindrance to the soul's search for truth. The soul can grasp the truth only by dissociating its rational function from the bodily senses, because the objects of its pure thought are Justice, Beauty, and other Forms, which transcend the bodily senses. The body is the source of all evils. It is subject to all kinds of disease, and breeds countless desires and fears, which in turn lead to war and civil discord. The acquisition of wealth is the universal cause of war, and we are compelled to acquire wealth for the care of the body. The soul can never seek what it loves, namely, wisdom and knowledge, until it is released from the chains of the body and purified from its contamination.

Since death can secure the liberation of the soul from the body, Socrates says, a philosopher should not fear but eagerly look forward to his death. This is an elaboration of what he had earlier said to Callicles. When Callicles said that the life of temperance was not a real living but as dead as the life of stones and corpses, Socrates wondered who was really alive and who was really dead (*Gorgias* 492e). In the *Phaedo*, he is restating the difference of their outlooks on life as the difference between the life of the soul and the life of the body. The Calliclean life of appetites is the life of the body; it is the life of war and strife. In contrast, philosophy is the life of the soul; it seeks what is truly akin to the soul. The life of the body is the death of the soul; the struggle to gratify bodily desires inevitably frustrates the aspiration of the soul. Hence, the life of the soul can be secured only by the death of the body.

Because the life and death of the soul are inversely connected with the life and death of the body, the criteria of being alive and dead are systematically opposed between Socrates and Callicles. What is alive by the criterion of body is what is dead by the criterion of soul, and vice versa. The same systematic opposition also affects our conception of virtues, according to Socrates. Consider the nature of courage. This is the virtue of having no fear for the death of one's body; it is the most obvious virtue for the philosopher. There is no reason for the philosopher to fear the death of the body; the philosopher eagerly waits for it. This philosophical sense of courage cannot apply to the lover of the body, who has every reason to fear its death. But even this person will have the courage to risk the safety of the body, if he or she is compelled to protect something of bodily value such as honor or wealth that can justify the risk. Hence, the same word *courage* covers two quite different virtues: courage in its vulgar sense and courage in its philosophical sense.

Likewise, Socrates says, there are two types of temperance, the virtue of tempering and controlling appetites. Temperance in its philosophical sense comes naturally to the philosopher, who despises the appetites. But the lover of the body has no reason to temper or control his or her appetite unless its satisfaction will eventually produce some unfortunate consequences that can outweigh the momentary pleasure of its gratification. The virtue of temperance for the lover of the body requires the calculation of future pleasures and pains against present ones. This is temperance in its vulgar sense, which Socrates identifies as an economy of exchange, "pleasures for pleasures, pains for pains, fear for fear"—in short, the exchange of the smaller for the greater goods in the world of the body (69b).

Socrates says that a philosopher would rather exchange all these virtues of the bodily world for the one true virtue of wisdom, and that this exchange alone can secure the true courage, temperance, and justice. The true virtue of wisdom is the virtue of knowing the Forms. This is not the virtue of wisdom that was claimed as the essence of all virtues in the *Laches* and the *Charmides*. The virtues of these two dialogues still belong to the popular or vulgar sense of virtue, because they are concerned with the affairs of the bodily world such as fighting in a battle or managing a household and a state. The vulgar virtue, Socrates says, is only an illusory appearance of true virtue, which is fit for slaves. The true virtue of wisdom becomes possible with the purification of the soul from the defilement of the bodily world and its initiation into the intelligible world. These two processes of spiritual perfection require the death of the body and the practice of philosophy. This Socratic view of death and philosophy makes sense only on the condition that the soul is immortal and that there is another world for the soul after death. Hence, the immortality of the soul and the existence of the other world become the central topics for discussion in the remainder of the dialogue.

Let us first consider the various arguments given for immortality. The first of them is the argument of opposites: everything is generated from its opposite, for example, the larger from the smaller and the smaller from the larger, the weaker from the stronger and the stronger from the weaker. Since this is the general principle governing the generation and corruption of all things, Socrates says, the living must come from the dead, and the dead from the living (72a). By the dead he means the souls of the dead. The souls of the dead must exist if the souls of the living are to come from them. Therefore the soul must survive the death of the body. In further support of this view, Socrates introduces the doctrine of recollection. If our knowledge comes by recollection, the soul must have existed before its birth in this world, because *recollection* means to recall what the soul had learned before its birth.

Socrates stresses two features of knowledge by recollection: its perfection and its priority to sense perception. For example, any two things can never be perfectly equal in the world of sense perceptions, but we have the knowledge of what it is to be perfectly equal. Hence, knowledge cannot be derived from sense perception. On the contrary, knowledge should be prior to sense perception. Without having the knowledge of true equality, we cannot recognize any two objects as equal or even approximately equal in the world of sense perception (75b). The same thing is equally true of our knowledge of Beauty, the Good, and Justice. If so, our knowledge also proves the existence of Forms, because they alone can be the objects of knowledge. Socrates says that these two things—the existence of Forms and the existence of the soul before its birth—stand or fall together (76e).

Even if his argument is sound, Socrates has only proven the pre-existence of the soul. But that is not strong enough to prove its post-existence, that is, the soul will continue to exist after the death of its body. For the latter proof, he offers the argument of affinity. There are two kinds of being, the visible objects of this world and the invisible Forms of the other world. The visible objects are mutable; the invisible ones are immutable. The soul is like the invisible objects, while the body is like the visible objects. Therefore, the soul is indestructible and immutable, while the body is destructible and mutable (79a–80b). When the soul is purified, it regains its affinity to the invisible world, and becomes like the gods and lives with them. On the other hand, if it is polluted and impure, it becomes like physical objects, heavy and ponderous. Such a polluted soul is dragged back to the visible world, and wanders around graves and monuments until it gets imprisoned in another body (81cd). Philosophy alone can deliver the soul from its imprisonment in the body.

At this point, Socrates pauses and invites objections from Cebes and Simmias. Simmias says that the relation of the body and the soul may be like the relation of a lyre and its harmony. Though its harmony is invisible, its existence is still dependent on the lyre, a visible object (86a). Likewise, though the soul is like the invisible objects, it may not be able to exist after the destruction of its body. Cebes' objection is different. Although the soul may survive its present body, it may eventually wear itself out after wearing a series of bodies (87d). Socrates disposes of Simmias's objection without much difficulty. His metaphor of a lyre expresses the view that the mind is an epiphenomenon of the body. In response to this view, Socrates simply cites the everyday phenomenon in which the soul opposes or controls the affections of the body. If the soul were only a by-product of the body, he says, this phenomenon would be totally unaccountable.

Socrates says that Cebes' objection is much more difficult to handle because it involves the question of causation (96a). To explain this point, he recounts the philosophical journey of his own youth. When he was young, he was deeply fascinated with natural philosophy because he thought it provided a splendid account of causation. However, he soon realized that there were many things that could not be explained by the theory of physical causation, for example, why the addition of one to one makes two. When he was losing his faith in natural philosophy, he heard of Anaxagoras's exciting doctrine that the mind (*nous*) is the cause of all things. Since the mind always aims at the best, he expected Anaxagoras to say that the mind directs and arranges everything for the best. But this expectation was soon dashed when he acquired Anaxagoras's works and studied them. Anaxagoras talked only of physical causes.

Socrates cites two sorts of things that cannot be explained in terms of physical causation. They are mathematical truth and human behavior. It is obvious that physical causation has no place in mathematics. As to human behavior, Socrates distinguishes between causes and conditions. Though physical entities provide the conditions for human behavior, they cannot be its cause. For example, Socrates is sitting in jail instead of running away to Megara or some other place. Though this behavior would be impossible without the support of his sinews and bones and other material conditions, Socrates says, none of these things is its cause. The real cause of his behavior is none other than his belief that he is doing the best (98d–99b). Socrates says that natural philosophers have not been able to see the vital distinction between causes and conditions.

Since he could neither learn about true causes from others nor discover them himself, Socrates says, he invented his own method of inquiry. This was to discover the truth of things by discourse instead of looking at them directly. This indirect method was only a second best, and its purpose was to avoid the danger of the direct method, which was similar to the danger of being blinded by looking directly at an eclipse of the sun (99de). This indirect method is the famous hypothetical method. It is to propose a hypothesis to account for something and see what consequences follow from the hypothesis. By using this method, Socrates says, he tried to give his own causal theory in terms of Forms as follows. First, he assumes the existence of Forms such as Beauty, the Good, and Largeness. Second, he assumes that they are the causes for phenomenal entities. For example, the Form of Beauty is the cause of all beautiful things, or rather the latter are made beautiful by participating in the former.

The theory of Forms and their participation can be restated in terms of presence. Instead of saying that all beautiful things participate in the Form of Beauty, we can say that the Form of Beauty is present in all beautiful things. The theory of participation is also a theory of predication. We can give the name (or predicate) of Beauty to some object by virtue of the fact that it participates in the Form of Beauty (102b). But how do all these theories contribute to the proof of immortality? They are used in the final argument for immortality, which is very hard to follow (102b–106d). The thrust of the argument may be summed up as follows. Beside the Forms, there are other causes (''subtle causes''). Since they are like the Forms, they are as indestructible as the Forms. One of these subtle causes is the soul whose indestructible character is life. Therefore, the soul cannot die.

Since the soul is immortal and indestructible, Socrates concludes, its care should be our primary and eternal concern (107c). When we arrive in Hades, we will be rewarded or punished for the way we have taken care of our souls. The virtuous souls will be allowed to go to a pure land of bliss, and the irredeemably wicked ones will be hurled into Tartarus for extinction. The curable ones will be punished for correction and redemption. The system of judgment for the dead is basically the same as was portrayed in the *Gorgias*. But the *Phaedo* presents one element that was not in the *Gorgias*. This is the elaborate picture of the earth and the other world. Nonetheless, both versions serve the same purpose of conveying Pythagorean faith in the cosmos that Socrates emphatically stated in the *Gorgias*. The object of this faith is not only the order of the physical universe, but the existence of moral order, that is, the virtuous are rewarded, and the wicked are punished.

How sound are the arguments for immortality? Traditionally, this has been regarded as the most important question in the *Phaedo*, and it has been the topic of many fine discussions and commentaries. Though I cannot add anything significant to this vast literature, I cannot avoid noting that those arguments are far from convincing, and are often outright flimsy. Keenly aware of their weakness, Plato seldom repeats those arguments in any other dialogues, even when he reaffirms his faith in immortality. Even in the *Phaedo*, those arguments are offered only as fables or likely stories. Perhaps to indicate this point, Socrates stresses the idea of fable at the opening of the dialogue. Noting the inseparable connection between pleasure and pain, he compares them to two creatures with one head, and says that this would have been a good material for Aesop's fable (60b). He also versified Aesop's fables as his way of complying with the repeated dream, which kept telling him to practice arts. The arguments for immortality are no more than a series of fables. In fact, Socrates presents his talk about the other world and life after death only as a myth or a plausible story (61e).

Every fable is supposed to carry a moral. What are the morals of the fables told in the *Phaedo*? I propose that they are meant to be an elaboration of the position Socrates took against Callicles in the *Gorgias*. In the *Phaedo*, the confrontation of Socrates with Callicles is restated as the battle between the life of the soul and the life of the body. The life of the soul can never be understood in the world of bodies, but only in the world of Forms, by virtue of which it has its own power of action and causation. The Forms are the essential constituents of the world of the soul as much as the material objects are the essential constituents of the world of the body. The soul is helplessly trapped in the prison of the body, and is defiled by its degrading appetites. To save the soul from its prison and cleanse it from its defilement is the function of philosophy. In the *Gorgias*, Socrates did not elaborate on this function of philosophy when he presented philosophy as a way of life.

In the opening section of the dialogue (58a–c), Plato sets up the salvic function of philosophy as the central theme by mentioning the annual pilgrimage from Athens to Delos as the cause for delaying Socrates' execution. This annual event took place in commemoration of Theseus's mission to Crete. In those days, Athens was under the rule of Crete, and every year she was forced to send seven young men and seven maidens as a tribute to the king of Crete, who gave them to the Minotaur to devour.[5] On the third of these sacrificial voyages, Theseus was the leader of the party of fourteen. Planning to kill the Minotaur, he took only five women and nine men, two of whom had to be disguised as women. They killed the monster and saved themselves. After this event, it became a sacred Athenian custom to send a mission to Apollo of Delos every year, and to allow no execution to take place in Athens from the time the ship is crowned at the outset of its voyage until it safely returns to Athens. This sacred custom delayed the execution of Socrates.

Though this story is told to explain why the execution was delayed, it sets the stage for Socrates' final talk with his friends before his death. In response to Echecrates' question of who were present at Socrates' final talk, Phaedo names two groups of people, nine native Athenians and five strangers, although there were a few others beside these. And the last two of the nine natives are two young men of aggressive temper, Ctesippus and Menexenus. These two seem to correspond to the two young men who were disguised as young girls in Theseus's party. As Ronna Burger points out, the number involved in these two groups of people coincide with the number of people Theseus had supposedly taken to Crete.[6] Kenneth Dorter suggests that Plato is trying to set up a parallel between the *Phaedo* and the story of Theseus.[7] In setting up this parallel, Dorter notes, Plato slightly changes the legend. According to the original legend, Theseus was included among the fourteen young people to be sacrificed. According to Plato's version, however, Theseus is not included in the fourteen. That is, Socrates is not included in the fourteen people named by Phaedo. By this alteration, Dorter astutely observes, Plato is telling us that the parallel in question is not a matter of coincidence but a product of elaborate design.

What message is conveyed by the parallel? According to Burger, it is supposed to tell us that Socrates' last conversation is presented as a reenactment of Theseus's victory over the Minotaur. What does the Minotaur stand for? Dorter says that it stands for the fear of death; in his last conversation, Socrates is trying to conquer the fear of death for himself and his friends.[8] In endorsing this view, Burger says, "The Minotaur that they must together confront is the childish fear of death that threatens to overcome all manliness."[9] But the Minotaur may stand for something much more basic than the fear of death. What is at stake in the *Phaedo* is something much more troublesome than the problem of death. It is the problem of life. The Minotaur should be taken as the symbol for the life of the body, the power of its appetites. It is like the mythical monster with the head of a bull and the body of a human. Plato often compares the unruly appetites to beasts and monsters.

The sacrificial tribute to the monster is a symbol of tyranny by appetites not only over the individual soul but also over the entire state. The Minotaur is a symbol of Cretan imperialism; it can also serve as a symbol of Athenian imperialism. The latter point is suggested by Delos as the destination of the annual mission. Delos was the initial center for the Delian League, which eventually became the Athenian empire. The annual tribute from Athens to Crete was not much different from the tribute that Athenian imperialists are now exacting from their subject states.[10] What the Athenians need is another Theseus, who can free and save them from the jaws of a far greater monster than the Minotaur, that is, their own imperial appetites. This new warrior is none other than Socrates the philosopher.

Socrates talks about a monster as soon as he is released from the prison chains and allowed to meet with his friends. Noting the inseparable connection between pleasure and pain, he says that they are like two creatures with one head. If Aesop had known of this, Socrates says, he would have composed a fable about a war between them and a god's attempt to reconcile them. When the god could not do it, he joined their two heads together (60c). In the *Gorgias*, Socrates stressed that the world of appetites is the world of pleasures and pains, and that it is the world of perpetual war. It is his mission to free and save the soul from this monster of aggression and predation. In this mission, the immortality of the soul, or rather its proof, serves as Ariadne's thread. By following it, Socrates can find his way out of the world of the body, just as Theseus found his way back to safety through the twisted labyrinth after killing the Minotaur.

If the liberation of the soul is the central message of the *Phaedo*, how effective is it as a Socratic response to the Calliclean challenge? It stands on the separation of two worlds, the world of the body and the world of the soul. These two worlds are governed by two different systems of value and two different principles of volition. The conflict of these two systems and principles was the conflict between two ways of living in the *Gorgias*, and their conflict is now resolved by the separation of the two worlds in the *Phaedo*. By this resolution, Socrates is willing to hand over the world of the body to Callicles, because it is the world of misery and degradation. He is only eager to get out of it and travel to the world of the soul. To accomplish this passage by the purification of the soul is the function of philosophy.

This is a highly negative response to the Calliclean challenge. It is built on hatred of this world and longing for the other world. Socrates has nothing but unmitigated contempt for the phenomenal world. Its only function is to imprison and defile the soul. In that case, Socrates can say to Callicles that all the power and glory of this world only lead to the misery and defilement of the soul. Pleasures and pains are no more than nails for riveting the soul to the body (83d). But such a negative response as this cannot be a satisfactory resolution of the Calliclean challenge. If the world of the body has no positive value, its existence is incompatible with Pythagorean faith in the rational order of the universe, which was the basic premise for Socrates' stand against Callicles in the *Gorgias*.

If the phenomenal world is by its own nature so evil, then people like Callicles must be its only natural products. If so, there is no point in reproaching them with indignation as Socrates did in the *Gorgias*. Socrates' critical stance in that dialogue makes sense only on the supposition that the phenomenal world is inherently good but has been contaminated by Calliclean greed and ambition. Instead of offering us the

wisdom of redeeming the phenomenal world from the tyranny of appetites, Socrates has urged us to hand over that world to Callicles and his
cohorts. Socrates cannot be said to reenact Theseus's mission to Crete,
which was to slay and subdue the monster. Instead he decides to flee
from it to the other world.

Even his Pythagorean friends are assembled only to form a chorus of
assurance; their function is limited to assuring his escape route to the
other world. This is quite unfaithful to their grand idea of *kosmos*, the
order and unity of the entire universe, including this world. This discrepancy between the Pythagorean idea and the Socratic escape is the
fatal flaw of the *Phaedo* as a response to the Calliclean challenge, and
Plato tries to redress this fatal flaw in the *Symposium*.

The *Symposium*

The *Symposium* takes an unusual format; it is not really a dialogue.
It is the story of a banquet at Agathon's house in celebration of his
victory at the tragedy festival. Having grown tired of drinking, the ban-
queters decide to give a series of speeches in praise of love (*eros*).
Some of the speeches are remembered and narrated by Aristodemus to
Apollodorus, who then relates them to Glaucon on their way from Phaleron to Athens. Let us go over those speeches.

Phaedrus says that love is the oldest god who gives the greatest
goods. Love provides the best guidance for living well especially by
giving us the sense of shame and sense of pride in acting well. One
feels the sense of shame more keenly in front of the boy one loves
than before anyone else. If inspired by love, even ordinary people can
overcome all fears. They can sacrifice even their lives for the sake of
love. Alcestis is the proof; she was willing to die to save her husband.
But Orpheus did not wish to die for the woman he loved, and he was
punished for that by the gods. When the sacrifice of one's own life is
made by the beloved as in the case of Achilles, it is even more admired
by the gods. They honor virtue more highly when it comes from love.
Phaedrus concludes his speech by reaffirming that love is the most an-

cient of the gods, the most honored, and the most powerful in helping both the living and the dead gain virtue and happiness.

Pausanias begins his speech by a critique of the previous speech. Phaedrus's praise of love was indiscriminate; he did not make the distinction between two kinds of love, the heavenly and the vulgar (or common). They come from two different Aphrodites. The heavenly Aphrodite is the daughter of Uranus, the god of heaven; the vulgar Aphrodite is the daughter of Zeus and Dione, and her name is Pandemos. The vulgar love is for the vulgar, who are more concerned with the body than with the soul, and who do not care whether their manner of love is noble or not. The heavenly love shuns wantonness and fickleness. His followers seek the intellectual association of the mind. To safeguard this noble relation of the lover and the beloved, Pausanias says, the city makes and enforces the laws of pederasty. He ends his speech by portraying the ideal relation of love as a partnership for gaining wisdom and virtue. The older of the two teaches the younger to become wiser and better, and the younger eagerly follows. This is the paradigm of heavenly love, and all other forms of love belong to the vulgar goddess.

Eryximachus begins his speech, commending Pausanias's distinction of two loves. As a student of medicine, he knows that the power of love is not restricted to the human world. It also operates in the world of animals and plants, and in the world of the gods as well. Health and harmony prevail where heavenly love rules; disease and destruction result where vulgar love prevails. This general principle is exhibited by the seasons of the year. When the elements are animated by the noble species of love, their mixture is temperate and produces good harvests. In contrast, when the seasons are controlled by the crude species of love, they produce hails and blights, death and diseases. All technical arts are in the service of heavenly love. Medicine restores the harmony of elements in the body; music creates love and concord between the various opposite elements. Even the rites of sacrifice are for creating harmony between humans and gods; hence the virtue of piety flows from love. So do the virtues of temperance and justice; even happiness and good fortune are gifts of love.

Unlike the natural scientist Eryximachus, Aristophanes begins his speech by giving a historical account of humankind. In the beginning, the shapes of human beings were quite different from their present shapes. There were three kinds of human beings: male, female, and hermaphrodite. The male sprang from the sun, the female from the earth, and the hermaphrodite from the moon. Each individual was round in shape and had two front sides, each of which had a pair of hands and legs. In the pride of their power, they attacked the gods, and Zeus came up with an idea that could weaken the human beings without killing them. This was to cut each of them in half. Ever since this massive operation, every human being feels the instinctual longing to seek and to be united with its other half, and this feeling is love. When a lover has the good fortune of meeting his or her other half, they are overcome with the feeling of belonging together and develop a lifelong bond of love. There is only one road to human happiness: we must bring our love to perfection by recovering our original wholeness. For this, love gives us the greatest hope of all.

Agathon begins his speech by citing one common fault of all the previous encomia. Instead of really praising the god of love, the previous speakers have congratulated human beings on the good things that come to them from him. To make up for this deficiency, Agathon compiles a list of glittering epithets for love: among the gods, he is the happiest, the youngest, and the most beautiful. He is also soft and delicate, supple and fluid. He is neither the cause nor the victim of injustice. He does no wrong to gods or human beings; he abhors violence. Beside the virtue of justice, he has the greatest share of temperance because he has power over pleasures and passions. He is also full of courage; he can even control Ares. He is the fountain of wisdom; all technical arts are derived from his wisdom. Before he was born, necessity was king among the gods. But since his birth, all good things have come to gods and humans alike through love of beauty.

In response to Agathon's speech, Socrates says that he was reminded of Gorgias. His speech was in the style of Gorgian rhetoric, which applies the most beautiful predicates to the object of discourse, whether they are truly applicable or not. Hence, Socrates feared that Agathon would end the speech by sending the Gorgian head against his own. This remark is evidently reminiscent of Gorgon's head and its frightful power of paralyzing anyone who sees it. Socrates feels the need of finding out how much truth or falsehood lies behind Agathon's Gorgian rhetoric. So he subjects Agathon to a brief cross-examination, and forces him to conclude that the god of love deserves none of the superlative attributes. Contrary to Agathon's speech, love does not possess beauty and goodness; that is why love perpetually seeks them. Socrates points out that the ultimate nature of love is desire, which arises from deficiency rather than from plentitude. In the *Lysis* (221de), he said that desire was the cause of love.

Socrates says that the art of love is the one thing he knows well, because he has learned it from the wise, renowned priestess of Mantinea, Diotima. He recounts the story of love as he learned it from her years ago. Love is not a god, but the desire (*epithymia*) and the spirit (*daimon*). He is the son of Poros (resourcefulness) and Penia (poverty). Born of a mortal and an immortal, love is himself neither mortal nor immortal. His existence lies in the domain of in-between; it is in between wisdom and ignorance. He is not tender and fair as usually supposed, but tough and rough, barefoot and homeless, like his mother. Like his father, he is vigorous and resourceful in pursuing what he needs. *Eros* is not beautiful as Agathon says, but loves and seeks beauty because he does not have it. Love is the desire for the permanent possession of the beautiful and the good. How does love seek its goal? By giving birth in beauty. All of us are pregnant in body and in soul, and we naturally desire to give birth as soon as we come to a certain age. Procreation is the way of mortals to achieve immortality; it is the mortal substitute for immortality.

While some people reproduce themselves in the world of bodies, others are pregnant in their souls. Some of them are the poets and the artists who leave their works for posterity and immortality. Warriors and statesmen achieve their immortality in honor and fame. Then there are those who achieve it in wisdom and other virtues. By far the greatest part of wisdom is the virtue of governing cities and households, which comprise justice and temperance. Hence, the laws of Lycurgus and Solon are finer progeny than any mortal children. But all these marvelous products belong to the lesser mysteries of love Socrates learned from Diotima; the final and the highest mystery of love is constituted by the ladder of love. A lover first falls in love with one body, and realizes that the beauty of one body is akin to the beauty of other bodies. So he must love all beautiful bodies. But he will soon see far greater beauty in the souls than in the bodies, and then appreciate the beauty of knowledge and wisdom. Finally, he will see Beauty itself, pure and absolute. This is the famous story of the ladder of love and its ascent (211bc).

At the top of the ladder, one finally sees the Form of Beauty, which surpasses all the beauties on earth. It never waxes or wanes; unlike earthly beauties, its beauty is perfect and complete. The contemplation of Beauty Absolute makes our life truly worthwhile. Moreover, only its contemplation can give birth to true virtue rather than its images. By begetting true virtue and nurturing it, one becomes fit to win the love of gods. Such a person can be said to be immortal if anyone is immortal among human beings. Therefore, Socrates concludes, there can be no better partner and helper for human beings than love, and we should devote ourselves to the things of love and exhort all others to do the same. At this point, Alcibiades arrives with his party of revelers, and interrupts the proceedings at Agathon's house. When he gets his turn to speak, he gives a eulogy of not love but Socrates.

Alcibiades compares Socrates to a statue of Silenus, whose inside is filled with tiny statues of the gods. Socrates also looks like the satyr Marsyas, who casts spells over people with his music. He does not need any musical instrument; his words are sufficient for the purpose. The power of his music is indeed extraordinary; his words captivate and transform everyone with the Bacchic frenzy of philosophy. His character and his virtues are equally extraordinary; they "go beyond my wildest dreams," says Alcibiades. When he was young, he once tried to seduce Socrates only to find that the man was totally impervious to temptations. In the battle of Potidaea, he witnessed Socrates' phenomenal courage and power to withstand the severe pains of cold and hunger in bare feet and an old cloak. During the horrible retreat from Delium, Socrates showed incredible composure and cheerfulness. For Alcibiades, there is nobody like Socrates; his ways are so strange and so unusual.

The Taming of *Eros*

The *Symposium* has long been read as a self-contained dialogue. Going against this tradition, I propose to interpret it as Plato's attempt to resolve the problem of the *Phaedo*. In that dialogue, as we noted, Plato saved the soul by disowning the body and the entire phenomenal world. For him, the body was only the prison of the soul, and the only way to save the soul from its contamination and defilement was to die in this world and fly up to the world of invisible Forms. If the world of the body is so irredeemably evil, we noted, its existence is incompatible with the Pythagorean faith in the rational order of the universe. Hence the problem of the *Phaedo* can be characterized as the problem of the body and the phenomenal world. To be sure, this is not stated as the central problem for the *Symposium*. But its central theme, love (*eros*), is essentially the problem of the body and the phenomenal world.

In the *Symposium*, Socrates identifies *eros* with desire (*epithymia*), the general form of appetition, and the basic force of the body. This nonrational dimension of the human soul, which was disowned in the *Phaedo*, is reinstated in the *Symposium*. In the *Phaedo*, Socrates was represented as the slayer of the Minotaur. In the *Symposium*, he does not slay but rides the beast. Hence, the *Symposium* is a reversal of the *Phaedo*. This thematic relation of the two dialogues is indicated by Apollodorus, who appears in the frame story of the *Symposium*. He is the man who plays a conspicuous role in the *Phaedo* without speaking a single word. At the opening scene of the dialogue, Phaedo mentions him as the one who was especially affected by the strong emotions of the day. And he never stops weeping and crying to the end. When Socrates finally drinks the hemlock, Apollodorus can no longer control his weeping and makes everyone else break down (*Phaedo* 117d). He is a man of intense emotion. At the opening of the *Symposium*, his nickname is said to be "the maniac", and his friend says that he talks like one, always furious with everyone, including himself, but not with Socrates.

The question of *eros* is the most suitable topic for Apollodorus, the man of intense emotion. Though he was given no chance to say a word in the *Phaedo*, he has the right to narrate the entire story of the *Sympo-*

sium. Whereas the *Phaedo* records a sober dialogue, the *Symposium* is a recollection of a drunken party. As Apollodorus comes alive in the *Symposium*, so does the Dionysian force of love and desire. Let us now consider how the dialogue resolves the problem of the *Phaedo*. In the *Symposium*, erotic love is the basic force for the ascent of the soul to the Form of Beauty. Sexual love is not independent; it is only a manifestation of the instinctual desire for procreation. By this ingenious stroke, Plato shows the common source for the two basic forms of human love that were displayed in the *Lysis*, namely, sexual love and parental love. The two are different manifestations of the same desire for procreation. Since the purpose of procreation is to create an extension of oneself, the definition of *eros* as the desire for procreation is consistent with the *Lysis* definition of love formulated in terms of what is akin to oneself.

The function of procreation is not restricted to the physical world; the world of the soul is a far more fertile field of procreation. In the world of the soul, the power of *eros*, the primeval force of the body, becomes one with love of wisdom. In the vision of Beauty, pure and absolute, the soul achieves the complete sublimation of *eros* into *philosophia*. This is a new way of resolving the problem of soul and body. In the *Phaedo*, the salvation of the soul is achieved by its separation from the body. Hence, the separation of soul and body is as important in that dialogue as the separation of the Forms from the phenomenal world. In fact, these two separations make no sense apart from each other, and the doctrine of immortality is only a corollary of these two separations. In the *Symposium*, on the other hand, the salvation of the soul is achieved by the joint operation of the soul and the body, and of reason and passion.[11] Hence, the notion of union is the pervasive theme of this dialogue.

The *Symposium* is a dialogue of union; the *Phaedo* is a dialogue of separation. The former redeems the world of body and its *eros*; the latter rejects them. These are two different ways of achieving the salvation of the soul. Although it is achieved by philosophy (love of wisdom) in both dialogues, love of wisdom takes different routes. In the *Phaedo*, the death of the body and its love is the necessary condition for fully realizing the love of wisdom. In the *Symposium*, what is required for realizing the love of wisdom is not the death of love but its service. For it alone can power the ascent to the world of Forms. The *Symposium* advocates the conversion of *eros* (instinctual love) to *philosophia* (love of wisdom).

This basic difference between the two dialogues may shed some light on the controversial issue of immortality in the *Symposium*. Whereas Socrates gives a series of proofs for immortality in the *Phaedo*, he never argues for it in the *Symposium*. In the latter dialogue, he talks about procreation as the mortal substitute for immortality, and makes the enigmatic remark that the one who gains the vision of Beauty is immortal if anyone is immortal among human beings. This remark has divided commentators into two camps. One camp wants to take it as an affirmation of immortality on the ground that this interpretation is consistent with the *Phaedo*, the *Republic*, and the *Phaedrus*.[12] The other camp is not persuaded by this argument; it wants to take the same remark as the denial of immortality.[13]

There is no satisfactory resolution of this controversy because both camps assume that immortality is the ultimate issue of the *Phaedo*. But the function of immortality is only instrumental for the realization of philosophy as the ultimate vocation of the soul. In the *Phaedo*, the separation of the soul from the body is the essential condition for the salvation of the soul, and its separation can be achieved only if it is immortal. Hence, the immortality of the soul is a critical issue. In the *Symposium*, on the other hand, the separation of soul and body is no longer necessary for the realization of philosophy as the ultimate vocation of the soul. Thus, the question of immortality is irrelevant for the central theme of this dialogue, and it never becomes a topic of serious discussion.

We noted earlier that the *Phaedo* should be read as a Socratic response to the Calliclean challenge. If the *Symposium* is a revision of the *Phaedo*, it should also be read as such a response. In fact, when Socrates presents philosophy as his love against Callicles' love of *demos* at *Gorgias* 481d, he also mentions Alcibiades, who plays an important role in the *Symposium*. To be sure, neither Gorgias nor Callicles is present in this dialogue, but they have a strong representation in the person of Agathon. Though he does not display the animosity of Callicles, there is a clear sense of contest between him and Socrates. As soon as

Socrates arrives and sits down next to Agathon, they talk about each other's wisdom. In concluding this small talk, Agathon says to Socrates that they will settle their respective claims of wisdom a little later with Dionysus as their judge.

In the meantime, the banquet turns into a contest of speeches, which culminates as a duel between Agathon and Socrates by the end of Agathon's speech. Socrates immediately labels it as Gorgian rhetoric, and exposes its hollowness by his interrogation. This is Socrates' initial victory over Agathon, and his final victory comes with his own speech, which overshadows Agathon's. By the time Alcibiades arrives on the scene, the contest is over, and when he takes the wreath off Agathon's head and uses it for crowning Socrates, he is finalizing the outcome without knowing what he is doing. If the contest between Socrates and Agathon is so important, what significance should be attached to the four speeches that precede theirs? We cannot answer this question without taking up the most baffling question on the *Symposium*: What is the principle that governs the progression of the six speeches?

Many scholars have tried to detect some ordering principle, but have not been able to give a convincing account.[14] This question has become one of the famously insoluble problems in Plato scholarship. Nevertheless, it appears that the six speeches are not thrown together at random. Each speaker, except the first, not only comments but also builds on the previous speeches. Though their limited perceptions of love have to be corrected and supplemented by the later speeches, their limitations appear to be not personal but representative of the speakers' social positions. For example, Pausanias is a lawyer who speaks from a legal perspective, while Eryximachus is a doctor who speaks from a scientific and technological perspective. The succession of these different perspectives surely gives some sense of cumulative progress in our understanding of love. But what kind of progression is involved in their succession?

As I see it, the succession of the six speeches appears to represent the progression of historical consciousness in ancient Greece. Phaedrus represents the mythical age, the earliest stage in the development of historical consciousness. His speech is full of mythological allusions; he quotes Homer and Hesiod, and other mythical authorities. Pausanias represents the later stage of the mythical age, the age of the lawgivers; he talks a great deal about the law. Even more important is his distinction between the two kinds of *eros*, heavenly and vulgar. This is indicative of the normative distinctions that constitute the world of human culture (*nomos*). He is concerned with the question of how things are done rather than that of what sort of things are done. Even his talk about homosexual love expresses his concern with the question of culture; homosexual love is a phenomenon of culture rather than of nature. Because of his concern with the *nomos/physis* distinction, some commentators have associated him with the normative relativism of the sophistic movement.[15] But that is unjustifiable. Unlike a sophistic relativist, he stresses the difference between good and bad laws.

Eryximachus represents the age of natural philosophy. As Stanley Rosen says, he reduces everything, even the psyche, to natural phenomena.[16] His theory of love as the harmony of opposites is reminiscent of natural philosophers, especially Empedocles and Hippocrates. He is the one who naturalizes the phenomenon of love. The god of love remains only in name; he really stands for what works by natural forces and principles. To understand these forces and principles is the foundation of technical arts such as medicine and music. Thus, the scientific ethos leads to the technological ethos. Aristophanes represents himself, the author of the *Clouds* and the critique of natural philosophy and other new learning. His story of the original human beings and how they were cut in half is a masterful parody of natural philosophy; he is telling Eryximachus that natural philosophers are spinning out their own myths in the name of natural science. At the same time he wants to show that the myths can have their own truths; there is some profound truth in his fable that love is the longing for the lost half of oneself. Even in his story, however, the love of god is also reduced to the natural force of attraction between human beings.

Aristophanes and Eryximachus represent two stages of scientific consciousness that have succeeded the mythical consciousness, whose two stages are represented by Phaedrus and Pausanias. Agathon and Socrates represent two stages of the humanistic consciousness that have succeeded the scientific consciousness. When Agathon says that all the speakers before him have spoken not about the god of love but only about his gifts, he is mainly reacting to the speeches of Aristophanes and Eryximachus. His criticism does not apply to the first two speakers, because both of them began their speeches with the god of love. He wants to repudiate the reduction of *eros* to natural phenomena by reinstating the god of love, but Socrates' critique of his speech shows that we cannot easily discard scientific consciousness and return to mythical consciousness. He acknowledges the scientific naturalization of *eros* in his assertion that it is not a god but a *daimon* and desire. But he shows a completely new way of humanizing *eros* by presenting it as the essential force for achieving the vision of Beauty, which secures our affinity with the gods.

Agathon and Socrates represent two different reactions to the age of scientific natural consciousness. One is emotional, and the other is rational. The emotional reaction represents the age of public theaters; it is the age of Gorgian rhetoric and demagogic politics. Agathon is the man who can enthrall the mass audience of thirty thousand with his speech, but feels stage fright for talking in front of a few intelligent people (175e, 194b). At *Gorgias* 502b–e, Socrates identified tragedy as the mother of demagogic oratory; if you strip away the musical elements of meter, rhythm, and melody from a tragic drama, you will have a demagogic speech. While Agathon represents the age of emotional persuasion, Socrates represents the age of rational discourse. He is the one who has invented dialectic, the art of talking person to person, and by question and answer. Despising the ignorant multitude, he respects the single person who is engaged in the discussion as his partner. The end of his talk is not emotional persuasion, but the acquisition of knowledge and wisdom. The art of dialectic is the art of philosophy. The succession of Socrates to Agathon represents the transition from the age of rhetoric to the age of philosophy.

If my account is correct, the six speeches form three pairs, which represent three different ages in the development of historical consciousness in ancient Greece. These three are the age of myth, the age of naturalism, and the age of humanism. The six speeches can also be regrouped in a somewhat different format, because of Aristophanes' flexible position. Insofar as he is critical of the age of scientific natural consciousness, he also belongs to the age of humanistic consciousness.

For that reason, we can divide the six speakers into two groups of three each. Whether the six speakers are divided into two or three periods, the order of their succession still indicates the progression of historical consciousness.

Alcibiades' speech demonstrates Socrates' philosophical consciousness not merely as a project or argument, but also as reality and fulfillment. Shortly after his speech, the banquet is broken up by the intrusion of a horde of revelers. Some of the guests leave, and Aristodemus falls asleep. When he wakes up, he finds Socrates talking with Agathon and Aristophanes. The fact that the first three speakers have already left and that only Agathon and Aristophanes are still talking with Socrates may indicate another historical fact. The two phases of consciousness represented by Agathon and Aristophanes were contemporaneous with Socrates, while the three phases represented by Phaedrus, Pausanias, and Eryximachus had come and gone before the age of philosophy represented by Socrates. Even the two ages of Agathon and Aristophanes will come to an end by the time the age of Socrates fully blooms, and this point appears to be indicated by the fact that the two poets also fall asleep and Socrates alone remains sober and awake until daybreak.

Some scholars have been tempted to read the succession of the six speeches by mapping them onto the various stages of ascent in Diotima's story.[17] This is a natural temptation because both of them are stories of ascent. But they are two different kinds of ascent or progression. One is historical; the other is philosophical. The philosophical ascent comes at the end of the historical progression. This dual perspective—historical and philosophical—is also useful for the resolution of the Socrates/Callicles conflict. In the *Gorgias*, this conflict was presented as an open confrontation between rhetoric and philosophy. It was pictured as a duel between the two protagonists, and Socrates could not deliver a knockdown argument against Callicles. In the new perspective of the *Symposium*, however, there is no real battle between the two. The age of philosophy simply supersedes the age of rhetoric, just as Socrates' speech overshadows Agathon's.

By this historicist reading of the *Symposium*, are we not making Plato too modern? We should be making a modernist out of him if we assume that historical consciousness is a modern invention totally unknown to ancient Greece. But that is to underestimate the historical sophistication of ancient Greece. The natural philosophers were already highly critical of the mythical consciousness, and the sophists further accentuated the historical consciousness by stressing the variability and historicity of all human conventions. As we saw in the last chapter, the *Ion* and the *Euthyphro* fully attest to Plato's own historical consciousness, and the *Symposium* should be read as his further elaboration. In one of his insightful observations, Stanley Rosen says, "in general, then, the *Symposium* is an evocation of the past, not in a historical but in a mythical sense."[18] I want to amend this statement and say that the *Symposium* is an evocation of the past not only in a mythical but also in a historical sense.

The transformation of historical consciousness from the age of mythical consciousness to the age of philosophical consciousness can also be characterized as the conquest of Dionysus by Apollo; it is the progressive transformation of the Dionysian into the Apollonian consciousness. This transformation is suggested by the name of the narrator for the dialogue. Though his temperament is highly emotional and Dionysian, he is called Apollodorus, "gift of Apollo." As Daniel Anderson notes, the *Symposium* is a record of a Dionysian event not simply because its speeches are made in a drinking party, but because the god of love is identified as Dionysus.[19] This Dionysian event takes place during the night, and only Socrates the Apollonian par excellence remains sober to the end. In fact, according to Alcibiades, Socrates never gets drunk whatever amount he may consume.

As dawn breaks and all other participants of the banquet have fallen asleep, Socrates alone still remains awake and sober. He goes to the Lyceum, washes up, and spends the day as usual. This is a perfect image of Apollonian sobriety, but the Apollonian spirit does not merely vanquish the Dyonisian spirit. The former transforms the latter. This transformation is best represented by Alcibiades' description of Socrates as the Marsyas who makes music with words rather than with flutes. Marsyas is a follower of Dionysus, but the word, or *logos*, is the possession of Apollo. The *eros* of Dionysus and the *logos* of Apollo come together in the making of Socrates and his love of wisdom.

Notes

1. Gregory Vlastos, *Platonic Studies* (Princeton, N.J.: Princeton University Press, 1973), 30–31.
2. Emile Benveniste, *Indo-European Language and Society*, trans. Elizabeth Palmer (Coral Gables: University of Miami Press, 1973), 277.
3. Diogenes Laertius, *Lives of Eminent Philosophers* (1.12).
4. Plato's real name was Aristocles. "Plato" was his nickname, which meant "broad".
5. This legend is fully recounted by Kenneth Dorter, *Plato's Phaedo* (Toronto: University of Toronto Press, 1982), 4–5, and Ronna Burger, *The Phaedo* (New Haven: Yale University Press, 1984), 17–20. There is some discrepancy between the two accounts. The human sacrifice was an annual event, according to Porter, but it took place only once every nine years, according to Burger.
6. Burger, *The Phaedo*, 19.
7. Dorter, *Plato's Phaedo*, 5.
8. Dorter, *Plato's Phaedo*, 86.
9. Burger, *The Phaedo*, 19. William Cobb interprets the Minotaur as the symbol of misology, "Plato's Treatment of Immortality in the *Phaedo*," *Southern Journal of Philosophy* 15 (1977):173–188, esp. 176.
10. The shift of naval supremacy and imperial power from Crete to Athens is mentioned at *Laws* 706ab.
11. For the cooperation of reason and passion, see J. M. E. Moravcsik, "Reason and Eros in the Ascent-Passage of the *Symposium*," in *Essays in Ancient Greek Philosophy*, John Anton and George Kustas, ed. (Albany: SUNY Press, 1971), 1:285–302.
12. For example, R. G. Bury, *The Symposium of Plato*, 2d ed. (Cambridge: University Press, 1932), xliii–xlvii; W. K. C. Guthrie, *A History of Greek Philosophy* (Cambridge: Cambridge University Press, 1975), 4:387–392.
13. For example, William Cobb, *Plato's Erotic Dialogues* (Albany, N.Y.: SUNY Press, 1993), 76; R. Hackforth, "Immortality in Plato's *Symposium*," *The Classical Review* 64 (1950):43–45.
14. For a representative summary of these attempts, see Bury, *The Symposium of Plato*, lii–lxiv.
15. For example, Bury, *The Symposium of Plato*, xxvii.
16. Rosen, *Plato's Symposium* (New Haven: Yale University Press, 1968), 101.
17. C. D. C. Reeve makes this point in "Telling the Truth about Love: Plato's *Symposium*," *Proceedings of the Boston Area Colloquium in Ancient Philosophy* 8 (1992):89–114.
18. Rosen, *Plato's Symposium*, 3.
19. Anderson, *The Masks of Dionysos* (Albany, N.Y.: SUNY Press, 1993).

CHAPTER THREE

Birth of the *Republic*

The *Protagoras*, the *Meno*, the *Euthydemus*, and the *Republic*

The *Phaedo* is a tragedy; the *Symposium* is a comedy. The former is filled with tears; the latter rollicks with laughter. One ends with a sunset, and the other with a sunrise. This is to state the differences of the two great dialogues from a literary rather than philosophical perspective. Such a literary perspective is suggested by the last scene of the *Symposium*. Socrates is trying to force Agathon and Aristophanes to admit that the same person can have the knowledge required for writing tragedy as well as comedy, and that a skilled tragedian can be a comedian as well (*Symposium* 223d). This remark has baffled some commentators for two reasons.[1] First, it is a radical idea in view of the fact that there was no poet in fifth century Greece who wrote both tragedy and comedy. Second, it goes against Plato's own claim that one can achieve excellence only by specialization (*Republic* 394e).

The baffling remark may make some sense if we take the *Phaedo* as a tragedy and the *Symposium* as a comedy. The same person who can write both tragedy and comedy is none other than the one who wrote these two dialogues. By the reference to the two genres of drama, Plato the author appears to state his own understanding of the vast difference

69

between the two dialogues. But the two dialogues advocate one ultimate goal for the human soul, that is, its perfection by philosophy. The question of how to reach this ultimate goal divides the two dialogues. The *Phaedo* shows the way of death; the *Symposium* shows the way of love. But the two dialogues share one common ground, the separation of Forms from the phenomenal world. In both dialogues, the fate of the soul hinges on this uniquely Platonic doctrine.

The World of Forms

Aristotle says that the Socratic definition gave the initial impulse for Plato's theory of Forms (*Metaphysics* 1086b1–5). Since the universal definitions Socrates was seeking in ethical matters could not be true of any sensible object, they must apply to entities of another kind (*Metaphysics* 987b1–8). Labeling those objects as Forms or Ideas, Plato maintained that they are invisible and eternal. As we noted in chapter 1, the Socratic definition goes through two stages: conventional and transcendent. The understanding of positive norms is sufficient for the conventional stage, but the transcendent stage requires more than that. It presupposes the existence of transcendent standards. Platonic Forms make their initial appearance as transcendent normative standards.

There are two kinds of normative standards: discursive and exemplary. A discursive standard can be given in a definition (*logos*), for example, the definition of courage as knowing what should be feared and what should be hoped for, as it is given at *Laches* 195a. On the other hand, an exemplary standard is an example that can serve as a standard; Socrates' valiant behavior at the battle of Potidaea is an exemplary standard, as recounted by Alcibiades at *Symposium* 221ab. These two standards are well known in law. Legal precedents are exemplary standards; legal principles are discursive standards. The discursive standard of courage says what it is to be courageous; its exemplary standard shows what it is to be courageous. The discursive standard is a universal; the exemplary standard is a particular. The former is abstract; the latter is concrete.

As long as Platonic Forms are conceived as abstract universals as

Aristotle says, there is no reason to separate them from the phenomenal world and install them in the supersensible world. In the early dialogues, Plato does not claim the separation of Forms because he takes them as abstract universals. At *Euthyphro* 6d, for example, Socrates talks about the Form of Piety as a universal without claiming its separate existence. There is nothing extraordinary about the theory of Forms as long as it remains a theory of abstract universals. But this theory takes on an extraordinary shape in the *Phaedo* and the *Symposium*, where the Forms are presented as paradigms (*paradeigma*) or exemplars. This is the doctrine of paradigmatic or exemplary Forms; they are not mere abstract universals but concrete particulars.

This doctrine can enhance the plausibility of extraordinary claims made about Platonic Forms. If Forms are concrete objects rather than abstract universals, they can be accepted as real entities because concreteness is an essential feature of being real. If they are real, they can surely exist in separation from the phenomenal world, and even become the objects of erotic love. It is hard to imagine abstract universals as objects of such love. If the Form of Beauty is only an abstract standard for setting forth what it is to be beautiful, it cannot arouse our emotion of love and ecstasy because it is not a concrete object of beauty itself. On the other hand, if it is such a concrete object, it can indeed be the object of erotic love. So Socrates says that the Form of Beauty is not only beautiful but more beautiful than anything on the earth. This is the controversial doctrine of self-exemplification and self-predication.[2]

This doctrine applies not only to the Form of Beauty but to all other Forms. The Form of Justice is just; the Form of the Good is good. Even the doctrine of self-predication is not sufficient to make the Forms the highest objects of erotic enchantment. They must be more beautiful than anything in this world. This may be called the doctrine of super-predication. They must be absolutely beautiful; this is the doctrine of absolute predication. It is one of Plato's favorite remarks that no earthly object is absolutely beautiful, that is, all earthly objects are beautiful only in some respects but ugly in others. The inevitable limitation and deficiency in the beauty of earthly objects provide the impetus for the erotic ascent to the world of Forms. If any earthly object were absolutely beautiful, it could fully satisfy our restless longing for perfect beauty and effectively terminate our erotic ascent.

In the *Phaedo*, Socrates argues for the existence of Forms as the objects of pure thought that goes beyond the domain of senses. In the *Symposium*, the Forms are much more than the objects of thought; they are the objects of erotic experience. An erotic enchantment with a supersensible object is a mystical experience. That is why the story of erotic ascent is told by a priestess as a story of the highest initiation mystery. This mystical experience of supersensible love may explain one especially strange feature of Socrates' behavior. When he comes to Agathon's house for the banquet, he stands on the neighbor's porch and goes into a trance. When Agathon asks Aristodemus to bring in Socrates, he says that the trance is one of Socrates' habits and that he does not want to disturb him (*Symposium* 175b). The story of Socrates' trance comes back in Alcibiades' speech (*Symposium* 220cd). These two incidents of trance mark the beginning and the end of the *Symposium*; they seem to say that the mystical vision of Beauty appears not only in Diotima's story, but in the living experience of Socrates.

Perhaps we should distinguish the mystical Socrates from the ethical Socrates, the familiar figure in the early dialogues. The mystical Socrates begins to take shape in the *Phaedo* and culminates in the *Symposium*. For the ethical Socrates, Platonic Forms are no more than discursive normative standards; for the mystical Socrates, they have to be exemplary standards as well. The doctrines of self-predication, superpredication, and absolute predication for Platonic Forms are required only for the mystical Socrates. Likewise, only the mystical Socrates requires the doctrine of separation, namely, that the Forms exist totally apart from the phenomenal world. Finally, there can be no erotic rapture for the ethical Socrates; such a rapture is the privilege of the mystical Socrates. Because of this rapture, he disdains everything earthly as he has demonstrated in casually spurning Alcibiades' beauty and erotic enticement.

Socrates' behavior under the conditions of extreme hardship as described by Alcibiades may appear to be the highest manifestation of asceticism. He is totally impervious to cold and hunger; he walks around in bare feet on the ice (*Symposium* 220b). That would indeed be an ascetic behavior for the ethical Socrates, but not for the mystical Socrates. The latter knows only erotic behavior. There is no need for the mystical Socrates to discipline himself like an ascetic because he has a far greater power in love. Nothing can really bother or tempt someone who is totally absorbed in an erotic enchantment. The erotic are much more powerful than the ethical; the *Symposium* eliminates the need for ethics. According to Diotima, everyone is moved by love, and love is always the love of the good and the beautiful. The only question that is left for us to decide is how far we can ascend on the ladder of love, and even this question is settled by the capacities of our love. The mystical Socrates is much more powerful and beautiful than the ethical Socrates. Erotics clearly surpasses ethics.

The Question of Community

Though erotics may perfect or even surpass ethics, it cannot replace politics. This is the critical problem with the *Symposium*. What would our life be like without politics even if we have perfect erotics? Erotics and ethics are matters of individual behavior, but politics concerns our community. We can fall in love or have an ecstatic experience as individual human beings, but not as a community. What can the mystical Socrates accomplish for the community as a political entity. Diotima says that one who has the wondrous vision of Beauty gives birth not to images of virtue, but to true virtue (*Symposium* 212a). Socrates' true virtue was indeed witnessed by Alcibiades at Delium and Potidaea, and it is largely comprised of the two virtues of courage and temperance (*Symposium* 219e–221c). But the virtue of justice is not even mentioned. To be sure, Diotima claims the immortal virtue and the glorious fame as the products of love, and gives the highest honor to the virtue of wisdom for governing cities and households. Moreover, she says that this virtue is comprised of temperance and justice (*Symposium* 208d–209a). But these virtues belong to the lesser mysteries of love, while Socrates' true virtue belongs to the greater or final mystery.

The distinction between the true virtue and the popular or vulgar virtue is not new with the *Symposium*; it was already made in the

Phaedo. As noted in the last chapter, Socrates said that the true virtue is the knowledge of Forms, while the vulgar or popular virtue is an art of exchange, "pleasures for pleasures, pains for pains, fear for fear"—in short, the exchange of the smaller for the greater goods in the world of the body (*Phaedo* 69b). But what relevance does the true virtue have for this world? Does it have anything to do with the question of justice? These are the difficult questions David Bostock has raised against the Socratic conception of so-called true virtue.[3] For the person who loves wisdom and nothing else, Bostock is convinced, the conventional conception of justice and other virtues can no longer have any relevance and significance.

The so-called true virtue should be totally egocentric; a true lover of wisdom is so absorbed in her pursuit of wisdom that she should be totally oblivious of others. Socrates is not only absorbed in his love of wisdom, but he is also truly self-sufficient. At *Lysis* 215ab, Socrates said that a truly good person cannot be a friend to anyone because she is sufficient to herself and does not need anyone else. A person of true virtue is such a person. In his praise of Socrates, Alcibiades never mentions his friendship with anyone; in fact, Socrates disdains all such relationships, even the traditional bond between the lover and the beloved. Socrates is a man of incredible arrogance (*hybris*); his true virtue makes him too superior and too self-sufficient to form any communal bond with others.

The so-called true virtue is apolitical; it transcends political bondage. But such an apolitical virtue cannot equip Socrates to meet the Calliclean challenge. In the *Gorgias*, as we already noted, the central point of contention between Socrates and Callicles is the question of justice, the political virtue par excellence. The problem of Athenian imperialism and moral decay did not come about as the failure of individual behavior; it was the result of collective political behavior. Hence, neither the ethical nor the mystical Socrates can deliver a satisfactory response to the Calliclean challenge. It is going to take a political Socrates. This point may have been anticipated by Socrates at the end of the *Gorgias*, where he says he will embark on politics in due course after practicing ethics.

Plato will present his political Socrates in the *Republic*. But the transition from the *Symposium* to the *Republic* is going to take a long journey of descent from the apex of erotic ecstasy down to the phenomenal world of civic affairs. For this descent, Plato writes three dialogues: the *Protagoras*, the *Meno*, and the *Euthydemus*. A theory of political art is much more difficult to formulate than a theory of ethical virtues. The problem of political art does not make its appearance until the *Protagoras* and the *Euthydemus*, and the political virtue of justice plays no significant role in the early dialogues and the two middle dialogues of the *Phaedo* and the *Symposium*, with the sole exception of the *Gorgias*. So I propose that the *Protagoras* not only introduces a new theme, but also thematically succeeds the *Symposium* and the *Phaedo*.

There are a number of thematic pointers that indicate the succession of the *Protagoras* to the *Symposium*. One of them is the personnel of the two dialogues. With the sole exception of Aristophanes, all the speakers of the *Symposium* reappear in the *Protagoras*. This has long been noted as a singular coincidence by many Plato scholars. But there is a significant age difference between the two appearances of these people. When they give their encomia of love in the *Symposium*, they appear as fully grown adults. In the *Protagoras*, they make their appearance as much younger people who are eager to imbibe the sophistic teaching. This fact alone makes the supposed dramatic date of the *Protagoras* much earlier than that of the *Symposium*. But their dramatic dates have nothing to do with their thematic relationship. The fact that most of the symposiasts reappear in the *Protagoras* as young students of the great sophists is Plato's thematic pointer for indicating that the education of youth is the central theme for the *Protagoras*. Aristophanes is excluded from this dialogue, because his presence would be inconsistent with his play the *Clouds*, a scathing satire on sophistic teaching.

How is the question of education related to the question of political art? For Plato, the political art is largely the art of education, that is, how to handle the problem of educating the future rulers and the future citizens in such a manner that they can properly function as members of their state. As we will see, the bulk of the *Republic* is taken up by the question of education. The theme of education is further indicated by another thematic pointer: Hippocrates, the impetuous young man who wakes up Socrates before daylight and begs for an introduction to Protagoras. He is identified as the son of Apollodorus no less than three times (310a, 316b, 328d). This should be taken as the author's suggestion that the identification carries some special significance. Apollodorus is the narrator of the *Symposium*; his role is to suggest the thematic succession of the *Symposium* to the *Phaedo*. Since the *Protagoras* opens with the problem of education for his son, it is natural to be regarded as the thematic successor to the *Symposium*.

These two thematic pointers have an educational tag, but there are two other thematic pointers that have a political tag. One is the two Homeric references Socrates makes in describing his sighting of Hippias and Prodicus among the many people assembled in the house of Callias (315bc). The other is the frame story for the dialogue. The Homeric references come from Odysseus's travel down to Hades, which has been known as the *Nekyia*. After one year of endless feasts at Circe's palace, Odysseus's companions call him aside and try to talk some sense into this man intoxicated with love and wine. They tell him that it is time to remember his home and the land of his fathers, if he is to be saved and return to it (*Odyssey* 10.471–472). Thus awakened from his erotic slumber, Odysseus begs Circe to keep her promise and let him find his way home. Granting his request, she advises him to go down to Hades and consult the soul of Tiresias about the way home. Among the dead, she adds, Tiresias alone has understanding while the rest of them are only flitting shadows.

When Odysseus travels to Hades, he meets the soul of Tiresias, which gives him the following advice and prophecy. His voyage back to Ithaca will be made difficult by Poseidon because he has offended the god. Even so, he might make his way home, after much suffering, if he can contain his desire and that of his men. When they approach the island of Thrinakia, they will see the cattle and sheep of Helios grazing there. If they do not molest the animals, they can get safely back to Ithaca; if they do molest the animals, they and their ships will be destroyed. Even if Odysseus himself escapes the destruction, he will return home late and ill in someone else's ship, having lost all his own. Then he will find troubles in his own house, and insolent men eating away his livelihood and courting his godlike wife with the bribery of gifts. He will take vengeance upon these men (*Odyssey* 11.100–118).

What is the relevance of this prophecy to the *Protagoras*? If this dialogue is to serve as the *Nekyia* of Socrates, we can set up the following parallel between his voyage and that of Odysseus. The ecstatic love of Socrates in the *Symposium* corresponds to Odysseus's erotic happiness in the palace of Circe. Like Diotima, Circe is a hierophant and priestess who directs the initiate into the deeper mysteries.[4] Socrates awakes from Diotima's erotic spell to return to the city of Athens, just as Odysseus awakes from Circe's erotic spell to return to the city of Ithaca. Odysseus learns from Tiresias that Ithaca has been besieged and ravaged by a host of greedy and insolent men. The situation of Ithaca is analogous to that of imperial Athens, because she is taken over by insolent men of greed and power. But when Odysseus gets back to Ithaca, he will clean up the place and restore the order, and Socrates will have a similar mission when he returns to Athens.

To be sure, Socrates does not go down to Hades; he only pays a visit to the house of Callias, one of the wealthiest closely connected to Pericles and his political circle. The guests assembled there are drawn from the governing class of imperial Athens. Hence, the house of Callias and his guests stand for the spiritually dead city of Athens. But who is going to play the role of Tiresias for Socrates and what instruction is he going to give? Whatever instruction he may give, it should be about political art, the art of governing the life of an entire city. The theme of political art is introduced in the frame story of the *Protagoras*. It occurs in a brief exchange between Socrates and an anonymous friend, who asks him how he has been getting along with his love Alcibiades. Though he was with the beautiful young man, Socrates replies, he scarcely took any notice of his beauty because he was so preoccupied with someone far better looking than Alcibiades. He then identifies this most beautiful person as Protagoras of Abdera (309cd).

On Socrates' scale of beauty, wisdom occupies the highest place; to be more beautiful means to have greater wisdom. Socrates talks as though Protagoras had the greatest wisdom. What sort of wisdom does he teach? When Socrates puts this question to him, Protagoras disdainfully speaks of the other sophists who teach the standard subjects such as arithmetic, astronomy, geometry, music, and poetry (318e). He is proud of teaching the wisdom of managing one's home and the affairs of one's city. This is none other than the wisdom of political art. Diotima called it civic virtue and assigned it to the lesser mysteries of love, far inferior to the intellectual virtue of *philosophia* in the final mystery of love. Socrates now looks upon it as the highest wisdom, but expresses his doubt about the possibility of teaching such a wondrous virtue. In general, he believes that virtue cannot be taught because he has never seen it done even by such an eminent statesman as Pericles. If Protagoras really knows the secret of teaching political art, then he surely deserves to be called the soul of Tiresias for Socrates.

The Question of Teaching

Protagoras tells the following myth to explain the genesis and nature of civic virtue. At the time of creation, Zeus gave Prometheus and Epimetheus the job of distributing natural talents and powers to all the species of animals. Epimetheus wanted to handle this assignment by himself, and Prometheus let him do it. He equipped some species with power, some with speed, some with claws or horns, some with thick hair and tough skins, and so on. By the time he came to human beings, he had used up all the resources. They were still naked and helpless, while all other species were properly equipped for survival. To make up for this mistake by Epimetheus, Prometheus stole technical arts from the immortals and gave them to human beings. But technical arts were not sufficient for their survival, because they were perpetually fighting with one another and were almost on the brink of extinction. To prevent this disaster, Zeus asked Hermes to take the two virtues of respect (*aidos*) and justice (*dike*) to humankind, because they were essential for living together in a city. He further decreed that every human being should have a share of these two civic virtues, and that anyone who did not should be killed for being a public pest.

This story, Protagoras says to Socrates, should explain the important difference between political excellence (virtue) and excellence in technical arts. Unlike the latter, political excellence is not a specialty for a few people, but a universal possession (322d–323a). Nobody can really be human without having a share in justice, temperance, and the rest of civic virtue, because these are the necessary conditions for social life. But civic virtue does not come by nature; it has to be developed by careful teaching. This is why people get angry with those who flout civic virtues, while nobody takes offense with the things that take place as a natural process such as being ugly or scrawny. This proves that virtue is acquired by teaching, which begins with little children and continues as long as they live. It is given by the nurse, the mother, the tutor, and the father; they teach the difference between the just and the unjust, the pious and the impious, the beautiful and the ugly. If children do not obey willingly, they are straightened out by threats and blows. It is the same method used to teach children how to speak and write. Everybody is a teacher of civic virtue, just as everybody is a teacher of language.

As Socrates says, Protagoras admits, children of distinguished parents do not always turn out as well as their parents. This familiar occurrence, however, proves not that virtue cannot be taught as Socrates claims, but the opposite. Because everybody can teach virtue, the children of distinguished parents do not have any advantage over others as far as civic education is concerned, though they may be given special education in horseriding or archery, which other children cannot afford to have. Why the children of distinguished parents do not always turn out well should be explained in terms of natural capacities and dispositions (327c). There is nothing to marvel about in the fact that bad sons are born of good fathers, and good sons are born of bad fathers (328c), because it is the outcome of a natural lottery.

This is Protagoras's lecture on the nature of civic virtue. First, there is the basic natural difference in our capacities and dispositions for virtue. Second, they have to be developed by teaching. Third, teaching is mainly a matter of training and disciplining, which requires no special skill. In response to this lecture, Socrates raises an unexpected question. Since Protagoras has mentioned several virtues, he wants to know whether they are one thing or many different things. Protagoras replies that they are one thing, and that the different virtues are its parts. Now Socrates asks him whether the different parts are like parts of a face (mouth, nose, eyes, and ears) or like parts of gold. Protagoras endorses the analogy of a face and its parts. Each of them is different from the others, and one person may have one part but not the others. This is the Protagorean doctrine of separability and distinguishability of different virtues, against which Socrates begins his move to reduce all virtues to wisdom or knowledge.

This reduction move is no surprise for us because we have already seen it implicitly in the *Laches* and the *Charmides*, and it leads to the identity of all virtues. Socrates' reduction takes several steps. First, he asks Protagoras to accept the view that justice and piety are the same. Though he senses some distinction between the two, Protagoras will let it stand (331c). Second, Socrates gives a long argument to show that temperance and wisdom are the same. Though this argument has been called fallacious by many critics, it is a highly reasonable view.[5] After all, the Greek word for temperance, *sophrosyne*, means the soundness of mind, and it was defined as self-knowledge in the *Charmides*. At any rate, Protagoras eventually accepts the identity of temperance and wisdom. At that point, Socrates begins to take him through the third step, the identity of temperance and justice. If this step is successful, he can establish the identity of justice, piety, temperance, and wisdom, leaving only courage unaccounted for.

Sensing the noose closing upon his neck, Protagoras begins to show his irritation and resistance. He wants to make long speeches, whereas Socrates insists on the method of short questions and crisp answers. Their contest of wills finally breaks up the argument, and Socrates threatens to leave. But they are restrained by Prodicus and Hippias, and Socrates and Protagoras agree to a new format of discussion in which Protagoras will ask questions instead of answering them. Now Protagoras says that the greatest part of education is to gain the ability to understand poetry (339a). This statement is consistent with his view that the art of sophists is an ancient one that goes back to the tradition of poetry in Homer, Hesiod, and Simonides, and that of prophecy in Orpheus and Musaeus (316d). As we saw in chapter 1, the transition from the poets to the sophists is the transition from theonomy to anthroponomy.

Protagoras gives his interpretation of Simonides' poem about the

maxim of Pittacus that it is difficult to be good. But his so-called interpretation is to show that the poem contradicts itself. Socrates counters
this negative interpretation by offering a positive one. Though there are
many interesting points in the two readings of the poem, we will pass
them over. Instead, let us take note of Pittacus and his maxim. At the
beginning of the sixth century, he was given dictatorial rule over Mytilene. When he heard that Periander of Corinth converted a similar office
into a tyranny, he renounced his office and power. That was the occasion when he pronounced the famous maxim that it is difficult to be
good. This was meant to express his anxiety over the fragility of human
virtue against the temptation of power and greed, which even impressed
Solon when he heard the story.[6]

Pittacus and Solon mark an important turning point in the historical
development of virtue in ancient Greece. Prior to this point, the Homeric virtues of courage and temperance had been predominant for Greek
heroes, because they were the virtues of a warrior. Pittacus and Solon
made civic virtues predominant; they were the virtues for governing a
city rather than waging war. In this new scale of virtues, justice takes
the highest place, and even temperance is reconceived in terms of justice. Simonides is a different poet from Homer. The latter sings the
virtue of warriors; the former talks about the virtue of civic leaders.
Hence, Protagoras's discussion of Simonides' poem further highlights
the civic dimension of his teaching. The importance of civic virtue is
demonstrated by the political crisis in the dialogue itself. When Socrates threatens to leave because Protagoras will not use the Socratic
method of short questions and answers, the dialogue is on the verge of
breaking up (335a–d). But it is saved by the intercession of their host
Callias and his friends, who ask them to be more tolerant of each other.
What is needed for continuing the dialogue is the civic virtue of *aidos*,
or respect, because a dialogue is a cooperative, social enterprise.

The importance of civic virtue is also highlighted by Socrates' account of philosophy in Crete and Sparta, perhaps the most outrageous
remark ever made in all of Plato's dialogues. According to Socrates,
these two cities have the longest and best philosophical tradition in all
of Hellas. Though they have more sophists than any other cities, they
hide and deny this fact. Moreover, they make pretense of ignorance to

prevent the others from discovering their secret wisdom for gaining ascendancy over other cities. The Spartans and the Cretans would rather have it thought that they owe their superiority to fighting and courage. Although this statement has been branded as a typical Socratic irony, it is in accord with Protagoras's earlier claim that the art of sophists is an ancient one that has been practiced under many different guises such as poetry, mystery religion, and even gymnastics (316d).

As we already noted, Socrates and Protagoras are chiefly concerned with the wisdom of civic virtue. Plato always had a high regard for the civic virtue of Crete and Sparta. At *Republic* 544c, when Socrates enumerates the four kinds of cities inferior to the ideal city, he picks Crete and Sparta as the best of the four kinds. In the *Laws*, Plato picks one Cretan and one Spartan as the two interlocutors for the Athenian Stranger, because Crete and Sparta have the two best known legal institutions. In the *Protagoras*, Socrates tells the story of Sparta's wisdom to explain the laconic style of Pittacus. Since the Spartans are trying to hide their wisdom, he says, they deliberately express themselves in short and terse statements. Some notable examples are: "Know thyself," and "Nothing in excess." The seven wise men of ancient Greece including Pittacus of Mytilene adopted the laconic style of speaking because they were lovers and emulators of Spartan culture. This is why his maxim "It is difficult to be good" is laconic and hard to interpret, according to Socrates.

Socrates praises the hidden wisdom of Spartans in deliberate contrast to the display (*epideixis*) of the sophists' shallow wisdom (320c, 328b). In this ironic contrast between the wisdom of sophists on display and the wisdom of Spartans under disguise, Socrates shrewdly designates the Spartan culture as the model for the emulation of the seven sages of Greece, whose wisdom and virtue in managing civic affairs are supposedly the specialty of Protagoras's teaching. Thus the Socratic irony may hide Plato's sincere admiration for the Spartan wisdom and culture. There are two sorts of irony: the irony of mockery and the irony of sincerity. The Socratic irony is an irony of mockery, if Socrates does not believe all those stories about the wisdom of Sparta but makes them up only to mock his opponent. In contrast, his irony is an irony of sincerity, if he believes everything he says about the wisdom of Sparta.

Textually, there is no way to determine which is the right interpretation of Simonides' poem, Socrates' or Protagoras's. Therefore, Socrates proposes to end the game of interpretation and get back to their original discussion. As soon as he takes over the role of asking questions, he tries to prove the identity of courage and wisdom. Although the four virtues they have discussed are quite similar, Protagoras says in response, courage is clearly different from other virtues. For there are many people who are unjust, impious, intemperate, and ignorant, and yet remarkable for their courage (349d). Against this objection, Socrates advances the following argument. Though confidence is often called courage, it may derive from knowledge or ignorance. Since ignorance-based confidence cannot be virtuous, courage must be based on knowledge, and the knowledge in question must be the knowledge of living well and ill, good and evil. He then identifies good and evil with pleasure and pain: *living well* means living in pleasure and *living ill* means living in pain (351b). This is hedonism: all pleasures are good insofar as they are pleasures, and all pains are bad insofar as they are pains.

Protagoras is reluctant to accept hedonism, because he feels, like the rest of the world, that some pleasures are evil. But Socrates asks why he should heed the opinion of the ignorant multitude that he disdains. Then Socrates proceeds to show that the multitude has no other standard for calling something good or evil than pleasure and pain, and that the computation of future pleasures and pains requires an art of measurement. This art can tell us which course of action can give us the best balance of pleasure over pain. Courage is this art, because it is concerned with the objects of fear and hope, which are matters of pleasure and pain. Since this art is a matter of wisdom and knowledge, courage is wisdom. This conception of courage is nothing new; we have encountered it in the *Laches* and then in the *Phaedo*, where it was presented as a vulgar conception of virtue. Socrates finally forces this conception of courage upon the resistant Protagoras, and concludes his argument that all virtues are reducible to wisdom.

The Method of Teaching

Protagoras and Socrates represent two opposite perspectives for understanding virtue. Protagoras presents a conventional understanding;

he names and describes virtues as given by convention. Because he is a conventionalist, he is mindful of what the multitude say about what is good and what is bad. Against his conventionalism, Socrates takes a transcendent approach and advocates the hedonistic calculus as a transcendent standard for deciding what is good and what is bad. At the end of the discussion, Socrates observes how absurd their respective positions have turned out. If virtue is knowledge as he has claimed, it can be taught. But he has maintained that it cannot be taught. On the other hand, if virtue is not knowledge as Protagoras has claimed, it cannot be taught. But he has maintained that it can be taught. That is, Socrates observes, both of their positions are self-contradictory.

This observation presupposes the Socratic conception of teaching, that is, only knowledge can be taught. However, there are two ways of teaching: Socratic and Protagorean. The object of Socratic teaching is knowledge; the object of Protagorean teaching is convention. The Protagorean method is to inculcate conventional belief and behavior in students by training and conditioning. The students do not have to know whether the convention is good or bad; on the contrary, the convention will tell them what is good and what is bad, when it is internalized by education. The difference between the two methods of teaching is neither recognized nor discussed in the *Protagoras*, but it becomes the central question in the *Meno*, the *Euthydemus*, and the *Republic*.

The *Meno* begins with the question of teaching, and this is the extraordinary feature of its abrupt opening. This dialogue has neither a frame story, nor a prefatory remark, and not even the ordinary formalities of salutation. Instead it begins with Meno's question to Socrates of whether virtue is acquired by teaching or by practice; or if neither by teaching nor by practice, whether it comes by nature or in some other way. This unusual opening has been one of the sore spots in Plato scholarship; nobody seems to know what to make of it. It is ignored by most commentators, even Paul Shorey and Paul Friedlander.[7] In my view, this is meant to establish the thematic continuity of the *Meno* with the *Protagoras*. The close thematic connection between the two dialogues has been astutely noted by Charles Kahn. He regards the *Meno* as "the direct sequel to the Protagoras" for the following reason. Both of them deal with the Socratic thesis that virtue is a kind of knowledge, and with the question of whether virtue can be taught.[8]

The identity of their thematic content, however, does not explain why the *Meno* should come after rather than before the *Protagoras*. The latter dialogue begins with the express intent to discuss the question of whether virtue can be taught, but spends most of its time in arguing whether all virtues are reducible to wisdom. Hence, the original question is still left untouched by the end of the *Protagoras*, and this untouched question is taken up by the *Meno*. Moreover, this question is handled on the premise that has been established in the *Protagoras*, namely, the reducibility of all virtues to wisdom. When Meno puts his abrupt question to Socrates, it looks as though he had been listening to the entire discussion of the *Protagoras*.

The opening question of the *Meno* mentions two ways of acquiring virtue. One of them is teaching and learning, and the other is practice. But how should we understand the nature of teaching and learning? This is the central question for the dialogue, and Socrates ingeniously takes Meno through the maze of this question. First, he gets Meno to define the nature of virtue on the pretext that the question cannot be settled without this definition. But the project of definition necessarily turns into a process of learning, and Socrates and Meno get involved in the paradox of definition, which becomes the paradox of learning, or the Meno paradox. Socrates resolves it by the doctrine of recollection, and then demonstrates this doctrine by using the slave boy. He holds that the boy has all along had true belief as part of his immortal soul, but he comes to recognize it by recollection. His learning process is not to acquire anything new, but to recollect what has already been in his soul unconsciously. It is a process for converting true belief into knowledge by rational articulation (97–98).

This is the theory of Socratic teaching and learning, about which we may note a few important points. First, it is a rational process, which is diametrically opposed to the Protagorean method of training and conditioning. Second, it cannot begin in a noetic vacuum; an inquiry cannot begin in total ignorance. Likewise, it is impossible to begin any definition without some predefinitional knowledge. Third, if every inquiry presupposes some prior knowledge, where does this prior knowledge come from? It can come from either an a priori or an a posteriori source. If it comes from an a posteriori source, the method of recollection is compatible with the Protagorean method of training. One can recollect what has been drilled into one's brain by training and conditioning. Fourth, if this is the only way of learning, there is no way to avoid normative positivism, because one can come to learn and recollect only what has been drilled into one's normative consciousness. By showing that there is some a priori source for recollection, Socrates secures the possibility of normative transcendence for the learning process, that is, our learning can take us beyond the domain of positive norms. This is the final and most important point about the doctrine of recollection.

These points are illustrated by concrete examples in the dialogue. In response to Socrates' request for a definition of virtue, Meno gives only examples of virtue rather than its definition. These examples constitute his predefinitional knowledge from the empirical source; they are derived from conventional wisdom. When Meno gives his first definition of virtue as the power of governing humankind, it is supposedly what he has gotten from Gorgias (73c). Again, its source is not a priori. Then Socrates gives two definitions of figure in order to illustrate how to formulate a definition of common essence: (1) figure is the only thing that is found always following color, and (2) figure is the limit of solid (75b-76a). Definition (1) is empirical, and has to be supplemented by a definition of color, which is also empirical. Definition (2) is not empirical; it is mathematical. Of these two definitions, Meno says he likes (1) better. Socrates replies that (2) is better, and adds that Meno would like (2) better, too, if he had been initiated into the mysteries. For Plato, the *initiation* means the initiation into the supersensible world of Forms.

The slave boy's performance is meant to illustrate a different kind of recollection from the one illustrated by Meno's performance. Though the slave boy's recollection has become a celebrated topic of philosophical discussion, nobody has recognized the recollection of the young Meno. The latter is a posteriori; the former is a priori. Their contrast is important for the dialogue. The a priori recollection by the slave boy does not resolve the problem of teaching virtue, though it may resolve the problem of teaching geometry. Teaching virtue may be much more difficult than teaching geometry. Although Socrates does not retract the assertion that virtue can be taught if it is knowledge, he suspects that there are no teachers and students of virtue (89e). Because Meno does not share this suspicion, they turn to Anytus for help on this new question.

Anytus disdainfully dismisses the sophists' claim to be the teachers of virtue, but says that any Athenian gentlemen can do much better than the sophists. How have the Athenian gentlemen gotten their virtue? Anytus says that they have gotten it from the previous generation, and that there have been many good men in the city. Socrates doubts that any of them have been good teachers of their own virtue, and names a string of eminent Athenians who have failed to teach their own children: Themistocles, Lysimachus, Pericles, and Thucydides. The mention of these four statesmen indicates that the *Meno* is concerned with the problem of teaching not ordinary virtues but civic virtues. The thematic role of the eminent Athenians is the same as that of Pittacus and Solon in the discussion between Socrates and Protagoras. They are all heroes of civic virtue.

Socrates' claim that even the Athenian statesmen could not teach virtue to their own children immensely offends Anytus. After warning Socrates not to speak ill of the Athenians, he leaves in a rage. Socrates and Meno continue their talk, and come to agree that if neither the sophists nor the Athenian gentlemen are teachers of virtue, there can be no other teachers. If so, Meno wonders, how has Athens had any good men at all? Socrates says that they are men of right opinion rather than of knowledge, and that right opinion can serve as a good guide for human life just as much as knowledge can (97b). But right opinion cannot be taught because it is not knowledge. It comes to us as a divine gift. Thus, the dialogue ends with a theory of right opinion instead of settling the question of teaching. Socrates does not altogether abandon his hope and says that, if there is someone who can understand and teach political art, that person will indeed be like Tiresias among the dead (100a). Here again the problem of teaching in this dialogue is firmly linked to the problem of civic virtue. Political art and civic virtue are treated as interchangeable in the *Meno* as well as in the *Protagoras*.

The Birth of Political Art

The reference to Tiresias is another thematic pointer that connects the *Meno* to the *Protagoras*. It directs our attention to Socrates' entrance into the house of Callias, where he made a couple of references to Odysseus's descent to Hades in describing Hippias and Prodicus. There, I propose, Socrates is making his own descent from the world of Forms to the phenomenal world just as Odysseus descended from the palace of Circe to Hades. In this descent, Socrates has been looking for his own Tiresias, and his reference to Tiresias at the end of the *Meno* shows that his search has been fruitless. Given this failure in his search, what step should he take next if he is to take on the role of Odysseus and reconstitute the social order?

Before taking up this question, let us note that the idea of Socratic descent to the phenomenal world can explain a couple of anomalies that have puzzled Plato scholars. One of them is the fact that in the *Meno* Socrates does not mention the Forms in his talk of recollection, whereas he stressed their connection in the *Phaedo*. If the *Meno* is a continuation of Socratic descent that began in the *Protagoras*, Socrates has reason to avoid all references to the Forms. There are no transcendent Forms in the phenomenal world. Nor does Socrates in the *Meno* link the concept of knowledge to the world of Forms as he does in the so-called middle dialogues. He talks about the difference between knowledge and opinion within the phenomenal world. You know the way to Larissa if you have traveled on it; you do not know it if you have not. But you can still obtain correct opinion from someone who knows the way (97ab). The knowledge of the way to Larissa is the knowledge not of a Form but of a phenomenal object.

The other anomaly is the fact that Socrates advocates hedonistic calculus in the *Protagoras*, and this appears to be inconsistent with his well-known critique of hedonism given in the *Gorgias* and other places. This anomaly can also be explained if we remember that he is on his journey of descent. At *Phaedo* 82ab, he introduced the distinction between true virtue and virtue in its popular or vulgar sense, and reaffirmed it at *Symposium* 212a. Only those who have seen the Forms can give birth to true virtue, while those without such a vision can have

only the vulgar virtue as an economy of exchange, "pleasures for pleasures, pains for pains, fear for fear"—in short, the exchange of the
smaller for the greater goods in the world of the body (*Phaedo* 69b).
Although all virtues are identical with wisdom in the Socratic reduction
scheme, the concept of wisdom is systematically ambiguous. It may be
either the wisdom of knowing the Forms, or that of knowing how to
manage the affairs of this world.

In the *Laches* and the *Charmides*, where the transcendent Forms were
not yet introduced, the virtue of wisdom was defined as the knowledge
of coping with the adversities of life and managing the affairs of households and cities. It is exclusively the wisdom of dealing with the world
of phenomena. But the *Phaedo* and the *Symposium* opened up a completely new world of Forms and presented a new conception of wisdom
as the power of disdaining this world and ascending to the other world.
The old virtue of wisdom is now branded as the vulgar virtue, and the
new virtue of wisdom is exalted as the true virtue. In the *Protagoras*,
however, Socrates cannot have true virtue but only the vulgar one, because he has descended to the phenomenal world, which can offer only
the empirical criteria of pleasure and pain. As he says, there is no other
standard for calling something good or bad (*Protagoras* 354cd). This
vulgar conception of virtue, as we will see later, will become the basic
principle for the construction of Magnesia in the *Laws*.

Unlike Odysseus's descent to Hades, however, Socrates' descent has
produced no positive results. He could not even find his Tiresias. This
is the puzzling feature of his descent. But the descent of Odysseus to
Hades is equally puzzling. Though Odysseus finds and talks with Tiresias in Hades, he does not get much useful advice from him about his
future travel to Ithaca. Only when he comes back from Hades to the
palace of Circe, does he receive a detailed instruction from Circe herself
about the Sirens, Scylla and Charybdis, and many other things that will
affect his voyage back to Ithaca (*Odyssey* 12.21–141). If she had the
advice Odysseus needed for the travel back to Ithaca, why did she send
him down to Tiresias in Hades? She could have spared him the whole
trip; his descent to Hades appears to be totally nonfunctional for the
epic journey. Does his descent serve any other purpose than that of

getting advice from Tiresias? This has been one of the most puzzling questions for Homer scholars.

The standard answer for this question is that the real function of Odysseus's descent to Hades is not to get advice and information from Tiresias, but to go through the experience of death and rebirth. Hades is the place of death; to descend to it means the experience of death, and to ascend from it means the experience of rebirth. This is the theme of the *Nekyia*.[9] By going down to Hades and coming back, Odysseus is dying as a hero of private adventure and enjoyment in the palace of Circe, and is reborn as a hero of public affairs and responsibility for the city of Ithaca. His new life is to have a new destiny, a new telos.[10] This motif of death and rebirth was common in Mediterranean mythology, and played an important role in mythical stories about gods and semidivine heroes, for example, Adonis and Osiris. Similar stories are told of Theseus, Heracles, and Orpheus. Odysseus's descent to Hades is clearly imitated by Aeneas's travel to the underworld in the Aeneid. The same motif of death and rebirth culminates in Dante's descent to hell and ascent to heaven in the *Divina Commedia*. In hell, he dies as a sinner to be reborn as a saint in heaven.

In Plato's dialogues, Socrates dies more than once; his trial and death are mentioned in more than one dialogue. Every time he dies, however, he is usually reborn for a new role. We have seen the death of Socrates in the *Phaedo*, but this event has more than one reference. Obviously, it refers to Socrates' death as a historical event, and the dialogue is supposed to describe it. But the narrated event also has a thematic reference, the death of the ethical Socrates. Thematically, the ethical Socrates was born in the *Apology*; his ethical career began with the divine mission from Delphi. This ethical Socrates lives through Plato's early dialogues, but dies in the *Phaedo*. In the other world, he will have no more ethical concerns because he will be free of the problems of the body. However, the death of the ethical Socrates is not the end of Socrates; Plato brings him back as the erotic and mystical Socrates in the *Symposium*. This is his rebirth. In Plato's hand, he gains a new form of immortality; he dies only to be reborn.

The death of the ethical Socrates was foretold by Callicles at *Gorgias* 486bc; his rebirth as the erotic Socrates was prepared by the *Lysis*.

When Socrates meets the two young boys, Lysis and Menexenus, he is about to ask which of the two excels in justice and wisdom. But he suddenly changes his mind, and starts asking questions about love (*Lysis* 207d). This indicates the change of his concern from the question of ethics to the question of love. Like Callicles of the *Gorgias*, Anytus of the *Meno* gives Socrates an angry warning and threat, which can be taken as an ominous foreboding of his trial and death (*Meno* 94e–95a). It is natural for us to associate Anytus's remark with Socrates' trial and death as a historical event, especially because Anytus was one of his accusers. But that historical event is not the only reference for the allusion; it is also thematically linked to the motif of death and rebirth embedded in the story of the *Nekyia*. Socrates is going to be reborn as a Tiresias, who has the knowledge of governing a city-state and the power of teaching it to others. This is my thesis of double reference. In Plato's dialogues, a description can have not only a historical but also a thematic reference. The historical reference is given by history, but the thematic reference is created by Plato.

The birth of the political Socrates will not take place until the *Republic*, but its advent is foreshadowed by the *Euthydemus*, just as the birth of the erotic Socrates is foretokened by the *Lysis*. The thematic connection of the *Euthydemus* to the *Protagoras* and the *Meno* is obvious; they are all addressed to the central question of whether virtue can be taught. The two sophist brothers of the *Euthydemus* make even a bolder claim than that of Protagoras and other sophists. Euthydemus and Dionysodorus say that they can demonstrate their method of teaching virtue (274ab). In the name of demonstration, the two sophist brothers subject the young Cleinias to three separate rounds of eristic argument. Interspersed between these three rounds, Socrates conducts two rounds of discussion with him. In the first round, which follows the first round of eristic argument by the sophist brothers, Socrates and Cleinias want to find out what is most important for securing our happiness. They come to agree that the use of good things is more important than the mere possession of them, and that knowledge is required for the right use of good things for our happiness. From this they conclude that knowledge is the most important thing for our happiness, and this is why philosophy (love of wisdom) should be pursued (282a–d). It is the only way to secure our happiness.

In the second round, which follows another round of eristic argument, Socrates and Cleinias resume their discussion by introducing the distinction between the art of making and the art of using. They agree that the art of making is useless without the art of using, which alone can secure our happiness. But who has the art of using, or rather whose art is it? In trying to settle this question, Socrates suggests that the art of generalship may be the highest. But the young Cleinias rejects it for the following reason. The art of hunting is not an art of using. Hunters know how to catch things but do not know how to use them. For example, the fishermen hand over their catch to the cooks. Even geometers and astronomers are not users but only hunters; they have to hand over their findings to the dialectician. The generals can capture cities, but they have to hand them over to the statesmen because they do not know how to use them.

While Socrates is narrating this event, Crito interrupts and expresses his wonder. He says he could not believe that all those marvelous things were said by the young boy, and that, if he is that smart, he needs no instruction from Euthydemus or anyone else (290e). The wondrous performance of Cleinias is the extension of the art of recollection from geometry to the domain of virtue as knowledge. Just as the slave boy came to recollect his insight into a geometrical figure under Socratic guidance, so does the young Cleinias recollect his insight into the nature of the art of using and its difference from the art of making. Neither of them needs education in the standard sense. When Socrates demonstrates the doctrine of recollection with an example of geometrical instruction in the *Meno*, our natural response is to wonder whether it is applicable to the teaching of virtue. This uncertainty is resolved by Socrates' demonstration in the *Euthydemus*; it is a dialogue of demonstration not only for the teaching method of the sophist brothers but also for that of Socrates.

With Socrates' guidance, the young Cleinias eventually identifies the kingly art or the statesman's art as the highest (291bc), but their inquiry gets into difficulties when they try to define the nature of this art. If the kingly art rules over everything, what does it produce? Surely it cannot produce the products of technical arts such as medicine. Since Socrates and Cleinias have decided that nothing is good except knowledge, the kingly art must produce some sort of knowledge. But what sort of knowledge? And what good can it do? These puzzling questions are remarkably similar to the difficult questions we encountered at the end of the *Charmides*. But there is a significant difference. In the *Charmides*, these questions were raised about temperance as the sovereign virtue. In the *Euthydemus*, they are raised about the political art as the highest art. This change foreshadows the conversion of the ethical into the political Socrates. Though temperance is the sovereign virtue for the ethical Socrates, it cannot be so for the political Socrates. The rebirth of the ethical Socrates as the political Socrates dictates a new order of virtues. Political virtue supervenes upon ethical virtue. This change is analogous to the one that takes place in the rebirth of Odysseus. Before his descent to Hades, he stands as the paragon of temperance, but he emerges from Hades as the master of political art for the city of Ithaca.

Because the *Euthydemus* provides the demonstration for the Socratic inquiry and teaching, it finally answers the question of whether virtue can be taught. It is this ideal of inquiry and teaching that becomes the guiding spirit for Plato's own Academy. In fact, this dialogue is closely linked, in terms of its aura, to the *Lysis*, which we have associated with the founding of Plato's Academy in the last chapter. The link between these two dialogues appears to be further suggested by the presence of Ctesippus in both of them. The Pythagorean theme of friendship or brotherly love that was introduced in the *Lysis* also reappears in the *Euthydemus*. The two sophist brothers form a partnership of cooperation like the one between Lysis and Menexenus. One is a partnership for inquiry, but the other is a partnership for eristic tricks. In either case, such a partnership is rare in Plato's dialogues.

Finally, the implied connection of the *Euthydemus* to Plato's Academy may explain the cryptic remark at the end of the dialogue about the writer of speeches who occupies the no-man's-land between the philosopher and the statesman (305bc). This remark is generally assumed to refer to Isocrates, who had established his own school before Plato did, and his school was the most important competition for Plato's Academy.[11] Like Plato, Isocrates was critical of the sophistic education.

But he was equally critical of the education that stressed the importance
of theoretical disciplines such as geometry and astronomy, as in Plato's
Academy (*Antidosis* 262–266). He firmly advocated that good education must be practical and that theoretical inquiry was useless. For these
reasons, there was a natural competition between his school and Plato's.

To make the competition even more intense, Plato and Isocrates con-
tended against each other as the true champions of philosophy. Let us
remember that these were the formative years of philosophy as an intellectual discipline. Plato presented his art of dialectic as the best way of
doing philosophy, while Isocrates championed his art of rhetoric as the
best way. This competition between Plato and Isocrates is important for
understanding the cryptic remark at the end of the *Euthydemus*. It
amounts to saying that Isocrates is neither a philosopher nor a statesman, but only a speech writer.

The *Republic*

This dialogue is set in the house of Cephalus, a wealthy merchant of
munitions. It consists of ten books. The first book, which serves as an
introduction, contains three rounds of argument, all of which are addressed to the nature of justice. In the first round, Cephalus gives Socrates his view of justice, which may be labeled as theonomic, that is, the
view that justice is to obey the laws given by the gods and that to
disobey them will bring about divine sanction. In the second round, his
son Polemarchus takes over the discussion and presents his view of
justice by citing Simonides' maxim that justice is to give everyone his
due (331e). This maxim is a much more general statement than the rules
of conduct Cephalus takes as his guide. The second round represents
the ethics of principles, while the first round represents the ethics of
rules. The former is a higher stage in the development of ethical consciousness than the latter. One may follow some rules without knowing
their *raison d'etre* until one understands the principles behind those
rules.

Though the general principles may stand on a higher level than the
specific rules, the former does not have all the advantage of the latter.

Whereas the rules usually tell exactly what should be done, the principles by themselves do not lay down such specific instructions. The rules are determinate; the principles are indeterminate. For example, the principle that justice is to give everyone his or her due does not tell us exactly what we should do in any particular situation. Therefore, we do not really know what a general principle means until it is fully interpreted. Thus the discussion between Socrates and Polemarchus turns into a game of interpretation, just the way another poetic statement of Simonides gave the impetus for such a game in the *Protagoras*. In Polemarchus's interpretation Simonides' maxim gets equated with the conventional view that justice is to benefit one's friends and harm one's enemies. But it is rejected by Socrates on the ground that the idea of justice as human excellence is incompatible with the notion of harming any human beings, even one's enemies, because to harm human beings is to make them unjust (335c–e). Thus ends the second round of discussion.

Provoked by this game of interpretation, Thrasymachus has been impatiently waiting to get into the argument. When he does, the third round of discussion begins. His view of justice is one with that of Callicles in the *Gorgias*: justice is the advantage of the stronger (338c). This is an important thematic pointer: in the *Republic*, Socrates is going to meet the Calliclean challenge, which he evaded in the *Phaedo* and in the *Symposium* by locating the ultimate destiny and happiness of the soul in the other world. In the *Gorgias*, Callicles admired the life of a tyrant, especially Archelaus, as the best exemplification of the ethos of power and greed. Socrates predicted his punishment in the other world if his deeds had been as unjust as Polus portrayed (*Gorgias* 525d). Book 10 of the *Republic* describes the dreadful punishment of a tyrant, Ardiaeus (*Ardiaios*), whose name and deeds were remarkably similar to those of Archelaus (*Archelaos*). This is another thematic connector between the *Gorgias* and the *Republic*.

The three rounds of discussion represent the three stages in the development of moral consciousness in ancient Greece, just as the six speakers in the *Symposium* represented the three stages in the development of historical consciousness. The Thrasymachus round of discussion represents the current imperial ethos of Athens, and the Cephalus round reflects the still lingering ethos of theonomy. The transition between these stages of moral consciousness is represented by the Polemarchus round. Whereas the poets and seers have the ultimate moral authority in the age of theonomy, their statements become objects of criticism and interpretation in the age of anthroponomy. What sort of sense and significance should be given to their statements is determined by the wisdom of their interpreters. I am making this point to highlight Plato's extraordinary interest in the development of historical consciousness, which has not been fully appreciated in Plato scholarship.

The remaining nine books of the *Republic* are again divided into three sections. In books 2, 3, and 4, Socrates enlists the help of Plato's two brothers Glaucon and Adeimantus for constructing an ideal state, the Kallipolis. This section introduces the theory that the soul is composed of three parts: intellect, emotion, and appetite. Corresponding to these three parts, the Kallipolis will have three social classes: rulers, warriors, and artisans. There is an isomorphism between the three parts of the soul and the three classes of the state. The four cardinal virtues are defined in reference to the three classes. Wisdom is the excellence of rulers; courage is the excellence of warriors; temperance is the proper order of these three classes. When each of these classes performs its role and achieves its respective virtue, justice obtains for the entire state. This theory of virtue equally applies to the individual soul because of its isomorphism with the state. This theory of virtue is notably different from Socrates' claim in the *Protagoras* and the *Meno* that all virtues are reducible to wisdom.

The next section consists of books 5, 6, and 7. The break between the first and the second section is suggested by Polemarchus's intervention at the beginning of book 5 (449b). His performance reminds us of the second round of discussion he undertook in book 1. With his intervention, the discussion turns into the question of wives and children, and eventually reaches the question of how to realize the Kallipolis. It is going to require a philosopher-king. For the education of a future philosopher-king, Socrates introduces the doctrine of Forms, the Divided Line, and the Cave, each of which turns on the demarcation between the visible and the invisible worlds. The aim of education is to enable students to transcend the visible world and ascend to the invisible Forms, by training them in the Pythagorean sciences and dialectic.

This program of higher education is preceded by elementary education, which is discussed in books 2, 3, and 4. Elementary education uses the Protagorean method of conditioning and practicing advocated in the *Protagoras*; the young children are tamed and molded into virtuous characters. However, the higher education uses the method of Socratic inquiry demonstrated in the *Meno* and the *Euthydemus*; it is essentially rational and dialectical. Elementary education is for the inculcation of civic virtues; it takes place before students become fully mature and rational. The higher education is for the development of political art; it is designed only for the most gifted who are destined to assume the leadership of the state.

The third section consists of the last three books. Socrates gives his theory of degeneration, that is, how the Kallipolis degenerates to inferior forms of government. Degeneration begins when the intellectual class loses control of the state to the other classes. When the warrior class becomes dominant, the Kallipolis deteriorates to a timocracy, in which the sense of honor rather than the virtue of wisdom is the highest value. When the artisan class becomes dominant, the state further deteriorates and becomes appetitive, because the artisan class corresponds to the appetite of the soul. The appetitive state can take three different forms: oligarchy, democracy, and tyranny. An oligarchy establishes one dominant value in the appetite of acquisition and accumulation. In democracy, all appetites are equal, and their equality leads to a chaotic state. Tyranny is finally introduced as a desperate measure for restoring some order to the chaotic state of appetites.

There are altogether five forms of government: the Kallipolis, timocracy, oligarchy, democracy, and tyranny. They achieve five different levels of justice and happiness. The ideal state is the best, while tyranny is the worst. These five forms of government can also account for the five forms of life for the individual soul because of its tripartite isomorphism with the state. A soul can be ruled by one of its three elements, just as a state can be ruled by one of its three classes. Moreover, the happiness and justice of the soul are also determined by the form of its government. Hence, the just person is happier than the unjust one. There is a proper reward and punishment for both the just and the unjust in this world as well as in the other world. The last book of the *Republic* is chiefly devoted to the institution of reward and punishment in the other world. It is described in the myth of Er.

The last person to be mentioned in the myth of Er is Odysseus; on the eve of his reincarnation, he chooses the quiet life of a private individual because he remembers the ills of his previous life of ambition (620c). The first sentence of the *Republic* also reverberates with the theme of his rebirth and return; Socrates says, "I went down (*kateben*) to the Piraeus yesterday with Glaucon, the son of Ariston." Jacob Howland points out its resemblance to Odysseus's statement to his wife on his return to Ithaca, "I went down (*kateben*) into the house of Hades to inquire about the return of my companions and myself" (*Odyssey* 23.252).[12] The association of these two statements has led to the obvious question: What symbolic significance should be attached to Socrates' trip down to the Piraeus? Some scholars have proposed that it is a prefiguration of the stories of descent in the *Republic*, especially the descent into the Cave and the descent of Er to Hades.[13] In describing the Cave, Socrates indeed quotes the description of life in Hades by the shade of Achilles (516d).

The magic phrase, however, is in the past tense ("I went down"). It may have a far more significant thematic reference to what has already taken place before the *Republic*, that is, Socrates' descent to the world of phenomena in the *Protagoras*, the *Meno*, and the *Euthydemus*. The house of Cephalus, in which the *Republic* is set, is interchangeable with the house of Callias, where Socrates described the assembled sophists and their company with a couple of allusions to Odysseus's descent to Hades. Both houses were closely associated with the Periclean circle; they stand for the wealth and power of imperial Athens. Eric Voegelin says that the Piraeus is the Hades for Socrates' descent.[14] The harbor town is the bastion of Athenian naval power, and glitters with the wealth of imperial Athens. It is the final terminus of Socrates' descent to the world of phenomena, which began in the *Protagoras*.

Socrates and company had come down to the Piraeus to watch the first festival in celebration of Bendis, the Thracian goddess, which turned out to be a vulgar spectacle and entertainment quite in tune with the crass materialism of the commercial city. The alien goddess Bendis has replaced the native goddess Athene as the symbol of Athenian ethos. The sense of sanctity and divinity has totally disappeared even from the domain of religious rituals. This is the height of Athenian degradation and makes life in imperial Athens look like life in the Cave and Hades. The Piraeus is the showcase for her decadent culture. For these reasons, I believe that the magic phrase ''I went down'' at the opening of the *Republic* refers to the long journey of descent Socrates had undertaken in preparation for the construction of the Kallipolis.

The *Republic* begins with Socrates on his way from the Piraeus to the city of Athens. This opening prompts comparison with the opening of the *Symposium*, which is narrated by Apollodorus on his way from Phaleron to Athens. The difference between Phaleron and the Piraeus has special significance for the Athenians of the fifth century. Phaleron used to be the chief harbor for Athens before the fortification of the Piraeus. Just as the Piraeus stands for the decadent days of imperial Athens, so Phaleron stands for the virtuous days of pre-imperial Athens. The Socrates of the *Symposium* was adequate for those virtuous days, but not for the decadent days. The malady of imperial Athens requires the drastic operation of reconstituting the entire city, which can be performed only by the Socrates of the *Republic*. The virtues of individual citizens are sufficient for their life if they are living in a just society. In an unjust society, however, their individual virtues alone can never secure their salvation and that of their city. In the *Gorgias*, Socrates said that a virtuous person could never be hurt by anything even if that person was crippled by torture, defamed, or butchered by his evil opponents. At *Republic* 496d, he drops this fanatic stand. When a virtuous person cannot cope with the evils of society, Socrates says, he has to keep quiet, mind his own business, and protect himself like someone taking refuge behind a small wall against a hail storm.

A Community of Brotherly Love

This is the vast distance Socrates has traveled from the *Gorgias* and the *Symposium* to the *Republic*, but there is one more important differ-

ence between the *Symposium* and the *Republic*. It is the question of
love. The *Symposium* is the world of rapturous love; the *Republic* is an
ideal rational state. If so, what happens to love in the *Republic*? Its
rational order appears to be incompatible with the rapture of love. In
the *Republic*, erotic love is replaced by brotherly love (*philia*). The
ideal state is a community of brotherly love or Pythagorean fellowship.[15] The members of the governing class do not have private property
or even their own families; they strictly follow the maxim that friends
have all things in common (423–424). Chiefly because of brotherly
love, the philosopher descends from Platonic Heaven into the Cave. He
sacrifices the happy life of contemplation and takes on the onerous duty
of administering the city.

In the *Republic*, the theme of brotherly love is highlighted by the
partnership of two brothers, Glaucon and Adeimantus, which reminds
us of Lysis and Menexenus in the *Lysis* and of Cebes and Simmias in
the *Phaedo*. This sort of partnership is rare in Plato's dialogues. It will
occur only once more in the *Laws*. In the *Republic*, the bond of fraternal
love is the spiritual foundation of a new political order. In the last two
chapters, we noted that a tribal state was a community of kinship and
friendship. Those days of primitive states were gone by the time of
imperial Athens, and the friendship based on kinship was not broad
enough to sustain the city-states. This social transformation is a hidden
motif in book 1 of the *Republic*. Polemarchus's interpretation of Simonides' maxim of justice (helping one's friends and harming one's enemies) was an acceptable way of living in the age of tribal states. One
had the duty of helping the members of one's own tribe, and harming
the members of the other tribes because they were natural enemies. That
is the way the Homeric heroes conducted themselves. But this simple
code of justice became unacceptable as soon as the members of different tribal groups became members of the same state, because a state
could not be sustained by the principle of mutual predation.

The maxim of helping one's friends and harming others naturally
leads to the problem of *pleonexia*, the ethos of acquisitive culture advocated by Thrasymachus. One has to take a bigger share than others, if
one is going to take good care of one's friends, the members of one's
family and tribe. When one takes a bigger share, one does so at the

expense of other tribes, one's natural enemies. Among the Homeric heroes, to demand and to take a bigger share than others is not a vice but a virtue. In the *Iliad*, Achilles never feels uneasy or ashamed in demanding a better share than Agamemnon. To demand and take a bigger share is a mark of the superior (*agathos*) man, because that is the best way to provide for one's family and friends.[16] However, this virtue of tribal culture became the most corrosive vice when different tribes were united into a single state of civil society. What was a virtue in a tribal society becomes a vice in civil society; in fact, it can turn the civil society into a state of nature in which everyone is at war against everyone else.

This type of social upheaval was not limited to antiquity. It became a serious problem for modern Europe with the emergence of civil society. The state of nature that preoccupied Hobbes was the state of acquisitive culture; the ethos of acquisition and aggression was on the brink of dissolving all civic bonds. Hobbes offered his theory of social contract as a solution for this problem: the principle of social cooperation for mutual benefit is better than the principle of mutual predation and destruction. In addition to this proposed solution, the seventeenth century considered another proposal: the appeal to the brotherhood of a nation-state, for example, all Germans should unite in a single nation because they shared the same heritage. This is the principle of national solidarity, which was often purveyed in the name of patriotism. There is a significant difference between these two proposals. The principle of national solidarity is an attempt to extend the sense of kinship and friendship from the tribal society to the nation-state. In contrast, the principle of social contract does not make such an emotional appeal; instead, it tries to find a rational basis for political order that transcends the emotional bond of kinship and friendship.

In Plato's days, these two proposals became familiar arguments in political circles. His foremost competition, Isocrates, argued for the ideal of pan-Hellenism as the best solution for the political despair of Athens and other Greek states under Persian domination. The Greek city-states could regain their power and glory only by putting an end to the feuds against one another and by uniting themselves under the leadership of Athens against the Persians. They should do so, Isocrates preached, because they were friends who shared the same bloodties.[17] The principle of social contract was advocated by many sophists. These two proposed solutions have left clear imprints in the *Republic*. In book 2, Socrates and his company take a careful look at the social contract argument for justice. In book 5, they consider the relation of the Greeks to the barbarians. Whereas the Greeks and the barbarians are natural enemies, Socrates says, the Greeks are friends to one another by nature. Therefore, the war between Greeks is a civil strife (470c).

For Plato, however, neither the principle of social contract nor the principle of pan-Hellenic solidarity can provide the foundation for a new political order. The principle of social contract can secure only the instrumental value of justice; justice is no more than a necessary means for securing social cooperation and promoting self-interest. Such a social means is a necessity for the weak and an irksome yoke on the strong (358e–361d). If the strong are strong enough to conquer and control the weak, they have no reason to make the contract with the weak to restrain themselves. Even if they have made such a contract, they have every reason to ignore or evade it if doing so will serve their interest better. As long as social contract is taken as an instrument of rational self-interest, there is no rational ground to abide with it as soon as its violation can serve self-interest better than compliance.

The principle of pan-Hellenic solidarity cannot offer any better prospect than the principle of social contract. It only shifts the line of hostility from one group of people to another, from the tribal boundary to the ethnic boundary. But it does not eliminate the cause of hostility and strife. If it is asked why the principle of solidarity should be accepted on any level, there can be two answers: (1) social solidarity is necessary for social cooperation and peaceful existence, and (2) social solidarity is good in itself. The first answer assigns only an instrumental value to the principle of social solidarity. Though the second answer recognizes the intrinsic value of social solidarity, there is no easy way to explain the rationality of such a value. Why should one Greek love another Greek more than she should love a barbarian, except for the instrumental value of coping with the barbarian aggression? In terms of kinship, the Greeks of different states are almost as alien to one another as they are to the barbarians.

The principle of ethnic solidarity had already been tried during the Persian Wars of the fifth century. Though it was successfully used in forming the Delian League and repulsing the Persians, it eventually led to the disaster of Athenian imperialism, as we saw in chapter 1. The patriotism of seventeenth-century Europe produced the same disastrous consequence. It became the fountainhead of national expansionism and imperialism, which eventually engulfed all the continents and oceans of the globe in a merciless game of aggression and predation during the nineteenth and twentieth centuries. The Holocaust was a gruesome product of the principle of ethnic solidarity.

Plato finds the spiritual basis for the new political order in the Pythagorean ideal of *philosophia*, the principle of brotherly love and fellowship in wisdom. This new principle transcends the natural boundaries of kinship and ethnic affiliations, because the world of wisdom stands above them all. This kinship in wisdom does not end at the boundary of humanity, but extends from the world of humans to that of the gods. By virtue of this cosmic friendship, Socrates can maintain that the virtue of justice is good not only as an instrument but as an end in itself. On the theory of social contract, justice can have no more than an instrumental value, because justice is the good of others. But justice cannot be the good of others in the world of Pythagorean brotherly love. Whereas a social contract brings together oneself and others into a scheme of cooperation for mutual benefit, the Pythagorean ideal of brotherly love turns oneself and others into a community of friends. Since a friend is an extension of oneself, justice in the Kallipolis cannot be the good of others. Socrates describes the Kallipolis as a community held together by a strong sense of kinship (463c–464a).

All these things concern the most difficult question in the *Republic*: What motive do we have to be just? This question of motivation is at the heart of Thrasymachus's and Glaucon's objection to the conventional pious view of justice. Brushing aside this view, they challenge Socrates to show that the virtue of justice has not only instrumental but also intrinsic value for the constitution of our happiness. The entire *Republic* is meant to be an answer to this question, and Socrates tries to cope with it especially with the doctrine of psychic justice in books 8 and 9. Psychic justice is the justice that obtains within the well-ordered soul. It is the good of the soul, just as health is the good of the body. This analogy was used by Socrates in his argument against Callicles in the *Gorgias*: justice is the health of the soul, while injustice is its corruption and its greatest evil (477c–478b). Hence, the doctrine of psychic justice is an elaboration of his response to the Calliclean challenge as well.

In the *Republic*, Socrates wants to establish the intimate connection between psychic and social justice. In the world of moral motivation, he holds, psychic justice naturally leads to social justice. But this claim can be taken in more than one way. First, the rule of reason that is essential for psychic justice can take two forms: formal and substantive. In the formal version, reason does not have its own ends and values; its only function is to secure an order among all the desires of the soul. By this standard, even a soul dominated by appetite can have a rational rule; a highly appetitive person or a cool villain can have a rational plan of life. Therefore, the rational rule of psychic justice must be interpreted in some substantive sense. If so, what ends and values does reason have on its own agenda? Should justice and the good of others be included in that agenda? Thrasymachus and Callicles can readily give a negative answer to this question. For this reason, Terence Irwin says that the *Republic* is an unconvincing answer to Glaucon and Thrasymachus.[18]

It may be possible for Socrates to make his case stronger by appealing to the world of Forms; the ends and values of reason are determined by its vision of the Good, which is essentially connected to the Form of Justice.[19] Even this move does not fully clinch the argument, because we can still raise another question: Why should one realize the Good unless it affects one's own happiness? This is the same question as why the philosopher should leave Platonic Heaven and go down to the Cave to take on administrative duties. This is perhaps the most intractable question Socrates has to face in the *Republic*. He first appeals to the philosopher's sense of justice; he should return to the state because he owes his upbringing and education to it. But to appeal to his sense of justice is to put the cart before the horse, because the question is precisely why he should be constrained by the sense of justice. Because Socrates' own answer turns out to be woefully deficient, many commentators have come to his aid with their own answers.

One of these answers is the replication argument, which is based on Diotima's story that every soul wants to reproduce itself to achieve immortality. The philosopher wants to go down to the Cave to replicate his psychic justice in other souls.[20] But this is a misapplication of the replication theory. In Diotima's story, the task of replication is restricted to the lesser mysteries of love; it is a surrogate for the true immortality that is achieved in the greater mystery of love. Since the philosopher has gone through the greater mystery, he has no need of replicating himself. If he wants to go down to the Cave, he should have some other business on his mind.

John Cooper gives a different reason for the philosopher's descent; he is a devotee of the Good, not his own good. As such a devotee, he wants to maximize the total amount of rational order in the world as a whole.[21] If the philosopher becomes a devotee of the Good rather than his own good, his reason becomes indistinguishable from the cosmic reason. He is no longer a private person with his own goals and ambitions. As an answer to Glaucon and Thrasymachus, this is too good to be effective, because they are concerned with the moral motivation of private persons and not of the cosmic reason. For these reasons, none of these proposed answers is as effective and as convincing as the one I proposed on the basis of *philia*. This answer has not been attempted largely because Plato scholars have never taken seriously the role of *philia* in his philosophy. Gregory Vlastos is one exception. He correctly repeats Socrates' description of the Kallipolis, "The ideal society of the *Republic* is a political community held together by bonds of fraternal love."[22] It is ultimately the bond of fraternal love that brings the philosopher back to the Cave.

The Pythagorean ideal of *philosophia* as a principle of social order also underlies Plato's doctrine of equality of women and men. In tribal communities, the distinction of men and women was as important as the distinction between friends and strangers. These two distinctions were the basic principles for the social fabric of antiquity. In the society of warriors, hunters, or farmers, the difference of two sexes was obvious; the men are usually endowed with bigger muscles and bones. However, this sort of natural advantage can no longer be considered as a relevant mark of superiority in the world of wisdom, and there is no reason to deny women their equality to men in a society of *philosophia*. For this reason, the equality of men and women is an essential feature of Plato's ideal state.

Though the Pythagorean ideal of brotherly love or friendship does not take its full effect until the *Republic*, its seed was already planted in the *Lysis*, where friendship was defined as the love of what is akin to oneself. The Pythagorean ideal is based on the kinship in wisdom. Though it is not even mentioned as a basic principle of justice in the *Republic* and seldom discussed in Plato scholarship, it has an over-whelming significance for the entire dialogue. Its special significance lies in presenting the *Republic* as Plato's political response to the Cal-liclean challenge. Even in the *Gorgias*, Socrates could not counter the Calliclean challenge without appealing to the Pythagorean ideal of uni-versal order and harmony, friendship and partnership (*Gorgias* 506d–508a). There he had no political philosophy of his own, and used the Pythagorean ideal only for buttressing his ethical ideals. These ideals could not add up to an effective response to the Calliclean challenge because the latter was not merely ethical but political.

In the *Republic*, Plato installs the Pythagorean ideal of brotherly love as the foundation for his political philosophy. The Kallipolis is a city of love (*philia*). It is the bond of love that ties together not only the three classes of the state into a harmonious whole, but also the three parts of the soul in each individual (589ab). This bond secures the hap-piness of both the soul and the state. The transition from the *Symposium* to the *Republic* can now be stated as the transition from erotic to frater-nal love. This transition has been achieved by Socrates' descent from the transcendent to the phenomenal world.

Notes

1. For different accounts of this point, see Diskin Clay, "The Tragic and Comic Poet of the *Symposium*," in *Essays in Ancient Greek Philosophy*, John Anton and Anthony Preus, ed. (Albany, N.Y.: SUNY Press, 1983), 2:186–202; R. E. Allen, *The Dialogues of Plato*, vol. 2, *The Symposium* (New Haven: Yale University Press, 1991), 170 n. 278.

2. For the self-predication of Platonic Forms, see John Malcolm, *Plato on the Self-Predication of Forms* (Oxford: University Press, 1991).

3. David Bostock, *Plato's Phaedo* (Oxford: University Press, 1986), 34.

4. Jean Houston, *The Hero and the Goddess* (New York: Ballantine Books, 1992), 183–184.

5. A representative critique of this argument is given by Gregory Vlastos in his introduction to Plato, *Protagoras* (New York: Macmillan, 1956), xxvi–xlv.

6. This account is given by Leonard Woodbury, "Simonides on Arete," *Transactions and Proceedings of American Philological Association* 84 (1953):135–63.

7. I know of only two exceptions. For A. E. Taylor, the abrupt opening shows that the *Meno* is Plato's early work. *Plato: The Man and His Work* (London: Methuen, 1926), 130. For Jacob Klein, "the suddenness of the question heightens its comical character." *A Commentary on Plato's Meno* (Chapel Hill: University of North Carolina Press, 1965), 38.

8. Kahn, "On the Relative Date of the *Gorgias* and the *Protagoras*," *Oxford Studies in Ancient Philosophy* 6 (1988):77.

9. The notion of rebirth is expressed by Circe's reference to Odysseus and his companions as rash men who have gone to Hades to die twice on their return from Hades (*Odyssey* 12.21–22). For a further discussion, see Douglas Frame, *The Myth of Return in Early Greek Epic* (New Haven, Conn.: Yale University Press, 1978), 39–49.

10. This point is well explained by Jean Houston, *The Hero and the Goddess*, 187–89.

11. For a description of Isocrates' school, see John Lynch, *Aristotle's School* (Berkeley: University of California Press, 1972), 48–54.

12. Jacob Howland, *The Republic: The Odyssey of Philosophy* (New York: Twayne Publishers, 1993), 48.

13. This view is well represented by Howland, *The Republic*, 48–49; Eric Voegelin, *Order and History*, vol. 3, *Plato and Aristotle* (Baton Rouge: University of Louisiana Press, 1957), 52–62.

14. Voegelin, *Plato and Aristotle*, 54.

15. This is often overlooked, but is well appreciated by Gregory Vlastos, *Platonic Studies*, 11; Gerasimos Santas, *Plato and Freud* (Oxford: Blackwell, 1988), 89–94.

16. For an account of Homeric ethos, see A. W. H. Adkins, *Moral Values and Political Behavior in Ancient Greece* (New York: Norton, 1972), 12–21.

17. Isocrates' speeches on pan-Hellenism are *Panegyricus* and *Panathenaicus*.

18. Irwin, *Plato's Moral Theory* (Oxford: University Press, 1977), 246–47.

19. For further discussion of this point, see C. D. C. Reeve, *Philosopher-Kings* (Princeton, N.J.: Princeton University Press, 1988), 140–44.

20. Irwin, *Plato's Moral Theory*, 242.

21. John Cooper, "The Psychology of Justice in Plato," *American Philosophical Quarterly* 14 (1977):151–57.

22. Vlastos, *Platonic Studies*, 11.

CHAPTER FOUR

The Self-Reflective Interlude

The *Phaedrus* and the *Cratylus*

Among Plato's works, the *Phaedrus* has the special distinction of being set in the open countryside. Outside the city walls, Socrates and Phaedrus meet by accident. First, Phaedrus reads a speech written by Lysias, which extols the advantage of having a nonlover for a friend rather than a lover (230e–234c). The association with nonlovers is much better and more beneficial because they are sober and prudent whereas lovers are imprudent and capricious. In response to this speech, Socrates gives his own, which describes the damages a jealous lover can inflict on his or her beloved, because the lover is a slave of appetite (237b–241d). These two speeches dovetail with each other. One praises the friendship of a nonlover and its advantages, while the other denounces the friendship of a lover and its disadvantages. Next, Socrates tells Phaedrus that they have committed a terrible offense in speaking ill of love, and he offers his recantation in an atonement for the offense. After the palinode, the two get into a discussion about the nature of rhetoric. This discussion is the second half of the dialogue, while the two speeches and the palinode constitute the first half.

The two halves of the dialogue are thematically divided. Love is the theme of the first half; rhetoric is the theme of the second half. The two halves are further divided by two styles of composition. The style of the first half is the same rhetorical style as that of the *Symposium*: the two speakers present their speeches. In the second half, this rhetorical style is replaced by the Socratic method of questions and answers. For these reasons, the *Phaedrus* reads like two separate dialogues stitched together into one, and the question of its unity has been one of the oldest problems in Plato scholarship.

What is it that holds together the two seemingly disparate parts of the *Phaedrus*? The standard answer for this question has been as follows. A lover must be able to speak persuasively to establish and cultivate a relation with the beloved. Therefore, the art of speaking well, rhetoric, is the natural topic to follow the topic of love. This answer is seriously flawed. It stands on the assumption that rhetoric is the best way of talking between the lover and the beloved. As a student of rhetoric, Phaedrus may subscribe to such a view, but Socrates has no reason to do so. For Socrates, the relation of the lover and the beloved is the relation of *philosophia*, and rhetoric is the worst way of cultivating wisdom. Beginning in the *Gorgias*, Socrates has repeatedly branded rhetoric as a technique of deceiving and misleading the gullible audience, while praising dialectic as the only reliable way of investigating the truths. By *dialectic* I refer not to the science of dialectic as defined in the *Republic*, but to Socrates' familiar way of talking by a series of short questions and answers as advocated in the *Gorgias* and the *Protagoras*. If Socrates has not abandoned his lowly view of rhetoric, he should simply say that the lover should use the art of dialectic rather than the dubious rhetoric, if he wants to lead his beloved to truth and wisdom.

Some may think that dialectic cannot be used for the conversation between lover and beloved, because the latter is usually too young. But Socrates has already used it for talking with very young children such as Cleinias in the *Euthydemus* and Lysis and Menexenus in the *Lysis*. In the *Phaedrus*, he is not talking about rhetoric because he wants to find the right way of talking between lover and beloved. He is talking about it because Lysias's speech is a piece of rhetoric and because he wants to investigate the nature of rhetoric. What is startling about this investigation, however, is that Socrates presents a completely different view of rhetoric from the one he had repeatedly stated before. Whereas he had said that rhetoric could never be anything more than a knack or empirical guesswork (*Gorgias* 462c), he now wants to transform it into a true art. This is a major reversal on his part, which cannot be explained by the usual interpretation of the dialogue. Perhaps, it can be explained if the *Phaedrus* is read as a self-critical work in which Socrates is reviewing some of the important theories he has already presented elsewhere.

Revision of the *Symposium* and the *Phaedo*

Let us compare the lover and the nonlover as described in the first two speeches of the *Phaedrus*. The nonlover has complete control of emotions and desires, because he is rational. He is not the slave of love but the master of himself (233c). There are two modes of ruling for the soul. One is by rational judgments and the other is by unruly passions. The former is called temperance, and the latter is love (237d–238d). The lover is overcome by passion; the nonlover is in control of it. Being rational and temperate, the nonlover avoids the evil of passions. In contrast, the lover is mad and the madness is called love. As Terence Irwin points out, the distinction between lover and nonlover is reminiscent of the distinction Socrates established between the rule by reason and the rule by passion in the *Republic*.[1] In his first speech, Socrates describes the domination of the soul by one of its desires exactly in the same way as he described the inner state of the unjust souls in books 8 and 9. The rational person educated in the ideal state should choose the nonlover over the lover, if that person wants to maintain the inner harmony of the soul. Thus, the first two speeches of the *Phaedrus* are reflexive of the *Republic*.

The distinction between the rational and the irrational rule of the soul is not the only thematic connection between the *Phaedrus* and the *Republic*. What brings these two dialogues even closer thematically is the notion of friendship (*philia*). In the last chapter, we noted the overriding significance of friendship in the *Republic*. The *Phaedrus* opens with a salutation to a friend ("My friend Phaedrus") and closes with a reference to friends ("Friends have all things in common"). Furthermore, the primary object of the first two speeches is friendship, and the difference between the lover and the nonlover is only incidental to it. These speeches raise the question: Which will be the better basis for friendship, the lover's irrational rule or the nonlover's rational rule? In the *Republic*, the concept of friendship was inseparably linked to the concept of rational rule. Thus, these two concepts thematically connect the two dialogues.

The *philia* (friendship) of the *Republic*, which is cool and rational, appears to be incompatible with the *eros* of the *Symposium*, which is intense and passionate. In the *Symposium*, *eros* was praised as the only way to the ultimate wisdom and the mystical vision of Beauty itself, but the friendship that is secured by rational rule appears to leave no room for erotic love in the life of a philosopher. If so, how should we understand the relation of *eros* and *philia*? In the *Phaedrus*, Plato is not just writing another dialogue on love, as many readers have thought. Instead he is reviewing from the perspective of the *Republic* what he has said about love in the *Symposium*. The *Phaedrus* is a dialogue of self-reflection and self-criticism. Let us now see what is eventually produced by this self-critical reflection.

In the palinode, Socrates wants to show that the incompatibility of *eros* and *philia* is only apparent, and that this appearance is attributable to a misunderstanding of *eros* and of rational rule. The temperance of the nonlover is only a slavish virtue; the reason of the nonlover serves only the instrumental function of promoting erotic appetite (256e–257a). Because it does not have its own aims and values, its rule is drastically different from the rational rule of the philosopher advocated in the *Republic*. Yet they are liable to be mistaken for each other, because both of them are called the rule of reason. In the previous chapter we distinguished between two types of rational rule: formal and substantive. The rational rule of the nonlover is the rule of formal rationality; the rational part of his or her soul has no substantive aims and values of its own. On the other hand, the rational rule of a philosopher is the rule of substantive rationality. If we overlook this distinction, we may mistake the ideal state for a community of loveless rationality, and the philosopher for a totally nonemotional being. Socrates wants to forestall this sort of misunderstanding about the life of reason by recanting his first speech and replacing it with his second speech.

Socrates wants to demonstrate the positive thesis that *eros* is an essential component of *philosophia* (love of wisdom), and that love is not ordinary madness as it is claimed to be in the first two speeches, but a form of divine madness. To explain the nature of this divine madness, Socrates talks about the immortal soul: it is like a charioteer and a pair of winged horses, which participate in the divine procession of gods and souls for the vision of eternal Forms. When the soul is reincarnated in this world, it no longer retains a clear memory of eternal reality. But the love of Eternal Beauty is revived by the sight of beautiful things in this world, and the eruption of erotic emotion is the manifestation of this revival. This mental state stands so far apart from the busy antics of humankind that it appears to be madness to most people (249d). It is indeed a possession that leads to the perfect mysteries of divine love. Hence, the erotic attraction of the lover to the beloved is the initial spark for *philosophia*, which is none other than the longing for the mystical vision of eternal reality.

To bring this longing to fruition, the lover and the beloved form a relation of mutual care and aid because the pursuit of wisdom is a communal enterprise of brotherly love. This is the basic difference between the *Phaedrus* and the *Symposium*. Though the ascent of the soul to the realm of eternal Forms is the ultimate end of *philosophia* in both dialogues, the ascent takes different forms. In the *Symposium*, the ascent is a solo flight; in the *Phaedrus*, it is a cooperative enterprise. Even in the divine world, the ascent takes place as a grand procession of countless souls. On earth, the communal bond for the philosophical procession takes its first step in the erotic bond between lover and beloved. Their love for each other develops into the relationship of teacher and disciple for the common love of Truth, Beauty, and Goodness (252–256).

In the *Meno*, Socrates said that there were neither teachers nor students of virtue (89e), but that assertion is disproven by the relationship between lover and beloved as teacher and student. The relationship of lover and beloved redefines the nature of *philosophia*; it means not only love (friend) of wisdom but love (friends) in wisdom. This bond of *philosophia* between the lover and the beloved is not limited to this world; it is the earthly extension of the celestial bond of fraternity that brings together the gods and the *daimones*, mortals and immortals, in the heavenly procession. Thus, the Pythagorean bond of brotherly love is the cosmic bond of *philosophia*, as Socrates argued in the *Gorgias*. The nature of this cosmic bond is extolled and celebrated in the *Phaedrus*.

In the *Symposium*, erotic relation does not lead to fraternal relation; according to Alcibiades, Socrates has never formed a bond of friendship with him. As we noted, he is too virtuous and self-sufficient to need a friend. What was called *philosophia* in the *Symposium* is really *erosophia*, and the *Phaedrus* converts *erosophia* into *philosophia*. The *Phaedrus* does this by taking us back to the *Lysis* and its ideal of friendship; we are reminded of this ideal by the resemblance of the two names involved, Lysis and Lysias. The two speeches about lovers and nonlovers resonate with the instruction Socrates gave Hippothales on how to deal with his beloved (*Lysis* 210e). Hippothales' relation to Lysis was erotic and self-seeking, and Socrates' love in the *Symposium* was not any less so. Self-seeking erotic love is replaced by brotherly love of fellowship in the *Republic*, and again in the *Phaedrus*. In that regard, the *Phaedrus* is a palinode of the *Symposium*.[2] This is why the idea of recantation is such an important theme in this dialogue.

In the *Symposium*, the notion of fellowship between lover and beloved is not totally unknown; it is an important element of Phaedrus's speech, and then becomes the climax of Pausania's speech. However, these speeches along with others are transcended by Socrates' story of Diotima. According to her, the fellowship between lover and beloved cannot be the ultimate end of the greater mystery of love, though it may function, like the love of bodies and souls, as an important step for ascending to the ultimate step. Friendship and fellowship are important in the *Republic*, because they alone can sustain the Kallipolis. Hence, Socrates disdains the notion of friendship and fellowship in the *Symposium*, but exalts it in the *Republic*. On this score, the *Phaedrus* reaffirms the *Republic* and revises the *Symposium*.

The *philosophia* of the *Republic* and the *Phaedrus* does not totally repudiate the *erosophia* of the *Symposium*; the mystical vision of Beauty and other Forms is retained equally in all three works. In the *Republic*, the vision of eternal Forms is evidently as enchanting and as rapturous as it was claimed to be in the *Symposium*. Socrates says that it is not easy for the philosopher to give up the contemplative life and undertake public service in the Cave. This difficulty does not become intelligible unless we recognize the superlative beauty of Forms and their power of attraction. If the Forms were merely abstract normative standards, the soul could never experience any rapture in its contemplation of those Forms or any difficulty in leaving them for the sake of practical works. If the philosopher's intellectual vision were limited to such skeletal Forms, he or she would be eager to descend to the Cave for their realization. For these reasons, we have to assume that the vision of Platonic Forms in the *Republic* is as arresting and as enchanting as it is supposed to be in the *Symposium*.

In the *Republic*, however, the mystical vision has a different effect; it is translated into the love of fellowship and the construction of the Kallipolis. This translation is reaffirmed in the *Phaedrus*, but the mystical vision is nothing new. It was already available in the *Symposium*. In that regard, Odysseus's travel down to Hades can stand as a perfect analogue to Socrates' descent from the *Symposium* to the *Republic*. In Hades, contrary to what Circe has told him, Odysseus does not get any useful advice from the soul of Tiresias on how to get back to his home. Strangely, Circe herself gives him that advice when he comes back to her palace from Hades. Why then did she send him down to Hades? The only plausible answer should be that she has all along had the knowledge and wisdom required for Odysseus's journey back to Ithaca, but her knowledge and wisdom do not become useful to him until his rebirth in Hades reorients his life as the responsible political chief for the city of Ithaca.

Diotima is Socrates' Circe and priestess. She has all along had the wisdom and knowledge Socrates needs for constructing the ideal state. The Pythagorean bond of *philosophia* is derived from the vision of Platonic Forms, which is already available in Diotima's world. One soul falls in love with another when the former sees an image of the Form in the other, because the image evokes the memory of the mystical vision of Forms (*Phaedrus* 250a-d). Even in the *Symposium*, the souls fall in love with each other by virtue of their longing for the eternal Forms, but their fellowship is not the ultimate end of their love. The mystical vision of the Forms that consummates their love dissolves their fellowship. In the *Republic*, on the other hand, the mystical vision lays the ground for the fellowship of the Kallipolis. By reaffirming the significance of fellowship, the *Phaedrus* revises the conception of love presented in the *Symposium*.

The *Phaedrus* not only revises the *Symposium*; it also revamps the *Phaedo*. The argument of immortality in the *Phaedrus* is essentially the same as the last of the many arguments Socrates gave in the *Phaedo*.[3] The final argument of the *Phaedo* was based on the premise that the soul is the cause that brings life to the body (105c–106e). The argument of the *Phaedrus* is based on the premise that the soul is the principle of self-motion (245c–246a). The principle of self-motion can be equated with the cause that alone can bring life to the body. The argument for the immortality of the soul in the *Phaedrus* only restates the final argument in the *Phaedo*. The *Phaedrus* also reaffirms the doctrine of recollection and reincarnation.

The two doctrines of immortality and recollection were missing from the *Symposium*, and their absence created a serious discrepancy between the two dialogues. In the *Phaedrus*, this discrepancy is dissolved and the central themes of the two dialogues are united into a single dialogue. Moreover, the picture of the other world in the *Phaedrus* is much brighter and more inspiring than the one in the *Phaedo*. For these reasons, the *Phaedrus* is not only a revision of the *Phaedo* and the *Symposium*, but their union. Even the title *Phaidros* can be read as a union of *Phaidon* and *eros*, the central theme of the *Symposium*.

The Knowledge of Phenomena

We have taken care of the first topic, the problem of love, in the *Phaedrus*. How should we handle the second topic, the problem of rhetoric? For that we have to go back to the theory of knowledge in the *Republic*. Knowledge is possible only for the world of Forms; for the world of phenomena, we can have only opinion. This is a drastic restriction of the domain of knowledge, which forecloses the possibility of natural science, or the scientific knowledge of phenomena. This appears to go against the list of four Pythagorean sciences Socrates prescribes for the program of higher education at *Republic* 525b—531c. This list includes not only arithmetic and geometry, but astronomy and harmonics. The last two belong to natural science; while the first two belong to mathematics. How can Socrates restrict the domain of knowledge to the world of Forms and yet regard astronomy and harmonics as sciences on a par with mathematics? Why does he not say that astronomy and harmonics are not really sciences because they are concerned with the world of phenomena? For these questions, Socrates provides a peculiar account of the two sciences of astronomy and harmonics.

He says that the visible patterns traced in the empirical heavens fall far short of true motions, and that they are not the objects of pure astronomy. They are the objects of empirical astronomy. The objects of pure astronomy are true motions that can be grasped not by sense organs but by reason and thought because they are not empirical (*Republic* 529cd). He makes the same claim for pure harmonics: its objects are not audible sounds and tones, but purely intellectual ratios of sounds and tones (*Republic* 531ab). This is a clear demarcation between the pure and the empirical versions of astronomy and harmonics.[4] The pure versions are concerned with intelligible objects; the empirical versions are concerned the sensible objects. This demarcation follows the corresponding treatment of the pure and the empirical versions of arithmetic and geometry (*Republic* 525d–527a).

Since pure astronomy is concerned with the nature of true motions, and their true swiftness and slowness, Socrates says, it dispenses with the empirical objects in the heavens (*Republic* 530b). If pure astronomy dispenses with the happenings in the visible heaven, what sort of science is it? Some commentators have interpreted it as something that goes well beyond the domain of mathematical sciences and comes very close to dialectic. Other commentators have seen it as a forerunner of modern astronomy, which employs the hypothetico-deductive model. These two accounts locate the objects of nonempirical astronomy differently. The second interpretation locates them in the physical world; hence it is in conflict with Socrates' description of pure astronomy. The first interpretation locates them in the domain of dialectic, the highest level of the Divided Line. In that case, astronomy and harmonics stand on a higher level than mathematics. This does not seem to fit into the Platonic scheme of sciences.

Recently there have been some efforts to locate the pure versions of astronomy and harmonics on the third level of the Divided Line. Ian Mueller says that the *Republic* assimilates astronomy to geometry.[5] Alexander Mourelatos says that pure astronomy should be understood as a general and pure kinematics, whose objects are the objects of *dianoia*.[6] If these two views are correct, they reduce the pure versions of astronomy and harmonics to mathematical sciences. But those purely mathematical versions of astronomy and harmonics are not natural sciences. The distinction between pure and empirical astronomy should not be confused with the distinction between theoretical and applied astronomy. Theoretical astronomy can be either pure or empirical. If it is empirical, it is a natural science. If it is pure, it is not a natural but a mathematical science. The distinction between pure and empirical astronomy is much like the distinction between the mathematics of physics and mathematical physics. The latter belongs to physics, but the former to mathematics.

The distinction between pure and empirical astronomy is like the distinction between pure and empirical geometry. Pure geometry is a priori; it is independent of empirical data. Empirical geometry is a posteriori; it is based on empirical data. Pure geometry belongs to mathematics; empirical geometry belongs to natural science. Let us now try to make the same distinction for astronomy. Though we are familiar with the notion of empirical astronomy, we do not know what it means to have pure astronomy. Socrates says that it studies the pure or true motion rather than empirical motion. What is the pure or true motion? Does it have any speed or location? If it does, it should have the pure speed and the pure location rather than the empirical ones. What is the magnitude of the pure speed? What is the nature of the pure location? The concepts of motion and speed make no sense once they are separated from the phenomenal world. In that case, the concepts of pure astronomy and pure harmonics make no sense either.

If pure astronomy is conceived by complete abstraction from the phenomenal world, it cannot be distinguished from mathematics. Differential equation can be regarded as a theory of motion, but it belongs to mathematics rather than to physics. Let us be clear about the distinction between the mathematics of physics and mathematical physics. The latter is an empirical science; the former is a mathematical science. If pure astronomy and pure harmonics totally transcend the world of phenomena, they are not natural but mathematical sciences. The four Pythagorean sciences of the *Republic* are four branches of mathematics, and the empirical versions of astronomy and harmonics do not belong to the domain of knowledge because they produce only opinions. This is consistent with Socrates' view in the *Republic* that there can be no true science or knowledge of phenomena.

This is the well-known Platonic distinction between knowledge and opinion, but it has some embarrassing consequences. To begin with, it is incompatible with the *techne* model of knowledge, namely, the idea that technical expertise is the model of knowledge. The *techne* model should not be confused with the *techne*-analogy, namely, the claim that the knowledge of virtue is analogous to technical knowledge. As Terence Irwin notes, the *techne*-analogy is rejected as early as the *Euthydemus*, because technical knowledge can have only instrumental value in contrast to the intrinsic value of virtue.[7] But the *techne* model is retained well to the end of the *Republic*. In book 10, Socrates talks about the technical knowledge of cobblers, farmers, and carpenters, and tries to explain the nature of technical knowledge in reference to Forms. For example, the carpenter derives his technical knowledge of making a bed from the Form of the Bed (*Republic* 596b). The pure knowledge of the Form is quite different from the technical knowledge of using it in making a bed. Their difference is on a par with the difference between pure astronomy and empirical astronomy. If empirical astronomy is not a true science or knowledge because it involves empirical data, neither can the technical knowledge of making beds be a true science because it also involves empirical data.

The *techne* model can have further complications, because in some cases technical knowledge appears to have nothing to do with the knowledge of Forms. Consider the knowledge of a navigator, who *knows* the way from Aegina to Athens (*Gorgias* 511d). His technical knowledge cannot be based on any Forms; there is no Form for the navigational route from Aegina to Athens. Then, how can it be called knowledge rather than opinion? Toward the end of the *Meno*, Socrates again talks about the difference between knowledge and opinion, and explains it with a perceptual model. One *knows* the way to Larissa if one has traveled on it. Though one has no knowledge of the way, one can still obtain correct opinion from someone who *knows* the way (*Meno* 97ab). The way to Larissa is the common object of both knowledge and the opinion, but it belongs to the world of phenomena. The knowledge of the way to Larissa is like the knowledge of a navigator. If so, there must be two ways of understanding the world of phenomena: knowledge and opinion. But how can a phenomenon be an object of knowledge rather than of opinion? Without answering this question, it will be impossible to maintain the *techne* model of knowledge.

The distinction between the pure knowledge of Forms and the technical knowledge of their application equally applies to the philosopher-king. Though he may have the pure knowledge of Justice and the Good, his knowledge of application cannot be pure because it involves the empirical data of the phenomenal world. By the strict standard of knowledge, his application is not knowledge but only opinion. To be sure, he is supposed to spend fifteen years in practical training after his study of dialectic. But does the practical training give him any *knowledge* of phenomena? The same question arises for the knowledge of the way from Athens to Larissa. Can one gain *knowledge* of it by simply traveling on it, though it is an empirical object? Can Socrates say that the philosopher-king has some special *knowledge* of application, which is not available to his unenlightened brethren in the Cave?

Finally, the distinction between knowledge and opinion also applies to Socrates' own talk in the *Republic*. How much of his talk is based on the Forms, and how much of it is concerned with the world of phenomena? How much of it belongs to the domain of knowledge, and how much of it to the domain of opinion? In books 2 through 4, the construction of the Kallipolis and the definition of the four cardinal virtues are based not on the Forms, but on the tripartite theory of the soul. But Socrates does not assert the existence of an eternal Form for the Kallipolis or the soul. Instead he lays out the tripartite theory of the soul on the basis of an empirical observation. In books 8 and 9, the tripartite theory of the soul again becomes the basis for the inquiry into the causes of degeneration for the Kallipolis and the virtuous soul. At the end of book 9 (*Republic* 592b), Socrates casually mentions the possibility that the model of the Kallipolis is laid up in heaven. But still he does not call it a Form.[8]

Between these two long stretches of soul-based empirical discourse, the Forms are introduced in books 5 through 7 for the discourse on the nature of philosophy and philosophical education. Socrates refers to this interlude as a digression as soon as he resumes the soul-based talk at the beginning of book 8 (*Republic* 453c). Most of the discourse in the *Republic* cannot qualify as scientific knowledge by Socrates' own standard of cognition. For it is based not on the Forms, but on the tripartite structure of the soul, which is an empirical entity. In that case, it should belong to the domain of opinion rather than knowledge.

The Problem of Rhetoric

The distinction between knowledge and opinion can be linked to the distinction between dialectic and rhetoric. In the *Gorgias* and the *Protagoras*, this distinction was introduced to differentiate two ways of talking. Rhetoric is Gorgias's and Protagoras's way of talking to a big audience by making long speeches. Dialectic is Socrates' way of talking; it is the method of question and answer between two speakers. In the *Republic*, however, Socrates redefines dialectic as the science of Forms. As a science of demonstration, dialectic makes an obvious contrast with rhetoric, which is an art of persuasion. If our talk about Forms belongs to dialectic, then our talk about the phenomena should belong to rhetoric, because the phenomena cannot be the objects of demonstrative knowledge. The distinction between dialectic and rhetoric should be equivalent to the distinction between knowledge and opinion. In that case, most of Socrates' talk in the *Republic* is a product of rhetoric rather than of dialectic. It is only for persuasion rather than demonstration.

In the *Gorgias*, Socrates repudiated the pretension of rhetoric to be an art, and branded it only as an empirical guesswork. He said that rhetoric aims not at the discovery of truth, but only at the gratification of appetites. This harsh critique of rhetoric should apply to Socrates' own performance in the *Republic*, if it belongs to rhetoric rather than dialectic. This is the embarrassing consequence of self-reflexivity for the dialogue. Here and there, in fact, he candidly admits that his account is only an opinion, and that only the god knows whether it is true or not (506c, 509c, 517b). But he says that a much better and truly demonstrative account can be obtained by taking the longer road of dialectic (*Republic* 435cd, 504b). That is, his account can be restated in the language of Forms, when he and his interlocutors finally get out of the Cave, ascend to the world of Forms, and master the science of dialectic. What has been presented in a rhetorical mode can be redeemed by the art of dialectic.

This hope of redemption by dialectic, however, never amounts to anything more than a dream, because the science of dialectic is only a dream to be realized by the birth of a true philosopher. Just compare Socrates' treatment of mathematics with his treatment of dialectic. Though dialectic and mathematics are presented as two branches of knowledge, his accounts of them are quite different. When he talks about mathematical sciences, he treats them as established disciplines. But when he comes to dialectic, he talks of it not as an established discipline but as a project for a science yet to be born. First, he gives a negative description; unlike mathematics, dialectic does not stand on unproven premises. Then he gives the positive description: dialectic moves from Form to Form until it reaches the highest Form, the Good, and gains the synoptic vision of all reality. What can Socrates say about the highest Form? Precious little. His account of the Good is so scanty that it has been a perpetual source of disappointment for many readers, and their disappointment has been most poignantly stated by George Grote: "He [Socrates] conducts us to the chamber wherein this precious and indispensable secret [the Good] is locked up, but he has no key to open the door."[9]

Grote's may be an overstatement; the Form of the Good may not be completely locked up. Though Socrates cannot talk about it in the same explicit manner in which he has discussed the nature of justice, temperance, and other things, he tries to convey some understanding of it by his allegory of the sun and the cave. He makes the candid admission that he has no knowledge but only some opinion of it (506c–e). He further confesses that our understanding of the Good is exceedingly feeble and perplexing. It is only a vague intuition (*apomanteuomene*), which is far from an adequate grasp of the Good (505e). To be sure, the philosopher-king must have a proper understanding of it before he can take on the task of governing the ideal state. In fact, the knowledge of the Good is the basic qualification for being a philosopher-king, but the existence of such a wise ruler is not an established fact. It is only a dream for the future. Thus, the notion of a philosopher king and that of dialectic as the science of Forms are no more than two nebulous dreams.

If the rhetorical discourse in the *Republic* cannot be transformed into the science of dialectic, it may be redeemed by converting rhetoric from empirical guesswork into technical art. This conversion operation, I propose, is Socrates' project in the *Phaedrus*. He constructs an imaginary response of rhetoric to its critics; the lady Rhetoric replies to the charge that she is not a true art but a mere guesswork. She says, ''I do not compel anyone to learn to speak without knowing the truth, but if my advice is of any value, he learns that first and then acquires me'' (*Phaedrus* 260e, trans. Harold Fowler). She concludes her defense with the statement that there can never be a real art of speaking without getting hold of the truth. Socrates lays down the requirements for converting rhetoric into an art. The first requirement is knowledge of the truth (259e, 262c). The second requirement is the method of collection and division, which gives the speech a clear and definite meaning (265d–266b). One requirement is methodological and the other is substantive.

The method of collection is to bring many particulars under a single Form. The reverse of this procedure is the method of division; it is to divide things into different Forms. Socrates illustrates it by using his own speech as an example. It divided madness into two kinds, ordinary and divine, and then further divided the divine madness into four kinds. Socrates gives another example to explain the method of division, which directly concerns the practice of rhetoric. To be an effective speaker, the orator must know what type of soul the audience has, for example, whether it is simple or complex, naive or cunning. The speaker has to know what type of soul is susceptible to what type of speech. Hence, the speaker has to know how to classify different types of soul, and their classification requires the method of division (270d–272a). What is noteworthy about this method of collection and division is that it is an empirical method; the Forms used by this method are not transcendent but empirical. The distinction of different types of souls is not based on the transcendent Form of the Soul any more than the distinction of its three parts is based on such a Form. The former is as empirical as the latter.

In the *Phaedrus*, the word *eidos* (Form) is used usually to refer to the empirical Forms such as the Form of the soul, while transcendent Forms are mentioned by their proper names, for example, "Justice itself," or "Temperance itself" (240a–250c). The word *eidos* plays an important role in both of the two occasions in which Socrates talks about the soul. The first occasion is his palinode, in which the Form of the soul is closely linked not only to the allegory of the charioteer and the two winged horses, but also to the power of a soul to affect and to be affected by another soul. The second occasion is Socrates' talk about the orator's knowledge of his audience, in which the Form of the soul is none other than its empirical nature (270b–271e). As Charles Griswold points out, the concept of Form in the *Phaedrus* is interchangeable with the concept of empirical nature (*physis*).[10] These two extended discourses by Socrates on the nature of the soul should remind us of the even more extended discourse on the nature of the soul and its relation to the question of justice in the *Republic*. This is another textual indication that the *Phaedrus* is meant to be a critical reflection on the *Republic*.

In the *Phaedrus*, it appears that Socrates is prepared to accept the empirical Forms as the objects of knowledge. An empirical Form should not be confused with a copy of a transcendent Form in the phenomenal world, although the latter may be called an empirical Form because it is in the empirical world. In its proper sense, however, an empirical Form has no counterpart in the world of transcendent Forms; for example, the tripartite structure of the soul is an empirical Form, which has no counterpart in Platonic Heaven. If there are empirical Forms in the phenomenal world, they surely can make possible the scientific understanding of phenomena, just as the transcendent Forms make possible the science of dialectic. Hence the recognition of empirical Forms is the most important step for establishing the science of phenomena and converting rhetoric from a mere guesswork to a true art. As we will see later in greater detail, the method of collection and division is the method for identifying and specifying the nature of each empirical Form. This method can lead to knowledge of the truth, the first requirement Socrates laid down for converting rhetoric into a true art. Since the method of collection and division is the second requirement, the two requirements are connected as means and end.

Though the empirical Forms can be the basis for the science of phenomena, such a science cannot meet the same rigorous criteria of knowledge that can be met only by the knowledge of transcendent Forms, for example, mathematical knowledge. Thus, Socrates is willing to relax the standard of knowledge for the new art of rhetoric. His relaxation of the cognitive standard is clearly indicated by his claim that he is giving a proof (*apodeixis*) for the immortality of the soul. The so-called proof cannot meet the rigorous standard required for mathematical proofs, because the soul is an empirical object. But Socrates still places an emphatic stress on his proof by referring to it with the word *apodeixis* and its cognates three times in a single passage at the outset of the proof (245bc).

Perhaps we should note one more thing about the method of collection and division. It is the same as the method of *diairesis*, which is extensively used in the *Sophist* and *Statesman*. Some commentators have said that this new method is enunciated for the first time in the *Phaedrus*.[11] But this is inaccurate. Socrates previously used it in his definition of rhetoric in the *Gorgias*. First, he divided the arts concerning the body from the arts concerning the soul, and then he divided the former into gymnastics and medicine and the latter into legislation and justice. In a parallel to this fourfold division of arts, he also divided all empirical guesswork into four kinds (*Gorgias* 464b–466a). At *Philebus* 16b, Socrates refers to the method of collection and division as the finest method he has always loved. Indeed, this method has been the central instrument for Socratic definition from the early to the late dialogues.

In the early dialogues, to be sure, the method of collection usually overshadowed the method of division, because Socrates was too obsessed with the common nature under definition to pay sufficient attention to the differentiae. Even Critias complained about this obsession (*Charmides* 165e). In the *Laches* and the *Charmides*, Socrates identified the common essence of courage and temperance as wisdom, but could not specify their differentiae. This tendency eventually led him to reduce all virtues to knowledge or wisdom in the *Protagoras*, the *Meno*, and the *Euthydemus*. This reductive tendency was clearly affiliated with the method of collection, which seeks the common nature. But this tendency is reversed in the *Republic*, where Socrates fully recognizes the differentiae of four virtues instead of trying to reduce them all to one virtue.

The recognition of differentiae is tied to the method of division, which is the indispensable complement to the method of collection. These two methods are brought into a good balance in the *Republic*, and the importance of their balance is reaffirmed in the *Phaedrus*. This is another textual indication that the *Phaedrus* is a reflection on the *Republic*. The first dialogue not only reflects on the shortcomings of the second, but also reaffirms its strong points. Such is also the case with the theme of *philia*, as we already noted. The method of collection and division and the nature of *philia* are the two positive thematic connectors between the *Republic* and the *Phaedrus*.

As a true art, Socrates finally maintains, rhetoric must be the art of living thought. In making this point, he stresses the important difference between written and oral speech. Written speech is dead; it can neither respond to questions nor defend itself against criticism (275d–276a). An example is Lysias's speech that was read by Phaedrus; one may memorize the whole speech without knowing what it really means. In that case, there is a complete divorce between speech and knowledge. Socrates says that speech can be written together with knowledge only in an intelligent soul (276a). An intelligent writing is not a substitute for thinking, but only a reminder for living thought. If this method of writing in the living soul is the true art of rhetoric, it turns out to be none other than the method of Socratic inquiry. This is the surprising outcome of the dialogue: the conversion of rhetoric into an art makes it indistinguishable from the Socratic method of inquiry. Rhetoric as a true art is none other than the *logos* of phenomena, the new art of talking about the world of phenomena.

The Socratic method of inquiry cannot dispense with the method of question and answer. Hence, the new art of rhetoric cannot differ from the science of dialectic in their mode of speech, though one is concerned with the world of Forms and the other with the world of phenomena. There is no longer any glaring difference between the two worlds, because each of them is a world of Forms. One is the world of empirical Forms, and the other is the world of transcendent Forms. There is a systematic affinity between the science of dialectic and the art of rhetoric. Each of them investigates a world of Forms with the same method of question and answer. No doubt, these two disciplines will require two different methods of investigation, that is, the a priori method of recollection for the study of transcendent Forms, and the empirical method for the study of empirical Forms.

In the early and middle dialogues, to be sure, the Socratic method of inquiry has usually been more closely associated with the a priori method of recollection than with the empirical method of investigation. But in the *Republic*, there is a clear shift of attention toward the empirical method as we noted earlier. Even in the empirical domain, living thought must be able to answer objections and defend itself against criticism if it is to be the thought of truth. Thus, it cannot dispense with the Socratic method of question and answer. Moreover, the same method provides the art of leading a soul (*psychagogia*) by the power of words (261a). This art is used by the lover for leading the soul of his beloved and for establishing their relation of friendship in wisdom. It is the art of *philosophia* that the old Socrates uses in talking with the young Glaucon and Adeimantus in the *Republic*. It is the same method of discourse that the philosopher-king will use in persuading the citizens of the Kallipolis, and that will be used in guiding the citizens of Magnesia in the *Laws*.

Socrates calls the new science of rhetoric the art of living thought and speech, which should be contrasted with that of dead thought and speech. But where can we find dead thought and speech? In the *Phaedrus*, the speech of dead thought is represented by Lysias's written speech, which cannot defend itself because it is abandoned by its author. Some commentators have said that this speech was Plato's parody of Isocrates.[12] In the formative days of philosophy as an intellectual discipline, as we noted in chapter 2, Isocrates was Plato's chief competition. He identified philosophy with his art of writing speeches (*Antidosis* 180–186, 270–271). Plato now characterizes the competition between him and Isocrates as one between a living dialogue and a dead monologue. So the dialogue ends with a critical remark about Isocrates.

The *Phaedrus* is a dialogue of *philosophia*. It should not end with the discordant note of a critical remark. Socrates ends it with a prayer to Pan to grant him a friendly concord within his soul, and Phaedrus joins in that prayer because friends hold all things in common. The prayer to Pan should remind us of the *Symposium*. As we noted in chapter 2, Socrates of the *Symposium* stands for the triumph of Apollo over Dionysus. Pan is a close associate of Dionysus, but his entourage of nymphs and cicadas is not confined to the dark hours of the night. In the *Phaedrus*, it makes its presence felt during the noon hours under the hot sun, the symbol of Apollo. The forces of light and darkness form the bond of harmony and friendship. The *Phaedrus* celebrates the *philia* of Apollo and Dionysus, which is even better than the conquest of Dionysus by Apollo.

Alienation from the Physical World

Unlike the world of Forms, the world of phenomena is chaotic, and this is the chief obstacle to elevating rhetoric to the same scientific level as dialectic. The problem of rhetoric is linked to the problem of how to cope with the world of phenomena. The linkage of these problems is intimated by the opening scene of the *Phaedrus*. Let us note two salient items in this scene. First, Phaedrus is out on a walk after listening for the whole morning to Lysias's lecture. He is taking the walk on the advice of his doctors, and his physical condition may represent the feeble state of rhetoric. The other salient item is Socrates' excursion to the countryside outside the city walls. This is a rare event for this man, who is famous for never leaving the city and who is too preoccupied with human beings to have any interest in trees and fields (230d). He breaks out in a rapturous adoration of natural beauty, the fragrance of flowering shrubs and the music of the singing cicadas. The entire landscape is shrouded in the mythical aura of nymphs and gods.

What is the significance of this event? The *Phaedrus* is the only dialogue that Plato sets in a beautiful natural scene. What is implied by this unique setting? These have been baffling questions for Plato scholars, but few have attempted to deal with them. F. M. Cornford is one of the few who have tried. By this magical setting, he says, Plato wanted to show the poetic and inspired Socrates, who had been unknown to his habitual companions. But this account is not quite satisfactory, because it does not explain why Socrates seeks inspiration in the countryside. As we noted in chapter 2, he can get into a trance almost anywhere, on the battlefield or on someone's portico. Though he may need some inspiration for delivering his two speeches, he has no need of it for the dialogical discourse with Phaedrus. But as Cornford says, "Throughout the dialogue, up to the prayer to Pan at the close, we are not allowed to forget the influences of nature and of inspiration which haunt the spot."[13]

Charles Griswold says that the beautiful scene is meant to serve the vital function of recollecting the Form of Beauty.[14] But Socrates says, on meeting Phaedrus, "You see, I am a lover of learning. Now the country places and trees won't teach me anything, and the people in the city do" (230d). If the trees and the open country cannot teach Socrates anything, they cannot help him in his recollection, either, because recollection is a method of learning. If the world of nature has become useful for teaching and learning, that is a drastic change for Socrates. In the *Phaedo*, he stated his disappointment with natural philosophers; ever since he has resolutely turned his attention from the world of nature to the world of human beings. When Phaedrus asks Socrates whether he believes the myth of Boreas's rape, he ridicules the natural philosophers' attempt to reduce all mythical events to natural phenomena (229c). What the natural philosophers have done with the mythical world is analogous to what Socrates has done to the world of nature. The natural philosophers have alienated the world of nature from human beings; Socrates has alienated the world of human beings from the

world of nature. They are alike in being victimized by their own alienation.

Socratic alienation was not Plato's invention, but an inheritance from
the sophists, who turned their attention from nature (*physis*) to culture
(*nomos*). The demarcation between these two has alienated the human
world from the natural world. In the *Phaedrus*, the wall that divides the
city and the countryside is the symbol for the demarcation between
nature and culture. In the *Republic*, Socrates has tried to build an ideal
city and bring all natural elements under rational control. It is a project
of control of nature by culture. He is determined to expel the poets from
the city because they can disrupt this project of rational control. He
proposes to impose a rigid reign over emotions and appetites. The Kallipolis is a war of conquest against the physical world; it is meant to
subdue and control all physical elements. In this Platonic struggle, nature is the ultimate enemy.

So far in this volume, we have tried to understand Plato's moves as a
series of responses to the Calliclean challenge. But the Calliclean challenge is the challenge of nature, the world of the body. In the *Gorgias*,
Callicles presented his principle of power politics as the basic principle
of nature that governs all animals and living beings. Callicles is a representative of physical nature and her unruly powers; the evil force in his
person is only an extension of physical forces. The Kallipolis is to be a
haven of human culture in the unruly wilderness of physical forces. It
is going to be built by eradicating all social institutions such as private
family and property that have emerged as manifestations of natural appetites. Its construction is supposedly a radical revolution that will get
rid of everyone more than ten years old and begin with a completely
clean slate. But there is no way to insulate this haven of culture totally
from the unruly forces of nature. The Kallipolis will eventually degen-
erate because of the genetic mistakes made in the breeding of children
(*Republic* 546a–d). Nature will eventually claim its dominion over culture.

If the war against the physical world can never be won, the Kallipolis
is a futile dream. Moreover, the idea of waging war against the physical
world goes against the Pythagorean ideal of love and harmony. The
ethos of conquest and subjugation infects the social order of the Kalli-

polis and the spiritual state of the soul. To be sure, Socrates has insisted on the theme of brotherly love that binds together the three classes of the Kallipolis and the three parts of the soul. But the philosopher's rule is going to be an absolute dictatorship over the lower classes. The dictatorship within the soul is equally rigid; it is reason's inflexible control over the nonrational parts, the elements of nature. This is the outcome of Plato's attempt to overcome the alienation of nature by conquest, but this project is self-defeating. There is no way to conquer nature by culture or to secure a total insulation of culture from nature as long as nature is the ultimate matrix for human existence and culture. This futile project has to be abandoned and be replaced by a better one.

The old project was based on the ethos of war and conquest; the new project should be based on the ethos of love and harmony. The old project presupposed the conflict of nature and culture; the new project should presuppose their unity and harmony. The transition from the old to the new project is symbolized by Socrates' excursion from the inside to the outside of the city. He can no longer keep the world of natural forces shut out of the city walls. His conception of nature has radically changed. In the *Republic* and before, he has had the incurable tendency of conceiving the physical world as something unruly and defiling. In the *Symposium*, the power of *eros* was the force of nature par excellence; it was identified as the force of darkness, the bacchanalian frenzy. In the *Phaedo*, the world of nature was identified as the world of the body, which defiled and imprisoned the soul.

The *Phaedrus* presents a completely new picture of nature: she is beautiful and enchanting. What is even more important than her beauty is the mythical unity of all her elements. This new sense of harmony and friendship also pervades the inner world of the soul. Just compare the charioteer and the winged horses with some of the imageries Socrates used to explain the relation of the three parts of the soul in the *Republic*. In book 9 (588cd), he constructs an allegorical model to describe the inner state of a tyrannical soul by putting together three parts. The first part is a beast with many heads; the second part is a lion; the third part is a human being. Surely, there can be no loving relation between these beastly elements even when they are properly subdued by the rational part. The *Phaedrus* not only replaces this beastly model with a humane one, but assigns a much more significant role to the nonrational elements. The two horses are the indispensable companions for the charioteer in his ascent to the supersensible world. This is a startling change in the conception of the soul.

In the *Phaedrus,* the disembodied soul is a composite entity; it is composed of the rational (the charioteer) element and the nonrational elements (the winged horses). As G. R. F. Ferrari points out, this is difficult to square with the views propounded in other dialogues.[15] In the *Symposium*, the *Phaedo*, and the *Republic*, it has been claimed that only the rational soul has access to the world of Forms. In the *Phaedrus*, the charioteer alone cannot even think of making his flight to the world of Forms without the assistance of the two winged horses. They provide all the force and energy required for his noetic ascent. If they stand for the forces of nature, then they present those forces in a highly positive light. This favorable picture of natural forces is, of course, in harmony with the beauty of nature, which highlights the setting of the dialogue. The *Phaedrus* marks Plato's radical transition from hatred and distrust of nature to love and trust of her.

The Language of Phenomena

Plato has to reconceive our relation to nature. Instead of rejecting her as our enemy, we should accept her as our friend. She should be the friendly matrix for the construction of the Kallipolis; she should be the mother of our city and our life. In that case, we have to understand her. But what sort of discourse (*logos*) do we need for understanding her? This is the central question for the *Cratylus*. In this dialogue, the name is taken as the basic unit of discourse; hence the topic of discussion is the theory of names. The nature and function of names is not a new topic for Socratic inquiry. In the previous dialogues, however, the function of names was linked to the world of Forms, for example, the word *justice* is the name of the Form of Justice. But the *Cratylus* is concerned with the names of phenomenal objects, and these names are taken as the basic units for the *logos* of phenomena. Thus, the *logos* of phenomena thematically links the *Cratylus* to the question of rhetoric in the *Phaedrus*.

In the *Cratylus*, Socrates joins a dispute between Cratylus and Hermogenes on the relation of names to objects. Socrates first talks with Hermogenes and then with Cratylus. Cratylus advocates naturalism: a name states the nature of its *nominatum*. In opposition to this view, Hermogenes advocates conventionalism: a name is a product of convention and has nothing to do with the nature of its *nominatum*. Hermogenes' conventionalism is extremely individualistic. When he talks about the convention of name giving, he does not mean any socially established convention. He holds that one has the power of giving any object whatever name one wants to give at any time. On this individualistic version of conventionalism, everyone will have his or her own private language, and there can be no communication between different people. However, Socrates gets Hermogenes to agree that the function of names is communication and distinction. By using names we exchange information, which is communication or instruction, and we distinguish things according to their natures (388b).

If the name is a convention to serve these functions, it should meet a certain requirement. Socrates explains this requirement by comparing the making of names to the making of shuttles. When a shuttle maker makes a shuttle, he cannot simply copy another shuttle already made by someone else. He has to know and consult the true Form of Shuttle, and has to realize the same Form in different materials. The materials for making names are sounds and syllables, the phonetic materials. Though different name makers, Hellene and barbarian, may use different phonetic materials, they may have to know the same true and proper Form of the name (390a). But who knows the true and proper Form? In the case of shuttles, it is not the shuttle makers but their users. In the case of names, it is the dialecticians who know the Form of the name (390c). By *dialectician* is meant simply someone who can ask questions and answer them, that is, anyone who can use language in conversation.[16]

Socrates calls the name maker the lawgiver (*nomothete*) or legislator (388e). To give a name to something is to give a law; a name belongs to law (*nomos*). To recognize language as a part of convention is a significant development on the demarcation between nature (*physis*) and culture (*nomos*). This demarcation has given us the impression that *physis* and *nomos* are two independent departments of our world. But their independence becomes questionable as soon as we recognize language as an element of *nomos*. In fact, language is not simply one segment of *nomos*, but rather the basic substratum of all *nomos*. Thus, there can be no direct access to *physis*; what we can know and say about *physis* totally depends on our language that belongs to *nomos*. Our access to nature has to be mediated by culture, and our knowledge of nature has to be a part of our culture. Since this important mediation depends on the function of names, it takes special skill to be the legislator who gives names.

On the supposition that communication and distinction are the two functions of names, Socrates persuades Hermogenes to abandon his individualistic conventionalism, which makes communication impossible. Then he takes Hermogenes through a long list of names, explaining how each of them describes the nature of its object. At the end of this etymological exercise, Socrates distinguishes between primary and secondary names. Secondary names can be analyzed into primary names, which are elemental. Socrates formulates a general proposition for all names, both primary and secondary: they are intended to reveal or represent (*deloun*) the nature of their objects (422d). This representational function is imitative; a name "imitates" the nature of its object by its letters and syllables (phonemes). This may be called the theory of phonemic imitation or representation, which requires the art of combining letters into syllables, syllables into names, names into phrases, and phrases into sentences. This is a constructivist view of language, which Socrates presents as his account of how language was developed by the ancients, the original legislators of names.

The Socratic constructivism should nullify the chief criticism against the *Cratylus*, namely, that it fails to recognize the elemental distinction between words and sentences. Socrates observes that the theory of phonemic imitation is truly outrageous and ridiculous (426b). For one thing, the number of phonemes is too small to cope with the number of things that have to be expressed by those phonemes and their combinations. At any rate, Socrates would like to know how his theory stands with

Cratylus. At this point, Hermogenes makes an interesting remark about Cratylus. Though he claims the correctness of names, he never explains what that correctness is. In fact, Hermogenes cannot even tell whether his obscurity is intentional or unintentional (427de). So Socrates has to find out what Cratylus really means, and thus the second half of the dialogue begins.

As it turns out, Cratylus holds two theses about names. First, only correct names are names. Incorrect names are not names at all; for example, *Hermogenes*, which means "born of Hermes," is not the name of Hermogenes, because he is not born of Hermes. The fact that people call him by that name makes no difference; it simply fails to be his name because it is incorrect. Second, the requirement of correctness cannot be met by Socratic theory of phonemic imitation; a name must be exactly like its *nominatum*. Here we have two theories of representation: (1) by resemblance and (2) by identity. Socrates shows the absurdity of (2). If an image is exactly like the original, he says, they cannot be distinguished from each other (432bc). The same difficulty will arise if the name is exactly like its object. If a name is not the same as its object, the former can only resemble the latter. There can be many things that can resemble an object, and any one of them can be picked as its name. Hence, it is a matter of convention to pick any one of them as its name. This is Socrates' argument for the inevitability of convention in the game of naming.

Cratylus does not easily give up his theory of representation by identity, which really means the identity between the meaning of a name and the nature of its object. He now insists that his theory of names can best account for the function of names for communication. Since the names are identical with their objects, one who knows the name also knows the object. Names can never fail to transmit information, nor can there be any other means of communication than names (435d–436a). He even claims that there is no other way of inquiry and discovery than using names. This is the absurd extremity of his naturalism; it takes names as substitutes for truth and reality. Socrates warns Cratylus that to rely on names as a means of inquiry and discovery is to incur the danger of being deceived, because the name giver has given names only according to his conception of things, which may be faulty. Even if the first legislator has given correct names, he must have known the nature of their objects without their names. So the critical question is whether things can be known without names (436a–438e). To put it another way, do we have any access to truth and reality apart from names?

This is the question of transcendence. We have noted that names belong to convention (*nomos*). If our access to truth and reality is totally determined by our names, we cannot transcend convention. In that case, there is no way to tell whether a conventionally given name is correct or incorrect. This goes against Cratylus's original claim that incorrect names are not names at all, because this claim presupposes the independent criterion for telling apart correct names from incorrect ones. Such an independent criterion is possible only if we can transcend convention and secure a direct access to truth and reality. This question leads to what Socrates calls the battle of names (438d). One party asserts that the names are *like* truth; the other party contends that they *are* the truth. By showing how absurd it is to hold the identity thesis of name and truth, Socrates manages to persuade Cratylus to give up his theory of names.

Let us note a few important developments in the *Cratylus*. First, the concept of *nomos* is radically extended by locating language in the world of *nomos*. In the early dialogues, the question of *nomos* was mainly normative; it was the basis of normative positivism, that is, the view that normative rules and standards are given by *nomos* rather than *physis*. In the *Cratylus*, conventionalism is no longer restricted to the normative dimension of human existence. It now pervades its cognitive dimension, because all our beliefs and knowledge are formulated in terms of names. So we have two forms of conventionalism: normative and cognitive. Since conventionalism is equivalent to relativism, the two forms of conventionalism are the two forms of relativism: normative and cognitive. The *Cratylus* extends the scope of conventionalism and relativism from their normative to their cognitive dimensions. This extension broadens the need of transcendent normative standards from the normative to the cognitive domains. In fact, the cognitive domain must have its own normative standards such as the standard of correct and incorrect names, or true and false beliefs. The concept of normative standard can no longer be contained within the ethical and political

domains. The concept of truth is not only descriptive but also normative; it is as normative as the concepts of goodness and justice.

The second point is the view that the names perform the two functions of communication and distinction. The shuttle analogy is very
effective for illustrating these two functions. Just as the shuttle goes
back and forth between the two sides of a loom, so do the names between two speakers. Furthermore, the shuttle performs the function of
separating threads in a loom, and the names perform the same function
of separating the objects to be named. This function of separation is the
function of distinction, which is closely linked to the method of division. This method is inseparable from the method of collection. When
a name separates or distinguishes something from other things, it also
performs the function of collection. For example, the name *horse* not
only separates all horses from all other objects, but also collects all
horses into one class.

In Socrates' hand, the two functions of communication and distinction become the basis for an effective critique of the two competing
theories of names. If names are as private as Hermogenes claims them
to be, they can never serve the function of communication. Hermogenes
may like to give the name *man* to what other people call horses, but this
new name cannot function as a means of communication until it is made
known to others by the use of some public language. The use of a
private or idiosyncratic language is ultimately dependent on some public language. Without the aid of public language, a private language can
only lead to linguistic solipsism. Cratylus's position is diametrically
opposed to Hermogenes'. On his theory, names are not only public, but
are directly connected to their objects. Their direct connection cuts out
the role of the linguistic subject. Though the role of the subject is never
mentioned in either of the two theories, it is the central point of their
difference. In Hermogenes' theory, the subject does everything; in Cratylus's theory, the subject does nothing.

By eliminating the role of the subject, Cratylus's naturalism removes
all the danger of subjectivism and linguistic solipsism. But his theory
of natural connection between the word and the object is not as simple
as Cratylus claims it to be. If the nature of the object is known, its
connection to its name should be transparent. If it is not known, how-

ever, the connection should be opaque. As Socrates points out, the real nature of objects is seldom known to the linguistic legislator, and the names are given in accordance not with the nature of things but with the legislator's conception of their nature. Hence, there is a natural tendency for obscurantism in the naturalist account of the relation between names and objects. This is the complaint that is lodged against Cratylus by Hermogenes at the beginning and the middle of the dialogue. Hermogenes charges him with dissimulation and mystification (383e–384a); he does not even know whether Cratylus's obscurantism is intentional or unintentional (472e).

Hermogenes' complaint against Cratylus is equally valid against the linguistic philosophy of today, which began with Frege's removal of the subject from the theory of meaning. His theory of sense and reference directly connects the meaning of a word to its object, and their direct connection has been motivated by his desire to avoid psychologism and subjectivism. Frege's program of subject-free semantics has inspired a long series of linguistic philosophers from Russell and Wittgenstein to Quine and Davidson. This long series has shared one common legacy, the attempt to claim an identity between the meaning of a word and the nature of its object. But this semantic attempt has produced a great deal of mystification and obscurantism. For example, Hilary Putnam and Saul Kripke say that the meaning of the word *water* is the ultimate nature of the liquid substance called water and that its ultimate nature is determined by the chemical formula H_2O. They also hold that the word had this meaning even before the discovery of the chemical structure of the water molecule.[17] This has been the meaning of the word *water* ever since the word was invented and placed in use. The identity of the meaning is fixed by the substance identity of water, which is expressed by the chemical formula.

The Putnam-Kripke thesis is a good example of the contemporary counterpart to Cratylus's naturalism: there is a direct relation between the word and the object, and the meaning of the word is determined by the nature of the object. This thesis is advanced on the premise that the ultimate nature of water is exhaustively described by the chemical formula. But that is surely a naive assumption; particle physics and quantum mechanics go deeper into the nature of material substances than the chemical theory of water. In that case, the meaning of *water* is determined not by the chemistry of the nineteenth century, but by the physics of the twentieth century. But even the physics of our century cannot promise the final theory about the nature of water and provide its substance identity. In that case, the real meaning of *water* turns out to be a phantom that has to be chased in the mythical land of final sciences.[18] Therefore, the real meaning of water turns out to be as obscure as the ultimate nature of matter.

For Cratylus, the two-term relation of the name and its object eventually degenerates to a one-term relation, because he claims their identity. He reduces objects to names by his claim that we can know nothing about the object except what we know about its name. This reduction leads to linguistic relativism: the world is constituted by our language, or everything we know is a function of our language. Hilary Putnam has eventually come to adopt this position, too. This is also the position of Jacques Derrida. His theory of writing is his theory of names. Under the strong influence of Edmund Husserl and Ferdinand de Saussure, he has also eliminated the subject from his theory of signs. In his case, the two-term relation of the name and its object degenerates to the two-term relation of a name to another name, a signifier to another signifier. It is impossible to get out of the chain of signification. Derrida says that there can be no access to the ultimate signified.[19] There is no way to avoid being imprisoned in one's own language. Thus, the most difficult question for all linguistic relativists has been: How can they get out of their own linguistic prison?

On this question, Socrates gives Cratylus some astute advice, which may serve our own need today. First, he tells Cratylus that the relation of a name to its object should be understood as a triadic relation rather than a dyadic one. The relation between the word and the object is not direct, but is mediated by the subject's conception of the nature of the object. Second, since it is impossible to name anything in the world of total flux, there must be something permanent for naming. These two items of advice are important not only for Cratylus but also for Socrates, if he wants to develop a theory of discourse for the world of phenomena, because they are the essential requirements for the names of phenomenal objects.

The problem of naming the phenomenal objects is quite different from the problem of naming that has become familiar in the previous dialogues such as the *Phaedo*, the *Republic*, and the *Phaedrus*.[20] In these dialogues, the transcendent Forms were taken to be the direct objects of names, and the phenomenal objects were named as only copies of those Forms. But that is highly unsatisfactory because not all phenomenal objects are named as such copies. For example, it cannot account for the name of the soul because its tripartite structure is not a copy of any transcendent Form. The tripartite structure is its own empirical Form. Socrates now realizes that the phenomenal object can have its name by virtue of its own empirical Form. His etymological exercises, which analyze the compound names into simple ones, are meant to show how to articulate the empirical Forms that have gone into the composition of those compound names. Thus, the *Cratylus* can be read as a prolegomena for a theory of names for the phenomenal objects, or rather the language of phenomena.

The distinction between the names of phenomenal objects and the names of transcendent Forms can now be linked to the distinction between the new art of rhetoric and the science of dialectic. The names of phenomenal objects constitute the language of rhetoric; the names of transcendent Forms constitute the language of dialectic. Without devising an adequate theory of names for the world of phenomena, Socrates can have no adequate language of phenomena. If there is no language of phenomena, there can be no way of converting rhetoric into an art and developing the science of phenomena. Thus, the problem of naming the phenomena becomes the most basic problem for the problem of securing the knowledge of phenomena. In the last chapter, we noted that the *Republic* was a dialogue of descent from the world of transcendent Forms to the world of phenomena. But this descent cannot be completed without securing the language of phenomena and thereby laying the foundation for the science of phenomena. In the *Cratylus* and the *Phaedrus*, Socrates self-critically recognizes the incompleteness of his journey of descent, and prepares the ground for its completion in the future dialogues.

For these reasons, Socrates is as self-critical and as self-reflective in the *Cratylus* as he was in the *Phaedrus*. Instead of taking a cold neutral position between Cratylus and Hermogenes, he clearly expresses his affinity and sympathy with the position of Cratylus. Hence, his critique of Cratylus is often a critique of his own position. He also warns Cratylus against the danger of self-deception (428d). If his position is highly similar to that of Cratylus, he also faces the same danger of self-deception. At the end of the dialogue, he advises Cratylus to go into the country. This is splendid advice for the man, who believes that to know an object is to know its name and that there is no other way of knowing. This is a clear syndrome of being insulated and alienated from the world of nature by the walls of culture. The alienation from nature is dramatically displayed by the total absence of scenery for the entire dialogue, which is in marked contrast with the beautiful natural scenery of the *Phaedrus*.

The poor Cratylus has been totally closed in by the wall of names. In the *Phaedrus*, we saw, Lysias's written speech was dead because it had been locked up inside the city walls, and Phaedrus had to take a walk outside the walls to regain his health. To write down a speech and memorize it instead of thinking through the object of discourse is like locking up the soul inside the walls of culture. Socrates showed why a good speech should be like a living creature with its own soul and body (*Phaedrus* 264c). The entire exercise in the *Phaedrus* was to find the secret remedy for restoring health and vitality not only to the sickly speech but also to the sickly soul, both of which are about to die from their alienation from the world of phenomena. In such an alienation, the death of the soul comes together with the death of the speech, and there is no better remedy for this malady than the wild country of beautiful trees and singing cicadas. Socrates knows this from his own experience of having suffered from the same malady and found the cure in the open countryside. Hence an excursion into the wilderness may well be the best remedy for the ailment of Cratylus.

Notes

1. Irwin, *Plato's Moral Theory* (Oxford: University Press, 1979), 238.
2. Martha Nussbaum gives a different account of the relation between the

Symposium and the *Phaedrus*. According to her, the *Phaedrus* alone expresses Plato's thought, and the *Symposium* does not. *The Fragility of Goodness* (Cambridge: University Press, 1986), 165–233. According to my account, Plato always gives the best exposition of his position as far as he can, though he may change it when he finds a better one.

3. For some strange reason, Guthrie says that it is a new argument. *A History of Greek Philosophy* (Cambridge: University Press, 1975), 4:419.

4. This point is fully discussed by Alexander Mourelatos, "Astronomy and Kinematics in Plato's Project of Rationalist Explanation," *Studies in History and Philosophy of Science* 12 (1981):1–32.

5. Mueller, "Ascending to Problems: Astronomy and Harmonics in *Republic* VII," in *Science and the Sciences in Plato*, John Anton, ed. (New York: Caravan Books), 103–22. 103, 110.

6. Mourelatos, "Astronomy and Kinematics," 6–7.

7. Irwin, *Plato's Moral Theory*, 92–93.

8. For a further discussion of this point, see Nicholas White, *A Companion to Plato's Republic* (Indianapolis, Ind.: Hackett, 1979), 39.

9. Grote, *Plato, and the Other Companions of Sokrates* (London: J. Murray, 1885), 4:213.

10. Griswold, *Self-Knowledge in Plato's* Phaedrus (New Haven, Conn.: Yale University Press, 1986), 88–92.

11. For example, R. Hackforth, *Plato's Phaedrus* (Cambridge: University Press, 1952), 137.

12. Gerard Ledger, *Re-Counting Plato: A Computer Analysis of Plato's Style* (Oxford: University Press, 1989), 117.

13. Cornford, *Principium Sapientiae* (Cambridge: University Press, 1952), 67.

14. *Self-Knowledge in Plato's* Phaedrus, 35.

15. *Listening to the Cicadas: A Study of Plato's* Phaedrus (Cambridge: University Press, 1987), 125–26.

16. This requirement has been misread and exaggerated by some commentators. For example, Guthrie says that the dialectician is the philosopher (*A History of Greek Philosophy*, 5:21). Allan Silverman says that the dialectician knows the essence of the object to be named and can give the definition of it. "Plato's *Cratylus*: The Naming of Nature and the Nature of Naming," *Oxford Studies in Ancient Philosophy* 10 (1992):38. Though these stiff requirements are associated with the notion of a dialectician in some other dialogues, they are not even mentioned in the *Cratylus*.

17. Putnam, *Mind, Language and Reality* (Cambridge: University Press,

1975); Kripke, *Naming and Necessity* (Cambridge, Mass.: Harvard University Press, 1972), 126–29.

18. This anxiety is expressed by Putnam, *Realism with a Human Face* (Cambridge, Mass.: Harvard University Press, 1990), 72.

19. Derrida, *Of Grammatology*, trans. Gayatri Spivak (Baltimore, Md.: Johns Hopkins University Press, 1976).

20. This point is well stressed by Allan Silverman, "Plato's *Cratylus*," 26.

CHAPTER FIVE

New Theory of Knowledge

The *Theaetetus*, the *Sophist*, and the *Statesman*

The *Republic* has given a two-world view: the world of Forms and the world of phenomena. The demarcation of these two worlds has led to the distinction between knowledge and opinion. We can *know* only the Forms, but can have only opinion or belief about the phenomena. As we saw in the last chapter, this is a troubling thought. If the phenomena cannot be known, the *Republic* itself becomes highly suspect because it is chiefly a discourse about two phenomenal objects, the soul and the state. If we can have no knowledge of phenomena, we can never find a scientific way of realizing the Forms in this world because such an enterprise cannot be given a scientific basis in the world of opinion. Without securing the knowledge of phenomena, we further noted, Socrates' journey of descent that began in the *Protagoras* cannot be brought to its completion. For these reasons, Socrates carefully examines the problem of knowing the world of phenomena in the *Theaetetus*.

The *Theaetetus*

In this dialogue, Theaetetus and Socrates try to define the nature of knowledge. They examine three definitions of knowledge: (1) it is perception, (2) it is true belief (*doxa*), and (3) it is true belief plus an account (*logos*). Socrates attributes the first definition to Protagoras, and situates it in the Heraclitean world of total flux. In such a world, nothing is stable enough to be known or even be named (183a). This point was stressed in the *Cratylus*, as we saw in the last chapter. Furthermore, every perception is relative to the perceiver, and that is a part of Protagorean relativism. In the last chapter, we distinguished between two versions of relativism, normative and cognitive, and noted that cognitive relativism is more basic and extensive than normative relativism. Though the more basic version of Protagorean relativism becomes the target of Socrates' critique in the *Theaetetus*, he does not overlook its link to normative relativism. If everything is relative to the perceiver and there is no objective truth, Socrates says, Protagoras cannot be any wiser than a tadpole (161cd).

The extended critique of Definition (1) reveals two basic defects. First, it cannot account for error because every sense perception is said to be true to the perceiver. Second, it restricts the domain of knowledge to immediate sensation of the present moment, and cannot account for our knowledge of the past and future. These two defects arise from the mistake of ignoring the function of the mind. According to the Protagorean theory, it is the sense organs that produce sense perceptions; against this, Socrates maintains that it is the mind that perceives with sense organs (184c). The mind also has to perform the task of putting together the reports from different senses. One and the same object can be the object of different senses; it may be seen, heard, or smelled. But the identity of such an object can be established not by any sense organs but by the mind alone. For this cognitive function, the mind has to employ the common terms such as *identity* and *difference, existence* and *nonexistence* (185a–e). In this cognitive process, the mind engages itself in a silent speech until its final decision and announcement, which is its judgment (*doxa*). The silent speech is the process of reflection.

Socrates suggests that knowledge should be understood in terms of the mind's reflection on sense impressions (186d). This suggestion leads to Theaetetus's second definition of knowledge as true judgment. Unlike sense impressions, which allow no room for errors, judgment can be either true or false. Since false judgment cannot be knowledge,

knowledge should be defined as true judgment. But how can we account for the phenomenon of false judgment? This is the question that worries Socrates for the moment. To make a mistake is to mistake one object for another. Given any two objects, we should either know both, know only one of them and not the other, or know neither of them. If both are known, it is impossible to mistake one for the other. If neither of them is known, it is equally impossible to mistake one for the other. If only one of them is known, it is also impossible to mistake the known for the unknown one, or vice versa. For these reasons, Socrates says, there is no way to explain how mistakes can ever take place (188a–b). Nor is it possible to explain it by Protagoras's doctrine that thinking falsely is to think what is not. Whereas to think what is not is to have no thought at all, false thinking involves some thought rather than no thought (189ab).

One class of mistakes can be explained as a mismatch between memory and perception (190e–195b). For illustration, Socrates introduces the allegory of a wax tablet. Our mind is like a wax tablet on which imprints are left by perceptions. When the mind tries to match one of its imprints with a presently perceived object, it can make a mistake; for example, it may match the imprint of Theodorus with Theaetetus as the perceived object. Though the allegory of a wax tablet can account for the mistakes made in matching thought with perception, it cannot explain the mistakes made in the operation of thought alone, for example, the mistake of thinking that the addition of five and seven makes eleven. So Socrates introduces the allegory of an aviary, but it also fails to explain the mistake. He then points out that they have been talking in a clumsy way. Though they do not yet know what knowledge is, they have used the distinction between being known and being unknown (How can a known object be mistaken for another object, known or unknown?). They have behaved as though they already knew what knowledge was.

With this observation, Socrates returns their discussion to Definition (2), but advances his reason for doubting its validity. Consider the difference between the knowledge of a witness and the true belief of a juryman. Definition (2) cannot account for this difference. Hence knowledge cannot be defined as true belief. To this objection, Theaetetus replies that he has heard of the distinction between knowledge and true belief. If he remembers correctly, knowledge is said to be true belief plus an account (*logos*). This is the third definition of knowledge, which marks a momentous change in Plato's theory of knowledge presented in the *Republic*. According to this theory, it is equally impossible for a witness or a juryman to have knowledge, because both of them are dealing with the world of phenomena, which cannot be an object of knowledge. The expression "the knowledge of a witness" would not have been allowed in the *Republic*. Evidently, the *Theaetetus* is seeking a theory of knowledge that can differentiate the cognitive state of a witness from that of a juryman.

With the third definition of knowledge, the discussion turns to figuring out what it means to give an account (*logos*). Socrates relates a theory of *logos* he once heard in a dream: the *logos* is the description of a complex entity in terms of its constituent elements. Because these elements are simple, they cannot be described but only be named. A description (*logos*) is a combination of names. This theory of *logos* ends in a paradox: the knowledge of a compound is based on the names of the elements that cannot be known. For example, the word *Socrates* can be known and described by analyzing it into syllables, and then analyzing those syllables into vowels and consonants. But the vowels and consonants themselves cannot be known. According to the dream story, we do know the word *Socrates*, but do not know the letters that make up the word. Knowledge is based on ignorance! "That is monstrous and absurd," responds Theaetetus (203d).

What is the moral of the dream story? Nicholas White says that we should not attach "too much importance to Plato's talk of atoms and compounds."[1] Gail Fine says that the dream story denies KBK, the principle that knowledge must be based on knowledge, and that in its place Plato advocates the interrelation model of knowledge.[2] According to this model, she says, "If the circle of our beliefs is sufficiently large, and the interconnections suitably comprehensive, the links in the circle are transformed from true beliefs into pieces of knowledge." The circular model is different from the linear one. The cognitive relation of elements and compounds is symmetrical for the circular model; the compounds are known in terms of elements, and the elements in terms of compounds. However, their relation is asymmetrical for the linear model; the elements must be known before the compounds. The linear model either terminates with the elements that cannot be known, or generates an infinite regress. Because this problem can be avoided by the circular model, it is favored by Fine.

The circular model is what is better known as the coherence theory of knowledge. On the other hand, the linear model is the axiomatic model. The structure of knowledge is like that of a pyramid whose base is a set of axioms or principles that must be known before the rest of the pyramid can be known. Going against Gail Fine, Julia Annas endorses the axiomatic model as the right way to interpret the dream story. She employs the Aristotelian distinction between two kinds of rational cognition: (1) the one that knows the elements of a science and (2) the one that is called reasoning or explanation, which can be equated with the *logos* of the dream story.[3] Since (2) is given in terms of (1), (2) cannot become knowledge until (1) also becomes knowledge. But the knowledge of (1) is the knowledge of elements that does not require reasoning or explanation. This linear model accepts KBK, and rejects the dream story, while the circular model rejects KBK and accepts the dream story. According to the linear model, KBK cannot be an epistemic option that can be accepted or rejected at our will. On the contrary, it is an axiom whose rejection would be monstrous and absurd, as Theaetetus says.

Theaetetus's response alone cannot settle the dispute between Fine and Annas. First, we had better hear the rest of the dream story; in fact, we have not yet seen the end of the story and its monstrous absurdity. In continuing the story, Socrates says that there are two ways of looking at a compound: it can be regarded as a sum of its parts, or as a whole that is more than such a sum. Theaetetus endorses the second view (205c): a compound has its own unity and identity that cannot be described by naming its parts. It is impossible to know a whole by simply knowing its constituent elements, for example, a syllable cannot be recognized by simply knowing its constituent vowels and consonants. In fact, the recognition of syllables was made much earlier than the division of syllables into vowels and consonants.

If a compound has its own unity and identity that cannot be reduced to the enumeration of its parts, there can be no *logos* for the whole any more than for its constituent elements, and the problem of knowing the compounds is on a par with the problem of knowing the elements. Socrates offers Theaetetus a choice between saying that both complexes and elements can be equally known and expressed, and that neither can be known or accounted for (205de). Whichever he may choose, for sure, he has to reject the dream story and its principle of asymmetry between the knowability of complexes and that of elements. If there is any asymmetry, Socrates says, it should be the other way around. In the experience of learning to read and write, one gets to know the letters well before getting to know the words in which they appear (206a). At least in the process of learning, the knowledge of elements is clearly prior to that of compounds. This passage appears to favor Julia Annas's axiomatic model over Gail Fine's circular model.

There is, however, one serious drawback with the axiomatic model; it cannot provide the *logos* of elements. According to the axiomatic model, the elements must be known without *logos*. On the other hand, the circular model can provide the *logos* of elements, but it has its own drawback. It cannot recognize the priority of elements to compounds in the process of learning. This defect, I propose, can be remedied by recognizing two circular models: (1) the circular model of elements and compounds, and (2) the circular model of elements only. According to (1), we know a compound by analyzing it into its elements, and know an element by identifying the various compounds in which it can be a part.[4] For example, we know the word *Socrates* by breaking it down to its seven letters, and know each of the letters by identifying all the syllables and words in which it is a part. There is a complete symmetry in the process of learning elements and compounds. If so, it denies the priority of elements to compounds in the learning process, which is stressed by Socrates.

There is one more weakness in the circular model of elements and compounds. It presupposes the knowledge of elements. Without knowing elements first, we can neither recognize a compound as a compound, nor analyze it into elements. So it appears that we cannot avoid admitting the priority of elements to compounds in the learning process and also in every cognitive process. Does that force us to abandon the circular model for the axiomatic model? Not before we try out the circular model of elements only. This model should be contrasted with the atomistic model of elements. According to this atomistic model, the knowledge of each element is independent of the knowledge of other elements. For example, the recognition of the letter *S* has nothing to do with the recognition of other letters. According to the circular model of elements, they are interdependent. For example, to know the letter *S* is to know how to discriminate it from other letters. There is no way of knowing any one letter without knowing the other letters; in fact, they are definable in terms of their mutual differentiation in a continuum.

The difference of these two models obtains not only in letters, but also in phonemes, musical notes, colors, and many other elements of perception. As we will see in the *Philebus*, all perceptual qualities are given in a continuum of colors, sounds, or smells, which is called the Indeterminate Dyad. Because all perceptual qualities are determined by the demarcation of such a continuum, each of them has not only its absolute value, but also its relational value. For example, the middle C in the musical scale has its absolute value that can be measured by its wave length. But the same middle C can have different relational values in a five-tone scale and in a seven-tone scale. For another example, the vowel *O* in the English language has an absolute vocal value. But this same vowel can have different relational values when it appears in other languages because their system of demarcating vowels is different from ours. The atomistic model of elements takes into account only the absolute values of perceptual qualities. For the circular model, however, the relational values are as important as the absolute values.

Of these two models, Gail Fine obviously favors the circular model of elements. But she does not seem to recognize the significant difference between it and the circular model of elements and compounds. For the *Theaetetus*, all we need is the circular model of elements. Socrates and Theaetetus can accept it together with the axiomatic model, which is compatible with either the atomistic model or the circular model of elements. The difference between these two models of elements lies with the problem of providing *logos* for elements. As we have already noted, it can be provided by the circular model but not by the atomistic model. But the *logos* of elements is different from the *logos* of a com-

pound. The *logos* of a compound is to describe its compositional complexity; the *logos* of an element is to describe its relation to other elements, or rather its distinction from other elements.

Two Principles of *Logos*: Identity and Difference

Francis Cornford says that the theory of *logos* in the dream story
"was certainly never held by Plato himself."[5] But it is right out of the
method of Socratic definition, which involves the analysis of a complex
into its constituent elements. At the beginning of the *Theaetetus*, Socrates defined mud as earth mixed with water (147c), and this definition
shows mud as a complex made of two simples, earth and water. But
this definition cannot become knowledge for anyone who does not already know the two simples. As long as the Socratic method of definition is taken as the cognitive paradigm, there is no way to explain the
cognition of simple elements. Hence the dream story is a critique of
Socratic definition; it forcefully raises the problem of the predefinitional
knowledge that was already touched upon in the Meno paradox.

The analysis of a compound into elements was fully discussed in the
Cratylus, where *logos* was associated with the distinction of primary
and secondary names. Since a secondary name is complex, it can be
analyzed into primary names. But primary names cannot be analyzed
because they are simple. *Logos* can be given to secondary names but
not to primary names; the objects designated by primary names cannot
be known. Thus the notion of *logos* in the *Cratylus* leads to the same
difficulty as the dream story does. If the simples cannot be known by
definition, they must be known directly. Let us call such a direct way
of knowing the Platonic intuition. In the dream story, I propose, Socrates is expressing his recognition that the method of definition is insuffi-
cient to give a complete account of human knowledge, and that it has
to be supplemented by a theory of intuition.

In the Socratic definition, the secondary names have long been the
primary objects of concern. For the first time in the *Cratylus* and the
Theaetetus, Socrates begins to see the importance of primary names in
his theory of knowledge. The primary names and the primitive elements

are linked to each other. In the dream story, the elements are said to be namable and perceivable (202b). But what kind of perception is involved in the perception of elements? It should be able to discriminate one perceivable element from another, and such a discrimination is a matter of intuition. But the intuition is bound to be discursive (*logos*), if it is made not in the atomistic but in the circular model of elements. Thus, Platonic intuition is always logos-bound, whether its object is perceptual or eidetic. This is its basic difference from the standard notion of intuition, which implicitly presupposes the atomistic model. Platonic intuition is also required for the cognition of a compound, if it is more than a sum of its parts as Socrates says. In fact, the intuition of a compound can take place on two levels: the intuition of the compound as a whole and the intuition of its elements.

Because Platonic intuition is discursive, it is radically different from the Protagorean sense-perception, which can admit no *logos*. Thus we have two ways of understanding the act of perception: (1) Protagorean sense-perception and (2) Platonic intuition. (1) is *logos*-free; (2) is *logos*-bound. (1) allows no room for errors because it is *logos*-free. In (2), however, errors can be made by its *logos*. But what is the nature of its *logos*? This question has yet to be settled. At the end of the *Theaetetus*, Socrates offers three possible meanings of *logos*: (1) any expression of thought in speech, (2) the enumeration of elements, and (3) the knowledge of difference. Socrates dismisses *Logos* (1) because it is too general to be of any use for the definition of knowledge. That leaves *Logos* (2) and (3).

In most commentaries, *Logos* (2) is taken to be a repetition of the dream story.[6] But it is not a repetition. Though both versions involve the notion of enumerating elements, they present two different problems. The dream story presents the problem of *knowing* a compound in terms of its elements. *Logos* (2) expands the scope of this problem by recognizing the elements as universals that can appear in other compounds. In the dream story, the letters *S* and *O* are mentioned as elements of *Socrates* but not of any other words or names. In *Logos* (2), the letter *theta* is recognized as a universal that can appear in *Theaetetus*, *Theodorus*, or any other names or words. In the dream story, Socrates never mentions the function of the elements as universals. For all he says, the elements of any given compound may never appear again in any other compounds.

If *Logos* (2) is an expansion of the dream story, so is *Logos* (3). There are two sides in the recognition of an element; one has to recognize not only its reappearance in different occasions, but also its difference from other elements. *Logos* (2) concerns the principle of identity (or universality), and *Logos* (3) the principle of difference (particularity). These two principles represent the two theories of perception that have been in contention against each other for a long time: essentialism and nominalism. It is the essentialist view that all perceptual objects are describable in terms of universals without remainder. This view leads to Leibniz's doctrine of the identity of the indiscernibles. In the nominalist view, on the other hand, the perceptual objects can never be adequately described in terms of universals, because they are particulars whose identity can never be captured by universals. In the essentialist view, the principle of identity is the basic principle of perceptual knowledge; all perceptual objects can be described by using the same set of universals. On the nominalist view, the principle of difference is the basic principle; the difference of perceptual objects and their particularity are irreducible and indescribable.

The *Theaetetus* admits the necessity of both principles, and their irreducibility is suggested by *Logos* (2) and *Logos* (3). Their irreducibility can explain the difference between the knowledge of a witness and the belief of a juryman. When a witness perceives a scene, she perceives it in all its particularity. Even when she recalls it from memory, her recollection is still associated with the particularity of the scene once perceived. However, when she describes it to the jury, she has to use a set of universals, which can never fully capture the particularity of the scene. This is what is missing from a juryman's belief, and this missing element is the deficient feature of his belief in comparison with the perceptual knowledge of a witness. Even for the domain of belief, however, the principle of difference cannot be completely dispensed with, because it is necessary even for the recognition of the difference between two universals.

The indispensability of these two principles, identity and difference, is suggested by the ending of the *Theaetetus*. This interpretation goes against the standard view that the *Theaetetus* ends with an *aporia*. The aporetic interpretation is textually correct because Socrates rejects the definition of knowledge that incorporates either of *Logos* (2) and (3). But let us find out what his rejection really amounts to. Socrates says that *Logos* (3) cannot be used for the definition of knowledge because its use will make the definition circular (210a). According to *Logos* (3), *logos* is the knowledge of the differentia. The definition of knowledge as true belief plus *logos* will be translated into "true belief with the knowledge of the differentia." The word *knowledge* appears in both the definiens and the definiendum, making the definition circular.

The problem of circularity is equally inevitable with *Logos* (2), though Socrates does not state it. As we noted earlier, *Logos* (2) is not a mere repetition but an expansion of the dream story. Their difference can be restated as the difference between the enumeration of elements and their recognition. A boy can enumerate all the letters in *Theaetetus*, though he may misspell the letter *theta* in *Theodorus*. In that case, Socrates says, he does not know that letter as a universal (208ab). Let us now suppose that the boy not only enumerates all those letters, but also knows them as universals. In that case, he can give a different kind of *logos* from the one that simply enumerates the letters. This is *Logos* (2), while the mere enumeration is the *logos* of the dream story. *Logos* (2) can be described as the enumeration of elements together with the knowledge of those elements. The definition of true belief plus logos will be translated into "true belief with the enumeration of elements together with the knowledge of those elements." This definition of knowledge is as circular as the one that employs *Logos* (3).[7]

This is not the first time we encounter the problem of circularity in the *Theaetetus*. The dream story was a story of circularity: the *knowledge* of a compound can be defined only in terms of the *knowledge* of elements. The same problem arises in the allegories of wax tablet and of aviary. Though they are meant to explain the nature of knowledge, Socrates has to use the distinction between knowledge and ignorance in their construction. He calls the circularity a shameless, vicious taint, but confesses the difficulty of avoiding it (196e). Somehow it is impossible not to use the words *know* and *knowledge* in the definition of knowledge. Finally, the problem of circularity makes its first appearance at the very beginning of the dialogue, when Theaetetus names many kinds of knowledge in response to Socrates' question, "What is knowledge?" Socrates does not simply complain about getting instances of knowledge instead of its definition. He also notes that the definition of knowledge, which ends with the phrase "knowledge of so and so" will make them go around on an endless road (147c). The inevitability of circularity in any definition of knowledge may indicate that it is indefinable. In that regard, it is like the elements.

It is indeed difficult to demonstrate that something is indefinable, because it has to be a negative demonstration rather than a positive one. If we can show that knowledge is simple, we can prove its indefinability because simples cannot be defined. But it is not easy to prove that knowledge is simple. In that case, the only way to demonstrate the indefinability of knowledge is to show that we cannot avoid the problem of circularity even in talking about it. In fact, the inevitability of circularity can be elucidated by the contemporary discussions of the problem of knowledge. Consider the familiar definition of knowledge as justified true belief. Since justification can be given in terms of reasons, this definition can be restated as true belief plus reasons, which turns out to be equivalent to the third definition in the *Theaetetus*, because reason and *logos* are equivalent. However, the reasons that can be given for the justification of a belief should be either known or believed to be true. If they are merely believed to be true, the justification is only a nexus of beliefs, which cannot be knowledge. On the other hand, if they are known to be true, the definition of knowledge as justified belief becomes circular because the justification is based on knowledge.

This point can be illustrated by the Gettier paradox, a devastating critique of the definition of knowledge as justified true belief. Gettier gives a formal statement of this definition: S *knows* that P, if and only if, (1) P is true, (2) S believes that P, and (3) S is justified in believing that P. It is also possible to restate (3) as "S has adequate evidence for P," or "S has the right to be sure that P is true." He introduces two additional points. First, it is possible for a person to be justified in believing a proposition that is in fact false. Second, if S is justified in believing P, and S correctly deduces Q from P, then S is justified in believing Q. These two conditions together with the definition of knowledge as justifed true belief produce the Gettier paradox.[8]

Let us suppose that S is justified in believing P, but P is in fact false, and that S correctly deduces Q from P, but Q happens to be in fact true. In that case, S is justified in believing Q, and S's belief of Q fits the definition of knowledge as justified true belief. But S's belief cannot be regarded as knowledge. Why? Gettier explains with the following example. Smith has strong evidence for the conjunctive proposition; (1) Jones is the man who will get the job, and Jones has ten coins in his pocket. From this premise he deduces the proposition: (2) the man who will get the job has ten coins in his pocket. He is justified in believing the premise because he has heard it from the company president. Since (2) is correctly deduced from (1), Smith is also justified in believing (2). But the job goes not to Jones but to Smith, who happens to have ten coins in his pocket. Hence, Smith's belief of (2) is justified belief, but nobody would call it knowledge.

In this example, a justified true belief (or knowledge) is based on the belief of a false premise. Here lies the essence of the Gettier paradox; knowledge is based on a false belief! The entire paradox revolves around the ambiguity of the word *justification.* The justification of a true belief can be given by a deduction from a premise that is either believed to be true or known to be true. If the premise is not known to be true, it can in fact be false, as it is in Gettier's example, although one may be justified in believing it. So understood, any justified belief is no more than a nexus of beliefs, which can be false or accidentally true. Even if one believes a proposition because of strong evidence, one has to rely on general empirical rules of evidence, which are known to be true or only believed to be true. If they are only believed to be true, the use of evidence cannot convert the belief in the original proposition into knowledge.

The important question for the Gettier paradox is whether the justification that goes into justified true belief is given in terms of knowledge or belief. As long as it is given in terms of belief, it cannot convert justified true belief into knowledge. If the justification is given in terms of knowledge, it can make the conversion. Thus, the Gettier paradox can be avoided by tightening the requirement of justification: the premise for the justification of true belief should not be merely believed but be known to be true. Then, the definition of knowledge as justified true belief becomes circular. Thus, the Gettier paradox leads to the same conclusion as Socrates' demonstration in the *Theaetetus*, that is, the definition of knowledge turns out to be inevitably circular, and this shows the indefinability of knowledge.

The Gettier paradox implicitly presupposes the correspondence theory of knowledge, but the problem of circularity cannot be restricted to this theory. The same problem can arise in the coherence theory of knowledge. Let us define knowledge as a set of beliefs plus their coherence. In that case, their coherence is either (1) known, or (2) only believed, or (3) neither known nor believed. For these three cases, the coherentist definition of knowledge takes on different shapes: (1) a set of beliefs plus knowledge of their coherence, (2) a set of beliefs plus belief of their coherence, and (3) a set of beliefs without knowledge or belief of their coherence. Definitions (2) and (3) cannot be definitions of knowledge, because they describe only a set of beliefs. Definition (1) is indeed a definition of knowledge, but it is circular. The same problem of circularity also arises in reliabilism. If knowledge is defined as true belief produced by a reliable mechanism of cognition, the reliability of the cognitive mechanism should be either known or not known. If it is known to be reliable, the definition turns out to be circular.[9] If it is not so known, the definition cannot be a definition of knowledge. Thus it is impossible to avoid the problem of circularity, whether we try to define knowledge in terms of correspondence, coherence, or reliabilism.

What is the upshot of all this? Knowledge can be defined in terms of either knowledge or nonknowledge such as belief or opinion. In the former case, the definition becomes circular. In the latter case, it cannot explain the mystery of how nonknowledge is converted into knowledge. This has led Bertrand Russell to conclude that knowledge can be defined only in terms of knowledge, and that knowledge so defined is only derived or derivative knowledge. Moreover, the definition of derivative knowledge must presuppose intuitive knowledge that cannot be defined, if the definition is not to fall into an infinite regress. To put it another way, intuitive knowledge is indefinable; though derivative knowledge is definable, its definition is circular.[10] Thus, the problem of definition forces us to acknowledge intuitive knowledge as the basis of all cognition. This Russellian conclusion is the final outcome of the *Theaetetus*.

By displaying the inevitability of circularity, the *Theaetetus* demonstrates the indefinability of knowledge. If we examine the text of the dialogue carefully, we will find that Socrates does not reject either *Logos* (2) or (3). What he rejects are the definitions of knowledge that use either of them, because their use makes the definitions circular. Because none of the proposed definitions of knowledge are accepted, the ending of the dialogue appears to be aporetic. But this appearance hides some important positive results. Beyond the indefinability of knowledge, the *Theaetetus* suggests two primitive ways of knowing: (1) knowledge by the principle of identity and (2) knowledge by the principle of difference. (1) is to know the identity of two things, and (2) is to know their difference. These two ways of knowing are two modes of intuition.

The knowledge of elements can be accounted for by (1) and (2). (1) is for the recognition of an element and its identity in different contexts, and (2) for the recognition of its difference from other elements. The knowledge of a complex can be achieved by the combined use of (1) and (2). In Plato's dialogues, (1) is much better known than (2); it is the basic method of Socratic definition, which establishes the identity of a Form shared by a countless number of instances. However, (2) gains its importance in the later dialogues. This shift of attention is indicated at the beginning of the *Theaetetus*, where Socrates uses the definition of mud as an example of definition. To this simple example, Theaetetus responds with his recounting of the complicated discussion on the distinction between square and oblong numbers (147d–148b). On the surface, this appears to be more like an example of classification than definition. However, it involves two definitions: the definition of lengths as the square roots of square numbers and of powers as the square roots of oblong numbers (148ab). While each definition establishes the identity of its definiendum, the two definitions together establish the difference of the two classes. So his example employs (1) and (2), while Socrates' example employs only (1).

The succession of Socrates' example by Theaetetus's indicates

Plato's recognition that (2) is as important as (1), and that the two are in fact inseparable. Their inseparability is also demonstrated by the second part of the *Parmenides*, in which the two categories of identity and difference are repeatedly employed in conjunction. These two categories continue to make their presence felt in all three definitions of knowledge in the *Theaetetus*. In the world of Protagorean sensation, Socrates says, nothing can be known because nothing ever appears the *same* to anyone (154a). When he introduces the operation of the mind for making perceptual judgment, he lists the categories of identity and difference together with the categories of likeness and unlikeness as its common notions (185a–e). He devises the allegory of the wax tablet to explain the nature of mistake in the recognition of perceptual objects, which involves the categories of identity and difference. These two categories underlie the two ways of knowing, (1) and (2), and the two types of *logos*, *Logos* (2) and (3). Let us rename these two as *Logos*-I (identity) and *Logos*-D (difference). The recognition of these two is the monumental accomplishment of the *Theaetetus*.

The Scope of Definition

There is one peculiarity of this dialogue that has bothered many commentators: the discussion of knowledge is restricted to the knowledge of phenomena. This restriction is never openly mentioned; even Socrates' original question, "What is knowledge?" is stated without any restriction on the scope of knowledge. In his first response to this question, Theaetetus defines knowledge by naming geometry and other sciences, and the crafts of the cobbler and other craftsmen (146c). As Socrates points out, these are instances of knowledge that do not constitute a definition of it, but these instances cover a much broader domain than that of perceptual knowledge. Nevertheless, Theaetetus comes back with his first definition of knowledge as perception. There is an obvious discrepancy between the definition and the instances, but Socrates does not register any complaint. Even when they reject the first definition, they do not extend the scope of their later definitions beyond the domain of perceptual knowledge. The restriction of their discussion

to perceptual knowledge is consistent from the first definition to the end
of the dialogue.

To be sure, this restriction may appear to be set aside in one instance,
when Socrates and Theaetetus talk about the nature of error in the addition of five and seven. Socrates stresses that this arithmetical operation
is different from the perceptual operation of adding five men and seven
men (196a). Surely, they are considering not empirical but pure arithmetic. To account for the nature of error in pure arithmetic, Socrates
introduces the allegory of aviary. Thus, the two allegories of wax tablet
and aviary appear to represent the two domains of knowledge, empirical
and nonempirical. However, the contrast between the two allegories
neatly corresponds to Hume's distinction between the matters of fact
and the relation of ideas. For Hume, the relation of ideas is no more
than the identity relation, and the sum of five and seven is identical
with twelve. Even a theory of perceptual or empirical knowledge has to
account for the relation of ideas, because the latter is essential for the
former. The nonempirical knowledge that is discussed in the *Theaetetus*
is restricted to this narrow scope, and does not represent the rich conception that includes all the Pythagorean sciences and the science of
dialectic as advocated in the *Republic*.

The restriction of knowledge to the perceptual domain in the *Theaetetus* is even more baffling, considering the fact that Theaetetus and
Theodorus are mathematicians, and that Socrates has touted mathematics as the best model of knowledge in other dialogues. But none of them
even mentions mathematical knowledge in their discussion except for
the famous example of making a mistake in the addition of five and
seven. Nevertheless, Theaetetus cannot altogether restrain the mathematical bent of his thought. When Socrates tries to explain the difference between definitions and instances at the beginning of the dialogue,
Theaetetus expresses his understanding of it with a mathematical example. Theodorus once showed Theaetetus and other students that the
square roots of numbers are sometimes commensurable and sometimes
incommensurable, by taking the first seventeen numbers one by one. To
formally state this distinction, Theaetetus says, they hit upon the idea
of dividing all the numbers into two classes: (1) the square numbers,
which can be produced by multiplying a certain number by itself, and

(2) the oblong numbers, which cannot be so obtained (147d–148b). By this example, Theaetetus now understands the difference between a definition and its instances as equivalent to the difference between a class and its members.

This episode clearly indicates the mathematical bent of Theaetetus. The same mathematical bent is equally manifest in Socrates' own thought. When he tries to account for the possibility of perceptual errors with the allegory of the wax tablet, he uses the same number seventeen in setting up the matrix of his combinatorics (192a–d). He considers the possibility of making mistakes in the domain of two objects on the supposition that each of the two objects is both known and perceived, not known but perceived, known but not perceived, or neither known nor perceived. Then he enumerates fourteen cases where mistakes are impossible, and three cases where mistakes are possible. They add up to exactly seventeen cases, and they are divided into three and fourteen, exactly the same division as that of the first seventeen numbers into three square numbers and fourteen oblong numbers.

In his enumeration of these cases of three and fourteen, Socrates employs such a complicated combinatoric method that it is hard to tell whether those two lists are complete. Though I cannot go into details, his method allows quite a few mistakes of both omission and repetition. Socrates simply employs this tricky method to produce seventeen cases to match the seventeen numbers of Theodorus. He could have used a much simpler method, but he does not.[11] This is a devilish trick Socrates plays on the innocent Theaetetus, who never questions his method of enumeration. What is the point of this mathematical trick? It clearly demonstrates Socrates' talent and delight in mathematical operations. But he does not introduce mathematics in the definition of knowledge. Instead, he is content to restrict the definition of knowledge to the domain of perception. Hence, this restriction cannot be attributed to his or his partner's incompetence in or distaste for mathematics. What is the reason for this restriction, then? This is perhaps the most baffling question for the entire dialogue.

Some commentators have tried to discount the restriction. In the *Theaetetus*, R. M. Dancy says, the word *aisthanesthai* (perception) has a much broader sense than that of sense-perception. In his praise of

Theaetetus, Theodorus says, "I've never perceived anyone as wonderfully talented" (144a, trans. Dancy). In explaining his art of midwifery, Socrates says to Theaetetus, "Have you perceived also that they are very skilled matchmakers . . . ?" (149d, trans. Dancy). In these two instances, Dancy says, the word *perceive* has a broad enough meaning to be replaced by the word *know*. Moreover, he says that the Greek verb *aisthanesthai* can be paraphrased as "being aware".[12] These two instances of expanding the meaning of the word *perception*, however, cannot explain the restriction of the discussion in the dialogue. For they appear not in the course of defining the nature of knowledge, but well before Socrates and Theaetetus begin their definition. Once the definition begins, the meaning of the word *perception* becomes clearly restricted to *sense-perception* instead of being allowed to have the broad meaning it had in those two occasions cited by Dancy.

There may be a better way of explaining the extended meaning of *perception* in those two occasions. It can be taken as Plato's rhetorical device for preparing his readers to accept Theaetetus's definition of knowledge as perception without much discomfort. If his readers were to retain the standard meaning of *perception* as restricted to sense-perception, they could not overlook the obvious inadequacy of the proposed definition and its deviation from the cited instances. Plato forestalls this expected sense of definitional inadequacy by deliberately using the word *perceive* in its extended sense not only once but twice in advance of the proposed definition. By this rhetorical device, Plato manipulates the natural response of his reader's semantic apparatus to the dialogical development, in which the nature of knowledge under inquiry is to be restricted to perceptual knowledge.

The Knowledge of Phenomena

What, then, is Plato's reason for this restriction? As we noted in the last chapter, Plato's restriction of knowledge to the world of Forms entails the impossibility of knowing the world of phenomena. When the young Theaetetus is introduced to Socrates, he says that he has been studying not only geometry, but also astronomy, harmonics, and arithmetic (145cd). Of these four subjects, two are mathematical sciences, and the other two are natural sciences. The *Republic* can account for the scientific character of arithmetic and geometry, but not of astronomy and harmonics, because these two involve the objects of the sensible world. To cope with this difficulty, Socrates had to argue for the distinction between the pure and the empirical versions of astronomy and harmonics. Though the pure versions are knowledge, he said, the empirical versions are only opinions. But the pure versions cannot be accepted as natural sciences, because they are really mathematics as we noted in the last chapter. That there can be no natural science is one of the fatal defects of the *Republic*. In the *Theaetetus*, Plato is trying to remedy this defect by demonstrating the possibility of *knowing* the world of phenomena.

Whereas Socrates said in the *Republic* that the phenomena can never be the objects of knowledge, he treats the knowledge of phenomena as an established fact in the *Theaetetus*. He casually acknowledges that a witness has knowledge of the facts, about which a jury can have only true belief (201b). This sort of admission could not have been made in the *Republic*. Even within the *Republic*, to be sure, it is indeed possible to gain knowledge of the Forms by studying the phenomena. But the knowledge of Forms so gained does not become the knowledge of the phenomena themselves. As far as the phenomena are concerned, they are forever destined to be the objects of mere opinion. In the *Meno*, Socrates talked about the possibility of converting belief into knowledge, but that conversion was restricted to the axiomatic knowledge of geometry and its recollection. Unlike the world of geometry, the world of perception is empirical, and the art of recollection cannot deliver empirical knowledge.

By the cognitive standard of the *Republic*, there can be no radical difference between a witness and a jury in their cognitive state. Both of them have only beliefs or opinions, which cannot be converted into knowledge by recollection. To be sure, the *Theaetetus* does not claim that all perceptions qualify as knowledge; in fact this claim is repudiated by the critique of Protagorean relativism. If perceptions cannot by themselves qualify as knowledge, what must be added to them? This is the ultimate question for the dialogue, and *Logos*-I and *Logos*-D are introduced to resolve this question. Though neither *Logos*-I nor *Logos*-D is of any use for Socrates and company in their attempt to define knowledge, they provide the two keys to perceptual knowledge. And these two keys can resolve the problem of the *Republic*.

These two ways of knowing are involved even in such a seemingly simple act as that of a frog catching a fly. The frog has to recognize the sameness of all flies and their difference from other objects. This act is not really simple but awfully complex; it requires a highly complex neural net. When a cow recognizes her baby calf, she also has to rely on the same two ways of knowing. She has to know that it is the same baby that she saw and smelled before, and that it is different from other babies. To recognize these two fundamentals of cognition is the ultimate purpose of going through what appears to be the futile effort of fleshing out all the contending definitions of knowledge. This is the prodigious achievement of the *Theaetetus*.

Going against the prevailing scholarship on the *Theaetetus*, I have given a positive account of its result. It is about time for us to consider the standard negative account. The classical case is Cornford's negative view of the dialogue. He says, "True knowledge has for its object things of a different order—not sensible things, but intelligible Forms and truths about them."[13] In his view, this is the necessary inference a Platonist should draw from the negative result of the dialogue, and it is in perfect accord with the *Republic*. According to this reading, the negative ending of the *Theaetetus* is meant to consolidate the positive theory of the *Republic*.

David Bostock makes a different response to the negative result: the dialogue fails to recognize the immense varieties of knowledge. Socrates and Theaetetus mistakenly assume that there is one single and unitary concept of knowledge. They do not even make such an elementary distinction as the one between knowing things and knowing that.[14] Myles Burnyeat tries to make a virtue out of this mistake. The moral of the negative dialogue is to demonstrate that there can be no simple definition of knowledge because there are so many different senses of knowledge and equally many senses of giving an account for true belief. Instead of a simple theory of knowledge, he says, we should construct a rich, complex theory by using all the materials provided in the

dialogue.[15] According to this reading, the *Theaetetus* is richly suggestive for our own inquiry, in spite of its negative ending.

Though Cornford and Burnyeat differ in assessing the outcome of the
dialogue, they agree on one point. They assume that the object of the
dialogical inquiry is the nature of knowledge unrestricted. Neither of
them recognizes the fact that the discussion in the *Theaetetus* is restricted to the problem of perceptual knowledge. They do not construe
the central question of the dialogue as it was conceived by Plato himself. This is the fatal defect in their respective readings. John McDowell
offers a third view on the negative outcome. According to him, the idea
of giving an account should be understood as the idea of providing an
explanation, which survives in the notion of dialectic given in the *Sophist*. The example of combining letters into syllables and syllables into
words is much like the dialectical skill displayed by the Eleatic Stranger
in the *Sophist*, namely, the art of combining and separating Forms. On
these grounds, McDowell concludes, "Now a conception of dialectical
knowledge like that of the *Sophist*, though of course it is not explicitly
set out in the *Theaetetus*, is not far beneath its surface."[16] This is a
highly suggestive view, but he has yet to explain how the art of *diairesis*
lies beneath the surface of the *Theaetetus*, and what kind of *logos* is
provided by this art.

Finally, let us take another look at Theaetetus's distinction between
square and oblong numbers. Just before giving his first definition of
knowledge, he uses it to show that he now understands what it means
to give a definition. That is quite strange because there can be much
simpler ways (for example, the definition of a circle or a triangle) of
showing it than the division of all numbers into two classes. It is a
distinction rather than a definition, though the two classes can be treated
as objects of definition after their distinction. For this reason, some
commentators have been tempted to see this mathematical episode as
Plato's tribute to Theaetetus's contribution to the theory of irrational
numbers. There are other commentators who are not fully satisfied with
this relatively simple account and try to descry much deeper significance for the episode.

Robert Brumbaugh says that the distinction between square and oblong numbers suggests the inherent incommensurability between

knowledge and opinion.[17] According to Kenneth Sayre, Theaetetus deliberately uses the word *power* (*dynamis*) in talking about the square roots of numbers so that it should be linked to the active and passive powers of perception in the first definition of knowledge.[18] Myles Burnyeat gives another account: we should see a parallel between the definition of knowledge and the theory of the irrationals as two extended enterprises. Just as Theaetetus's work on the irrationals was an extended work that had to be sustained with stamina and dedication, so is the inquiry into the nature of knowledge in the dialogue bearing his name.[19]

Here is my own interpretation. Let us take the distinction between square and oblong numbers as an analogue to the difference between the knowledge of Forms and the knowledge of phenomena. Until Theaetetus's contribution to the irrationals, there was no way of computing the square roots of oblong numbers.[20] There was no knowledge of those roots, but only opinions. But his method of computation can now give us the knowledge of the irrationals. Hence, Theaetetus's method is analogous to extending mathematics to the study of nature. The difference between the square roots of square numbers and those of oblong numbers is like the difference between geometry and astronomy, mathematics and natural science. Though mathematics can be used for natural science, the latter cannot be reduced to the former. There is no way to give a mathematical account of a natural event or object without remainder. This is very much like the problem of computing the square roots of oblong numbers; the computation is only an approximation to the true value, which cannot be made without remainder.

Socrates illustrates the art of approximation by the attempt to describe Theaetetus (209bc). If he is described as a man with a nose, eyes, and mouth, he cannot be distinguished from any other man. We can make the description more specific: he is a man with a snub nose and prominent eyes. But Theaetetus of this description cannot be distinguished from Socrates. Whatever degree of specification we may try to give the description, it can never fully capture the uniqueness of Theaetetus, because we always have to rely on universals for the specification. In that regard, our knowledge of a perceptual object is just like our knowledge of the irrationals. Our specification has to stop somewhere, and it is good enough for our purpose if it can help us avoid confusing one person with another, or one perceptual object with another. The art of specification is the practical art of approximation. The science of phenomena can never achieve the precision of mathematics or the science of Forms.

Though our knowledge of phenomena is only an approximation, it is different from guesswork or mere opinion because it is governed by the method of computation and specification. On the other hand, our knowledge of mathematics and Forms is not simply an approximation. It grasps the truth in its completeness. For this reason, the contrast between square and oblong numbers is analogous to the contrast between the knowledge of Forms and the knowledge of phenomena. Just as irrational numbers cannot be reduced to rational numbers, the knowledge of phenomena cannot be reduced to the knowledge of Forms. But the study of irrational numbers was made into a scientific enterprise by Theaetetus's method of computing those numbers. For the science of phenomena, we need the Theaetetus of natural science.

The *Theaetetus* is Plato's call for the new science of phenomena. Because this new science can be born only by the application of mathematics to the world of phenomena, its possibility is discussed by a group of mathematicians. At the beginning of the discussion, Socrates presents his question not only to Theaetetus, but to all the mathematicians present, especially Theodorus. The old eminent mathematician wants to be excused from the arduous inquiry (146b), and Socrates has to turn to the young mathematician Theaetetus for the discussion. This shift from Theodorus to Theaetetus represents the shift of emphasis from pure mathematics to its application to the world of phenomena. The application may be far more important than pure mathematics itself. Whereas the *Republic* praised pure mathematics as the basic science for preparing the soul's ascent to the science of dialectic, the *Theaetetus* stresses the importance of taking pure mathematics down to the world of phenomena. This descent of mathematics will be fully realized in the *Timaeus*.

It may be instructive to compare the three definitions of knowledge with the Divided Line of the *Republic* (509f–510a). All three of them belong to the lower half of it. The lowest level of the Divided Line,

which consists of only images (*eikasia*), corresponds to the first definition of knowledge as perception. The next higher level, which consists
of opinion (*pistis*), corresponds to the second definition of knowledge
as true belief. The Divided Line has nothing that corresponds to the
third definition. If we want to locate it in the Divided Line, we have to
place it higher than the second lowest level but lower than the third level
of reasoning (*dianoia*). This extra level is the knowledge of phenomena,
whereas the level of *dianoia* is the knowledge of Forms. But the two
levels are alike in making use of reasoning or *logos*. The level of perceptual knowledge can be regarded as an extension of *dianoia*, just as
the science of irrationals can be regarded as an extension of the science
of rational numbers.

This extension of *dianoia* to the world of phenomena is the descent
of *logos* from the world of Forms to the world of phenomena, and this
descent is the epistemic dimension of Socrates' descent, which began
in the *Protagoras*. In this dialogue, his descent was chiefly concerned
with the normative problem of civic virtues; in the *Theaetetus*, its epistemic dimension is getting spelled out. In both the epistemic and the
normative dimensions of Socratic descent, Protagoras the sophist functions as the champion of the world of phenomena, and Socrates tries to
take over this function from him. In the *Protagoras*, he tried it by advocating the unity of all Protagorean virtues; in the *Theaetetus*, he tries it
again by doing something Socrates never does in any other dialogue,
that is, taking on the special chore of explicating and defending the
Protagorean theory of perception to the best of his ability.

The descent of *logos* to the world of phenomena establishes the possibility of natural science, and revises Socrates' gloomy picture of the
physical world presented in the *Republic*. In that regard, the *Theaetetus*
reaffirms Socrates' reorientation toward the world of nature, which
began in the *Phaedrus*. But his conception of nature is not anything like
the romantic view of nature given in the *Phaedrus*. Whereas this dialogue presented nature as a world of beauty and enchantment, the
Theaetetus recognizes the inevitability of evils in this world (176a). In
this sober view of nature, Socrates neither denounces nor exalts it.
Though we have to live with the evils of this world, we still have to
know it. To establish the possibility of knowing the world of phenom-

ena, Socrates revamps the concept of belief (*doxa*) in the *Theaetetus*. The word *doxa*, which is usually translated as belief or opinion in the *Republic*, is also usually translated as judgment in the *Theaetetus*. This translational difference reflects the change that takes place in the meaning of the word *doxa*.

In the *Republic*, Socrates established a systematic contrast between *doxa* and *episteme*, which corresponds to his demarcation between the sensible and the intelligible worlds. The difference between *doxa* and *episteme* is like the difference between the blind and those with sight (*Republic* 484c). Socrates says, ''Even the best of opinions are blind'' (*Republic* 506c). Unlike *episteme*, *doxa* has no epistemic justification; it is not a product of intelligence. It is a piece of information one passively receives from someone else without really knowing why. One may also gain *doxa* as a product of indoctrination, superstition, or even ideological manipulation. One can never be the master of one's own *doxa*. As long as one lives in the domain of *doxa*, one is enslaved to the prevailing opinions of his social world. In the *Theaetetus*, this negative meaning of *doxa* is replaced by a positive one. In its new meaning, the word *doxa* can no longer be translated as *belief* or *opinion*. It is not something passively received from someone else, but rather something actively made by the agent. This active notion of *doxa* is given by Socrates' description of it as the soul's dialogue with itself, asking itself questions and answering, affirming and denying, and finally making a decision (*Theaetetus* 190a). And the decision can be rational if the soul's conversation is rational.

This is the theory of rational *doxa*, the *doxa* plus *logos*, and its *logos* is provided by *Logos*-I and *Logos*-D. The possibility of rational *doxa* about the phenomena is the possibility of the knowledge or science of nature. To realize this possibility is to vindicate the Heraclitean thesis that the world of phenomena is governed by *logos*. Though it is a perpetual flux, it is not a chaos but *kosmos* (order). This is the Pythagorean faith that was proclaimed by Socrates in the *Gorgias*, and this faith is being redeemed epistemologically in the *Theaetetus*. As we will see later, it will be redeemed cosmologically in the *Timaeus*. This is the final step in Plato's journey of descent, which will nullify the distinction between the pure and the empirical versions of astronomy. Here is a new picture of astronomy given in book 10 of the *Laws* (893cd, trans. Pangle):

And we learn, at any rate, that in this rotation such motion carries the largest and the smallest circles around together, distributing itself proportionately to the small and the large, being less and more according to proportion. That is how it has become a source of all wonders, conveying the large and small circle at the same time, at slow and fast speeds that are in agreement, an effect that someone would expect to be impossible.

This passage has often been compared with the passage of *Republic* 529d, which makes an emphatic distinction between pure and empirical astronomy. There is a noteworthy difference between the two passages. The *Republic* passage demarcates the True Motion, the Slowness itself, and the Swiftness itself from their empirical counterparts. The former are said to belong to the domain of *dianoia*, while the latter are said to belong to the visible world. The former alone are the proper objects of pure astronomy; the latter are only the objects of empirical astronomy. No trace of this demarcation can be found in the passage from the *Laws*. Instead of Motion, Slowness, and Swiftness, it speaks of only plural "slow and fast speeds." These are empirical objects; there is only the empirical science of astronomy. For Plato, we should note, astronomy is not simply astronomy, but natural science par excellence.

The *Philebus* talks about the knowledge of the divine sphere, for example, the knowledge of justice itself, as pure knowledge free of mixtures (62a). This may sound like the revival of the distinction between pure and empirical science. But the distinction between pure and impure science in the *Philebus* demarcates pure science not from empirical, but from applied science. Empirical science is not the same as applied science; for example, a great bulk of astronomy is pure science that may find no application in our life, although it is definitely empirical. Hence, the *Philebus* is not talking about the same type of pure science that was discussed in the *Republic*. Moreover, the *Philebus* stresses the unity of pure and applied science; their unity is the only way to find one's way home (62b).

The *Sophist* and the *Statesman*

Logos-I and *Logos*-D were already contained in the method of collection and division introduced in the *Phaedrus*. The method of collection is based on the principle of identity, and the method of division on the principle of difference. Socrates presented these two methods in his proposal to transform rhetoric into a true art that could be used in talking about the phenomena scientifically. In the *Theaetetus*, he presents *Logos*-I and *Logos*-D as two principles for the knowledge of phenomena. Thus, these two are the thematic connectors between the *Theaetetus* and the *Phaedrus*. Even more important thematically, they further connect the *Theaetetus* to the *Sophist* and the *Statesman*, in which the Eleatic Stranger employs the two methods of collection and division for the definition of sophist and statesman.

Without this thematic connector, it is hard to explain the continuity from the *Theaetetus* to the *Sophist*. At the end of the *Theaetetus*, the three participants make an agreement to meet again for further discussion. At the beginning of the *Sophist*, they come together "according to yesterday's agreement," but Theodorus has brought a visitor from Elea. Since the discussion of the previous day was inconclusive, we should expect them to continue their inquiry on the same topic and perhaps obtain some help from the new visitor from Elea. But nobody even mentions the inquiry of the previous day. Instead, Socrates asks the Eleatic Stranger to explain what the people of Elea think about the sophist, the statesman, and the philosopher. From then on, the Eleatic Stranger takes charge of the discussion for the definition of sophist, and this new discussion is presented as completely independent of the discussion in the *Theaetetus*. On the surface, thematically, the two dialogues appear to be independent and discontinuous. But this appearance of discontinuity only hides the thematic continuity to be established by *Logos*-I and *Logos*-D.[21]

In the *Sophist*, the Eleatic Stranger gives many definitions of sophist, each of which is produced by the method of collection and division. By the standard of Socratic definition, these definitions are not definitions. Stanley Rosen is forthright in telling us that the Eleatic Stranger produces a variety of perceptive descriptions, but no definition.[22] But the

Greek word *logos* can be translated as description or definition. Let us consider all those descriptions of sophist: (1) a hired hunter of rich young men, (2) a merchant of learning and knowledge, (3) a retailer of the same wares, (4) a salesman of one's own products, (5) an athlete in disputation, (6) a purifier of the soul, and (7) a maker of semblances and false conceit (231de). These descriptions are on a par with descriptions of Theaetetus such as 'Theaetetus is intelligent' or 'Theaetetus is a mathematician.' All of them are propositions or judgments. One set of them describes a single individual, and the other set describes a class of individuals.

There is no basic difference between these two sets of propositions, because both of them describe the objects of the phenomenal world. But the Eleatic Stranger appears to recognize some important distinctions between these two sets of descriptions. He identifies *diairesis* with the familiar art of dialectic, and consigns the judgments about Theaetetus ('Theaetetus sits' and 'Theaetetus flies') to the also familiar domain of *doxa*. The implied demarcation between *doxa* and dialectic appears to be his restatement of the demarcation between *doxa* and *episteme* in the *Republic*. But this impression is highly misleading for Plato's new epistemology. There is no basic difference between *diairesis* as a method of defining the nature of a class and *doxa* as a method of forming judgments about a single individual. In both cases, the individuals of the phenomenal world and their classes are the ultimate objects of description.

The multiplicity of descriptions in the definition of sophist has been a source of grave dissatisfaction for many Plato scholars. By the Socratic standard, the Eleatic Stranger should present only one definition, namely, the definition that captures the essence of sophist, and reject all the other definitions. However, none of his definitions appear to capture the essence, nor does he reject any of them. In fact, he accepts them all. That surely goes against the Socratic method. Let us call the method of the Eleatic Stranger the Eleatic method, and try to identify its basic difference from the Socratic method.

About their difference, Cornford says that the Socratic method moves upward from instances to the definition, while the Eleatic method moves downward from a genus to species.[23] Though this is a correct description, it leaves out the most important difference between the two methods. It concerns the objects of definition. The eidetic entities are the objects of Socratic definition; the phenomenal objects are the objects of Eleatic definition. The essence of an eidetic object can be defined in a single definition, for example, the Form of triangle can be defined as a plane figure bound by three sides. This is the nature of an essential definition that is sought by the Socratic method, but the nature of a phenomenal object cannot be captured by a single definition. As the Eleatic Stranger repeatedly says, it is complex and many-sided (223c, 226a). Hence, each description can give only one side or facet of its many-sided character. All the different descriptions can be true of the sophist.

Stanley Rosen's complaint does not stop at the multiplicity of the Eleatic definitions, but extends to the Eleatic Stranger's inability to distinguish between "better and worse" definitions. From this, he concludes that the Eleatic method is much inferior to the Socratic method. He counsels us to read the art of *diairesis* as Plato's vindication of Socratic method against the Eleatic charges, which began in the *Parmenides*.[24] But the Eleatic Stranger never implies that all the different definitions of sophist are equally valid and valuable. In fact, there is a procedure of evaluating all the definitions and selecting the best one. Let us go over this procedure, step by step.

First, the Eleatic Stranger clearly indicates his reservation about the sixth definition, namely, the sophist as a practitioner of the art of purifying the soul. He is afraid of calling the practitioners of this art sophists, because that would give the sophists too high a meed of honor. He also says that *elenchus* is the greatest and the most effective method of purification, and that it confutes the vain conceit of wisdom (230d, 231b). The art of purification achieves an effect exactly opposite to what the sophists achieve, namely, instilling the vain conceit of wisdom in the innocent youth. The Eleatic Stranger treats the sixth definition as an error of resemblance, that is, the mistake of not recognizing the difference between a dog and a wolf because of their superficial resemblance (231a).

The sophists and the purifiers look alike because both of them employ the method of disputation. Hence, one can be mistaken for the other, and this mistake is related to the warning Socrates gave at the opening of the dialogue that the true philosophers sometimes wear the guise of sophists (216c). The Eleatic Stranger's description of the art of purification is almost interchangeable with Socrates' description of philosophy as purification at *Phaedo* 82cd, and of his art of midwifery at *Theaetetus* 210c. If the practitioners of this art are to be called sophists, the Eleatic Stranger says, their art is the sophistry of noble lineage (231b). It is hard to think of any better way of establishing a clear demarcation between the sophists and the purifiers like Socrates.

Though the sixth definition is clearly false, the other five definitions are more or less true. The Eleatic Stranger does not treat them as equally valid and valuable. Some of them are meant to be obvious and superficial, while others are meant to be probing and profound. Before giving the seventh and final definition, he sums up the first six definitions. In that summation, he restates his reservation about the sixth definition, and singles out the fifth definition (the sophist as an athlete in disputation) as the most revealing one (232b). The reexamination of this definition leads to the formulation of the final definition (the sophist as the maker and master of images and semblances in knowledge), and it is endorsed by Theaetetus as the most accurate statement about the object of their definition (233d).

Now that we have the final definition of the sophist, we can reevaluate all the other definitions in reference to it. The sixth definition should be rejected because it is incompatible with the final definition. The rest are compatible with it. The sophist of the final definition can be (1) a hired hunter of rich young men, (2) a merchant of learning and knowledge, (3) a retailer of the same wares, (4) a salesman of one's own products, or (5) an athlete in disputation. But the converse is not always true. For example, a merchant of learning and knowledge is not always a maker of images and semblances. It is possible for someone to sell real learning and knowledge rather than the counterfeits. Hence, none of the first six definitions is a complete one, while one of them is outright false. So we may regard the first six definitions as a preliminary survey for formulating the final definition. Thus, there are two stages in the definition of sophist.

Let us now compare these two stages with the two stages we observed in the Socratic definition of the early dialogues. We marked the two stages as conventional and as transcendent. The conventional stage was the examination of conventional ideas, and the transcendent stage went beyond conventional wisdom in search of transcendent truth. The preliminary definitions of sophist definitely belong to the conventional stage; they only describe the various conventional notions about the sophist. The final definition is the transcendent stage, which transcends the conventional conceptions. This transcendence would not be possible, if there were no access to reality except the names of objects as Cratylus claimed in the *Cratylus*. In fact, the definition begins with the name *sophist*. But this name yields many different preliminary descriptions of sophist, because it has many different meanings in its conventional usage. And these different meanings are spelled out by the art of *diairesis*. The method of *diairesis* does not stop there, but moves on to the transcendent stage.

In the *Statesman*, the Eleatic Stranger seeks the definition of statesman. Since he uses the same method of collection and division, his attempt looks like a repeat performance of what he did in the *Sophist*. Because of this, the *Statesman* has been regarded as tedious and repetitious; it has been called the weary dialogue.[25] However, the *Statesman* is not simply a repetition of the exercise already performed in the *Sophist*. The later dialogue presents a new problem in the art of definition that was not encountered in the earlier one. In the *Sophist*, the Eleatic Stranger was faced with the problem of generating one final definition from the six preliminary ones. This is the problem of unity and identity; the problem of how to make one out of many. In the *Statesman*, he faces exactly the opposite problem of distinction and differentiation. Every definition of statesman he gives turns out to be overinclusive; it covers too many competitors for the statesman. The Eleatic Stranger has to find a way to demarcate these competitors from his definition of statesman. This is the problem of differentiation and distinction, which requires *Logos*-D. On the other hand, the problem of uniting all the different definitions of sophist into one requires *Logos*-I.

The definition in the *Statesman* also goes through two stages, whose division is marked by the myth of two ages. The first definition includes not only the statesman but also the herder of pigs (266a–e). On the occasion of this obvious error in definition, the Eleatic Stranger talks about two sources for this sort of mistake. The first is the problem of empirical insensitivity, and the second is the problem of analogical paradigms. To explain the first point, he recounts the myth of two ages. The first age is the age of Cronus, in which the world is governed by the gods. By the end of the first age, the world reverses the direction of its rotation, and every process of growth and decay also gets reversed. This is the age of Zeus, in which the divine governance of the world is terminated and the world is left to its own devices. The beginning of human society and government in the age of Zeus looks very much like the myth Protagoras told to explain the genesis of human society under the aegis of Zeus (*Protagoras* 320c–322d). The myth of two ages is an extension of this Protagorean myth; Plato has just added the age of Cronus to the age of Zeus.

After giving the myth of two ages, the Eleatic Stranger says that the definition that fails to see any distinction between the statesman and the pig herder would have been correct for the age of Cronus but incorrect for the age of Zeus. In the age of Cronus, there was a vast difference between the herders and the animals in their charge because all the herders were gods, whether the herded animals were humans or pigs. In the age of Zeus, however, the huge gap that separates the pigs and their herders does not exist between the humans and their herders. This is why the first definition of the statesman is correct for the age of Cronus but incorrect for the age of Zeus. The Eleatic Stranger and the Young Socrates have wound up with this definition because they have over-looked the important difference in the empirical conditions of the two ages. This difference can be detected not by the method of recollection but by the method of empirical observation. Perceptual knowledge is essentially empirical, as advocated by the *Theaetetus*.

The second problem is the problem of analogical paradigms. The Eleatic Stranger gives an exposition on the use of paradigms (277a–279a). He says that nothing can be demonstrated without using a para-digm, and that without the use of a paradigm everything looks like a dream. The herder is a paradigm for defining the statesman; the hunter is a paradigm for defining the sophist. Both of them are analogical para-digms, which are obviously different from the mathematical paradigms of the *Republic*. The mathematical paradigms belong to the classical logic of classes, but the analogical paradigms belong to the logic of analogical resemblance. These two logics are basically different in their semantics. In the classical logic, the class boundaries are definite and determinate; given any class, everything is either definitely included in it or excluded from it. For example, something either belongs to the class of birds or not. There are no borderline cases, no slippery slope arguments, nor the sorites paradox.

The logic of analogical resemblance is semantically opposite to the classical logic of classes. In the logic of analogical resemblances, the class boundaries are indefinite and indeterminate; there is no way to avoid borderline cases, slippery slope arguments, and the sorites paradox. We can bundle all of these problems together and call them the problems of semantic indeterminacy. In the *Phaedrus* (262ab), Socrates showed how slippery slope arguments are used by the rhetoricians to mislead and deceive their audience. The art of rhetoric thrives in the world of semantic indeterminacy. The logic of resemblance is infected with semantic indeterminacy, while the logic of classes enjoys semantic determinacy.

The difference between the two logics can be further elucidated by the principles of identity and difference. In the classical logic of classes, the two principles have different domains. If two things belong to the same class, they are governed by the principle of identity. If they belong to different classes, they are governed by the principle of difference. In the logic of resemblance, the principle of identity has to be replaced by the principle of resemblance, which stands somewhere between the principles of identity and difference. The categories of *like* and *unlike* are different from the categories of *identity* and *difference*. When two things resemble each other, they are also different from each other. Unlike the categories of *identity* and *difference*, the categories of *like* and *unlike* do not reign over two separate domains, but always operate in conjunction. Resemblance and difference are matters of degree, whereas identity and difference are matters of kind or class.

The problem of resemblance underlies the problem of predication that annoyed Socrates at *Republic* 479b. He notes the strange fact that the application of a predicate always involves the application of its opposite, for example, what is small is also large, and what is light is also heavy. There is no determinate boundary between being small and being large, being light and being heavy. These predicates are applied to the phenomenal objects because they are copies of the Forms as their paradigms, but the copies are never identical with but only resemble their originals. Because *likeness* cannot be separated from *unlikeness* in the relation of resemblance, the application of a predicate cannot be separated from the application of its opposite. In the logic of resemblance, when the principle of likeness overrides the principle of unlikeness in the comparison of two things, they will be assigned to the same class. When the relation of two principles is reversed, the two things will be assigned to different classes. When neither principle can dominate the other, the two things become the borderline cases that belong to the indeterminate zone between the two classes.

The logic of classes and the logic of resemblance respectively represent the world of Forms and the world of phenomena. Throughout the *Sophist* and the *Statesman*, the Eleatic Stranger uses the logic of resemblances, because he is defining the phenomenal objects. He exclusively relies on paradigms of the phenomenal world such as a hunter and herder, and mentions the once-touted mathematical paradigm only to make fun of it. He first reminds the Young Socrates that he and his friend Theaetetus are interested in geometry (266a). He then proceeds to employ the square root of two feet in producing a definition that places the humans and the pigs in the same class. He calls it a famous joke. His use of mathematics is much like the ridiculous use of mathematics in the humanities and social sciences, and even in natural sciences in our day.

Many of us are tempted to build mathematical models for no other reason than our blind faith that those models are the only legitimate tools for all inquiries. The mathematical joke is especially important, because the objects of definition in the *Sophist* and the *Statesman* are not transcendental but phenomenal. There is no transcendent Form of sophist or statesman; the different Forms (or kinds) of hunters and herders, sophists and statesmen, are all empirical. In the last chapter, we noted that the objects of inquiry for the science of phenomena are the empirical Forms. But these Forms are too complex and too indeterminate to be neatly described by mathematical tools. This is another way of saying that they cannot be the objects of exact sciences. This is the basic difference between the world of Forms and the world of phenomena.

Truly exact science is possible only for the world of Forms, for example, mathematics; all sciences for the world of phenomena are more or less inexact. To elucidate this point further, the Eleatic Stranger uses the arithmetical attributes of being two-footed and four-footed in his definition schemes. The paradigm of bipeds shows the resemblance between humans and birds; the two paradigms of bipeds and quadrupeds show the difference between humans and pigs. However, neither of these mathematical paradigms is of any use in identifying the essential nature of human beings. When the Eleatic Stranger divides the art of measurement into two kinds, one of them is quantitative and the other is normative (284e). The former handles mathematical quantities such as number, length, depth, breadth, and thickness; the latter involves qualitative terms such as *moderate, fitting,* and *timely,* all of which belong to the logic of resemblance.

There is one more reason why the logic of resemblance is much more difficult to use than the classical logic of classes. The logic of resemblance can map out many different lines of resemblance and difference. For example, humans (the featherless bipeds) are like birds in having two legs, but unlike them in not being feathered. And we may not be able to know how many lines of resemblance and difference there are between any two objects. But we have to decide which of these lines are significant and which are not. This decision can be made only by our purpose of definition and our sense of reality. Though the logic of resemblance is much more unwieldy than the classical logic of classes, it is the only way to gain a decent description of the infinitely complex phenomena. This is another reason why the description of phenomena is like the computation of irrational numbers. We can only hope to have decent approximations, which are accurate enough to identify and distinguish things for our practical purposes.

So we come back to the two great principles of identity and difference, which underlie *Logos*-I and *Logos*-D. These two principles have become Plato's overriding concern ever since their initial appearance in the guise of the method of *diairesis* in the *Phaedrus*. In the *Theaetetus*, they have been transformed into the two basic ways of knowing. In the *Sophist* and the *Statesman*, the two principles of identity and difference constitute the new method of dialectic. In the *Sophist*, *identity* and *difference* are officially accepted as two of the five ultimate categories. In the *Parmenides*, they provide the categoreal basis for the dialectic of the One and the Many. Without these two categories, there can be no distinction of the One from the Many, or of the Many from one another. In the *Philebus*, they will provide the categoreal basis for the divine method of introducing order into the Indeterminate Dyad (15d–17d). In the *Timaeus*, they will constitute the basic principles for the construction of the World-Soul (35a). They are the same basic principles of cognition for the World-Soul as they are for the human soul (37bc), and perhaps for the souls of the frogs and the pigs as well.

Except for the doctrine of Forms, there is no other doctrine that receives such repeated attention and emphasis in Plato's works as the doctrine of *identity* and *difference* does. In the late dialogues, as a matter of fact, this doctrine takes on the same significance as the doctrine of Forms did in the middle dialogues. It is the ultimate ground of all *logos* and knowledge, especially the *logos* of phenomena. At *Theaetetus* 180ab, Socrates observed how discourse had become impossible for the radical Heracliteans; at *Cratylus* 383e–384a, Hermogenes said how the discourse of another Heraclitean Cratylus had deteriorated to a game of dissimulation and mystification. This later Heraclitean tendency goes against the original spirit of Heraclitus's own teaching. He had stressed not only the flux of the phenomenal world, but also its *logos*. Plato's effort to devise a suitable *logos* of phenomena is his effort to restore the original spirit of Heraclitean legacy.

Notes

1. *Plato on Knowledge and Reality* (Indianapolis, Ind.: Hackett, 1976), 179.

2. Fine, "Knowledge and *Logos* in the *Theaetetus*," *Philosophical Review* 88 (1979):366–97.

3. Annas, "Knowledge and Language: the *Theaetetus* and the *Cratylus*,"

in *Language and Logos,* Malcolm Schofield and Martha Nussbaum, eds. (Cambridge: University Press, 1982), 95–114, esp. 113.

4. Fine, "Knowledge and *Logos* in the *Theaetetus*," 386.

5. Cornford, *Plato's Theory of Knowledge* (London: Routledge, 1935), 143.

6. For example, John McDowell in his translation of Plato, *Theaetetus* (Oxford: University Press, 1973), 252.

7. This is the view of John McDowell, trans., Plato, *Theaetetus*, 254.

8. Gettier, "Is Justified True Belief Knowledge?" *Analysis* 23 (1963), 121–23.

9. For further discussion, see William Alston, "Epistemic Circularity," *Philosophy and Phenomenological Research* 47 (1986):1–30.

10. Bertrand Russell recognizes the problem of circularity in the definition of knowledge and the importance of intuitive knowledge. *The Problems of Philosophy* (Oxford: University Press, 1959), 132–33.

11. A standard method is shown by Brian Fogelman and D. S. Hutchinson, " 'Seventeen' Subtleties in Plato's *Theaetetus*," *Phronesis* 35 (1990):303–6.

12. Dancy, "Theaetetus' First Baby: *Theaetetus* 151e–160e," *Philosophical Topics* 15 (1987):61-108.

13. Cornford, *Plato's Theory of Knowledge*, 162.

14. Bostock, *Plato's* Theaetetus (Oxford: University Press, 1988), 268–70.

15. Burnyeat, The *Theaetetus* of Plato (Indianapolis, Ind.: Hackett, 1990), 240.

16. McDowell, trans., Plato, *Theaetetus*, 259.

17. Brumbaugh, *Plato's Mathematical Imagination* (Bloomington: Indiana University Press, 1954), 40.

18. Sayre, *Plato's Analytical Method* (Chicago: University of Chicago Press, 1969), 60–61.

19. Burnyeat, "The Philosophical Sense of Theaetetus' Mathematics," *Isis* 69 (1978): 510-12.

20. His method of computation is the method of reciprocal subtraction and proportion. Wilbur Knorr, *The Evolution of the Euclidean Elements* (Dordrecht: Reidel, 1975), 255–73; D. H. Fowler, *The Mathematics of Plato's Academy* (Oxford: University Press, 1987), 31–42.

21. Mitchell Miller gives a different account of the connection from the *Theaetetus* to the *Sophist* and the *Statesman. The Philosopher in Plato's Statesman* (The Hague: Nijhoff, 1980), and "Unity and *Logos*: A Reading of *Theaetetus* 201c–210a," *Ancient Philosophy* 12 (1992):87–111.

22. Rosen, *Plato's Sophist* (New Haven, Conn.: Yale University Press, 1983), 141.

23. Cornford, *Plato's Theory of Knowledge*, 185.

24. Rosen, *Plato's Sophist*, 208.

25. Guthrie, *A History of Greek Philosophy* (Cambridge: University Press, 1978), 5:164.

CHAPTER SIX

New Theory of Forms

The *Parmenides* and the *Sophist*

In the *Parmenides*, Plato subjects his theory of Forms to a rigorous critique. This dialogue is divided into two parts. In the first part, the old Parmenides takes the young Socrates through a series of questions about the theory of Forms, and demonstrates its absurd consequences. When the young Socrates candidly confesses his inability to cope with those consequences, the old Parmenides attributes his difficulties to his youth and immaturity, and prescribes a system of dialectical exercises for his metaphysical education. These exercises constitute the second part of the dialogue; they consist of accepting eight hypotheses one after another and following through the logical consequences of each. These dialectical exercises are the most obscure and enigmatic pieces Plato ever wrote, and no one has been able to give an intelligible and satisfactory account of them. Before tackling this enigmatic part of the dialogue, let us consider the first part.

The Theory of Forms and Parmenides' Critique

Let us go over the series of questions Parmenides raises against the theory of Forms. First, he wants to know the scope of Forms. Are there

Forms of not only Justice and Beauty, but also Man, Fire, or Water, and even Hair, Mud, Dirt, and many other undignified objects (130bc)? Socrates has never clearly defined the scope of Forms. In the *Symposium*, he talked about only the Forms of Beauty, Goodness, and Justice. In the *Phaedo*, in addition to these ethical and aesthetic Forms, he also talked about the mathematical Forms such as Odd and Even, Equality and Largeness, and then the Forms of Fire and Snow, Hot and Cold. In the *Republic*, he even talked about the Form of Bed. Now Parmenides is suggesting a further extension of their scope to such undignified things as mud and dirt. Since these Forms are not much different from Fire and Snow, Socrates has no good reason to object to the proposed extension, and he feels quite uneasy about it. Parmenides points out that his uneasiness is not governed by any rational principle.

Without resolving this problem, Parmenides questions Socrates about the doctrine of participation. Though this doctrine has been used by Socrates in other dialogues, it has never been fully explained. How can a Form, which is supposedly one and indivisible, be in many things? This is not a difficult question if the Form is understood as an abstract entity. However, Socrates has claimed its concreteness; this is the doctrine of paradigmatic Forms, as we noted in chapter 3. It is also the doctrine of reification. In Aristotle's words, this means to regard the Form as a substance rather than as a predicate or attribute of something (*Metaphysics* 987b23). With the reification of Forms, the doctrine of *part*icipation literally means having a *part*, that is, an object has a share or piece of a Form as its own constituent. A Form can be in many things only by dividing itself into many parts and parceling out each of those parts to each of the many phenomenal objects. Obviously, this account of participation is absurd, but its absurdity only reveals the absurdity of Platonic reification.

Platonic reification also leads to the doctrine of self-predication and the third man argument (131e–132b). If the Form of Largeness is itself large (self-predication), there must be another Form, which is shared by the Form of Largeness and large things. To meet these objections, Socrates proposes that each Form be understood as a thought, which can exist only in a mind (132b). On that supposition, Parmenides responds, each Form must be a thought of something, and this object of thought, which is the same in all cases, must have exactly the same characteristics that he has attributed to the Form. By converting a Form into a thought, Socrates cannot get rid of the Form because a thought requires a Form for its object. To meet this objection, Socrates now says that a Form should be conceived as a pattern whose likeness is copied by the phenomenal objects. On this conception of Forms, the participation should be understood as the relation of copies to their original pattern (132d). But Parmenides points out that the relation of likeness between the original and its copy leads back to the third man argument.[1]

These are indeed formidable objections to the theory of Forms. But Parmenides says that there is an even more serious objection than these, namely, the Forms are unknowable if they are truly separate existences. His argument is as follows. Take the master-slave relation, for instance. A master is the master of a slave in this world, but not of the Form of Slave. On the other hand, the Form of Master is the master of the Form of Slave, but not of any slave in this world. The Forms are related only to one another, and the phenomenal objects are also related to one another. But there is no relation between the Forms and the phenomena, but only total separation. This is the doctrine of separation. Parmenides now points out that the same separation should obtain between the Form of Knowledge and the phenomenal knowledge. The Form of Knowledge knows only the Forms and never the phenomenal objects, while the phenomenal knowledge knows only the phenomenal objects and never the Forms. Since we have only phenomenal knowledge, we can never know the Forms.

Two points stand out in Parmenides' critique: the separation of Forms and their reification. These two problems involve two different conceptions of the Form: (1) as abstract and (2) as concrete. As an abstract entity, the Form is a universal; as a concrete entity, it is a paradigm or exemplum.[2] It is the unique feature of Plato's theory of Forms that they are at once an abstract universal and a concrete particular. This feature is indeed strange. It goes against our commonsense understanding that the demarcation between abstract universals and concrete particulars is exclusive each of the other. But Plato does not thrust this strange feature directly to his readers; he rather leads them gradually into his strange doctrine first by advocating the doctrine of self-predication and then the doctrine of self-exemplification. Here are two well-known instances of self-predication from the *Protagoras*:

(1) Justice is just.

(2) Piety is pious.

The doctrine of self-predication does not automatically translate into the doctrine of reification. These two sentences can be interpreted in such a way that they can dispense with the separate existence of Forms. Though there are more than one way of doing it, I will cite only Gregory Vlastos's theory of Pauline predication. He takes its paradigm from St. Paul's statement, "Charity is kind." Vlastos renders this statement as:

(3) Charity is such that anyone who is charitable is
     [necessarily] kind.[3]

He shows many other Pauline statements that can be parsed in this manner: "Love is blind," "Justice is impartial," "Honesty is rare," etc. No doubt, the same interpretation can be given to Sentences (1) and (2).

The doctrine of Pauline predication construes the subject term of (1) and (2) not as a substantive but as an attribute, which can be distributed to whoever has it. Its purpose is to avoid mistaking the abstract noun *justice* for a substantive, or rather the mistake of its reification. The same purpose can be achieved by replacing the noun with an attributive phrase, "to be just":

(4) To be just is just.

This is roughly what Constance Meinwald calls the *pros heauto* (in relation to itself) predication in distinction from the *pros ta alla* (in relation to others) predication.[4] No doubt, as she claims, this is the best way to get rid of the third man argument. She is absolutely correct because this argument arises from the reification of Forms.

Pauline predication is perfectly acceptable for the *Protagoras*, because this dialogue does not assert the separate existence of Forms. But it is not for the *Phaedo* and the *Symposium*. When Socrates says, "Beauty is beautiful" in these dialogues, he is not stating the truism that to be beautiful is beautiful, but that there is the Form of Beauty and that it is beautiful. This is Platonic predication. Though both Pauline and Platonic predications involve self-predication, they are radically different about their subject terms. In Pauline predication, the subject term is only a universal; in Platonic predication, it is not only a universal but also a particular. It is a paradigm. In Platonic predication, self-predication amounts to self-exemplification. Strictly speaking, even these two are not enough for Platonic predication; it requires super-predication and super-exemplification (The Form of Beauty is more beautiful than any of its instances), and absolute predication and exemplification (the Form of Beauty is absolutely beautiful in every respect).

Though Platonic predication sounds outlandish, it is essential for Plato's theory of knowledge and experience in his middle dialogues. No doubt, the theory of Forms was initially introduced to support the Platonic view that there are normative standards and a priori truths that transcend the empirical world, and that our knowledge of them cannot be accounted for without accepting the separate existence of Forms. But their separate existence need not be taken to be anything more than their independence of the world of phenomena, and there is no need to assert the doctrine of paradigmatic Forms, that is, they are not simply abstract universals but concrete paradigms. For all the a priori or transcendental functions of Forms in the normative and cognitive domains can be well discharged by the abstract Forms. But the *Phaedo* and the *Symposium* assign one more function to the transcendent Forms. It is the experiential function: the Form of Beauty is not only an abstract concept of beauty, but also a concrete object of aesthetic experience. Its absolute exemplification means that it alone can give the absolutely fulfilling aesthetic experience.

The experiential function is required for the mystical or erotic Socrates, whereas the normative and the cognitive functions are sufficient for the ethical and the political Socrates. But the experiential function is far less plausible than the normative or cognitive function. However, Socrates cleverly used the Form of Beauty in explaining the experiential function, and in giving it some semblance of plausibility. He often compares the Forms to mathematical objects, whose beauty is well recognized by his audience. By this comparison, he shrewdly advances a plausible argument for self-predication and self-exemplification for the Form of Beauty. But the absurdity of Platonic predication becomes obvious, as soon as we try to extend it to other Forms than the Form of Beauty. For example, how can the Form of Justice exemplify the attribute of justice?

At *Republic* 500c, Socrates indeed says that the Forms do no wrong to each other. In a sense, this statement is a truism; the Forms can never inflict any injury on each other because they are eternal and inanimate entities that can never be hurt by anything. But Socrates makes this assertion as a proposition of self-exemplification for the Form of Justice and other Forms, that is, the Form of Justice exemplifies the attribute of justice in its relation with other Forms. Such an exemplification, however, makes sense only in a community of agents who can interact with one another, but the Form of Justice does not belong to such a community. Since it can never be an agent of just or unjust acts, its self-exemplification is absurd. For the same reason, it is equally absurd to say that the Form of Master is the master of the Form of Slave, that is, the former orders around the latter, or to say that the Form of Knowledge knows all the Forms, as Parmenides suggested to the young Socrates (*Parmenides* 134b). To know something or to be a master is a conscious act that cannot be performed by the Forms, which are eternally unconscious entities.

The absurdity of self-exemplification, which arises from the conception of Forms as concrete paradigms, is in the center of Parmenides' critique. Though the Young Socrates cannot cope with this critique, Parmenides concedes that it is equally impossible to dispense with the Forms altogether, because their elimination will destroy the significance of all thought and discourse (135c). This is the transcendental argument for the existence of Forms: they are the necessary conditions for the possibility of thinking and talking. If Socrates wants to keep the Forms, Parmenides says, he should be able to give a better account of them. To this end, he recommends a series of stiff dialectical exercises, which constitute the second part of the dialogue.

Eight Categoreal Systems

The dialectical exercises revolve around eight hypotheses, which are exceedingly obscure and opaque. Consequently, there have been a wide spectrum of interpretations, ranging from the Neoplatonic view that those exercises constitute the process of emanation from the ultimate One, to the simple view that they are dialectical tricks.[5] Instead of examining these conflicting interpretations, I would like to offer my own. I will take the eight hypotheses as eight categoreal systems. By "a categoreal system" I mean a system of primitive predicates such as Aristotle's or Kant's categoreal systems. This is a semantic interpretation that should be distinguished from an ontological one. To explain their difference, let us take the theological problem of God on the semantic and ontological levels. On the semantic level, we want to know what sort of predicates should be employed in our conception of God. On the ontological level, we want to know which of these predicates is really true of God. Since semantic investigations can be ontologically noncommittal, they can serve as preliminary exercises for the ontological exploration.

The distinction between these two approaches will become clearer and take on greater significance as our discussion progresses. But for the moment I want to stress that the central issue of the *Parmenides* is not ontological but semantic. As we already noted, Parmenides and Socrates are chiefly concerned with the problem of accounting for the possibility of discourse, the most important problem in semantics. But the ontological problem is going to be settled not in the *Parmenides* but in the *Sophist*. It is my thesis that the *Parmenides* offers a series of semantic exercises in preparation for the important ontological decisions to be made in the *Sophist*. These semantic exercises are given in the eight hypotheses, and they are all *hypothetical* because they are meant to explore all the semantic possibilities of different categoreal systems without making any ontological commitment. In another word, they are only hypothetical considerations.

The eight hypotheses are divided into two groups of four, each of which can be further divided into two groups of two. The first two hypotheses, H_1 and H_2, are concerned with the One; the second two, H_3 and H_4, are concerned with the Many (or Others). These four hypotheses constitute the first tetrad. The remaining four hypotheses are again divided into two groups of two. H_5 and H_6 are concerned with the One;

H_7 and H_8 are concerned with the Many (or Others). These four hypotheses constitute the second tetrad. Let us first examine the first tetrad.

Though the One is the common topic for both H_1 and H_2, it is different in the two hypotheses. The One of H_1 is described as the absolute unity, which has no parts (137c). The One of H_2 is described as having parts; it is a whole of parts (142d). It is a complex unity in contrast to the simple or absolute unity of the One in H_1. Such an absolute unity can be neither in motion nor at rest. It can be neither the same as nor different from itself or another. It cannot even have a name or be spoken of; it can never be an object of knowledge and opinion. H_1 totally eliminates the possibility of discourse. The One of H_2 yields exactly the opposite result; it can be described in many different ways because it is complex. One and Being are its two parts. Beginning with these two, Parmenides deduces a multitude of other parts: *limited* and *unlimited*, *identity* and *difference*, *motion* and *rest*, *equality* and *inequality*, and the other categories, all of which are denied of the One of H_1.

The semantic implication of H_2 is the opposite of that of H_1. Whereas nothing can be said about the One of H_1, too many things can be said about the One of H_2 and many of them lead to contradictions. In that case, H_2 should also make discourse impossible. But Parmenides dissolves the contradictions of H_2 by installing H_{2a}, which distributes the contradictory predicates over different times—for example, the One can have existence at one time and no existence at another (155e). With the dissolution of contradictions, H_2 can provide a sound semantic basis for discourse. H_1 and H_2 are semantically opposite. The predicates that cannot be assigned to the One of H_1 can be assigned to the One of H_2. The second hypothesis secures the possibility of discourse, while the first hypothesis assures its impossibility.

Kenneth Sayre regards the examination of H_1 as Plato's critique and rejection of Parmenides. He points out that the eight sets of attributes denied of the One in H_1 are derived from the attributes Parmenides claims for Being in his *Way of Truth*.[6] But these attributes cannot be predicated of the Parmenidean One, if it is the absolutely simple unity as Parmenides claims. Hence his doctrine of Being should be rejected. Though this is an acute observation, there is another way of reading the first two hypotheses. Instead of taking them as the rejection of Parmenides' doctrine of Being, we can take them as two ways of interpreting it. H_1 is the semantic interpretation of the Parmenidean One as an absolute unity, and H_2 is its interpretation by the attributes Parmenides himself uses in informally talking about the One. The incompatibility of the two hypotheses reveals the contradiction between the two accounts of Being given in the *Way of Truth*, the formal and the informal.

Sayre makes another interesting suggestion: H_2 is a strong defense of Pythagoreanism, especially its two basic theses that *unity* generates number and that number is constitutive of sensible things. And he adds that there has been a history of Eleatic attempts to discredit these two theses.[7] Indeed, the generation of number is a salient feature of H_2, and it can be taken as a Pythagorean trait. But Sayre overlooks an important point. Whereas the One of H_2 is primitive, the One of Pythagorean tradition is derivative. It is generated from the two primal principles of *limit* and *unlimited*.[8] In H_2, however, *limit* and *unlimited* are not prior to the One. They arise along with other predicates in the categoreal specification of the One. In H_2, moreover, number is generated from two and three, which are generated from the complexity of the One, namely, its three features of *being* and *oneness*, and their *difference* (143a–e).

In H_2, the One does not generate its parts, but already contains them as its parts. Nor are the sensible objects generated by number. As we will see shortly, the One is already conceived of as an empirical object. It is already one whole with two parts, namely, its *being* and its *unity*. Each of these two parts is in turn a whole with two parts, because its *being* must have its own *unity* as well as its own *being*. Likewise, its *unity* must have its own *being* as well as its own *unity*. This process of dividing a whole into parts goes on like an endless chain reaction, and this chain reaction generates the indefinite multitude and then number. In H_2, the generation of number simultaneously employs a monad and a dyad, whereas the Pythagorean method employs only the monad.[9] The complex One of H_2 with its two parts (*being* and *unity*) is a combination of a monad and a dyad into a single entity.

At this point, perhaps, we should be clear about the nature of categoreal deduction in the *Parmenides*. The parts and whole in the One of H_2 are not generated any more than the absolute unity of the One of H_1 is.

They are postulated by the two hypotheses. On that condition, Parmenides considers what sort of predicates are required for describing each of the two Ones. His method of deduction is at once hypothetical and transcendental. Hence, it should not be confused with the Pythagorean method of deduction, which generates everything from the One, which is in turn generated from the *limit* and the *unlimited*.[10] This generative method was further elaborated by the various versions of Neoplatonism, which spin out the whole world from the One. No such generative procedure is involved in the Platonic method of categoreal derivation. The generative derivation is an ontological operation; the categoreal derivation is a semantic one.

The Pythagoreans and the Eleatics had a long dispute over the question, "Which is primary, *being* or *number*?" The Pythagoreans maintained the primacy of *number* over *being*, by claiming that *number* can generate all things. On the other hand, the Eleatics maintained the primacy of *being* over *number*, by claiming that *being* must be presupposed by *number* (without *being*, *number* cannot *be*). H_2 can be read as a proposal for resolving this dispute. If the Parmenidean Being is a whole with parts, those parts cannot be distinguished without number.[11] If so, the concept of number is presupposed in the concept of being. On the other hand, the concept of being is equally presupposed by the concept of the Pythagorean One. Without the concept of being, the number cannot be said to *be*, nor can the different numbers *be* differentiated from each other. Since the two concepts of being and number presuppose each other, there is no point in asserting the priority of one over the other. This is a typically Platonic reconciliation of the two schools; it avoids reductionism by accepting the legitimate claims of both views in its synthesis.[12]

Kenneth Sayre has taken the first two hypotheses as Plato's position on the ancient battle between the Eleatics and the Pythagoreans.[13] In his view, the first hypothesis is Plato's attack on the Eleatics; the second hypothesis is his defense of the Pythagoreans. But we can find a better account. Instead of associating H_1 with Eleaticism and H_2 with Pythagoreanism, we should take the two hypotheses as two ways of interpreting Parmenidean Being, as I suggested earlier. Instead of simply endorsing Pythagorean constructivism in H_2, Plato modifies it in such a way as to reconcile the Pythagoreans with the Eleatics on the ontological question of number. He does not take side with either of the two camps, but finds a way to reconcile their differences.

Before going further, let us note that there are two different approaches for understanding the eight hypotheses. One way is the historical approach. This is the attempt to find out which philosophical school of ancient Greece is represented by each of the eight hypotheses, for example, whether Pythagoreanism is represented by H_2. The other way is purely formal. This is to take the eight hypotheses as purely formal schemata for a categoreal system. I prefer this approach to the historical one, because I believe it was Plato's own. From my formal perspective, it is only a matter of accidental interest whether any of the eight hypotheses represents or even resembles any ontological system of ancient Greece.

Let us now consider H_3 and H_4. H_3 is associated with H_2; H_4 is associated with H_1. The One of H_1 as the absolute unity without any parts is accepted for the semantic account of H_4 and its Many (or Others). Because the One is the absolute unity, it can have no relation with the Many. Neither can the Many have unity because they are totally separated from the One. They can have neither likeness nor unlikeness, be neither in motion nor at rest, and neither come to be nor cease to be. They can have no properties or relations at all (159d–160b). In that case, nothing can be said or known about them. The semantic consequence of H_4 is exactly the same as that of H_1, because they stand on the same notion of the One.

The One of H_2 as a complex unity is the basis for the semantic interpretation of H_3. The Many of H_3 partake in the One of H_2 in two ways (157b–e). They are parts of one whole, and each of them is a whole having its own parts. If the Many are shown to be parts of one whole, H_3 is equivalent to H_2. H_2 starts out with the One and shows that it is a whole having many parts. This dialectical process is reversed by H_3, which starts out with the Many and shows that they belong to the One as its parts, or that each of them is a One. Hence all the predicates that are derived in H_2 are accepted in H_3 (158e–159b). H_2 and H_3 are semantically equivalent, just as H_1 and H_4 are.

In summing up the result of his discourse on the first four hypotheses,

Parmenides says, "Thus, if there is a One, the One is both all things and nothing whatsoever, alike with reference to itself and to the Others" (160b, trans. Cornford). This statement has been a puzzle. He talks as though the One had been the common topic for the four hypotheses, but this is clearly inconsistent with the text of the dialogue. In the first two hypotheses, the topic of discussion was indeed the One. But the discussion clearly shifted to the topic of the Many in the last two hypotheses. In summing up the result, Parmenides appears to have forgotten one of the two topics in his own discourse. But this is justifiable in our interpretation. The Many turns out to be no more than the Many of Ones, each of which has to be the One of either H_1 or H_2.

In H_5 and H_6, the discussion returns to the One. But the One ("if the One is not") of these two hypotheses is different from the One ("if the One is") of the first two hypotheses. The former are the nonexistent Ones; the latter are the existent Ones. What is meant by "the nonexistent One" or "the existent One"? Since Parmenides does not explain these terms, we can only infer their meanings contextually. In the first four hypotheses, Parmenides has consistently restricted the notion of being to the phenomenal world (141e, 152a). Hence, the One in these four hypotheses can be any phenomenal object such as a rock, a tree, an atom, or the entire physical world.

This interpretation may appear to be incompatible with Parmenides' statement that the One of H_1 has nothing to do with time, and that it has never become, is becoming, or will become (141e). In fact, this statement has been the source of the Neoplatonic interpretation that the One is the Form of the Good or God that transcends the space-time world.[14] But Parmenides' statement in question can be construed either ontologically or semantically. If it is taken ontologically, the Neoplatonic interpretation is correct. If it is taken semantically, it means something quite different, that is, the temporal categories do not apply to the One of H_1 because its absolute simplicity allows no predication. Though the One may well be in time, we just cannot say that it is in time. It is not a question of where the One is, but a question of what categories can be applied to it.

While the One of the first four hypotheses is phenomenal and immanent, the One of the last four hypotheses is transcendent. It is "the nonexistent One''. It does not exist in the space-time world, for example, a Platonic Form or an eidetic entity. This interpretation is supported by Parmenides' illustration of ''if the One is not.'' He says this statement is like ''if *largeness* does not exist,'' or ''if *smallness* does not exist'' (160c). *Largeness* and *smallness* are two well-known examples of Platonic Forms; in H_2, Parmenides said that neither of them can be in the One (149e–150d). If the One of H_2 is existent in space and time, while *largeness* and *smallness* are not existent in space and time, the latter cannot be in the former.

Though the One of H_6 is transcendent and the One of H_1 is phenomenal, they are semantically equivalent. The One of H_6 has neither being, nor properties, nor relations. Just like the One of H_1, it cannot be an object of discourse, knowledge, opinion, or perception (164ab). At the outset, the One of H_5 behaves like the One of H_2. It can be an object of discourse and knowledge, because it has most of the properties and relations that are attributed to the One of H_2. But when it comes to the question of being, its categoreal scheme gets more complicated than that of H_2. The One of H_5 must have being in some sense, though it is said not to exist (161e). So Parmenides concludes that the One has existence and nonexistence. Likewise, the One is both in motion and at rest, and comes to be and ceases to be (162e–163b). It appears that the One of H_5 is trapped in a nest of contradictions. Parmenides does not try to dissolve them by spreading the contradictory predicates over the different moments of time as he did for the contradictions of H_2. This method would not work for the One of H_5, because its predicates transcend the temporal domain.

The contradictory predicates of H_5 can be parceled out into the two worlds of transcendence and immanence; for example, the One is not in the phenomenal world but it is in the transcendent world. It can take the following predicates: *knowable, same* and *different, of this one character* (rather than another), *like* and *unlike, equal* and *unequal, being* and *not-being, transition from being to not-being,* but *no locomotion* or *alteration* in space and time (160b–163b). These predicates are different from those assigned to the phenomenal One of H_2: *whole* and *parts, limited* and *unlimited, plurality* and *number, shape* and *extension, place* and *location, motion* (locomotion and alteration) and *rest, same* and *different, like* and *unlike, contact* with itself and others, *equality* and *inequality, temporal predicates* (older and younger), *epistemic predicates* (knowable and perceivable), *combination* and *separation, increase* and *decrease, assimilation* and *dissimilation* (142c–157b). The temporal and spatial predicates, especially locomotion and alteration, are included in this set of predicates, but excluded from the other set.

The Many of H_7 are semantically linked to the One of H_5. Unlike the One, however, the Many are not eidetic but existent entities, that is, they exist in the phenomenal world (164b). They are the masses or the multitude of material objects. Each of the Many appears to be one or the smallest unit, but turns out to be many. It is indefinitely divisible. These masses appear to have the properties and relations that can be described by the categories of H_2 and H_3, namely, *unity* and *plurality, odd* and *even, limited* and *unlimited, great* and *small, equality* and *inequality, likeness* and *unlikeness*. But none of them truly applies to the Many; they only appear to participate in those Forms (164e–165d). They make up the world of *appearance*.

The difference between H_3 and H_7 can be explained by the Democritean and the Kantian conception of matter. Democritus claims that the physical world consists of absolutely indivisible atoms; Kant claims that there are no such atoms and that every physical object can be further divided. The Democritean atoms are the Many of H_3; each of them is truly one. The Kantian objects are the Many of H_7; each of them only appears to be one. The unity of a Democritean atom is physical and real; it is a One that cannot be physically divided. The unity of a Kantian object is not physical but conceptual or eidetic; it is a One *as* a stone or *as* a tree, that is, by virtue of the eidos or concept of a stone or a tree. The eidetic unity for the Many of H_7 is provided by the One of H_5. But the eidetic unity of a physical object is different from the eidetic unity of an eidos or concept itself. The latter unity is real, but the former unity is only apparent. A stone or a tree appears to be one entity, but it can be divided into many entities.

The Many of H_8 have neither the real unity of H_3, nor the apparent unity of H_7. They have no unity whatsoever, whether it be eidetic or physical. Since they are totally devoid of unity, nothing can be said or known about them. No properties and relations can be assigned to them, and not even the appearance of having any properties and relations. Semantically, the Many of H_8 are as elusive as the One of H_6. This is not a coincidence. The semantic interpretation of H_8 presupposes the One of H_6. Unlike the One of H_5, the One of H_6 cannot provide the eidetic or apparent unity to the Many of H_8 because the One is totally separated from the Many. The One of H_6 is too simple to have any communion with the Many of H_8. Hence the Many cannot be the objects of knowledge or opinion (166a). Under the last hypothesis, so Parmenides concludes, there is nothing at all. The Many of H_8 are as good as nothing; so is the One of H_6.

These eight hypotheses exhaust all the possible categoreal systems. So the Parmenidean exercises turn out to be a systematic examination of all the possible categoreal schemes. That may explain the role of the young Aristotle as Parmenides' respondent in these exercises. Many things have been written about the identity of this young man, but I am inclined to identify him with the Aristotle of the *Categoriae*, the first treatise for a systematic account of categories. By the time Plato was writing and reading the *Parmenides* in his Academy, probably, the young Aristotle was already there and showed special interest in the subject. His metaphysical training might have begun with rigorous categoreal exercises like the ones we find in the *Parmenides*, and that might have paved the way for the development of his logic.

The unique feature of Aristotle's logical treatises, the *Organon*, is that it opens with the *Categoriae*. Since this treatise deals with such metaphysical concepts as *substance* and *accident*, it appears to be misplaced by our modern standard. Many modern logicians and metaphysicians have felt that the *Categoriae* is a part of Aristotle's metaphysics rather than of his logic. Here, however, lies the basic difference between his logic and modern formal logic. The *Categoriae* provides the semantic basis for his theory of predication (or proposition) and inference in his *Organon*, whereas such a semantic basis is disavowed by modern logic because it is meant to be purely formal and syntactic. Aristotle's logic is not purely formal or syntactic like modern logic; it is constructed on a well-defined semantic basis. In my view, his conception of a semantically based logic is a Platonic legacy. Plato not only examines the different categoreal systems in the *Parmenides*, but also maintains in the *Sophist* that a system of categories is the semantic basis for the art of predication and discourse (*logos*).

Let us consider the mutual relation of all the eight hypotheses. H_8 is the complement to H_6. Together they show the impossibility of talking about the One and the Many, as H_1 and H_4 have done. But the One of H_1 is opposed to the One of H_6. The former is transcendent; the latter is immanent. And yet they are alike in being the absolutely simple unity, which cannot be talked about. H_8 is the counterpart to H_4; they take the Many as the absolute plurality without any unity, which is equally impossible to talk about. The One of H_5 is opposed to the One of H_2. The former is transcendent; the latter is immanent. But they are alike in having a complex unity. H_7 is the counterpart to H_3; they take the Many as an assemblage of the many Ones. But each of the Many in H_3 is truly one, while each of the Many in H_7 only appears to be one.

These mutual relations of the eight hypotheses can be derived from the combinatorics of the two pairs of predicates that can be assigned to the One: simple and complex, and transcendent and immanent. The One can be either simple or complex, and either transcendent or immanent. By combining these two pairs, we can produce four different Ones: (1) the simple and immanent One, (2) the complex and immanent One, (3) the simple and transcendent One, and (4) the complex and transcendent One. These four Ones are distributed to the four hypotheses of H_1, H_2, H_5, and H_6. These four Ones then determine the nature of the Many in four different ways, which are represented in the four hypotheses of H_3, H_4, H_7, and H_8. Each of these four hypotheses is paired up with each of the other four: H_1–H_4, H_2–H_3, H_5–H_7, and H_6–H_8.

Of these four pairs, neither H_1–H_4 nor H_6–H_8 is acceptable as a categoreal system, because they make predication impossible. As I said before, a categoreal system is a system of predicates (the Greek word *kategoria* means a predicate). In spite of all the difficulties about the Forms, Parmenides said, they cannot be rejected because we can neither think nor talk without them (135c). If a categoreal system is for the sake of thinking and talking, there is no point in retaining H_1, H_4, H_6, or H_8. On the other hand, H_2, H_3, H_5, and H_7 can be employed as instruments of thinking and talking. Hence they are acceptable. Thus, the eight hypotheses divide themselves into two groups of four, one group to be rejected and the other group to be retained. All and only the hypotheses to be retained (H_2, H_3, H_5, and H_7) are designated by prime numbers. This is indeed intriguing. But this result is achieved by an elaborate maneuver in the enumeration of the eight hypotheses. The first two hypotheses are enumerated in the sequence of simple (the simple One) and complex (the complex One). If this sequence is to be repeated in the enumeration of the remaining hypotheses, the eight hypotheses will be lined up as follows:

Figure 1

1. the One (s + p)   2. the One (c + p)
3. the Many (s + p)   4. the Many (c + p)

5. the One (s + t)   6. the One (c + t)
7. the Many (s + p)   8. the Many (c + p)

The expression (s + p) stands for "simple and phenomenal"; (c + p) for "complex and phenomenal"; (s + t) for "simple and transcendent"; (c + t) for "complex and transcendent". In Figure 1, the sequence of simple and complex is repeated in the enumeration of eight hypotheses. But this repeated sequence does not appear in Plato's own enumeration:

Figure 2

1. the One (s + p)   2. the One (c + p)
3. the Many (c + p)   4. the Many (s + p)

5. the One (c + t)   6. the One (s + t)
7. the Many (c + p)   8. the Many (s + p)

In Figure 2, the first two hypotheses are given in the sequence of simple and complex, but this sequence is reversed in the enumeration of the third and the fourth hypotheses. Though the fifth and the sixth hypotheses again talk about the One, they do not repeat but reverse the sequence of the simple One and the complex One in the first two hypotheses. The last two hypotheses repeat the complex/simple se-

quence. There is no way of telling when Plato will use the simple/
complex or the complex/simple sequence in lining up each of the four
pairs of hypotheses. It appears that his only motive is to mark the four
retained hypotheses with prime numbers. What is the significance of
marking them with prime numbers? Prime numbers cannot be factored
except by themselves and one, which was not considered as a number
by the ancient Greeks. That they cannot be factored means that they are
irreducible; the Ones of the four retained hypotheses are irreducible,
just like prime numbers, though they are not simple but complex.

The Positive Dialectic

To demonstrate the irreducibility of the four prime numbered hypotheses is the positive result of the dialectical exercises in Part 2 of the
Parmenides. This positive result can be refined further. H_2 and H_3 are
semantically equivalent and convertible to each other. The One of H_2,
when multiplied, becomes the Many of H_3; each of the Many, when
separated, becomes the One. We can combine these two hypotheses into
one and label it as $H_{2=3}$. The relation of H_5 and H_7 is somewhat different; they presuppose each other. As we have already seen, the Many of
H_7 derive their unity from the One of H_5. On the other hand, the nonexistent One of H_5 can participate in existence via the Many of H_7. This
is how the predicates of being and nonbeing become applicable to the
One of H_5, as Parmenides says (162b). Thus H_5 and H_7 are mutually
dependent; neither of them can function without the other. They should
be combined into one categoreal system and be labeled as H_{5+7}.

The mutual dependence of H_5 and H_7 makes possible the participation relation between the world of Forms and the world of phenomena.
The same relation of mutual dependence does not obtain between H_6
and H_8. The One of H_6 is too simple, too absolute, and too aloof to
allow any communion between itself and the Many of H_8. Hence, there
is no participation relation between H_6 and H_8, and the Many of H_8
cannot even belong to the world of appearances. The unbridgeable
chasm between the One of H_6 and the Many of H_8 is the same sort of
absolute separation between the Forms and the phenomena that Parmen-

ides says makes impossible our access to the world of Forms and the gods' access to the sensible world (133a–134e). The characterization of the One of H_6 is exactly the same as the description of Forms in the *Phaedo*, the *Symposium*, and the *Republic*, that is, they are absolutely simple and transcendent.

The four retained hypotheses can be reduced to two: $H_{2=3}$ and H_{5+7}. They have different ontological scopes. $H_{2=3}$ is restricted to the phenomenal world; H_{5+7} covers both the phenomenal and the transcendent worlds. Let us now consider the scope of categories for these two systems. Since H_2 is equivalent to H_3, all the categories applicable to the One of H_2 are also applicable to the Many of H_3, because each of the Many is a One. The two categoreal systems have the same scope ($H_2 = H_3$). The categories of H_{2a}, which is an extension of H_2, also belongs to H_3. This point is important to stress. Because Parmenides does not repeat all the categories of H_2 and H_{2a} in his discussion of H_3, he may give the wrong impression that H_2 and H_3 have two different sets of categories. The categoreal scope of H_3 is in turn the same as that of H_7, because the Many of H_7 are the same as the Many of H_3 except in one regard. Each of the Many in H_7 is not truly one but only appears so, whereas each of the Many in H_3 is truly one. But this difference does not affect the scope of the categories. Hence H_7 is identical in its categoreal scope with H_2 and H_3, but H_{5+7} is broader than all of them because it is the addition of H_5 to H_7. In its categoreal scope, H_{5+7} is equivalent to H_{2+3+5}. Thus, $H_{2=3}$ is incorporated into H_{5+7}.

This is the final outcome of the Parmenidean dialectical exercises. This positive result goes against the traditional understanding of Part 2 of the dialogue. Though there have been many interpretations of the dialectical exercises, few of them have recognized any positive result. Most commentators assume that Parmenidean exercises are meant to discredit the eight hypotheses by exposing their contradictions. But there are two different accounts of these contradictions: the theory of internal contradictions and the theory of external contradictions. The theory of internal contradictions holds that each of the eight hypotheses generates its own internal contradiction. The theory of external contradictions locates contradictions not in each of the eight hypothesis, but in the conjunction of one with another, that is, in lining them up in four pairs of two competing hypotheses.

The theory of external contradictions regards the eight hypotheses as four pairs of antinomies in the same way the eight cosmological theses are paired up into four antinomies in Kant's *Critique of Pure Reason*. In this view, the important question is whether the antinomies are real or apparent. Those who regard the antinomies as real assign a serious purpose to the Parmenidean exercises. On the other hand, those who take them as apparent or specious antinomies look upon those exercises as frivolous games.[15] The antinomy theory is obviously true. For example, H_1 is a contradictory of H_2. H_1 entails that nothing can be said about the One; H_2 entails that many things can be said about the One. Given this contradiction, the important question is whether it can be resolved. If the contradiction is apparent, it is not even a problem. All we have to do is show that it is not a real contradiction. If the contradiction is real, it can be resolved by rejecting one of the paired hypotheses. For example, the contradiction of H_1 and H_2 can be resolved by the rejection of H_1. The same method can resolve the contradictions of the other pairs. Hence, the theory of external contradictions does not discredit the Parmenidean exercises.

The theory of internal contradictions can indeed discredit the Parmenidean exercises, because it locates the contradictions within each hypothesis.[16] Let us now see how well this theory holds up. It cannot apply to the four hypotheses, which permit no predication whatsoever, because there can be no contradictions without predication. On the other hand, each of the other four hypotheses appears to suffer from its internal contradictions. But these can be resolved. As we noted, the internal contradictions of H_2 are neatly dissolved by H_{2a}, and those of H_3 can be handled in the same manner because H_3 is equivalent to H_2. The internal contradictions of H_5 can be resolved by recognizing the two worlds of transcendence and immanence as two separate domains of predication. The distinction of these two domains functions just like the demarcation of time into different moments for resolving the internal contradictions of H_2. The internal contradictions of H_7 can be resolved in the same way those of H_3 are resolved, because the Many of H_7 are in space and time just like the Many of H_3.

Most commentators assume that the negative thrust of the dialectical exercises is not only set by Zeno's negative tone at the opening of the dialogue, but confirmed by Parmenides' two summations of his own discourse. He gives one summation in the middle and another at the end of the exercises, and both of them describe the One and the Others (Many) with contradictory predicates. Here are two summations.

(1) Thus, if there is a One, the One is both all things and nothing what-soever, alike with reference to itself and to the Others.

(2) To this we may add the conclusion: it seems that, whether there is or is not a One, both that One and the Others alike are and are not, and appear and do not appear to be, all manner of things in all manner of ways, with respect to themselves and to one another (160b, 166c, trans. Cornford).

These statements appear to be self-contradictory, but they are elliptical statements. Though the *One* and the *Others* have different senses in different hypotheses, they are jumbled together in the two summations. Since this semantic entanglement produces the apparent contradictions, they can easily be dissolved by disentangling the different senses of the *One* and the *Others*.

Traditionally, the *Parmenides* and the *Theaetetus* have been read as two massively aporetic works among Plato's late dialogues. Each of them has been understood to end in a tremendous *aporia*: the *Parmenides* in the mutual contradictions of the eight hypotheses, and the *Theaetetus* in the conflicting accounts of *logos*. But these are gigantic misreadings. Let us look at the structure of the two dialogues. Each of them consists of two parts. In the first half of the *Theaetetus*, knowledge is defined as perception; in the second half, it is redefined in terms of judgment. There is a positive ascent in the transition from the first to the second half of the dialogue. The definition of knowledge as percep-tion surely leads to an unacceptable *aporia*: every perception is true and there can be no room for error. The second definition of knowledge is not meant to be a mere substitution, but is designed to resolve the *apo-ria* of the first definition by providing an epistemic apparatus to account for the occurrence of errors. Hence, the transition from the first to the second definition of knowledge is a Platonic ascent from a lower to a higher level of understanding. Finally, as we have seen, the conflicting accounts of *logos* given at the end of the dialogue constitute a set of constructive proposals for future inquiry rather than an aporetic ending.

The *Parmenides* also consists of two parts. The first part ends with Parmenides' critique of the theory of Forms and Socrates' admission of the difficulties in maintaining the theory as it stands. The second half is designed to show the source of these difficulties. The Young Socrates has proposed and used his theory of Forms without articulating the categoreal scheme that has to be presupposed for the theory. The second half of the dialogue presents and examines eight categoreal systems, which can give different interpretations to the theory of Forms. Some of them produce exactly the same difficulties that have been admitted as inevitable by the Young Socrates. But there are other categoreal systems that can avoid those difficulties. This sort of categoreal discrimination is the positive result of the dialectical exercises, which provides an impressive metaphysical sophistication and education for the young Socrates.

Furthermore, there is a qualitative difference in the mode of discourse between the two parts of the dialogue. In the first half, the mode of discourse is informal and unsystematic; in the second half, it is formal and systematic. The first half employs metaphors and similes; the second half sticks to abstract technical terms. Hence the transition from the first to the second half is again a Platonic ascent; it is an ascent from an informal to a formal and systematic discourse. Finally, the examination of the eight hypotheses does not yield a series of massive contradictions, but produces a highly selective set of categoreal schemes.

In this volume, I have all along maintained that there are no purely negative dialogues in the Platonic corpus, and that the so-called aporetic endings always hide some positive result. The *Parmenides* and the *Theaetetus* are no exceptions to this unfamiliar thesis. They present two sets of constructive proposals instead of ending with two big skeptical conclusions. The *Parmenides* proposes semantic models, and the *Theaetetus* constructs epistemic models. Now these two sets of models have to be linked to an ontological scheme, because the semantic and the epistemic models can make sense only in the ontological context. This final step of ontological commitment is made in the *Sophist*.

The Ontological Decision

In the *Sophist*, the Eleatic Stranger reviews the ontological dispute between monists and pluralists, and wants to clarify the semantic problem in this dispute (243e–245e). How should we understand the meaning of the word *being*? This semantic question establishes the thematic connection between the *Sophist* and the *Parmenides*. This is the same sort of question that was encountered with the problem of the One and the Many in the *Parmenides*. And it is now linked to the controversial ontological issue between the two camps of monists and pluralists.

The Eleatic Stranger says that the pluralists assert the existence of more than one entity, for example, the Hot and the Cold, but they apply one and the same word, *being*, to both of them. How should we understand the meaning of this term? It cannot be identified with only one of the two elements. If *being* is identified with the Hot, the Cold cannot be said to be, and vice versa. There is one word, *being*, to describe more than one thing; this is the obvious disparity between the word and its objects. This is the semantic problem for the pluralists. The Eleatic Stranger proposes two alternatives: (1) *being* should not be identified with either of the two elements, but be treated as a third thing which is shared by the two elements, or (2) *being* should be identified with the sum of the two elements.

The monists assert the existence of only one thing. The Eleatic Stranger takes note of the fact that they make use of two names in speaking of the One or the All. When they say, "The One is," they have to use at least two words, *one* and *being* (244c). This is exactly the same problem that we encountered with the One of the Parmenidean exercises. The monists start out with one entity, but end up with two. This is exactly the opposite of the problem for the pluralists, who start out with a plurality and end up with a unity. Even if the monists want to accept only one name for the One in order to avoid the pluralistic consequence, they still have to contend with two things, the object and its name. They can avoid this consequence only by refusing the distinction between the name and its object or claiming their identity (244d).

Furthermore, the monists have to account for the relation of the One and the Whole. From Parmenides' own description, the Eleatic Stranger points out, the One is a mass of a well-rounded sphere. It looks like a whole with many parts (244e). In that case, the Parmenidean Being cannot be a simple unity. The Eleatic Stranger wants to know whether *being* is a whole or not. If *being* is a whole of parts, the monists have to accept pluralism because a whole is made of many parts. On the other hand, if *being* is not such a whole, the monists have to accept two separate entities, namely, *being* and the *whole*, which is another form of pluralism. The monists can avoid these pluralistic consequences by denying *being* to the *whole*, that is, by saying that the *whole* has no *being*. Such a denial will make Being itself deficient because it will be deprived of *being* a whole. If *being* is not a whole, moreover, there can be no coming-into-being, and no definite numbers because all these things take the relation of parts and whole (245cd). We have also encountered these difficulties of the monists in the Parmenidean exercises.

This brief discussion of monism and pluralism is a review of the first two hypotheses of the *Parmenides*. Let us consider the difficulties of monism. If *being* is not a whole with parts, the Eleatic Stranger says, it can neither be named nor be spoken of. This was the conclusion Parmenides reached in his examination of H_1. Nor can the One be an object of knowledge or discourse. So *being* as a simple unity is the same as the One of H_1, and it is rejected by the Eleatic Stranger. His rejection amounts to the joint rejection of H_1 and H_4, because they all employ the same notion of the One as a simple unity. Moreover, their rejection entails the rejection of H_6 and H_8. If *being* is taken as a complex entity, it is the same as the complex One of H_2. It is accepted by the Eleatic Stranger as the solution for the monist's semantic paradox. The acceptance of H_2 is also the acceptance of H_3 and $H_{2=3}$, because they are all equivalent.

The Eleatic Stranger has proposed two solutions for the semantic problem of pluralists: (1) *being* should be identified with the sum of the two elements, or (2) it should be assigned to a third thing that is shared by the two elements. In the first solution, the pluralists begin by accepting only the Hot and the Cold. At that point, they need only H_3; the Hot and the Cold are the Many of H_3. By the time they accept the Hot and the Cold as parts of a Whole, however, their H_3 becomes H_2, because the Whole is the One of H_2. This is the same categoreal development that we noted in the Parmenidean dialectical exercises, that is, H_3 can maintain its categoreal coherence only by accepting the complex One of H_2 as its complement. By this dialectical move, H_3 becomes equivalent to H_2. The first solution leads to $H_{2=3}$, and it is the same solution as that of the monists. In this regard, monism and pluralism are convertible. The pluralists who accept the sum of the Many as reality are *de facto* monists, while the monists who acknowledge the parts of the One are *de facto* pluralists.

In the second solution, the pluralists introduce a third thing that is shared by the two original elements (the Hot and the Cold). The third element cannot be an existent or phenomenal entity like the two original elements. It is an eidetic entity, the One that is not. This is the One of H_5. We have said that H_5 requires H_7. The Hot and the Cold can now be identified with the Many of H_7. In the second solution, the pluralists begin with H_7 (the Hot and the Cold), and join it with H_5 (the third thing). Hence the second solution leads to H_{5+7}.

Up to this point, the Eleatic Stranger has only rehearsed the result of Parmenidean exercises, reminding us that $H_{2=3}$ and H_{5+7} are the only semantically viable categoreal systems. Which of these two systems should be adopted? This question requires his ontological decision, and it is given in his story of the battle of gods and giants (246a–251a). The giants are the materialists, who recognize nothing but material elements. For them, $H_{2=3}$ is sufficient. The Eleatic Stranger advances a few arguments against its adequacy. First, though the materialists regard only the tangible material objects as true beings, every one of them can be shattered and pulverized (246b). If so, no material object is truly a One; at best, it can have the appearance of being a One. In that case, the right categoreal system for materialism is not H_3, but H_7. But the H_7 cannot stand alone; it has to depend on H_5. Thus we arrive at H_{5+7}.

Against the materialists, the Eleatic Stranger maintains that there are other things beside the body, namely, the soul. Unlike the body, the soul has intangible and invisible qualities such as justice and wisdom

(246e–247b). But the materialists can respond with the claim that the soul is just another type of material object or an epiphenomenon of matter. In that case, the Eleatic Stranger would like to know what is the quality that is common to both the body and the soul, and by virtue of which both are said to have being. He suggests that the common quality must be the power to act and be acted upon (247e). This common quality is analogous to the third thing that is shared by the Hot and the Cold in the Eleatic Stranger's previous discussion of pluralism.

With this inconclusive argument, the Eleatic Stranger turns his attention to the idealists. He observes that they would not easily accept the power of acting and being acted upon as the essential criterion of *being*. For them, such a power belongs to *becoming* and is incompatible with *being* (248c). But the idealists claim to have communion with *being*, and even know it. Such a communion with *being*, the Eleatic Stranger points out, should involve the power of acting and being acted upon *being*. If the world of *being* is truly immutable as the idealists claim, it should be devoid of life and intelligence. Since that is an unreasonable conception of *being*, the power of action and motion should be accepted as an essential feature of *being* as well as of *becoming*. On the other hand, if everything is subject to motion and change, intelligence should be equally impossible. Hence, knowledge and intelligence presuppose not only something permanent but also the power of action.

For these reasons, the Eleatic Stranger concludes, the idealist view that the true reality is absolutely immutable is as unreasonable and unacceptable as the materialist view that everything is mutable. So, like a child begging for "both," the philosopher who values knowledge and intelligence has to accept both the changing material objects and the unchanging eidetic objects (240d). This amounts to his endorsement of H_{5+7}. His argument is transcendental: it alone can account for the possibility of life and intelligence. This is the same type of argument that we encountered in the *Theaetetus* and the *Parmenides*. This is Plato's repeated transcendental argument for ontological dualism, but his dualism should not be confused with his old two-world view. His ontological dualism only claims two different types of elements for the constitution of one world.

The expression $5+7$ in H_{5+7} appears to have long been on Plato's mind. At *Theaetetus* 196a, Socrates uses $5+7$ as an example in his discussion of how errors take place. This example is presented in conjunction with the allegory of the wax tablet, which is meant to mirror the operation of our memory. Plato may be calling upon the mnemonic resources in the wax tablets of our own memory. He may be telling us that $5+7$ is a secret key for recognizing the relevance of the *Theaetetus* and the *Parmenides* to the ontological discussion in the *Sophist*. Am I reading too much into the $5+7$ of the *Theaetetus*? It might have been a product of casual thought and coincidence. In fact, Plato does not even number the eight hypotheses; the numbers have been assigned to them by the commentators.

On the other hand, Plato installs quite a few thematic pointers in the *Theaetetus*, which indicates its close connection with the *Parmenides*. The most obvious one is Socrates' refusal to talk about Parmenides' doctrine of Being, though he mentions his fictional meeting with the reverend sage of Elea in his youth, which sets the stage for the *Parmenides* (183c–e). Much less obvious than this passage is the repeated use of the phrase ''some one thing (*hen ti*)'' for indicating any object of thought, perception, and judgment at *Theaetetus* 188e–189a. This clearly resonates with the One (*hen*) of the *Parmenides*. This thematic connector is further associated with the necessity of common terms such as *being* and *nonbeing*, *identity* and *difference*, *likeness* and *unlikeness* for our thought and discourse (*Theaetetus* 185a–186c). This passage reinforces the transcendental argument Socrates gave for the existence of Forms in the *Parmenides*, and these common terms are none other than the central categories presented in the examination of the eight hypotheses.

The transcendental argument is further negatively echoed in the *Theaetetus*, when Socrates laments over the equal impossibility of talking with the radical Heracliteans and the radical Parmenideans. It is impossible to talk with the Heracliteans, because nothing remains stable in their hand. Since the meaning of their questions and answers perpetually change, they cannot settle anything even with one another (180ab). But Socrates points out that the situation is not any better with the opposite camp, the Parmenideans (180e). It is equally impossible to talk with them because they claim that the All is an absolute unity. The very possibility of sensible discourse is getting undermined by the Heraclitean doctrine of perpetual flux and the Parmenidean doctrine of absolute unity and immobility. Socrates stresses the importance of taming and avoiding these radical schools and of securing the semantic basis for rational discourse.

Part 2 of the *Parmenides* can give a semantic account of the radical Parmenideans and Heracliteans. The radical Parmenideans subscribe to H_1, and the radical Heracliteans to H_4. Discourse becomes impossible with either of these categoreal systems, because they allow no predication. The problem of discourse appears even in the dream story of the *Theaetetus*, where Socrates describes the whole as composed of its parts, and the parts are the elements that cannot be further divided (201d–202c). They can be named but not described; each of them behaves like the One of H_1. On the other hand, the whole is like the complex One of H_2; it is predicable. *Logos* can be given for the whole, but not for the elements. The possibility of discourse is the common topic that hovers over not only the *Parmenides* but also the *Theaetetus* from the beginning to the end.

Then, there is the mud that sticks to both dialogues. At the beginning of the *Theaetetus*, Socrates shows Theaetetus what it means to give a definition, by taking the definition of mud for an example (147c). In the *Parmenides*, the Form of Mud (*pelos*) is used as an example to illustrate the Forms of undignified objects (130c). Forms and definitions are convertible. When we put all these thematic pointers together, it seems unlikely that $5+7$ is only a casual thought that has nothing to do with the thematic connection of the two dialogues. What appears to be casual and even trivial in Plato's writing is often an ingenious contrivance of his devilish genius. Finally, let us note that the conceptual scheme of H_{5+7} is not totally new in Plato's philosophy. Although it unifies into one categoreal scheme the temporal and the eternal elements, which were separated into two worlds in the *Republic*, it is still the same conceptual scheme that has all along been underlying Plato's conception of a human being as composed of the body and the soul. Even in the conception of the soul, Plato has always recognized both the temporal and the eternal elements. In adopting H_{5+7}, he transforms his dualistic conception of human beings into a cosmological scheme.

The acceptance of H_{5+7} still leaves one more problem unresolved. While nothing can be said about the absolutely simple One, as we noted, the many predicates that can be assigned to the complex One may be incompatible. The compatibility and incompatibility of Forms concern the art of combining or blending Forms, which is identified with the science of dialectic by the Eleatic Stranger (253d). He notes that there are three contending schools: (1) no Form can be combined with another Form, (2) every Form can be combined with every other Form, and (3) a Form can be combined with some Forms but not with others. School (1) cannot account for the existence of statements, because there can be no statements without the combination of Forms. School (2) cannot discriminate the acceptable from the unacceptable statements, for example, the contradictory or nonsense statements. Hence, school (3) alone is a reasonable position, and it is endorsed by the Eleatic Stranger (252e). As a way of explaining how (3) works out, the Eleatic Stranger shows the various ways in which the five ultimate Forms, *being*, *motion*, *rest*, *identity*, and *difference*, can and cannot combine with one another.

By the combination of Forms, the Eleatic Stranger shows how his chosen categoreal systems can account for the possibility of discourse. Hence, the problem of discourse not only thematically connects the *Parmenides* and the *Theaetetus* to each other, but further establishes their thematic relation to the *Sophist*. This thematic relation is echoed in the battle of gods and giants, which is the basis for the Eleatic Stranger's ontological deliberation for his categoreal choice. For this battle is none other than the battle between the two camps of Parmenideans and Heracliteans, which Socrates describes as the common menace for the possibility of rational discourse in the *Theaetetus*. This possibility is finally secured by the Eleatic Stranger, who brings the Parmenidean categoreal exercises to its completion. Thus the Stranger plays the thematic role of connecting the *Parmenides* to the *Sophist*.

With this accomplishment, the Eleatic Stranger fully deserves Socrates' reference to him at the beginning of the dialogue as "not a stranger but some god" (216a). This description in turn resounds back to the hypothetical admiration Socrates had entertained for the dialectical feat of combining and separating Forms in the *Parmenides*. He had said,

"But, as I said just now, if he begins by distinguishing the Forms apart just by themselves—*likeness*, for instance, and *unlikeness*, *plurality* and *unity*, *rest* and *motion*, all the rest—and then shows that these Forms among themselves can be combined with, or separated from, one another, then, Zeno, I should be filled with admiration" (129de, trans. Cornford). This marvelous feat of combining and separating Forms is exactly what the Eleatic Stranger performs in the *Sophist*.

Some scholars have interpreted Socrates' initial response to the Eleatic Stranger quite differently. They have seen it not as an expression of admiration but as one of suspicion and distrust.[17] To be sure, Socrates expresses his fear to Theodorus, "Your companion may be one of those higher powers, who intends to observe and expose our weakness in philosophic discourse, like a spirit of refutation" (216b, trans. Cornford). But this fear, which was expressed well before the Eleatic Stranger takes charge of the discussion, is completely assuaged by his performance. He turns out to be anything but the spirit of contention and refutation. Socrates indeed encountered such a spirit in Parmenides and Zeno in the *Parmenides*. Hence, Socrates' initial response to the appearance of the Eleatic Stranger is his way of connecting the two phases of the Eleatic contribution to Plato's philosophical development: the negative (or critical) and the positive (or constructive).

Socrates' reference to the Eleatic Stranger as "not a stranger but some god" deserves some further attention. Socrates goes on to say that it is not much easier to discern philosophers than gods, because both of them take on so many different shapes. This should explain why the sophists also take on so many different shapes. Since they are the counterfeit philosophers, they should take on as many different shapes as the philosophers do. As Stanley Rosen points out, these remarks of Socrates allude to *Odyssey* 17. 485–487.[18] This is the episode in which Odysseus, disguised as a stranger, returns to Ithaca. But he is not really a stranger.[19] This may be true of the Eleatic Stranger. He is talking about the separation and combination of Forms, which is quite strange to Platonic Socrates who advocates the radical separation of Forms. Nevertheless, the Eleatic Stranger still represents the old familiar doctrine of Forms. He is no more a stranger to Socrates and his friends than Odysseus was to the people of Ithaca.

Notes

1. It is my regret to give only a sketchy summary of these difficult problems. Excellent and extended discussions are available in Francis Cornford, *Plato and Parmenides* (London: Routledge, 1939); R. E. Allen, *Plato's Parmenides* (Minneapolis: University of Minnesota Press, 1983); Mitchell Miller, *Plato's Parmenides* (Princeton: University Press, 1986); Constance Meinwald, *Plato's Parmenides* (Oxford: University Press, 1991).

2. This distinction is fully discussed by John Malcolm, *Plato on the Self-Predication of Forms* (Oxford: University Press, 1991).

3. Vlastos, *Platonic Studies* (Princeton: University Press, 1973), 408.

4. Meinwald, "Good-bye to the Third Man," Richard Kraut, ed. *The Cambridge Companion to Plato* (Cambridge: University Press, 1992), 365–96.

5. A good summary of traditional interpretations is given by W. G. Runciman, "Plato's *Parmenides*," in R. E. Allen, *Studies in Plato's Metaphysics* (New York: Humanities Press, 1965), 149–84, esp. 167–84. For more recent interpretations, see the works by Miller, Allen, and Meinwald cited in note 1.

6. Sayre, *Plato's Late Ontology: A Riddle Resolved* (Princeton: University Press, 1983), 50–51. The eight sets of attributes are (1) limit and the unlimited, (2) shape, (3) place, (4) motion and rest, (5) same and other, (6) similar and dissimilar, (7) equal and unequal, and (8) temporal order.

7. Sayre, *Plato's Late Ontology*, 52–53.

8. For a detailed account, see, Walter Burkert, *Lore and Science in Ancient Pythagoreanism*, trans. Edwin Minar (Cambridge: University Press, 1972), 33–35.

9. This point is confirmed by Aristotle's description of Plato's relation to the Pythagoreans. Though Plato agreed with the Pythagoreans on many points, he says, Plato differed from them in "positing a dyad and constructing the infinite out of great and small, instead of treating the infinite as one" (*Metaphysics* 987b25–27, trans. W. D. Ross).

10. The view that the Pythagorean method generates physical objects is supported by Aristotle's account in *Metaphysics* 1091a12–16. For a fuller discussion, see Cornford, *Plato and Parmenides*, 17–18.

11. This point is stressed by the Eleatic Stranger at *Sophist* 238b: what is and what is not cannot be conceived apart from number.

12. The Eleatic-Pythagorean dispute is still alive in the contemporary discussion on the definition of natural number. The set theoretic definition is a continuation of the Pythagorean tradition. It implicitly asserts the primacy of sets and numbers over the domain of objects and properties. This is especially so with

Zermelo's derivation of natural number from the null set. Since no objects or properties are contained in the null set, his definition appears to make natural number independent of any ontological consideration. But the Eleatics can still revive the Parmenidean objection to the Pythagoreans by pointing out the inevitability of using the concept of being even in talking about the null set. One has to say, "There *is* a null set," or "Let us assume the *existence* of a null set."

13. Sayre, *Plato's Late Ontology*, 49–62.

14. For the Neoplatonic interpretation, see Cornford, *Plato and Parmenides*, 131–34. Glenn Morrow and John Dillon, trans., *Proclus' Commentary on Plato's Parmenides* (Princeton: University Press, 1987).

15. The view that the antinomies are real and serious is well represented by Gilbert Ryle, "Plato's *Parmenides*," *Mind* N.S. 48 (1939):129–51, 303–25. The other view is equally well represented by Cornford, *Plato and Parmenides*.

16. This view is endorsed by Julius Moravcsik, "Forms and Dialectic in the Second Half of the *Parmenides*," in Malcolm Schofield and Martha Nussbaum, eds., *Language and Logos* (Cambridge: University Press, 1982), 135–58; *Plato and Platonism* (Oxford: University Press, 1992), 129–67. He does not exempt any of eight hypothesis from self-contradiction.

17. For example, Stanley Rosen, *Plato's Sophist*, 61–69, and Rosen's interpretation is endorsed by Nicholas White in his review of this book. *Journal of the History of Philosophy* 23 (1985):422.

18. Rosen, *Plato's Sophist*, 62.

19. Mitchell Miller gives an elaborate account of the Homeric allusion: the Eleatic Stranger conceals himself and comes to Athens to restore philosophy in the same manner Odysseus disguises himself as a stranger and comes to Ithaca to restore its political order. *The Philosopher in Plato's Statesman*, 10–14.

CHAPTER SEVEN

Platonic Construction

The *Statesman*, the *Philebus*, the *Laws*, and the *Timaeus*

In his new ontology, Plato still accepts Forms along with the phenomenal world. This goes against the view that the Forms are no longer important or are even abandoned in his late dialogues. How is his new ontology different from the old one? In the first place, Plato has abandoned his previous two-world view. In the *Republic*, he advocated the existence of two separate worlds, the visible world of material objects and the invisible world of Forms. With H_{5+7}, these two worlds become two sets of elements for the constitution of one world. With the fusion of the two worlds into one, Plato no longer resorts to his old rhetoric of self-predication and self-exemplification, super-predication and super-exemplification, and absolute predication and absolute exemplification. He stops saying such things as ''The Form of Beauty is beautiful,'' or ''The Form of Beauty is more beautiful than any beautiful thing on earth,'' or ''The Form of Beauty alone is truly and absolutely beautiful.''

The Art of Construction

Whereas the idea of separation was predominant in Plato's old theory of Forms, the idea of combination becomes central in his new theory.

The art of combining the letters of the alphabet into words is Plato's favorite analogy in explaining the combination of Forms. Socrates makes use of this analogy at *Theaetetus* 203a, and the Eleatic Stranger does the same at *Statesman* 278a. The art of combining Forms is the art of construction, which produces new Forms. For example, the Form of herding human beings is produced by combining the Form of herding with the Form of human beings. Such a Form is a composite or derived Form, which should be distinguished from an underived or primitive Form. A primitive Form can be said to be simple, but to call it a simple Form is confusing. As we have already seen, an absolutely simple Form can never combine with another Form.

A primitive Form must be a complex One, because it can combine with other Forms. But it cannot be a composite Form, because it cannot be constructed by the combination of other Forms. For a constructed Form is not primitive but derivative. There is an element of complexity in both a complex Form and a composite Form. But they involve different types of complexity. The complexity of a composite one is compositional, while the complexity of a complex Form is relational. The complexity of the Form of Sameness lies in its relation to the Forms of Being and Otherness. In its own essence, it is still simple. By contrast, the Form of a human being as a featherless biped is not simple in its essence, because it is composed by the union of the Form of being featherless and the Form of being biped. Hence it has compositional complexity as well as relational complexity.

The distinction between the primitive and the derived Forms may help Socrates answer the tough question Parmenides posed about the scope of Forms, that is, whether there is Form of Man, a Form of Fire, a Form of Water, and a Form of Hair or Mud or Dirt (*Parmenides* 130c). In the *Theaetetus*, as we already noted, Socrates defines mud as earth mixed with water (147c). Whatever is definable is compositional, and a compositional Form can be constructed. On the other hand, because the primitive Forms cannot be constructed, they cannot be defined, either. They are the objects of not definition but intuition. The intuition of primitive Forms is Platonic intuition. The primitive Forms can be used for the construction of definable or derivative Forms. Their construction is Platonic construction.

Platonic constructivism brings a tremendous economy and flexibility to the theory of Forms. Without it, Plato would have to accept not one Form of Mud, but an infinite number of them. For there is an infinite variety of mud, which can be represented only by an infinite number of Forms, for example, the Potter's Mud, the Oven-maker's Mud, the Brick-maker's Mud (*Theaetetus* 147a). This is the problem of eidetic proliferation. In book 10 of the *Republic*, Plato appears to be already concerned with this problem. Socrates says that the god makes the Form of Bed and that he makes only one Form of Bed (597bc). This remark is often dismissed by most commentators as strange talk, which is out of line with the theory of eternal Forms presented in books 6 and 7. Surely, it is a way of controlling the eidetic population of Platonic Heaven. But it is not a good way of coping with the problem on the metaphysical level, because it is a *deus ex machina*. It does not explain why the god makes only one Form of Bed instead of many Forms such as the Wooden Bed, the Metal Bed, the Soft Bed, the Hard Bed, and so on. Platonic constructivism is a much better way to cope with this problem, because it can construct an indefinite number of Forms of Bed from a few primitive Forms.

The distinction between primitive and derivative Forms leads to the distinction between two ways of knowing: intuition and definition. A derivative Form can be known by definition because it can be defined, but a primitive Form cannot be known by definition because it cannot be defined. It must be known by intuition. The method of definition must presuppose the method of intuition, and this was the moral of the dream story in the *Theaetetus*. In the middle and late dialogues, Plato begins to appreciate the importance of intuition, whereas he was obsessed with the problem of definition in the early dialogues. When the Eleatic Stranger talks about the primitive Forms of Being, Motion and Rest, Identity and Difference, he never thinks of defining them. Intuitive recognition of these Forms are taken for granted. The doctrine of intuition can also resolve the paradox of definition in the *Meno*. The elements that go into any definition must be known either by a further definition or by intuition. The paradox can be resolved only by the doctrine of Platonic intuition.

Though the doctrine of intuition is only implied by the paradox of definition in the *Meno*, it becomes fully operational in the *Republic*. In fact, the transition from Socratic definition to Platonic intuition is made in that dialogue. Book 1 of the *Republic* reads like a typical Socratic dialogue. Socrates engages his interlocutors in the definition of justice, and shoots down the proposed definitions one after another. But the discussion takes an unexpected turn in book 2, when Socrates and his company begin to construct a state. This is the beginning of Platonic constructivism. Only after constructing an ideal state, they define the four virtues of wisdom, courage, temperance, and justice in reference to its social structure. In this process of definition, Socrates describes the nature of justice, "Further, we have heard many people say, and have often said ourselves, that justice is to perform one's own task and not to meddle with that of others" (433a, trans. Grube).

Gregory Vlastos takes this statement as the definition of justice, therefore a representation of the Form of Justice.[1] In the *Republic*, he explains, the problem of justice arises in the context of cooperation and reciprocity. By division of labor and by exchange of goods and services, all the participants do their parts and receive their benefits. This is the basic idea of justice, which governs the construction of the ideal state. What is remarkable about this basic idea is that it is not presented as the result of a laborious definition. One of the comical moments in the *Republic* is the way Socrates and his interlocutors locate the virtue of justice. After picking up the three virtues of wisdom, courage, and temperance, Socrates puts on the air of initiating a big hunt for the final virtue of justice, and exhorts Glaucon and Adeimantus not to let their biggest quarry get away (432bc).

This is a ploy familiar in the Socratic game of searching for a definition. But the aroused expectation ends in an anticlimax, when Socrates says that the object of their search has been rolling right in front of their feet all this time (432d). When Glaucon confesses not to know what he is talking about, Socrates says that they have been using the idea of justice all along in constructing the ideal city. If they have had it all along without the labor of special instruction or definition, they must have gotten it by their commonsense intuition. Hence Socrates attributes the idea of justice to the popular view; it is a common property of all human beings.

The description of justice as a cooperative enterprise, in which all the participants do their parts and receive their benefits, may even look like a definition of justice. But it is not really a definition. The description is correct only on the condition that their parts and their benefits are justly allocated. By spelling out this condition, the description should read, ''Justice obtains in a cooperative enterprise, when all the participants do their justly allocated parts and receive their justly distributed benefits.'' The description of justice can be given only in terms of justice; the intuition of justice is ineliminable in any discourse about justice. This is what is meant by the claim that the Form of Justice is primitive, or that its nature cannot be defined but only be intuited.

The Form of the Good is even more difficult to define than the Form of Justice. Socrates cannot give even an informal or contextual description of this Form, as he does for the Form of Justice. He can give only an analogical description of it by comparing it to the sun (517c). Platonic intuition is essentially vague; it is inarticulate and indeterminate. Hence it is radically different from Aristotelian intuition (*nous*). The latter is articulate and determinate; it is like Descartes' clear and distinct ideas. To express the vagueness of intuition, Plato is careful in choosing the words for its description. He uses *apomanteuomene* for the epistemic contact with the Form of the Good (*Republic* 505e), and *apomanteuesthai* for the same contact with the Form of Being (*Sophist* 250c). These two words are derived from *manteis* and *manteia*, which are associated with the idea of divination. Though the word *manteis* or *manteia* appears frequently in Plato's dialogues, the use of the words beginning with *apomanteu* is limited to these two occasions. They are highly unusual in Plato's lexicon.

Since the Form of the Good and the Form of Being are the two highest Forms, their intuition should be the vaguest, and be in need of interpretation and articulation like oracles and divinations. Plato may be trying to convey this point by using the two unusual words, *apomanteuomene* and *apomanteuesthai*. If the intuition of primitive Forms is vague, it should be articulated. The method of definition is a method of articulation; it articulates our intuition of the object under definition by naming its constituents. But this analytical method of articulation is inapplicable to the intuition of primitive Forms, because they are compositionally simple and indefinable. Their articulation requires a synthetic method, which is the method of construction. This is the method used in the *Republic* for the construction of the Kallipolis; its construction is a way of articulating the Form of Justice.

The *Republic* marks the transition from Socratic definition to Platonic construction, just as it marks the transition from Socratic definition to Platonic intuition. These two transitions are concurrent because Platonic intuition and Platonic construction are two indispensable partners to each other. After the *Republic*, intuition and construction become the overriding concern for Plato to the end of his long career. The *Cratylus* shows the construction of secondary names from primary ones. The *Sophist* is concerned with the problem of constructing propositions and definitions by the combination of names or Forms. The same constructive process governs the problem of definition in the *Statesman*. In fact, these two dialogues show that the Socratic definition is only a product of Platonic construction.

The construction in the *Sophist* is of a different kind from the one in the *Statesman*. The former is descriptive; the latter is normative. The normative construction produces normative ideals or standards; the descriptive construction produces propositions or definitions for describing the existing entities. On the surface, the definition of statesman may look like the definition of sophist; it may appear that both of them are meant to describe the actual entities, the statesmen and the sophists, respectively. But the concept of a statesman is a normative ideal, whether there are real human beings corresponding to this ideal. On the other hand, the concept of a sophist is not a normative ideal, because the sophist is only a counterfeit philosopher. It is a degradation of an ideal.

Because the concept of a statesmen is a normative ideal, it takes on different shapes in the two ages of Cronus and Zeus. What is an ideal statesman for the age of Cronus is not ideal for the age of Zeus. The ideals have to be adjusted to the changing empirical conditions, and this adjustment is an essential feature of normative construction. The concept of a sophist can also take on many different shapes in different circumstances, but for a different reason. The different circumstances can give different shapes to the degradation of an ideal, and the *Sophist* has to construct many different definitions to capture all the different shapes and functions that can be assumed by the sophists. But those definitions are still descriptive. The distinction between normative and descriptive constructions is the important factor that differentiates the *Statesman* from the *Sophist*, although many commentators have regarded the *Statesman* as a weary continuation of the same boring definitional exercise that began in the *Sophist*.

The distinction between these two types of construction underlies the Eleatic Stranger's talk about two types of measurement (283c–285e). One of them directly compares two objects for the determination of their relative length or weight, and the other compares the two objects in reference to a standard. The first is empirical and descriptive; the second is normative. The latter is called the method of due measure or norm (284d). It requires normative standards. What sorts of standard are they? Are they positive or transcendental standards? These questions are not raised in the *Statesman*. But he talks about the elements and their combination for the art of construction (278b–d), and mentions the *genesis* of standards (*pros ten tou metrion genesin*). By this, we may assume, he is referring to the construction of normative standards from primitive Forms. The Eleatic Stranger goes on to say that the notion of due measure and that of technical arts stand or fall together. For Plato, the technical art is an art of normative construction.

The Method of Construction

In the *Sophist* and the *Statesman*, the art of construction is described as the art of combining Forms and compares it to the art of weaving. This combinatory art has usually been understood as the precursor of Aristotelian method for defining species in terms of genera and differentiae. In the *Philebus*, however, he sets forth a radically different method of construction. It is called a gift of the gods to human beings or the divine method (14c, 16c). It requires three constituents: (1) the unlimited, (2) the limit or measure, and (3) the cause to effect their union or mixture (27a). The divine method introduces order into the phenomenal world of indeterminate manifold. For example, human vocal sounds constitute one continuum, which can be divided into a system of vowels and consonants. This division also sets up the measure or standard for each vowel and consonant. For another example, the continuum of musical sounds can be divided into a system of intervals, a harmonic scale (17a), and this division also sets up the measure or standard for each musical note. The measure or standard is a paradigm, for example, the paradigm of red; whatever resembles it will be called red. This is the process of imposing a system of paradigms on a continuum.

The principle of continuum rules all qualitative predicates such as *large* and *small*, *heavy* and *light*, *hot* and *cold*, and so on (14d). Each of the attributes designated by these predicates is continuous and indeterminate, that is, it can always be more or less. For example, something heavy can always be heavier or less heavy. An indeterminate continuum such as these can be organized into an ordered whole by its demarcation into many segments, and such a demarcation requires the concept of a unit (the One), and produces a system of paradigms that are called measures or standards. Such a system of paradigms is the ontic basis for the logic of paradigms. Since the relation of a paradigm to the instances in the domain of indeterminate continuum is the relation of resemblance and difference, the logic of paradigm is the logic of resemblance.

Kenneth Sayre regards this process of demarcation as Pythagorean, and associates it with the Pythagoreanism of hypothesis 2 in the *Parmenides*.[2] To be sure, the metaphor of mixing is Pythagorean, whereas the metaphor of weaving is Eleatic. As we have noted in the last chapter, however, hypothesis 2 does not simply restate Pythagoreanism, but considerably modifies it. But even this modified categoreal system is not semantically powerful enough to underwrite Platonic constructivism in the *Philebus*. It requires H_{5+7}. The basic difference between the two categoreal systems lies with the Many. In H_3, each of the Many is a really discrete One; in H_7, each of the Many is only an apparent One, which is a segment in a continuum. But the segment is not the ultimate One; it can be further divided into many Ones.

The truly discrete One of $H_{2=3}$ is not a continuum. In the *Philebus*, the continuum of sounds and other phenomenal properties cannot produce any truly discrete Ones when they are divided into different segments. These segments only appear to be Ones, while the concept of a unit or measure transcends them. This concept is the *limit*; it is the One of H_5. On the other hand, the continuum are the *unlimited*; its segments are the Many of H_7. Hence the union of the *limit* and the *unlimited* requires H_{5+7}. This interpretation of the *Philebus* is supported by Aristotle's observation that Plato diverged from the Pythagoreans in making the One and the numbers separate from things (*Metaphysics* 987b30). The One and the Many are separated from each other in H_{5+7}; they are joined in H_2 and H_3.

The divine method of construction may appear to be based on H_2, because H_2 resembles H_7. But there is the difference between what is and what appears to be. The One of H_2 is truly one, and so is each of the Many of H_3. But each of the Many of H_7 only appears to be one, and this is the nature of the Many in the *Philebus*, which excludes any true definiteness (24c). Let us elucidate this point by considering the individuation of the Many. In $H_{2=3}$, their individuation is real; there is a real boundary between different individuals. In H_{5+7}, individuation is not real but only apparent; there is only an apparent boundary between different individuals. What is the nature of the boundary between two vowels *o* and *u*, or between two consonants *b* and *p*? It is not really real but only apparent, because it is an indeterminate line in a continuum. Such an indeterminate line belongs to H_{5+7}, but not to $H_{2=3}$.

To be sure, the Platonic constructivism of the *Philebus* greatly resembles Pythagorean constructivism; both of them give order (the *limit*) to the *unlimited*. For the sake of convenience, I will use the label "Pythagorean constructivism" to refer to both or any other version of constructivism that deals with the indeterminate continuum. This Pythagorean interpretation of the divine method is not universally accepted. Though I cannot discuss all the other competing interpretations, I should at least mention the long line of scholars who have tried to assimilate the divine method to the Eleatic Stranger's art of weaving in the *Sophist* and the *Statesman*.[3] According to this interpretation, the divine method is just like the method of collection and division, which begins with the concept of a genus and keeps dividing it until we reach the concept of an *infima species*. For the sake of convenience, let us call it the Aristotelian interpretation, and note the difference between the two interpretations. In the Pythagorean interpretation, the divine method produces elements such as the letters of the alphabet; on the Aristotelian interpretation, it produces *infirma species*.

The elements are simple; *infirma species* are complex. The latter is defined by the combination of Forms; a species is defined in terms of a genus and differentiae. Furthermore, the boundaries of elements are indeterminate, but the boundaries of species are determinate. In the Pythagorean interpretation, the divine method divides an indeterminate continuum into elements; on the Aristotelian interpretation, it divides a genus into species. A genus is not a continuum, but a collection of discontinua or simply a collection of discrete species. The Pythagorean interpretation requires the logic of an indeterminate continuum and resemblance; the Aristotelian interpretation requires the logic of discontinua or classes. Given these differences, the Pythagorean interpretation appears to have a better textual support than the Aristotelian interpretation. Especially, the two examples Socrates gives in his illustration—the division of phonemes and musical notes—clearly favor the Pythagorean interpretation.

The theory of indeterminate continuum together with Pythagorean constructivism can resolve the paradox of participation that was discussed in the *Phaedo*. Simmias participates in the Form of Smallness when he is compared with Phaedo (Simmias is smaller than Phaedo). But he also participates in the Form of Largeness when he is compared with Socrates (he is larger than Socrates). How can one and the same person participate in two contradictory Forms, Largeness and Smallness, at the same time? At *Republic* 479ab, Socrates tries to resolve this question by his doctrine of partial participation—*ou mallon* (more or less)—someone can participate never absolutely but only partially in the Form of Largeness or Smallness. At *Theaetetus* 182a, Socrates introduces the concept of quality (*poiotes*) such as hotness and whiteness, and this concept becomes the basis for the concept of an indeterminate continuum. Every quality can be more or less; there can be neither the minimum nor the maximum of any quality. Every quality participates in the two Forms of Largeness and Smallness. The concepts of Largeness and Smallness are the two basic concepts for the constitution of an indeterminate continuum. Hence the latter is called the Indeterminate Dyad, or the Great (or Large) and the Small.

The doctrine of participation can now be replaced by the doctrine of construction. In the *Phaedo*, the attributes of Simmias were explained by participation, that is, he participates in the Forms of Largeness and Smallness. This sort of direct participation in the Forms is not advocated in the *Philebus*. The Forms of Largeness and Smallness are used in constructing the concept of a human being, a horse, or a house. In reference to such a concept, we can say that someone is a large person, that this is a small house, or that my horse is relatively small, that is, in relation to other horses. Predication is not a direct participation in the Forms; it always presupposes a set of implied references to some standards or other objects, which are products of Platonic construction.

When Socrates introduces the divine method for solving the problem of One and Many, he mentions two different levels of discourse. One is the level of phenomenal objects; for example, Protarchus is one by nature but many because he is composed of many parts (14d). On this level, Socrates says, the problem of One and Many is trivial and childish, but it becomes a difficult problem on the transcendent level, which is beyond generation and corruption. This is the second level of discourse for the problem of One and Many: it involves the unity and plurality of Forms such as Man and Ox, Beauty and Goodness (15a). These two levels of discourse coincide with the two categoreal levels of H_{5+7}. But Socrates' handling of the divine method is quite strange. After explicating its intricate character, he does not proceed to use it for the discussion on hand. Instead he recounts a dream story to the effect that the good is neither pure pleasure nor pure knowledge, but their mixture (20b–23b). Then he introduces another method to explain the problem of mixing.

The second method divides all things into four kinds: the limit, the unlimited, the mixture, and the cause (23b–27b). Though this method also involves the *limit* and the *unlimited*, it is evidently different from the first or the divine method. The differentiation of these two methods has been a topic of controversy, and many theories have been proposed for its resolution.[4] These two methods construct two different sorts of things. The construction of a musical scale is governed by the first method, and that of a musical composition by the second method. For another example, the distinction of vowels and consonants into a phonological system is governed by the first method, and the combination of those vowels and consonants into a word, phrase, and sentence is governed by the second method. The first method belongs to the art of distinction and classification, and the second method to the art of combination and production.

Let us use the two labels *eidetic* and *ontic* to differentiate these two modes of construction. The divine method is for eidetic construction; the other method is for ontic construction. To establish a system of colors or sounds is to establish an eidetic system. It does not create colors or sounds, but installs a system of paradigms or concepts for their demarcation and recognition. Without such an eidetic distinction, the color spectrum would remain an undifferentiated continuum. But to construct a sentence or sonata is not simply eidetic but ontic; it does not merely distinguish such elements as letters and sounds, but puts them together to make an object. These two modes of construction are not independent of each other. The eidetic construction generates the elements, which are required for the ontic construction. These two phases of construction are essential for every technical art, and Socrates presents his two methods as a way of illuminating the nature of all technical arts (16c). These two modes of construction, eidetic and ontic, together constitute the theory of Platonic construction.

Of these two modes of construction, only the ontic construction was fully recognized in the *Sophist* and the *Statesman*. It is what the Eleatic Stranger calls the art of weaving or combining Forms. If there is to be an art of weaving, however, it requires the art of making threads. The latter is a more basic art than the former, and the *Philebus* introduces the more basic art as the divine method. There is an element of confusion because both arts involve the same two elements of the *limit* and the *unlimited*. But these two elements do not have the same meaning for the eidetic and the ontic constructions. In the demarcation of different musical notes, for example, the *unlimited* is the undifferentiated musical scale, from which each discrete note is generated as a measure or standard by the application of the *limit*. Though each note gains a definite value in this eidetic construction, it becomes an item in the domain of the *unlimited* for an ontic construction. If I want to use different notes for a musical composition, I have to treat them as a domain of the *unlimited* because there is an indeterminate number of ways for using each of them. What is determinate on the level of eidetic construction becomes indeterminate on the level of ontic construction.

The eidetic construction extends the basic categories of H_5, insofar as it establishes the conceptual distinctions of empirical elements. To put it another way, it generates the empirical concepts or Forms by applying the transcendent concepts or Forms of H_5 to the empirical manifold. For example, the empirical concepts of sounds and colors are generated by eidetic construction, in which the primitive concepts of H_5 function as the *limit* and the empirical manifold as the *unlimited*. Now the empirical manifold is the Many of H_7. Hence the eidetic construction connects H_5 with H_7, thereby producing H_{5+7}. The eidetic construction not only produces, but also expands H_{5+7}, insofar as the empirical concepts are not already contained in it. Now the ontic construction is the extension of the eidetic construction, because the ontic construction produces its objects by using the elements provided by the eidetic construction. Thus, the categoreal system of H_{5+7} turns out to be the ultimate basis for all Platonic construction. Let us now see how the theory of Platonic construction is operative in the *Laws* and the *Timaeus*.

The Construction of Magnesia

Let us now look at the construction of Magnesia. The city is designed to have 5,040 citizens, who are divided into four classes on the basis of property. The city is also divided into twelve tribal units, each of which contains four property classes. Magnesia is to be governed by the General Assembly and the Council of Elders, whose membership is limited to 360. A subcommittee of one twelfth of the Council is to exercise executive powers for one month at a time. All these organizational arrangements involve numbers, and these numbers are the Pythagorean limits for the organization of indeterminate continua.

Consider the division of all citizens into four property classes. The property differentials constitute an indeterminate continuum; some citizens can have more or less property than others. Such an indeterminate continuum can be divided into any number of units, depending on the size of the basic unit. The Athenian Stranger fixes as the basic unit the minimum amount of property required for decent living in Magnesia, and uses this basic unit as the measure or standard for defining the lowest class. Those who have two times the basic unit constitute the next higher class; those who have three times more, the third class; those who have four times more, the richest class (744a–d). Nobody is allowed to have more than four times the basic unit. It is an eidetic construction to establish the basic unit for the differentiation of property classes; it is an ontic construction to employ the same basic unit for the organization of the four-class structure.

The composition of the city in terms of tribal units also requires the two modes of construction. The distinction of each tribe from others is an eidetic construction; to assemble only twelve tribes for the composition of a city is an ontic construction. How many tribes should be in a city? How many property classes should be allowed in a city? These are the questions of measure. In fact, the notion of measure is somewhat ambiguous because it can be operative on both levels of construction, ontic and eidetic. For example, what should be the basic requirement for decent living in Magnesia? This is the question of measure that belongs to eidetic construction. On the other hand, how many property classes should be allowed is the question of measure that belongs to ontic construction. One is the eidetic measure; the other is the ontic measure.

Though we have treated the twelve tribes as elements for the construction of Magnesia, each tribe itself is composed of 420 citizens or households. The citizens and their households function as elements for the construction of a tribe, and the number 420 is the ontic measure for this construction. To restrict the membership of the Council of Elders to 360 is also an act of construction that requires an ontic measure, because its membership can be larger or smaller than 360. The same method of construction is employed to set up not only the general political framework of Magnesia, but also the particular institutions such as the system of education, the judiciary, and the penal code. Their construction also requires the notion of ontic measure, and this notion was discussed in both the *Statesman* and the *Philebus*. This central notion for Platonic construction is the notion of the right measure or mixture, or more simply the golden mean.

Let us look at some examples of the right measure or mixture. The governing structure of Magnesia is said to be the golden mean or the right mixture of authority and liberty,[5] and its system of election is a mixture of balloting and lottery, which respectively represent monarchy and democracy (756e). The Nocturnal Council is a mixture of young and old, new learning and old experience (951d). The property law is a mixture of public and private holdings; though the land remains the common property of the whole city, it is divided into allotments for private use. A marriage requires a good mixture of opposing genetic endowments, if it is going to produce good children (773a). Justice is a mixture of prudence, temperance, and courage (631c). The law is effective when it is a mixture of persuasion and compulsion. In short, the well-constructed state must be well mixed like a good drink (773d). This theme of mixing well for the right measure constitutes the final section of the *Statesmen*, where the Eleatic Stranger explains the nature of royal art as the blending together of two temperaments, the gentle and the courageous, for the constitution of a state. The same art of mixing well is the art of Platonic construction that was elaborated in the *Philebus* in the guise of the divine method and the fourfold distinction. The same art is now used for the construction of Magnesia. Platonic construction is the construction of proper measures.

The construction of proper measures requires two elements, knowledge of transcendent Forms and knowledge of empirical facts, because it involves the *limit* and the *unlimited*. The *limit* is derived from the Forms, and the *unlimited* is provided by the empirical world. Let us now consider how the two forms of knowledge, empirical and transcendent, operate in the construction of Magnesia. It has been controversial whether the existence of transcendental Forms is accepted in the *Laws*.[6] Though we cannot take up this issue here, we can safely assume that the presence of Forms is fairly evident in this dialogue. As R. F. Stalley points out, however, the theory of Forms in the *Laws* is quite different from the one given in the *Republic*.[7] The Athenian Stranger does not say that the Forms are truly real, while the world of phenomena is only apparently real. There is no sharp separation of Forms from phenomena. Though the Form transcends the concrete particulars, it is not a concrete paradigm, but an abstract universal. It provides the unity of many particulars, for example, the unity of virtues (963a–965e), and it is the linchpin in the question of One and Many (965b). The Forms of the *Laws* can be described as the Ones of H_{5+7}.

For the cognition of Forms, the Athenian Stranger never uses the discursive method of definition or argument. Instead, he simply appeals to our intuition. Consider the way he handles the Thrasymachean thesis that justice is the advantage of the stronger because justice means to obey the laws laid down by the stronger to promote their own interest (714c–715c). He handles this thesis in a much simpler way than Socrates does at *Republic* 338c–347a. Socrates tries to refute the thesis with a series of arguments. In the first argument, for example, he says that the thesis is defeated by the fact that just acts as defined by Thrasymachus can sometimes turn out to be harmful to the stronger, because the stronger may not know their own interests in laying down the laws. This argument is as flimsy as to say that the definition of medicine as the art of curing sickness is invalidated by the fact that medicine sometimes fails to cure sickness. Socrates' other arguments against Thrasymachus are not any better than the first one; they are all futile in refuting the Thrasymachean thesis.

The concept of justice belongs to our basic intuition, and it is futile to try to prove that some basic intuition is wrong, because, unlike arguments and proofs, the basic intuitions are not subject to proof or disproof. The Athenian Stranger makes no such futile attempt, but simply says that the laws designed for the advantage of one social group rather than of the whole community are not true laws. In such a community, the word *justice* is an empty name (715bc). His method is not argumentative but *intuitive*; it appeals to our basic intuition of justice. Anybody with a sound intuition of justice can immediately see that the advantage of the stronger is injustice, although it is often disguised as justice. If one cannot see it, one cannot be proven wrong by argument because all arguments are constructed on our basic intuitions.

This is not to say that the *Laws* always appeals to our intuition rather than to reasoned arguments. The Athenian Stranger readily employs arguments whenever he has to deal with the problems that cannot be settled by intuition. In book 10, for example, he advances elaborate arguments for theism against the atheists. The existence of gods and their concern with humankind are clearly not matters of intuition. He also advances many arguments in support of the thesis that the virtuous are happier than the vicious (660–662, 716–717, 732–734, 742). Whether or not virtue is always rewarded with happiness is surely another question that cannot be settled by intuition. On the other hand, he wastes little argument to prove such an intuitively obvious point that the laws should not serve the private interests but promote the good of the entire state (715ab).

The basic intuition is the intuition of transcendental Forms, but it is not sufficient for Platonic construction. It also requires empirical knowledge, because it has to make use of the *unlimited* as much as the *limit*. In this regard, it is like musical composition, which requires not only the transcendent knowledge of aesthetic ideals but also the empirical knowledge of musical instruments and their capacities. Let us now see how the Athenian Stranger makes use of empirical knowledge. By historical reflection on Persia and Athens, he establishes his thesis that the absolute and undivided power leads to tyranny, and the lawless liberty to anarchy (693d–703d). By a similar reflection on the history of Sparta, he shows that the mixture of authority and liberty produces the due measure for government (691c–693c).

The historical and empirical investigations, however, are not sufficient for constructing the normative standard (due measure) for government, because they are limited to the causal account of institutions. By the causal account, we can tell that tyranny follows from the absolute power, but not that tyranny is bad. The latter is a normative judgment that requires normative intuition. Thus, the normative intuition of transcendental Forms and the empirical knowledge of historical facts are two essential elements of normative construction.

It is hard to overstate the importance of empirical and historical knowledge in the *Laws*. Experience is so essential for the development of practical wisdom that old age becomes almost equivalent to wisdom. The wisdom of the old is highly respected. All the important positions such as the Guardians of the Law and the members of the Nocturnal

Council are given to the old citizens. Even in music and dance, the third chorus of old people is more important than the first (young boys) and the second (young men) choruses (665d). In matters of government, the Athenian Stranger says, one's vision is dullest in youth, and keenest in old age (715de). For this reason, he has two old men for his partners of dialogue in contrast to the two young partners of Socrates in the *Republic*. The importance of empirical knowledge is further stressed by the proposal that the knowledge of empirical astronomy should be included in the qualification for being a member of the Nocturnal Council. As we noted before, the *Republic* made an emphatic distinction between empirical and pure astronomy, and recommended only the latter as fit for the education of the future Guardians. In the *Laws*, that distinction is forgotten, and pure astronomy is not even mentioned.

The empirical Forms also play an important role in the construction of normative standards. When the Athenian Stranger begins to reflect on the historical experience of Persia and Athens for enlightenment, he calls their constitutions the two matrices (693d), that is, they are the empirically produced models or Forms. These empirical models are two ideal types that represent two qualities of liberty and authority, and each of these two qualities is a continuum like pleasure and pain, hot and cold. Hence the construction of a due measure by a mixture of liberty and authority requires the technique of Pythagorean construction and the logic of continuum. In his discussion of homicide in anger, the Athenian Stranger uses the same logic of continuum in making the distinction between voluntary and involuntary acts. He says that no act in anger is either totally voluntary or totally involuntary, and that every act in anger is partly voluntary and partly involuntary (867a–c). Instead of the voluntary/involuntary dichotomy, he uses the category of resemblance, for example, some acts resemble the voluntary more than the involuntary. There is no clearer boundary between voluntary and involuntary for the acts of anger than there is between hot and cold. This is a highly innovative way of handling perhaps the most difficult question in metaphysics, namely, the problem of free will and determinism.

The logic of continuum makes the constructivism of the *Laws* different from the constructivism of the *Republic*. The division of the three classes for the Kallipolis is made in an analogy to the tripartite division of the soul, and there is a natural difference between the three parts of the soul. By contrast, such a natural difference is not involved in the division of the four classes for Magnesia. All of them have the same qualification of owning properties, and their only difference lies in the quantity of their property. This quantitative difference lies in an indeterminate continuum, which can be divided into any number of segments. Hence the citizens of Magnesia can be divided into any number of classes. The fixing of these numbers is more or less arbitrary, whereas there was a natural basis for dividing the state into three classes in the *Republic*. Thus, the Kallipolis admits a radical difference and inequality among the three social classes, but Magnesia recognizes a basic equality of all citizens.

The classical logic of classes governs the construction of the Kallipolis, and the logic of continuum governs the construction of Magnesia. The logic of classes is a logic of discontinua; it presupposes a clear discontinuity or demarcation between different classes. The logic of discontinua is useful for the demarcation of natural kinds, because their demarcation is usually distinct. On the other hand, the logic of continuum is useful within the boundary of each natural kind. Consider the demarcation between two natural kinds, sounds and colors; nobody would think of using the logic of continuum for talking about their demarcation from each other. Within the boundary of each natural kind, however, we have to rely on the logic of continuum and resemblance rather than on the logic of discontinua or classes.

In the *Republic*, the three social classes are treated as though they were three natural kinds or three species of human beings. Since each of these three species is supposed to develop only one of the three parts of the soul by specialization, none of them is allowed to be a complete human being. This has been recognized as one of the most serious flaws in the *Republic*.[8] The *Laws* rectifies this flaw by employing the logic of continuum and resemblance as the basic instrument for social organization. Though Magnesia is not an egalitarian society, it is a society of proportional equality (757bc). All citizens proportionately enjoy the basic equality in material possession and political participation.

The Construction of the Physical Universe

In the *Laws*, the Pythagorean ideal of constructed order is not restricted to the ideal city, but extends to the motion of the heavens. Here is a picture of its circular motion:

> And we learn, at any rate, that in this rotation such motion carries the largest and the smallest circles around together, distributing itself proportionately to the small and the large, being less and more according to proportion. That is how it has become a source of all wonders, conveying the large and small circle at the same time, at slow and fast speeds that are in agreement, an effect that someone would expect to be impossible. (893cd, trans. Pangle)

This general principle of circular motions is again based on the notion of continuum ("being less and more") and that of proportion, which arises from Pythagorean construction. Book 10 of the *Laws* gives a synoptic view of the physical universe, which derives its central ideas from H_{2a} of the *Parmenides*. This hypothesis lays out a general theory of locomotion and alteration, combination and separation, increase and decrease in size, assimilation and dissimilation, and generation and corruption.[9] As we noted earlier, H_{2a} is an extension of H_2, which is incorporated into H_{5+7}, Plato's ultimate categoreal scheme. H_{5+7} is the basis for Plato's Pythagorean constructivism.

The synoptic view of book 10 of the *Laws* is fully spelled out in the *Timaeus*, the story of creation by the Demiurge. His method of construction is exactly the same art of mixing and blending that is spelled out in the *Philebus* and used for the construction of Magnesia. The construction of the World-Soul requires the operation of blending on two levels (35a). First, there is the blending of the indivisible *being* and the divisible *being*, the indivisible *identity* and the divisible *identity*, and the indivisible *difference* and the divisible *difference*. These three operations produce the intermediate *being*, the intermediate *identity*, and the intermediate *difference*. The blending of these three produces the World-Soul. The distinction between the indivisible and the divisible corresponds to the Pythagorean distinction between the *limit* and the *unlimited*. The intermediate *being*, *identity*, and *difference* are the mixtures of the *limit* and the *unlimited*, and the World-Soul emerges as the final mixture of these mixtures.

The *Timaeus* recognizes three distinct entities, Being, Space, and Becoming (52d). Being is the *limit*; Space is the *unlimited*; Becoming is their mixture. These three elements are also essential in the construction of primary bodies (53c–55c). The Demiurge constructs them by molding primitive matter in the shape of four eternal atomic patterns: fire, air, water, and earth. The eternal pattern is the *limit*; the original matter is the *unlimited*. Since the eternal patterns clearly belong to Plato's old theory of Forms, they have generated a controversy for Plato scholars. Whereas the Forms seem to disappear from the other late dialogues, they seem to reappear in the *Timaeus*. How should we account for this inconsistency in the late dialogues? G. E. L. Owen has tried to resolve this question by reassigning the *Timaeus* from the late to the middle dialogues.[10] But this move cannot be supported by textual evidence.

The *Timaeus*, however, does not resurrect Plato's old theory of Forms in its entirety; it is restricted to the creation of primary bodies. If Timaeus were to adhere to the old theory of Forms, he would say that the eternal Forms were also the models for the creation of trees and plants, animals and humans, body and soul, and even gods and stars. But the eternal Forms are not even mentioned in the creation of so many other things than the primary bodies. The only eternal pattern for the creation of all these things is that of an eternal Living Being (37cd). This Form is as general as the Form of the Good or Being. In Plato's new theory of Forms, as we noted, only the most general Forms are admitted as primitive Forms. Hence, the Form of the Living Being is perfectly acceptable for the new theory as much as the Forms of Being, Identity, and Difference are.

The eternal Forms of primary bodies, to be sure, cannot easily be accommodated within Plato's new theory of Forms. How then can we account for their presence in the *Timaeus*? I propose the following account. The conversation of the *Timaeus* is said to have taken place, by agreement, the day after the discussion on the best form of society, and Socrates gives a brief summary of the discussion, which can readily be identified with the *Republic* (*Timaeus* 17c-19b). That is, the *Timaeus* is presented as a continuation of the *Republic*. Although this is an incredible pretense, we will not discuss its significance until chapter 8. For the moment, let us see what Plato has to do to keep up this pretense. Since the theory of paradigmatic Forms is a prominent feature of the *Republic*, its reappearance in the *Timaeus* can make the latter dialogue appear to be a continuation of the former. This is his literary or expository device to render the dramatic date of the *Timaeus* credible.

Though the theory of primary bodies and their eternal Forms is a remnant of the old theory of Forms, it is not totally incompatible with Plato's new theory of Forms, because it can be restated in the new theory of Platonic construction. All the primary bodies are constructed from two basic triangles, the right-angled isosceles and the right-angled scalene (53d). These two triangles are differently combined to produce the four atomic shapes of the pyramid, the octahedron, the icosahedron, and the cube. But none of them is permanently fixed. Each of them can disintegrate to their basic triangles, and the latter can recombine to produce different atomic structures. Combination and separation, composition and decomposition, are the essential features of atomic structures. In that case, there is no reason not to regard the four eternal models of atomic structure as the works of divine construction. Although they are created by the god, they can still be called eternal because divine creation takes place prior to the creation of time itself. At *Republic* 597c, Socrates had no qualm in saying that the god made only one eternal Form of Bed.

The two basic triangles that make up all the atoms are more primitive than the atomic structures. But even those triangles would not have been regarded as eternal entities by the Pythagoreans. After talking about the construction of primary bodies, Timaeus says that the principles more remote than these are known to the god and such men as the god favors (53d). An account of these remote principles is given in the *Laws*: "Clearly, when the original cause, obtaining growth, proceeds to the second transformation, and from this to the next, and, when it arrives at the third, it allows of perception by perceivers. By this transformation and change everything comes into being" (894a, trans. Pangle).

This passage restates the original Pythagorean theory of construction: a point is transformed into a line, which is transformed into a plane, which is transformed into a solid, which is finally transformed into a visible physical object. This passage is sometimes taken to indicate that Plato accepts the Pythagorean theory that perceptual objects are created from geometrical entities.[11] But the primary bodies of the *Timaeus* cannot be reduced to spatial properties because they are composed of not only spatial properties, but also the original matter that is already contained in the Receptacle. But this passage is important for indicating that even the triangles are not primitive entities, but products of construction.

If the triangles are constructed, then the Forms of primary bodies should be doubly so because they are constructed from the triangles. On the other hand, if they are not constructed, but eternal patterns, they will remove all constraints on the eidetic population, and Platonic Heaven will be populated with an infinite number of eidetic objects. This may be the strongest argument for the view that even the so-called eternal patterns of primary bodies are works of construction. Already in the *Republic*, as we noted, Socrates talked about the construction of the Form of Bed by the god, though he was not even thinking of the construction of the physical world. But the *Timaeus* constructs not only the primary bodies but even the souls, and the construction of composite Forms seems to be consistent with this cosmic program of construction.

No doubt, the *Timaeus* repeatedly reiterates the demarcation between Being and Becoming, the hallmark of the middle dialogues, and this demarcation has more than anything else reinforced the view that this dialogue retains Plato's old two-world view. But the dyad of Being and Becoming of the middle dialogues is expanded to the triad of Being, Space, and Becoming. In this new triad, Becoming emerges as the blending of Being and Space, and this blending produces one world with two elements in place of the two worlds. As William Prior points out, the demarcation between the Forms and the phenomena is handled quite differently in the *Timaeus*. In the *Republic* (508c, 509d, 517b), the Forms are placed in the intelligible space (*noetos topos*), while the phenomena are situated in the perceptual space. The demarcation of these two spaces, which represents Plato's old two-world view, is rejected in the *Timaeus*. "By insisting on the non-spatiality of the

Forms,'' Prior says, "Plato clearly (more clearly than before) shows
his awareness of their abstract nature."[12] The abstract Forms need not
constitute a separate and independent universe, and this is the important
difference between the Forms as concrete paradigms and the Forms as
abstract universals.

Reason the Demiurge

This is the Platonic version of Pythagorean constructivism, which
governs the construction of both the physical universe and Magnesia. It
is literally the divine method, because it belongs to the god, the Demiurge. This divine artisan is reason personified (*Timaeus* 47e); it is none
other than what is described as the cause and agent of mixture and
creation (*demiourgoun*) at *Philebus* 26e, 27b. The construction of Magnesia is the extension of this constructivist reason; its laws are the dictate of reason.[13] The human beings can construct their cities and laws
only insofar as they participate as rational beings in the cosmic reason
of construction. This is to follow in the footsteps of God, who is the
measure of all things (716c), or to obey the immortal element in our
humanity (714a). Thus, the principle of rational construction links together the *Laws* and the *Timaeus* in one joint project of construction.
Since this principle is expounded as the divine method in the *Philebus*,
this dialogue functions as the bridge between the *Laws* and the *Timaeus*.

The *Philebus* is also the bridge that connects the *Statesman* to the
Laws. The *Statesman* ends with a description of royal art as the art of
blending and weaving; in the *Philebus*, this art is restated as the art of
mixing, the art of Pythagorean construction. In the *Laws*, this art is used
for the construction of Magnesia. In the *Philebus*, to be sure, the art of
construction is introduced to facilitate the discussion on the role and
place of pleasure in the constitution of the human good. But the problem of pleasure, especially how to manage it, is the leading question
that opens the inquiry into the art of legislation in the first book of the
Laws. Although the laws of Sparta and Crete are well designed for
the cultivation of courage, the Athenian Stranger points out, they are
inadequate for the cultivation of temperance.

Courage is the virtue for controlling pain in the face of overpowering fear; temperance is the virtue for controlling excessive pleasure. The Spartan and the Cretan laws do not really teach the youth how to cope with the problem of overpowering pleasures; instead they force the young to stay away from excessive pleasures. Hence, their virtue of temperance is the virtue of abstinence. In place of this negative virtue, the Athenian Stranger advocates the need of cultivating the positive virtue of temperance, by fully exposing the young to the experience of strong pleasures, for example by participating in a drinking party (636–651). Thus the question of pleasure is the thematic connector between the *Laws* and the *Philebus*.

In the *Laws*, the question of pleasure and pain is not an independent question; it is linked to the question of courage and temperance. The Athenian Stranger says that these two virtues are equally important for the ultimate goal of self-control, because pleasure and pain are the two springs of human nature (636d). The role of these two virtues for self-control is precisely the last topic of discussion in the *Statesman*; as we already noted, the Athenian Stranger describes the royal art as the art of blending tenderness and courageousness, the two basic dispositions for the constitution of temperance and courage. The importance of these two virtues is the thematic connector between the *Laws* and the *Statesman*. Thus the *Philebus* thematically links the *Statesman* with the *Laws*. This complex thematic role may also explain one special feature of the *Philebus*; it not only opens but also ends *in medias res*. Because this dialogue is a thematic bridge between the *Statesman* and the *Laws*, it can begin and end in the middle of discussion.

Getting back to Platonic constructivism, let us note that it really begins with the construction of the Kallipolis in the *Republic*. But the method of its construction is quite different from the one we have just examined, because they are based on two different theories of Forms, the old and the new. In the old theory, the Forms are said to be concrete paradigms; in the new theory, they are supposedly no more than abstract universals. The former is the theory of determinate Form; the latter is the theory of indeterminate Forms. Elsewhere I labeled these two theories as the skyscraper version and the bedrock version of Platonism.[14] The skyscraper version paints a lavish picture of Platonic

Heaven: it is adorned with a complete system of normative rules and standards. The bedrock version does not paint such a lavish picture; its modest claim is that Platonic Heaven gives only the primitive Forms. The difference of these two versions can perhaps be better understood in terms of mathematical Platonism. The skyscraper version claims that Platonic Heaven contains the complete edifice of mathematics from arithmetic and geometry to calculus and topology. On the other hand, the bedrock version holds that it contains only the basic mathematical ideas, and that mathematical systems have to be constructed from those basic ideas. Constructivism is essential for completing the bedrock version of Platonism.

The distinction between the bedrock and the skyscraper versions also obtains for the classical and the medieval theories of natural law, because it is another version of Platonism. In the skyscraper version, natural law is understood as a complete system of eternal rules and standards for the government of human behavior. In its bedrock version, natural law only provides the basic precepts for constructing a normative system. Aquinas appears to subscribe to this view of natural law in his distinction between its primary and secondary precepts. He says that primary precepts are self-evident and ungenerated, and that secondary precepts are derived from primary ones by practical reason. In that case, primary precepts belong to the bedrock foundation of natural law, and secondary precepts to its superstructure, the skyscraper. The former are objects of intuition; the latter are products of construction.

In the skyscraper version, the Forms are fully determinate; they are more real than their copies in the phenomenal world. For example, the Form of Beauty is more beautiful than any beautiful thing in this world. The nature of Forms is described by the doctrine of self-exemplification, super-exemplification, and absolute exemplification. All these hallmarks of the skyscraper version are gone from the bedrock version. The Forms are now conceived as essentially indeterminate. At *Statesman* 285d–286b, the Eleatic Stranger admits that the greatest and noblest conceptions are difficult to comprehend because they cannot be given any images. The images are much more determinate than those conceptions. In the *Phaedo* and *Republic*, Socrates held exactly the opposite view: the Forms are much more intelligible than the sensible objects, because the latter are indeterminate (always more or less so and so), while the former are determinate.

The two types of Forms present different problems for their realization. To realize a determinate Form in the world of phenomena is to copy it; it is the art of replication. But the art of replication cannot realize an indeterminate Form, because a copy of indeterminate Form would be also indeterminate. Its realization requires some determinate shape, which can be given by the art of articulating and specifying indeterminate Forms. This art was used in the definition of sophist and statesman, and further elaborated in the divine method of the *Philebus*. It is also the art of combining Forms or weaving them. This art governs the construction of Magnesia. On the other hand, the art of replication governs the construction of the Kallipolis; it is said to reproduce the eternal pattern laid up in heaven (*Republic* 592b).

In these two arts of articulation and replication, the knowledge of Forms plays different roles. In the art of replication, the knowledge of Forms is the most important thing because it alone guarantees the right replication of Forms in the phenomenal world. If you know the Form, you can replicate it in the phenomenal world; if you do not know it, you cannot replicate it. How well you can replicate a Form depends on how well you know it. In the art of articulation and creation, the knowledge of Forms cannot play such a decisive role because it is as indeterminate as the Forms themselves. The most important thing for this art is the power of transforming indeterminate Forms into determinate Ones. Thus, we have two models of realizing the Forms in the world of phenomena: the model of replication and the model of articulation.

The model of replication is like the act of building a house in accordance with a detailed blueprint. The model of articulation can also be compared to the act of building a house, but there is no detailed blueprint for its construction. It is guided only by an indeterminate concept of a house. These two models demand different skills from the builder; the model of articulation places a far greater burden on the builder than the model of replication. Hence the two models differ in ranking the relative significance of the theoretical and the practical or productive knowledge. In the model of replication, theoretical knowledge is supreme, and practical knowledge is derivative. The latter is only a copy of the former. In the model of articulation, theoretical knowledge is not really knowledge, but only the concept of an indeterminate ideal or principle such as the ideal of justice or the principle of equality. On the other hand, practical knowledge has the power to convert an indeterminate concept or principle into a determinate object, action, or institution in the phenomenal world.

The model of indeterminate Forms and their articulation becomes fully operational in the *Laws*. In the construction of Magnesia, the Athenian Stranger constantly appeals to experience and history; he builds on the legal traditions of Athens, Sparta, and other Greek cities. There is no hint of direct recourse to transcendent Forms. The operation of the Nocturnal Council is no different; it makes extensive use of the experience of its members. They even consult the citizens who have traveled abroad and studied the laws of other states, especially when those laws are superior to their own. These measures would have made no sense for the philosopher-king of the *Republic*, whose decision is supposedly guided by his knowledge of Forms, which is claimed to be far superior to any empirical knowledge. Whereas the knowledge of Forms is determinate in the *Republic*, it is indeterminate in the *Laws*. Unlike the former, the latter cannot serve as a direct guide in the practical domain until it is given determinate content in the domain of experience and history.

The *Statesman* is the watershed; it looks backward to the *Republic* and forward to the *Laws*. From this dual perspective, the Eleatic Stranger gives two definitions of royal art, which is separated by the myth of two ages. These two definitions present two different accounts of political art. Charles Griswold has made an instructive comparison of these two accounts.[15] In the first definition, the Eleatic Stranger begins with the distinction between gnostic and practical knowledge, and places political science together with arithmetic in the camp of gnostic knowledge. The distinction between gnostic and practical knowledge restates the distinction between theoretical and practical knowledge of the *Republic*. In the second definition, Griswold says, the Eleatic Stranger treats political science as a branch of practical art.

In the first definition, political art is treated as a branch of theoretical knowledge; in the second definition, it is treated as a branch of practical knowledge. In my view, the first definition goes with the model of replication, and the second definition with the model of articulation. Griswold further points out that the first definition of a statesman is accompanied by the analogy of shepherding, and the second definition by the analogy of weaving. The art of weaving makes fabric, but the art of shepherding does not make sheep. The latter belongs to the model of replication, and the former to the model of articulation. Just like a shepherd watching his flock of sheep, the statesman can, in the model of replication, gain his knowledge by simply inspecting Forms (*Republic* 500c). In the model of articulation, the Forms are not the objects of the highest knowledge, because they are only the materials to be used for weaving. The highest knowledge belongs to the art of combining Forms. Hence the art of weaving is the royal art.

Finally, I want to point out an important ambiguity lurking in the notion of an eternal model for the Kallipolis. The ambiguity lies in the claim that the model is said to be not a Form and yet eternal. If it is eternal, it is the model for the art of replication. On the other hand, if it is not a Form, it can also be regarded as a model constructed by the art of combination and articulation. Though there is no easy way to resolve this ambiguity, it may as well be taken to indicate that the *Republic* already contains the substantive ideas for the theory of indeterminate Forms and the art of their articulation, while formally advocating only the theory of determinate Forms and the art of their replication. In that case, the *Republic* should mark the transition from the skyscraper version to the bedrock version of Platonism. And the transition appears to be inevitable, because the notion of articulating indeterminate Forms is far more plausible than the notion of replicating determinate Forms. The latter is only a carryover from the *Symposium*, which had to make the Forms fully determinate to be the direct objects of aesthetic experience.

Notes

1. Gregory Vlastos, *Platonic Studies* (Princeton: University Press, 1973), 117–23.

2. Sayre, *Plato's Late Ontology* (Princeton: University Press, 1983), 133–86.

3. A critical summary of this interpretation is given by Gosling in Plato, *Philebus* (Oxford: University Press, 1975), 160–65.

4. Here are some notable examples. R. Hackforth regards the first method as logical and the second method as ontological. *Plato's Examination of Pleasure* (Cambridge: University Press, 1945), 21. Stuart MacClintock says that the difference between the two methods corresponds to the distinction between the order of knowing and the order of being. "More on the Structure of the *Philebus*," *Phronesis* 6 (1961):46–52. A full comparison of the two methods is given by Dorothea Frede in her introduction to Plato, *Philebus* (Indianapolis, Ind.: Hackett, 1993), xxxiii–xxxix.

5. The Athenian Stranger talks about the mixture of monarchy and democracy rather than that of authority and liberty. But the latter is his real concern, as R. F. Stalley explains in his *Introduction to Plato's Laws* (Indianapolis: Hackett, 1983), 120.

6. For a good discussion of this issue, see Guthrie, *A History of Greek Philosophy* (Cambridge: University Press, 1975), 4:378–81.

7. *Introduction to Plato's Laws*, 135.

8. This point is fully discussed by Stalley, *Introduction to Plato's Laws*, 109–10.

9. For a fuller discussion, see Cornford, *Plato and Parmenides* (London: Routledge, 1939), 197–99; Allen, *Plato's Parmenides* (Minneapolis: University of Minnesota Press, 1983), 261–73.

10. Owen, "The Place of the *Timaeus* in Plato's Dialogues," in R. E. Allen, *Studies in Plato's Metaphysics* (New York: Humanities Press, 1965), 313–38.

11. Aristotle was the first to read the *Timaeus* in this manner (*De caelo* 299b15–300a19). A more recent representative is John Burnet, *Greek Philosophy: Thales to Plato* (London: Macmillan, 1914), 344.

12. *The Unity and Development in Plato's Metaphysics* (La Salle: Open Court), 91–92.

13. This point is stressed by Glenn Morrow, *Plato's Cretan City* (Princeton: University Press, 1960), 544.

14. T. K. Seung, *Intuition and Construction* (New Haven, Conn.: Yale University Press, 1993), xii–xiii.

15. Griswold, "Politike Episteme in Plato's *Statesman*," in *Essays in Ancient Greek Philosophy*, John Anton and Anthony Preus, ed. (Albany, N.Y.: SUNY Press, 1989) 3:141–67.

CHAPTER EIGHT

Platonic Thematics

The *Gorgias* is Plato's problem set; it sets forth the basic issues that will occupy Plato's attention throughout his long illustrious career. At the center of this problem set stands the Calliclean challenge. In our thematic journey, we have tried to interpret his dialogues as a series of responses to this challenge. The first response was ethical, the second was erotic, and the third was political. These three were represented by three different Socrateses. The first is the ethical Socrates, who inquires into the nature of virtue in the early dialogues. The second is the erotic or mystical Socrates, who emerges in the *Lysis*, and ascends to Platonic Heaven in the *Phaedo* and the *Symposium*. The third is the political Socrates, who descends to the world of phenomena in the *Protagoras* and the *Meno*, inaugurates political art in the *Euthydemus*, and creates the Kallipolis in the *Republic*. The succession of these three Socrates is a record not only of Plato's development of his own ideas, but also of his own critique of those ideas.

Plato replaced the ethical Socrates with the erotic Socrates, because he realized that the ethical Socrates could not meet the challenge of Callicles. For the sake of the mystical and erotic Socrates, he had to assert the existence of Forms as an independent world of absolute beauty, and to define *philosophia* as the love of that world. This new love defines the life of the erotic Socrates. Even within the erotic cycle, Plato's self-criticism remains relentless; his dissatisfaction with the *Phaedo* leads to the *Symposium*, in which he tries to reinstate the role of desire and appetite in the name of *eros* instead of renouncing them. But even the *Symposium* cannot really meet the challenge of Callicles, because the erotic Socrates is ill-equipped to cope with the social dimension of human life. In order to remedy this defect, Plato finally introduces the political Socrates in the long detour of the *Protagoras*, the *Meno*, the *Euthydemus*, and the *Republic*. The transition from the *Symposium* to the *Republic* is the transformation of *eros* into *philia*, the Pythagorean ideal of love and order introduced in the debate between Socrates and Callicles in the *Gorgias*. This transformation endows *philosophia* with its social dimension, and the ideal state of the *Republic* emerges as the city of this new *philosophia*.

The three cycles of the ethical, the erotic, and the political Socrates can be labeled as the cycles of *arete* (virtue), *eros* (erotic love), and *philia* (brotherly love). In the *Charmides*, temperance was established as the supreme virtue for the ethical cycle; in the *Republic*, justice is installed as the supreme virtue for the political cycle. Hence, the transition from the ethical to the political cycle can be seen as the supervenience of justice over temperance. But the virtue of temperance does not easily yield its old place. Though it is replaced by justice as the supreme virtue in the *Republic*, it is not reduced to the virtue of any one class or one part of the soul such as the virtue of wisdom or courage. Socrates could have defined temperance as the virtue of the artisan class just as he defined wisdom as the virtue of the governing class and courage as the virtue of the warrior class. Instead he defines temperance as a virtue of all three classes working together, that is, their harmony (*Republic* 431e). In this definition, temperance duplicates the function of justice. This anomaly can be explained as a residual effect of the old sovereignty the virtue of temperance had in the ethical cycle. Its sovereignty is almost reinstated in the *Laws*, as we will see later in this chapter. One way or another, the virtue of temperance retains its overriding significance throughout Plato's writings. So does the figure of Odysseus appear and reappear at every critical juncture of his writings. After all, temperance was the virtue of Odysseus.

The *Republic* is not only the end of the cycle of *philia*; it is also the culmination of all the three periods. It preserves and perfects everything Plato has accomplished in all three cycles of *arete*, *eros*, and *philia*.

This culmination is followed by the *Phaedrus*. It is Plato's dialogue with himself, where he takes stock of all his previous works. He becomes especially concerned with his stringent demarcation between the world of Forms and the world of phenomena, and with his disdainful treatment of the latter. This radical dualism recognizes the existence of order and beauty only in the intelligible world, and consigns the sensible world to the reign of disorder and disharmony. Such a view of reality not only goes against the Pythagorean ideal of universal order in the cosmos, but endorses the basic premise for Callicles' philosophy of power politics, that is, the physical world is only fit to be the beastly theater of ruthless struggle for power and survival.

If the physical world is such a hideous place as this, it cannot serve as the matrix for the construction of a decent community. In this case, the flight to the other world may be the only way out of it, but the way out is also an escape from the Calliclean challenge. There is no other way to meet this challenge except by embracing the world of phenomena as the matrix of our existence. This requires the birth of a political Socrates, who can descend to this world and establish a decent social order. For this enterprise, he has to acquire a positive understanding and appreciation of this world. In the *Phaedrus*, the affirmation of this world is an important topic for Plato's self-critique, and continues to be so in the *Cratylus*. In these two dialogues, as we saw in chapter 4, Socrates begins the search for the *logos* of phenomena, the art of talking about this world. Previously, he had been chiefly concerned with the *logos* of Forms, the art of talking about the Forms, which was called the science of dialectic in the *Republic*. For the sake of distinction, the art of talking about the phenomena has to be associated with rhetoric, and the question of how to transform rhetoric into a true art becomes one of the important topics in the *Phaedrus*.

In the *Sophist* and the *Statesman*, the *logos* of phenomena is finally devised and presented as the art of *diairesis*. But this art is now called the art of dialectic, and described as the art of combining and separating the Forms. Thus the art of talking about the Forms and the art of talking about the phenomena come together and become one art of *diairesis*, which is the art of Platonic construction. This fusion of the two arts has been prepared by the new theory of Forms developed in the *Parmenides* and by the new theory of knowledge suggested in the *Theaetetus*. In fact, these two new theories fuse the world of Forms and the world of phenomena into one world whose ontological structure is delineated by the categoreal structure of H_{5+7}.

The fusion of the two worlds is a metaphysical move that initiates the metaphysical cycle in Plato's dialogues. This cycle comprises the four dialogues of the *Parmenides*, the *Theaetetus*, the *Sophist*, and the *Statesman*. I propose to call them the Eleatic Tetrad because Eleatic legacy plays the central role in those dialogues. The Eleatic Tetrad divides itself into two dyads. The *Parmenides* and the *Theaetetus* constitute the first dyad, and the *Sophist* and the *Statesman*, the second dyad. The first dyad is a rigorous critique of the two-world view, which prepares for the constructive work in the second dyad. Yet the *Sophist* and the *Statesman* are only prolegomenas for further works. The *Statesman* does not construct an ideal state or constitution, but only specifies the requirement for such a construction. Likewise, the *Sophist* does not give a system of ontology and cosmology, but only sketches out a categoreal scheme that will be required for such a system.

These preparatory works lay the foundation for Plato's final works in another group of four dialogues, the *Laws*, the *Philebus*, the *Timaeus*, and the *Critias*. I would like to call them the Pythagorean Tetrad because the Pythagorean constructivism is the pervasive theme of these dialogues. The Pythagorean Tetrad can also be divided into two dyads. The first dyad is normative; the second dyad is descriptive. The *Laws* and the *Philebus* constitute the normative dyad; the *Timaeus* and the *Critias* constitute the descriptive dyad. In these two dyads, Plato presents his final response to the challenge of Callicles.

From the *Republic* to the *Laws*

The division of labor between the *Philebus* and the *Laws* is marked by the divide between ethics and politics. The topic of the *Philebus* is what is good for human beings and what is the proper place of pleasure in the human good. The topic of the *Laws* is the problem of legislation for a political community. The separation of ethics and politics in these two dialogues repairs the most grievous defect in the *Republic*. In this dialogue, Plato tried to use the same model of discourse for talking about ethics and politics because he believed in the structural isomorphism between the soul and the state. He wanted to maintain the thesis that the same four virtues of wisdom, courage, moderation, and justice should obtain for both the soul and the state. But this premise of structural isomorphism overlooks the most obvious difference between the soul and the state. The question of justice cannot arise between the different parts of the soul because they can never attain the required difference in personhood. Whatever difference there may be among the different parts of a soul, none of them can function as an independent agent.

The unity of a soul is much more stringent than the unity of a state. The unity of a soul is the unity of a single person; the unity of a state is a unity of many persons. The unity of a state should allow enough room for the difference of persons, but the ideal state is designed to function as though it were a single person. By the celebrated analogy between the soul and the state, the *Republic* not only eliminates the distinction of persons, but imposes an excessive demand for the unity of the state. It eliminates the institutions of private property and private family among the members of the governing class. It allows no distinction between *mine* and *thine* not only in the distribution of material possessions, but also in the experience of pleasures and pains. In the ideal state, everything should be *ours* (*Republic* 463–464). In such a unitary community, the problem of justice is dissolved. It cannot even become a problem.

The structural analogy also inordinately magnifies the difference between the governing class and the governed. Within the human soul, there is an enormous cognitive difference between intellect and appetite. If the difference between the governing and the governed classes is to mirror the difference between intellect and appetite, the governing class should be like the gods and the governed should be like the brutes. The two classes should be like two different species. Gregory Vlastos called this glaring class difference Plato's bifurcation of the human race, and attributed it to his bifurcation of the whole universe into the two domains of sensible and intelligible objects.[1] But the bifurcation of the universe need not dictate the bifurcation of the human race, if the intelligible world is accessible to all the human race rather than to only a few philosophers. It is not the bifurcation of the universe, but the structural analogy of the state to the soul that dictates the bifurcation of the human race.

The question of whether the bifurcation of human race is acceptable or not depends on the empirical character of human nature, that is, whether human beings are born with such glaring differences in natural endowments that their classification is like the classification of gold, silver, and bronze as Socrates says in the *Republic*. But Socrates does not pay much attention to the empirical nature of humanity and the world in the construction of the Kallipolis. On the other hand, the construction of Magnesia is securely based on empirical knowledge, as we noted in the last chapter. This is perhaps the most important factor that accounts for the extensive difference between the *Laws* and the *Republic*. Before considering their difference, however, let us stress the common premise for both works: the government should be entrusted to those who have the knowledge and intelligence for governing a state.

The rule of wisdom is the common ideal for the construction of both the Kallipolis and Magnesia. In implementing this ideal in the *Republic*, Socrates completely ignores the empirical conditions, and only tries to combine political power with philosophical wisdom, which leads to the ideal of a philosopher-king, which in turn leads to the ideal of his absolute power. Since the philosopher-king is wise enough not to abuse his power, he thinks, his power should be free of all political constraints. Thus, he hops from one ideal to another, without paying attention to the empirical conditions that are required for their realization. For example, he does not even consider whether there can be any real human beings wise and virtuous enough to live up to such a lofty ideal as that of the philosopher-king. Instead he only claims that the realization of the ideal state depends on such a man of wisdom being invested with the power of government.

The Athenian Stranger operates differently; he hops back and forth between the ideal and the real. He pays special attention to the empirical conditions. Whenever he find the ideals too high or too demanding for the real world, he readily makes the compromise. About absolute power, for example, he notes that no mortal can wield it without becoming swollen with insolence and injustice (713c, 875a–d). Even if human beings can gain the theoretical knowledge of justice and a correct understanding of jurisprudence, he warns, they would never be able to restrain their private interests and pursue the good of all if they are given the positions of unconstrained power (874e–875c). It is their human nature, especially their instinctual feelings of pleasure and pain, that will ultimately drive them to a blind pursuit of private interests, if their powers are unaccountable. This universal natural propensity can be controlled by placing all public officials under the constraint of law.

The Athenian Stranger insists that every officer should be held accountable, and be subject to scrutiny before his appointment and to audit after his tenure. In Magnesia, the office of scrutinizer is one of the highest positions, which is accompanied with the highest honors. Without these legal constraints, he says, even those who have the knowledge of right government cannot overcome the power of appetite. Such is the nature of mortal beings, he declares (875b). The rule of law is required because of the universal propensity for the pursuit of self-interest. As an ideal, the rule of a wise statesman would indeed be far better than the rule of law, because the latter is only a poor copy of the former, only if we could find a person of wisdom who could transcend self-interest (875cd). Since there are no such human beings in this world, the Athenian Stranger is willing to settle for the rule of law as the second best.

The empirical consideration also enters in the conception of *philia* that binds together Magnesia. In the Kallipolis, wisdom is the bond of *philia* and fellowship. The Guardians and their Auxiliaries can constitute a community of brothers and friends, only because they share the same philosophical wisdom. They need nothing else. On the other hand, the artisans cannot participate in the fellowship of *philia*, because they lack philosophical wisdom. This purely intellectual conception of *philia* is overhauled by the Athenian Stranger; he recognizes the importance of emotional and natural elements in *philia*. To this end, he not only endorses but emphasizes a few elements that were not allowed or were ignored in the *Republic*. Whereas the *Republic* abolishes the natural institution of family for the class of Guardians, the *Laws* accepts it, along with the tribal organizations, as the most basic institutions for social solidarity and cohesion.

The Athenian Stranger also recognizes the importance of social equality for *philia*. Citing the ancient proverb, "Equality breeds friendship," he says that slaves and masters can never be friends (757a). The relation of the governing and the governed in the *Republic* is not much better than the relation of masters and slaves in the domain of political rights. Plato now realizes that the Kallipolis cannot be a community of *philia*. The Athenian Stranger says that such a community requires not only the wisdom of the ruler but also the willing consent of the ruled. But the willing consent can be given only by free people. This is a remarkable change not only from the *Republic* where the consent of the governed was not even considered as a problem, but even from the *Statesman* where the importance of informed consent was recognized with considerable ambivalence. Though the Eleatic Stranger admits that it is better to rule with the consent of the governed than with force and violence, he still holds that a true statesman has the right to govern with or without the consent of the governed (*Statesman* 293a–c; 296a–d).

The equality of all citizens is one of the recurrent themes in the *Laws*. Although the Athenian Stranger does not advocate the equality of women to men as vocally as Socrates does in the *Republic*, there is no textual evidence to assume that the former's position is any weaker than the latter's. The *Laws* prescribes substantively equal programs of education for both sexes (804d–805a) and makes women eligible for public offices (785b). But the principle of equality goes well beyond gender boundaries; it does not allow glaring difference between rich and poor, or between ruler and ruled. The autocratic power of the philosopher-king is replaced by an elaborate system of checks and balances, which diffuse the power of government from the Council of Elders to the Nocturnal Council, from the lowest to the highest courts, from the magistrates to their examiners and scrutinizers. Even the system of election incorporates the use of lots for the sake of equality and solidarity (757de).

In the *Laws*, liberty and equality are admitted as two essential elements for the constitution of *philia* in addition to wisdom. Without equality and liberty, the Athenian Stranger says, it is impossible to avoid disaffection and resentment among the masses and to promote the solidarity of all citizens. Liberty and equality are indispensable for achieving the harmony of feelings (757de, 773c). In the *Republic*, wisdom functions as the single base for supporting the community of *philia*; in the *Laws*, this single base is replaced by the tripod of wisdom, liberty, and equality. The three ideals of the French Revolution, liberty, equality, and fraternity, are already implicitly present in the constitution of Magnesia. Whereas fraternity has turned out to be the least important of the three ideals in the development of modern liberal traditions, it is the ultimate end of Magnesia.

The *Laws* is so radically different from the *Republic* that some commentators have thought it could not have been written by Plato.[2] Of course, this sort of response presupposes the naive view that the *Republic* is the most perfect summation of Plato's philosophy. In that view, anything that gravely diverges from the *Republic* could not have been written by Plato. But anyone who recognizes grievous deficiencies in the *Republic* would welcome and endorse the notable difference between the two political works. But there has been a repeated attempt to discount the difference between the two works and reclaim their unity.[3] What is really the exact relation of the *Laws* to the *Republic*? This has been one of the controversial questions in Plato scholarship. It appears that Plato anticipated his readers' perplexity on this question, and tried to explain it by his myth of the two ages (*Statesman* 269c–274e). Plato makes it clear that this myth is purely his own concoction. The Eleatic Stranger makes a special attempt to discourage the Young Socrates from associating it with some traditional myths.

Here is the outline of the myth. The history of the universe repeats the cycle of two ages, the age of Cronus and the age of Zeus. During the age of Cronus, the universe rotates in one direction with divine assistance. At the end of this age, the god relinquishes his control, and the universe reverses the direction of its motion and begins to move with its own force. This new cycle is the age of Zeus. In the age of Cronus, the god personally governs human beings and all other animals by appointing divine demons as their shepherds. It is the age of peace and prosperity, and there is no personal possession of wives and children. Nor is there any need for political institutions; political decisions are made directly by the divine ruler. In the age of Zeus, however, the divine government is terminated, and the whole universe is engulfed in an ever-increasing disorder. In this chaotic age, human beings and other animals are left to their own devices.

The Eleatic Stranger tells this story to facilitate the definition of royal art (*Statesman* 269c). What then is the relevance of this myth to the royal art of government? After finishing the myth, the Eleatic Stranger tells the Young Socrates that they have been making a mistake on a grand scale in their definition of statesman (274e). Whereas they were supposed to define the statesman for the present cycle of history, they were giving a definition suitable for the other cycle. The statesman who can govern without a constitution belongs to the age of Cronus. There is no point of having a constitution if there is a wise ruler who can personally administer the state. In the age of Zeus when the divine ruler departs from the scene, the world has to run in accordance with the instructions it has received from him. The constitutions are the instructions; they are only substitutes for his practical wisdom. But these substitutes become a necessity for the age of Zeus, because there are no longer divine rulers.

The age of Cronus and the age of Zeus represent the celebrated distinction between the rule of man and the rule of law that has become a enduring fixture of our political language. Their difference is explained by the Eleatic Stranger as follows. Because the circumstances are variable from case to case, it is impossible to design laws that can fit every case. Since laws have to be drafted only for the average cases in mind, they can never do justice to all cases (294b–295a). The impersonality of law is the source of inevitable injustice, and government by law can only be an approximation to complete justice. But this sort of injustice can be avoided under the personal government by a wise ruler, who can take into account the special circumstances of every case. The personal government by a wise ruler is the best form of government, and the impersonal government by law is the second best. Since the best form of government is unavailable to our age, the Eleatic Stranger and the Young Socrates have to settle for the second best. Their mistake on a grand scale was to look for the very best, whereas they could realize only the second best.

This is the same mistake that was made in the *Republic*, for the Kallipolis clearly belongs to the best form of government that is fit only for the age of Cronus. In the *Laws*, the Athenian Stranger constructs an ideal constitution with the aid of his two friends, while they were on the way to the cave and temple of Zeus (625b). Evidently, it is meant for the age of Zeus. He is also cognizant of the age of Cronus and its happy government under the divine ruler (713b–e). He repeats the distinction between the best and the second-best form of government. His description of the best form fits the ideal state of the *Republic* (739c–e). In this ideal state, all citizens are friends, who have everything in common. Everything private from joy to sorrow is excluded from all aspects of life. But he adds that such a marvelous city is inhabited only by gods or their children. Thus the *Republic* is consigned to the age of Cronus. This is Plato's ingenious way of saying that he has seen a systematic deficiency in the *Republic* and is trying his best to repair it in the *Laws*.[4] The *Republic* is for the rule of man; the *Laws* is for the rule of law.

Though the Eleatic Stranger in the *Statesman* tries to define a statesman suitable for the age of Zeus, as George Klosko correctly points out, the requirements for such a statesman are hardly distinguishable from the requirements for being the philosopher-king of the *Republic*.[5] In both cases, a single individual should embody all the virtues and knowledge for governing the state. Whereas the availability of such a superhuman, a moral saint and a political sage in one person, is the premise for the construction of the Kallipolis, its unavailability is the premise for the construction of Magnesia. Because the philosopher-king is a moral saint and a political sage at once, he is placed above the law, and the rest of citizenry should be kept out of the business of government because they do not know enough about it. Since such a sage-saint is not available for the construction of Magnesia, his individual wisdom is replaced by the collective wisdom of public officials and deliberative bodies, which require the participation of all citizens in the affairs of government. Nevertheless, political art is a matter of wisdom in both cases; as Glenn Morrow puts it, the rule of philosophy prevails in both the *Republic* and the *Laws*.[6]

In the *Republic*, the royal art is the art of individual wisdom; in the *Laws*, it is the art of collective wisdom. The collectivization of political wisdom in Magnesia is achieved by the institution of laws. The *Republic* places the philosopher-king above the law; the *Laws* places all public officials under the law. The *Republic* fails to see the importance of laws; they are said to be unnecessary in a good state and useless in a bad state. Hence the philosopher-king should be allowed to work without legal constraints. His virtue is assumed to be sufficient for the task, but this naive faith in the perfection of human virtue and wisdom is resolutely rejected by the *Laws*. The instinctual feelings of pleasure and pain are so powerful and so persistent that no public official can guard against them without the aid of laws. To this extent, Plato accepts Callicles' beastly view of humanity, but does not capitulate to his beastly principle of power politics. Instead, he proposes the law as the effective institutional force to control the instinctual force of pleasure and pain. Thus, the law is Plato's concession for the frailty of human beings, and his second hope for their salvation from the grip of their own appetites.

Plato's Ever-Lasting Achievements in the *Laws*

It has been Plato's grave misfortune to have the *Republic* mistaken for his greatest work by his admirers and critics alike. Even such a relentless critic as Karl Popper brands Plato as the father of totalitarianism largely on the basis of the *Republic*, while discounting and dismissing the great achievements in the *Laws*.[7] But the *Republic* was a relatively immature work; as we already noted, it was written by Plato, who was still immature not only metaphysically but also politically. It was composed at the initial stage of Plato's long journey of descent from the world of Forms to the world of phenomena. Though this journey of descent began with the *Protagoras*, it was not even halfway through by the time Plato wrote the *Republic*. Its completion required a new theory of knowledge and a new theory of Forms, which Plato had to work out in a long series of dialogues after the *Republic*.

Though the *Republic* represents the relatively immature Plato, its dazzling poetic language has enthralled most of his readers and blinded them to the far greater importance of his later and more mature works, especially because these later works are presented in much plainer language. The poetic beauty of the *Republic* has been mistaken for its philosophical profundity, and this mistake has been Plato's greatest misfortune. No wonder, Plato was always distrustful of poetry and repeatedly warned us against its power of deception and seduction. What, then, are Plato's great achievements in the *Laws*? Though this is not an easy question, I will say the following.

First, Plato's rule of law is the sovereignty of the law: the law is the supreme ruler. The Athenian Stranger says that all the magistrates are the servants to the law (715d). This view of sovereignty appears to be antithetical to the doctrine of popular sovereignty, the foundation of modern liberal democracies. But the concept of popular sovereignty is highly ambiguous, because it is not easy to identify the will of the people. Popular sovereignty may be nothing more than the authority of the ruling majority, which make political decisions on the basis of their private pleasure and interest, or their prejudice and ignorance. If the laws are framed in such a partisan politics, Plato holds, they have no authority to be obeyed. The laws should be made only for the common good, and this legislative function belongs to reason (713a, 714a, 715b). Hence, the sovereignty of the law is the sovereignty of reason and the philosophical wisdom.

Although the sovereignty of the law sounds alien to modern ears, the sovereignty of reason has become the most important element in Rousseau's and Kant's conceptions of the state and the law. For Rousseau, the formation of the general will is the essential requirement for the passage from the state of nature to the state of civil society.[8] But the general will is not the will of all; it is not the will of the people in any simple aggregation. It is the will common to all; it aims at the common or general good.[9] The function of the general will is identical with the function of reason in the *Laws*. Moreover, Rousseau holds that human beings become truly free only by obeying the general will, while they are slaves as long as they obey their private wills. This notion of freedom is further amplified by Kant's doctrine of autonomy: we can free ourselves from the chain of desires and passions only by obeying the moral laws we prescribe for ourselves. He also holds that the moral laws are the dictates of pure practical reason.[10] Thus his conception of moral law turns out to be a restatement of Plato's conception of law as the dictate of reason.

Second, the system of checks and balances that is introduced into the political structure of Magnesia is Plato's ingenious invention. To be sure, the Athenian Stranger does not claim it as his own invention, but proposes it as a lesson we should learn from the historical study of Persia, Sparta, and Athens. Though the notion of checks and balances may have already been operative in some political institutions, Plato was the first to give it a theoretical formulation. It is addressed to the most difficult problem in political philosophy, namely, how to control political power. It served as the guiding idea for the Federalists in designing the Constitution of the United States. Theoretically, the notion of checks and balances has been appropriated so firmly by a distinguished series of writers from Aristotle and Polybius to Montesquieu and James Madison that we do not even think of giving the credit for its invention to its original author.[11]

Third, Plato was the first to stress the importance of striking a right balance between competing values. In colloquial terms, this is the notion of the golden mean, which we associate with Aristotle rather than Plato. Again, this notion is not really Plato's invention; it may be found in the commonsense wisdom of any society, ancient or modern. But Plato was the first to give a theoretical account of why the problem of balancing competing values is inevitable in human life. In his view, human life is always an arena of competing values, and their conflict can take place not only between different persons and social groups, but also within every single individual. In the *Statesman*, the Eleatic Stranger says that there is an inevitable conflict between the two natural dispositions for courage and temperance, and that this conflict takes place not only within every single individual but also between two groups of people, the violent and the gentle. Moreover, he points out that the natural conflict between courage and temperance goes against the usual view that all virtues are friendly and harmonious with each other (306bc).

In Plato's view, the conflict of virtues and dispositions is not an isolated event. As we will soon see, conflict is a cosmic principle; his conception of conflict is as pervasive as that of Heraclitus. He does not simply accept the conflict of competing values as the inevitable cosmic principle, but tries to find the best way to resolve it. He finds it in the art of striking a right balance between competing values, and this difficult art is the heart of the royal art, as described by the Eleatic Stranger in the *Statesman*. The royal art of weaving does not only bring together the different elements for the constitution of a state, but also strikes the right balance between their competing claims and values. In the *Philebus*, the concept of right balance is restated as the concept of right mixture; it stands at the top in the ranking of all good things (66a).

In the *Laws*, the notion of balancing competing values becomes the most pervasive principle of organization on both the individual and the social levels. This is the ultimate ideal embodied in the virtue of temperance (*sophrosyne*) that is extensively discussed by the Athenian Stranger in the first two books of the *Laws*, though it is usually understood to be no more than self-control or moderation. The control of our desires and dispositions can be achieved without striking a right balance of them, but such a control cannot be the ultimate end of our life because we want to find the best way to realize them rather than simply to control them. We can find the best way in the virtue of temperance, if it is understood as the art of striking a right balance between competing values. The right balance is the optimal balance that achieves the best realization of all competing values. Understood in this delicate sense, temperance is the most pervasive virtue in the *Laws*; in this regard, Ernest Barker by no means overstates the case by his provocative claim that temperance is the ''mainspring'' of the *Laws*.[12]

If temperance is understood as the virtue of right balance, it is the final refinement of the idea that Socrates presented in his debate with Callicles in the *Gorgias*. In this debate, as we noted in chapter 1, Socrates takes temperance as the ultimate virtue to counter Callicles' thesis that the excellence of human life consists in the totally unrestrained gratification of appetites. In the *Gorgias*, however, Socrates does not yet stress the importance of balancing competing values, evidently understanding temperance solely as the virtue of self-control. Hence, this virtue has no special attraction or justification as an end in itself, though it may have some instrumental value. This is why Callicles scoffs at the very idea of self-control. As soon as temperance is understood not simply as the virtue of self-control, but as the art of striking a right balance between competing values, it shows itself as the ultimate art for achieving the optimal realization of all our values. It is the virtue that fulfills the principle of optimality, which must be accepted as the first principle for any system of ethics. Even Callicles cannot afford to disdain it.

The principle of striking a right balance has also become a permanent fixture of practical philosophy. Almost every important decision in constitutional law involves the problem of finding a right balance between competing values. For example, the Supreme Court has to weigh many competing values, freedom of press against national security, or freedom of speech against public safety. In *Roe v. Wade*, the Court had to strike a balance between the protection of fetal life and the liberty of pregnant women. But the idea of striking a right balance does not necessarily mean giving equal weight to competing values. In Plato's words, it means to give proportionate weight to the competing values, that is, to give each of them the weight they deserve. In some cases of competing values, the principle of right balance may mean to protect one value at the expense of the other. *Brown v. Board of Education of Topeka* was such a case; the Supreme Court protected the value of racial desegregation at the expense of the value of freedom of association.

The conflict between competing values has often been mischaracterized as a contradiction, especially by the Marxists and the Critical Legal Scholars. For example, Duncan Kennedy says that our legal system is systematically infected by the contradiction between two incompatible ethical positions, individualism and altruism.[13] Individualism advocates the primacy of individuals over society; it stresses the importance of individuals as the agents of rights, initiatives, self-reliance, and well-being. Society is only an instrumental framework for promoting these individualistic values. Altruism advocates exactly the opposite doctrine, the primacy of society over individuals. Society should not be regarded as a mere instrument, because it has its own ultimate end that is much nobler than individualistic values. Its essential function is to be a community of mutual care and respect.

Though individualism and altruism are mutually incompatible, Kennedy says, both of them have been accepted as the basic principles of liberalism. Consequently, their contradiction permeates the liberal legal tradition. He has further expanded the scope of their contradiction; it is not unique to modern liberal tradition but common to all societies.[14] In Kennedy's usage, individualism and altruism are two competing systems of value, and their conflict is inevitable and persistent in every legal and ethical system. But it is a mistake to conclude that every legal and ethical system is infected with contradictions. This is the mistake of overlooking the difference between conflict and contradiction. A contradictory ethical or legal system nullifies itself, just as a contradictory statement does. But the competition of values does not nullify those values; it simply demands the practical wisdom of striking a balance. On the other hand, the problem of contradiction is not a matter of practical wisdom but a logical problem. It makes no sense to say that we can save a contradictory statement from itself by striking a right balance. Nor is there any point in getting alarmed over the fact that every legal system is riddled with competing values, because life itself is a perpetual conflict of values. This is Plato's enduring insight into human life.

Because the art of striking a right balance is highly delicate and sometimes highly complex, many political philosophers have felt the temptation of reducing all values to one kind. With such a reduction, the complex art of balancing can be replaced by the simple art of maximization. This is the road the utilitarians have taken; they reduce all values to the single value of utility and maximize it for every case. But this reduction is possible only in theory. Even the utilitarians have to contend with the conflict between different kinds of utility, for which they cannot find any other solution than the art of striking a balance. John Rawls has taken a different approach. Instead of reducing all values to one, he recognizes two values, liberty and equality, and forestalls their conflict by prescribing their lexical order (the priority rule), that is, the principle of liberty always takes priority over the principle of equality.[15] Though this mechanical procedure can indeed avoid the difficulty of striking a balance, it can surely produce many unwise decisions. For example, this procedure could overrule the *Brown* case.[16] There is really no substitute for the difficult art of striking a balance.

From Culture to Nature

Though the role of pleasures and pains, appetites and feelings, was systematically denigrated in the *Republic*, it is given a positive value in the *Laws*. The Athenian Stranger says, ''Nothing is so native to men as pleasure, pain, and desire; they are, so to say, the very wires or strings from which any mortal creature is inevitably and absolutely dependent'' (732e, trans. A. E. Taylor). He goes on to say that pleasures and pains are so important for human beings that even the noblest life cannot be praised without reference to its pleasures and pains (733a). What is the proper place of pleasure in human life? In the *Philebus*, Socrates tries to settle this question by finding their right place in the human good, that is, what is good for human beings. To this end, he constructs the notion of the human good in the same way the Athenian Stranger constructs an ideal constitution for the good of a state. He stresses that the human good cannot be composed of a single element such as pleasure or knowledge (21–22).

The feeling of pleasure and the rule of reason are two basic elements for the constitution of the human good. Since pleasure and pain are the *unlimited*, they cannot become good and beautiful until reason introduces order by mixing them with the *limit*. Though reason is the cause or the agent for the production of this mixture, it cannot perform this task without using the unlimited domain of pleasure and pain. The latter is the indispensable material to be used for the mixing of the human goods. This is the final answer to the challenge of Calliclean hedonism; the Socrates of the *Philebus* handles it with a far greater authority and dexterity than the Socrates of the *Gorgias* did. The thematic connection between these two dialogues is indicated by Protarchus, a former student of Gorgias, who refuses to take any position contrary to that of his former mentor (*Philebus* 58ab). The *Philebus* turns out to be quite contrary not only to the *Gorgias*, but also to the *Phaedo*, the *Symposium*, and the *Republic*. Whereas these dialogues praised the purity of wisdom and warned against the corrupting power of pleasure, the *Philebus* endorses a proper mixture of wisdom and pleasure as the highest form of the human good.

The clash between Socrates and Callicles in the *Gorgias* was a duel between reason and appetite. This duel was further intensified in the *Republic*, where Socrates advocated a radical revolution and an absolute conquest of appetite by reason. The *Philebus* shows that the duel stood on the wrong premise that either pleasure or wisdom was sufficient for the human good. This premise is proven false by demonstrating that the life of pleasure totally devoid of wisdom and the life of wisdom totally devoid of pleasure are equally inconceivable. In the *Laws*, the problem of pleasure and pain is restated in terms of the universal war for survival in the animal kingdom. Cleinias says that what is generally called peace is only a fiction and that every state is by nature forced to wage an undeclared war against every other state (626a). In response, the Athenian Stranger says that the universal war is not limited to the relation between different states, but takes place between villages, between households, and between individuals, and that it takes place even between the different parts of each individual soul.

The ultimate cause of this universal war is the mighty strings of pleasure and pain that control all human beings like puppets (644e) for self-gratification and self-aggrandizement. In the *Gorgias*, Callicles described the entire world of nature as a theater of aggression and predation for the gratification of appetites. There are two ways to cope with this universal war, according to the Athenian Stranger; one is the way of conquest and victory, and the other is the way of friendship and reconciliation (627e–628e). In fact, the laws of Sparta and Crete are designed as instruments of war and conquest; hence they develop only the virtue of courage and neglect the other virtues. The way of friendship and reconciliation has to begin within the soul of each individual; the war between the different parts of the soul should be ended by bringing them into friendship and harmony. Their friendship is the Pythagorean *philia*; their harmony is the concord of reason and emotion, which is the virtue of temperance (*sophrosyne*).

The concord of reason and emotion is the highest form of knowledge and wisdom; their discord is the lowest form of ignorance and folly (689ab). Discord and folly arise in the soul of a person who hates what she judges to be noble and good and who loves what she judges to be evil and unjust. Concord and wisdom arise in the soul of a person who loves what she judges to be noble and good and who hates what she judges to be evil and unjust. As George Klosko points out, this is a strange characterization of wisdom and folly, which cannot be found in Plato's other dialogues.[17] Since the concord of reason and emotion is temperance, the highest form of wisdom is temperance. Conversely, the vice of intemperance is the highest form of folly. Since wisdom is the basis of all virtues, temperance leads to all virtues. This is why Ernest Barker called temperance the mainspring of the *Laws*.

To be sure, this is an extraordinary view of temperance, but it is not introduced for the first time in the *Laws*. In the *Charmides*, temperance was defined as the knowledge of oneself, the sovereign virtue for governing the household and the state. In the *Gorgias*, temperance was taken as the ultimate virtue, from which all other virtues were derived. This extraordinary role of temperance is being reaffirmed in the *Laws*. Moreover, the way of temperance is the way of peace and friendship (*philia*), which encompasses all the divine goods and virtues, whereas the way of war and conquest requires the development of only one virtue, courage (630e–631d).

The Athenian Stranger proposes to construct a law that can function as a way of peace and friendship and that can develop all virtues. Such a law is an instrument of friendship and cooperation rather than war and conquest, because it promotes the common good rather than private gains. However, such an instrument is inconceivable to any mortals who are blinded by their private interests; it can be appreciated only by those who can recognize the importance of common goods that transcend private desires and passions, by rising above the level of beastly existence and taking a divine perspective. Hence, the law is regarded as a manifestation of the immortal element in human beings (714a). For the same reason, it can secure divine goods for the mortals.

The law is the golden and holy string that can control the beastly strings of pleasure and pain (645a). The law can achieve this task only by education. It can mold the character and emotion of all citizens in such a virtuous manner that they will love what is just and noble, and hate what is unjust and ignoble. This cultivated sense of loving justice and hating injustice is the golden and holy string of the law; it is just another name for the power of virtue, the inculcation of which is the central function of the law. The *Laws* proposes an education state just as much as the *Republic* does, and the aim of education in both cases is the cultivation of virtues. In both cases, it is Plato's credo that only the cultivation of virtues can save human beings from the misery of beastly existence and elevate them to the divine world of peace and concord.

The Athenian Stranger says that the law is a better guide for attaining happiness than greed and vice. He makes this assertion on two grounds. First, the life of virtue is a far better guide to happiness than the life of vice (732e–734e), and the life of virtue can be inculcated by the law. Second, the law is called a public calculation of pleasure and pain (644cd); it is a much more effective way of figuring out the pleasure and pain of all citizens than the blind working of appetites. Thus, the law closely ties the function of virtue to the hedonistic calculus of pleasure and virtue. The hedonistic calculus was introduced by Socrates as the common measure of all goods and evils at the beginning of his descent to the phenomenal world (*Protagoras* 354de). Before this introduction, he had maintained an emphatic distinction between virtue in the true sense and virtue in the vulgar sense (*Phaedo* 69b; *Symposium* 212a). The vulgar virtue was supposedly concerned with the problem of managing pleasure and pain in the phenomenal world; the true virtue was the virtue of knowing and loving the beauty of Forms. But the *Laws* drops the notion of true virtue as completely and as resolutely as the notion of pure astronomy and harmonics.

In Magnesia, the life of pleasure and pain is firmly linked to the life of virtue by the power of law. This is the final response to the Calliclean challenge. In the *Gorgias*, Callicles maintained that pleasure was the highest good and pain was the ultimate evil, and that the virtue of a superior human was to secure the good and avoid the evil by the unrestrained gratification of desire. Moreover, it is the justice or law of nature that entitles the strong to exploit the weak, but this natural sense of justice has been contaminated by the conventional sense of justice that has been framed by the weak to control the strong. However, the *Laws* shows that the life of Calliclean virtue is the life of beasts that can only plunge the state into a war of private interests. Such a state is no longer a community of love, but a battleground for civil war. Callicles' natural justice is the law of beastly instinct that can lead us only to misery rather than to happiness. Only by replacing his law of instinct with the law of reason can we elevate human existence from the beastly to the divine level.

The imagery of war and conquest in the *Gorgias* is replaced by the sense of friendship and cooperation in the *Laws*. The same sense of friendship and cooperation between reason and appetite was already prefigured in the harmony between Apollo and Pan, which we noted in the *Phaedrus*. The *Laws* also celebrates the marriage of Apollo and Dionysus (665a, 672d). The sense of friendship and cooperation between reason and appetite is reaffirmed in the story of the *Timaeus*. Originally, the physical world was a chaotic mass (the unlimited), but was transformed into a world of order and beauty by the Demiurge. The sense of natural beauty and order was already prefigured in the *Phaedrus*, where Socrates broke out in a rapturous adoration of the natural beauty manifest in trees and grass, the fragrance of flowering shrubs, and the music of the singing cicadas. Now the *Timaeus* gives a formal explanation of natural order and beauty, which is also informally stated in the *Laws* (897–903) and the *Philebus* (28d–30e). This formal explanation endows the physical universe with a sense of friendship and community between rational and material elements (32c, 88e), and lays the ground for the friendly relation between nature and culture.

The conversation of the *Timaeus* is said to have taken place, by agreement, the day after the discussion on the best form of society, and Socrates gives a brief summary of the discussion, which can readily be identified with the *Republic* (*Timaeus* 17c–19b). But there is a problem with the ideal state; it is still lifeless and motionless. Socrates reminds his visitors that their assignment is to give it a sense of real life by placing it in the real world. What is strange is the manner in which this assignment is carried out. Instead of talking about the ideal state, Timaeus tells the story of creation by the Demiurge, and Critias follows it up with his story of two ancient cities, Athens and Atlantis. How do these two stories accomplish the assignment? This has been the baffling question about the *Timaeus* and the *Critias*. Perhaps we can answer this question by taking the two ancient cities as primitive versions of the Kallipolis and Magnesia.

In the prehistoric Athens, the military class was set apart from artisans and husbandsmen. They were provided with what was necessary for their maintenance and training. They had no private property, and whatever they had was regarded as common property. Critias adds, ''they followed in all things the regime we laid down yesterday when we were talking about our hypothetical Guardians'' (*Critias* 110d, trans. Desmond Lee). Atlantis was founded by Poseidon, and governed by ten kings, who had descended from him. Though each of the ten kings had absolute power in his own region, the distribution of powers and privileges among them was determined by the laws engraved on the pillars in the temple of Poseidon. They assembled in the temple to consult on matters of mutual interest and injury. They had a government by council like that of Magnesia. In the council, they made their decisions in accordance with the laws of their father (120bc). Theirs was a government of law like the government of Magnesia.

The division of Atlantis into the ten kings' territories resembles the division of Magnesia into the twelve tribal regions. In Atlantis, each household is given an allotment of land, just as it is in Magnesia. Again, as in Magnesia, the physical layout of Atlantis was highly geometrical: the capital city was composed of a circular citadel surrounded by two rings of land and three rings of water (*Critias* 113de). In Magnesia, the whole country is divided into twelve equal sections by twelve lines radiating from the citadel (*Laws* 745bc). Both Atlantis and Magnesia are works of Pythagorean construction. The Council of the Kings met alternatively every fifth and sixth year, thereby showing equal respect to both odd and even numbers. The respect for numbers was also Pythagorean. To be sure, the story of Atlantis is also a story of her degeneration, but she thrives as long as the citizens obey the laws. Her degeneration begins when her citizens neglect the divine element in their souls and cannot bear prosperity without moderation (120d–121c).

The Cosmic Moral Order

If Atlantis and Athens of the *Critias* are the primitive versions of Magnesia and the Kallipolis, they can demonstrate the feasibility of realizing these two ideal cities. In the *Republic*, Socrates was duly concerned with the realizability of the Kallipolis; in the *Laws*, Magnesia presents the same problem. This is the sort of problem that cannot be resolved by discussion alone, though Socrates tries to settle it by discussion in the *Republic*. The best way to resolve it is to appeal to history. If history has already produced two cities that resemble the two ideal states, as Critias says, she has amply demonstrated their realizability in this world. This is the ''historical'' demonstration of their realizability, and it becomes Critias's part of the assignment, that is, to give the ideal city a sense of real life by placing it in the real world. Timaeus's part of the assignment is to provide the natural basis for this historical demonstration. He gives an account of the physical world and its order in such a manner that Mother Nature can be accepted as the matrix for the construction of ideal cities. In that case, the order of human society can be regarded as an extension of the natural order of the physical world created by the Demiurge.

The dual perspectives of nature and history demonstrates the harmony and partnership between the world of nature and the world of human beings or culture. Nature is the basis for building culture; culture is the extension of nature. This unitary and harmonious view of nature and culture is Plato's revision of the sophistic demarcation between nature (*physis*) and culture (*nomos*). With this demarcation, the sophists in general implied that culture is something unnatural or even anti-natural. Nature is original and primitive; culture is only a human fabrication. Against this sophistic view, Plato argues for the continuity and unity of nature and culture. Nature is a product of construction as much as culture is, and even the World-Soul and the human souls are products of construction (*Timaeus* 35a; *Laws* 892ac, 894d, 967d).

To celebrate the unity of nature and culture, Plato stages the entire dialogue of the *Laws* in the open country. We saw such a natural setting only once before in the *Phaedrus*. Although the natural setting for this dialogue is refreshing and beautiful, its participants are far from healthy and vigorous. They are out in the countryside to take therapeutic exercises for their sickly constitutions. By contrast, the Athenian Stranger and his two companions are hale and sound enough to walk the whole distance from Cnossus to Mount Ida. They are planning to build the city of Magnesia as an integral feature of nature. Their plan reflects the faith in the unity of nature and culture, which was expressed by Socrates' Pythagorean claim in the *Gorgias* that the universe is a *kosmos*. This claim was made in response to the distinction between the law of nature and the law of culture, which Callicles maintained on the basis of the sophistic demarcation between nature and culture. If there is such a demarcation, the physical world cannot be anything but a theater of conflict and chaos, as Callicles maintains, because it is governed by the blind physical forces. On the other hand, if nature is a product of intelligent creation, it should be governed by the principle of order and harmony as Socrates claimed in the *Gorgias*.

Socrates said that Callicles could not appreciate the cosmic order because he neglected geometry (*Gorgias* 508a). His faith in the cosmic order is spelled out by the *Timaeus*, a geometrical account of the universe. Such a well-ordered physical universe should be in harmony with the order of human culture and society. The *Republic* never recognized the importance of harmony between the physical world and human society. On the contrary, it was a daring attempt to protect a city by building the walls of culture against the turbulent world of nature. In the *Phaedrus*, Plato began to suspect that this was a terrible mistake. He now remedies it by building the city of Magnesia in the countryside. He further supports the unity of nature and culture by presenting the two cities of Atlantis and Athens as historical products of nature and by situating history itself in the matrix of nature. The unity of nature and culture is celebrated by the assignment of Timaeus and Critias to give the lifeless ideal city a sense of real life by placing it in the real world (*Timaeus* 19b–20c). They provide the ontological link between the ideal city and the physical world, and between culture and nature.

In that case, why are these two dialogues presented as a continuation of the *Republic*? Though these two dialogues are said to take place according to a previous agreement supposedly made in the *Republic*, this dialogue says nothing about such an agreement. Timaeus and company were not even present for the discussion in the *Republic*. Hence the implied connection between the two dialogues has been a puzzle. Francis Cornford says that the summary of the ideal state at the beginning of the *Timaeus* refers not to the Kallipolis of the *Republic*, but to some other discussion on the same topic. The latter discussion allegedly took place on the festival of Athena, whereas the discussion of the *Re-*

public was conducted on the festival of Bendis.[18] These two festivals were separated by the interval of two months. According to this view, Socrates conducted two dialogues for constructing the same ideal city. And that is quite a strange sequence of events.

The strange sequence of events, of course, is Plato's fabrication to give an air of plausibility to the claim that the *Timaeus* is a continuation of the *Republic*. When he was writing the *Republic*, he never thought of providing the physical basis for the Kallipolis. So he presented the *Republic* as a self-contained work. But when he comes to construct Magnesia, he recognizes the need for situating those ideal cities in the physical and historical world. He also realizes that the self-containedness of the *Republic* is its serious deficiency. What is the best way to repair this deficiency? He can present the *Timaeus* as a continuation of a dialogue similar in its content to the one in the *Republic*. By this ingenious literary device, he uses the *Timaeus* to provide the physical basis for both the Kallipolis and Magnesia at the same time.

The notion of cosmic order proclaimed by the *Timaeus* and the *Critias* is quite alien to the *Republic*. On the other hand, this notion permeates both the *Laws* and the *Philebus*. The *Timaeus* and the *Critias*, in fact, complement the *Laws* and the *Philebus*. Since there are neither textual nor thematic grounds for connecting the *Republic* directly to the *Timaeus* and the *Critias*, their connection must be understood as an indirect one. If we are right in assuming that the *Laws* and the *Philebus* constitute the revision of the *Republic*, then we can see that the *Timaeus* and the *Critias* are required for this revision. In this revision, Plato situates his two ideal cities in history and then locates history itself in the matrix of nature. To this end, he inserts the story of creation by interrupting Critias's story of the two ancient cities, which begins right after the introductory remarks of the *Timaeus*. This interruption has long been a puzzle; it is Plato's literary device for embedding his view of human history in the context of the physical universe.

The Pythagorean Tetrad—the *Laws*, the *Philebus*, the *Timaeus*, and the *Critias*—does not only revise but complete the *Republic*. This completion can provide the final response to the Calliclean challenge. In the *Gorgias*, Callicles represents not merely the world of greed and power, but the entire physical universe. As Callicles says, greed and power are the universal force of all living beings in nature. Hence, the final response must include a reasonable account of the physical world and its relation to the human world. Thus, the Pythagorean Tetrad completes the journey of descent that began in the *Protagoras*, and this completion is indicated by the travel plan for the Athenian Stranger and his two friends in the *Laws*. Their journey from Cnossus to Mount Ida belongs neither to descent nor to ascent. It takes place on the flat land; they cannot go down any lower.

The journey of descent began with the reference to Odysseus's descent to Hades, where he found the spirit of Tiresias and sought his counsel on how to find his way back to Ithaca. After foretelling the difficulties Odysseus will face on his way home and in recovering his wife and his city from the throng of her suitors, Tiresias tells Odysseus what sort of life he should seek after his return to Ithaca: he should resettle in a land away from the sea and seafaring, and make his living in farming. Then he will live a happy life to his old age. This prophecy is fulfilled almost to the letter in the *Laws*. Magnesia is a farming community to be established away from the sea. It is not an accident that both Odysseus and the Athenian Stranger have to guard against the danger of the sea. Odysseus's suffering came from the Trojan War; the disaster of Athens came from her imperial expansion. Seafaring was the common cause of both disasters. The Athenian Stranger lists a catalogue of evils that a city on a seashore breeds in the human souls (705ab), and supports his distrust of navy and sailors by quoting the authoritative words of Odysseus at Troy (706b–e).

The story of descent from the *Protagoras* to the *Laws*, however, cannot end with the establishment of Magnesia. It has to take one more big step and answer the question, ''What sort of moral order governs the universe?'' This is one of the most important but neglected questions in moral and political philosophy. In the *Gorgias*, Socrates took a fanatic stand by claiming that one can be virtuous even in a totally immoral world. He can take such a fanatic stand because he believes that his soul can never be harmed by other people's immoral acts. In the *Phaedo* and the *Symposium*, he tries to secure a haven for the virtuous soul in the world of Forms so that it can never be adversely affected by anything that takes place in the phenomenal world. In the *Republic*, the moral life of a virtuous soul is relocated in a just society in this world, but the just society has to be situated in a moral universe, which can guarantee the happiness of the virtuous and the punishment of the wicked. The justice of human beings is not self-sufficient; it has to be protected by the justice of the gods. This link of human to divine justice is reaffirmed in the *Laws*; the system of penal code in book 9 is followed by the doctrine of divine justice in book 10.

The same problem arises in Kant's moral philosophy. It begins with his notion that moral will is the ultimate source of all moral values and that it is totally self-sufficient. Kant says that its noumenal existence and moral value can never be affected, even if it encounters the misfortune of losing all its efficacy in the phenomenal world. In the dialectic of practical reason, however, Kant comes to recognize the indispensability of a moral order in the universe for the life of virtue. A similar recognition was made much earlier by the ancient Chinese sages, who had conceived Heaven as the impersonal moral order of the universe that sustains the moral and political order of human beings. Similarly, the Stoics claimed that the entire universe was morally governed by a rational deity. This claim was rather amazing because they were at the same time subscribing to the Socratic ideal of self-sufficiency for the virtuous soul. In their view, even the interior equanimity of a virtuous soul could not be sustained without its harmony with the macrocosm.

The moral order of the Platonic universe is linked to its geometrical order. At *Gorgias* 508a, Socrates said that Callicles knew nothing about the cosmic moral order because he had neglected the study of geometry. In the *Republic*, Socrates installed the study of geometry as the basic step for the ascent to the world of Forms. In the *Timaeus*, it becomes the final step in the descent to the world of phenomena; the ultimate nature of the physical universe can be understood only in the language of geometry, because it is the language of the god who makes and rules the entire universe. The *Meno* has already shown that geometry can be used for descent as well as for ascent. Socrates used it for the slave boy's recollection on his journey of descent. When the *Theaetetus* called for the birth of natural science, it really advocated the use of geometry for the study of phenomena. This is why the entire dialogue was conducted in the presence of an eminent geometer Theodorus. At

Laws 893c–897c, the Athenian Stranger takes the geometric view of the universe as a visible manifestation of its divine governance.

For the Athenian Stranger, cosmology is the basis for constructing moral theology against the atheistic view that there are no gods, and the immoral view that the gods do not care about the justice of human beings even if they exist. The education of Magnesia should make sure that all citizens believe that the virtuous are properly rewarded and the wicked are duly punished by the gods. Without this belief, the rule of law and justice cannot be sustained. Hence the crime of impiety is the most serious one; it is the crime of subscribing to atheism and other associated doctrines that can undermine the belief in the divine governance of the universe (907–910). For the same reason, knowledge of moral theology is the most important requirement for becoming the Guardians of the Laws (966cd). In the constitution of Magnesia, the doctrine of the laws and the doctrine of the gods are inseparably intertwined. Although the law is Plato's concession for the frailty of human beings, it is also a gift from the gods. This divine gift also secures the unity of nature and culture, because nature is also a work of the god.

The Role of Theaetetus in the Platonic Corpus

In Plato's dialogues, with the exception of Socrates, nobody is given such a conspicuous role as the young man Theaetetus. His role is extraordinary for more than one reason. To begin with, he is one of the two central speakers retained from one major dialogue (the *Theaetetus*) to another (the *Sophist*). This point becomes even more conspicuous, considering the fact that Socrates moves from the foreground to the background in the same transition from the *Theaetetus* to the *Sophist*. Plato's singular treatment of Theaetetus does not stop there. When Theodorus presents Theaetetus to Socrates at the beginning of the dialogue, he describes the young man with a series of superlatives: "I assure you that, among all the young men I have met with—and I have had to do with a good many—I have never found such admirable gifts. The combination of a rare quickness of intelligence with exceptional gentleness that I should have hardly have believed could exist, and I have never seen it before" (144a, trans. Cornford).

The combination of these two traits is what was characterized as the truly philosophical temperament by Socrates in the *Republic* (485a–487a). He also lamented how rare it was to find both of these two traits in one and the same person.[19] Theodorus makes the same observation in his praise of Theaetetus:

In general, people who have such keen and ready wits and such good memories as he, are also quick-tempered and passionate; they dart about like ships without ballast; and their temperament is rather enthusiastic than strong; whereas the steadier sort are somewhat dull when they come to face study, and they forget everything. But his approach to learning and inquiry, with the perfect quietness of its smooth and sure progress, is like the noiseless flow of a stream of oil. It is wonderful how he achieves all this at his age. (144ab, trans. Cornford)

At the beginning of his talk with Theaetetus, Socrates says to him, "I can assure you that, often as Theodorus has spoken to me in praise of a citizen or stranger, he has never praised anyone as he was praising you just now" (145b, trans. Cornford). This statement is to underscore the fact that Theodorus's praise of Theaetetus is not only intended to be exceptional and unprecedented by the speaker, but is accepted as such by Socrates himself. In all his dialogues, Plato never uses this sort of superlative in praising any other human being. Even Socrates' praise of Glaucon and Adeimantus (*Republic* 367e–368a), though generous, pales by comparison with the lavish praise of the young Theaetetus. Why does Plato take such an extraordinary measure in building up the character of this young man? The natural answer to this question may very well be that the lavish praise is Plato's tribute to Theaetetus, especially because this dialogue opens with the story of his impending death.

Though this answer may be true, I want to propose another theory. I believe that Plato is setting up the young Theaetetus as his own *persona*, that is, an ingenious mask for himself. The character traits and the personal background of Theaetetus resemble those of Plato's own to a remarkable extent. As a student of the great mathematician Theodorus, Theaetetus the young man is studying geometry and other mathematical sciences. Mathematics was indeed an important element of Plato's early education. He was also exposed to the Heraclitean doctrine of flux through his association with Cratylus, according to Aristotle's account (*Metaphysics* 987a31–32). After Socrates' trial and execution, he is supposed to have taken refuge with Euclides in Megara, and then traveled to Cyrene to see Theodorus.[20] The same sequence of Euclides and Theodorus introduces the young Theaetetus in the dialogue.

When Theodorus meets Socrates, the former presents the young Theaetetus as an orphan, whose sizable inheritance has been squandered by his trustees. Socrates notes that his father, Euphronius of Sunium, was a man of great substance (*Theaetetus* 144c). Later he compares Protagoras's doctrine of perception to a helpless orphan, because its author is dead and there is no one to protect it (164e).[21] This episode seems to describe what has eventually become of the Heraclitean legacy for the young Plato, when he became associated with the later Heracliteans such as Cratylus. They have killed the *logos* of Heraclitus, who had advocated the order of the phenomenal world in spite of its flux. The *logos* of Heraclitus was the great substance of his doctrine, which has been squandered by its trustees and custodians. There is an implied parallel between the Heraclitean legacy and Theaetetus's inheritance. By the time the young Plato got to know the Heraclitean doctrine, it had already been wasted by its custodians. Thus, the financial status of the young Theaetetus reflects the intellectual status of Plato as a young Heraclitean.

By the time Theaetetus gives the definition of knowledge as perception in the *Theaetetus*, he is taking the Heraclitean position. Socrates' articulation of this definition in terms of Protagorean relativism describes the chaotic state of the radical Heraclitean school, which cannot allow the distinction between true and false perceptions, and which destroys the very possibility of all sensible discourse. The rest of the dialogue is the story of how Socrates can lead him out of this intellectual abyss; hence it is the story of what the Socratic art of delivery can do for the young man in a dire strait. Thus, Socrates appears as Theaetetus's deliverer at a critical juncture of his career. Though Socrates can do nothing to deliver him from his financial strait, he can do something for the intellectual salvation of the troubled young man, because he is an astute physician of the soul.

Theaetetus's spiritual and intellectual inheritance from his father is even more impressive than his financial inheritance. Benitez and Guimaraes say, "Perhaps, then Socrates is most interested in Theaetetus's psychic inheritance, and his concern is whether it may be squandered as well."[22] The intellectual inheritance and endowment of Theaetetus constitute the young man's stellar prospect, as portrayed in Theodorus's praise at the opening of the dialogue.[23] Hence, to save Theaetetus is not only to help him out of his intellectual crisis, but also to guide him to fulfill his impressive intellectual promise. He will eventually accomplish these two goals by recovering the great Heraclitean legacy, the *logos* of phenomena. He will secure the *logos* of phenomena by appropriating the theory of Forms from the Parmenidean tradition. Thus, the young man Theaetetus stands for the awesome prospect of redeeming and reconciling the two great philosophical traditions of ancient Greece. This prospect is foreshadowed by the frame story of the *Theaetetus*. Though the discussion of knowledge is conducted from the Heraclitean perspective, it is recorded and preserved by the Parmenideans of Megara. The awesome prospect finally begins to materialize when the young Theaetetus comes under the tutelage of the stranger from Elea in the *Sophist*. This story may well reflect the philosophical journey Plato had gone through in his youth and the ambitious project he had undertaken for the future of philosophy.

For these reasons, I am tempted to identify the young Theaetetus as the mask of the young Plato. This identification may further be supported by the unusual combination of the same extraordinary talents that can be found in both Theaetetus and Plato. They also share the same city for their residence; the opening exchange of the dialogue between Socrates and Theodorus underscores the presentation of Theaetetus as the best specimen of Athenian youth. Finally, Plato's most ingenious dialogical device for setting up the young Theaetetus as his persona is Socrates' story of midwifery. When the young man experiences his initial difficulty in formulating the definition of knowledge, Socrates compares his perplexities to labor pain. The birth of an idea is like the birth of a baby; it has to be conceived, nurtured, and delivered by the soul. Socrates says that he is not only a son of a midwife, but also practices the same art (149a). But his art is different from the ordinary art of midwifery; it assists the soul in labor pain (150b).

Socrates' maieutic art has traditionally been interpreted as his familiar art of dialogical interrogation. In that case, Theaetetus is neither the first nor the only one to be assisted by this art, because he exercises it in every dialogical encounter. In fact, he says, he has been practicing it for a long time and helped a great number of young people with various results (150e–151b). Why does Plato then stage Socrates' story of midwifery as a major episode in the *Theaetetus*? Why is it not even mentioned in the other dialogues? In the *Theaetetus*, the story of Socrates' maieutic art is not only a major episode in the dialogue, but a recurrent theme. Time and again, Socrates reminds the young man that he is in the throes of labor pain (160e–161a, 184b). It is a leitmotif that runs throughout the entire dialogue. At the end of the dialogue, he again stresses his function as a midwife and even advises Theaetetus about his future conception (210bc).

There are two ways of interpreting the theme of Socratic midwifery. On the surface, Socrates exercises his art in articulating and delivering Theaetetus's conception of knowledge as he has done in many other dialogues. On a deeper level, however, the role of Socrates as a midwife stands for a special event that takes place only in this dialogue, that is, the birth of Theaetetus as a philosopher. Plato appears to point to this deeper significance by linking Theaetetus's sense of perplexity to his sense of wonder. In response to Theaetetus's experience of wonder, Socrates says, "That shows that Theodorus was not wrong in his estimate of your nature. This sense of wonder is the mark of the philosopher" (155d, trans. Cornford).

The birth of Theaetetus as a philosopher is linked to the death of Socrates. At the end of the dialogue, Socrates once more recounts his role as a midwife and then says, "Now I must go to the portico of King Archon to meet the indictment which Meletus has drawn up against me" (210d). This is the last time Socrates alludes to his impending trial and death in Plato's dialogues. In the course of our thematic journey, we have noted that Socrates dies more than once, and that every occasion of his death serves a different function. But this one is especially different from the others. In the two previous occasions—the *Gorgias* and the *Meno*—the allusion to his impending trial and death was made in the course of debate by his opponents, namely, Callicles and Anytus. In the *Theaetetus*, the allusion has nothing to do with the thematic content of the dialogue; it is made as an independent announcement by Socrates himself after the debate is over. In the *Gorgias* and the *Meno*, the allusion appears as part of the debate; in the *Theaetetus*, it is attached to the end of the debate. At the ending of the dialogue, the pronouncement carries a tone of finality.

The tone of finality may indicate that this time the death of Socrates will not lead to his rebirth. We have noted that the death of the ethical Socrates led to his rebirth as the erotic and mystical Socrates, whose death in turn led to his rebirth as the political Socrates. The Socratic cycle of birth and rebirth has finally come to an end. But the theme of his death cannot be dissociated from the theme of birth and rebirth. Though he must go to stand trial, he still makes the arrangement to meet again with Theodorus and Theaetetus at the end of the *Theaetetus*. This is indeed strange. Why does he couple the allusion to his death with the agreement for another round of discussion? The next round takes place in the *Sophist*, where Socrates drops out of the foreground and fades away into oblivion. That is his philosophical death. However, Socrates is immortal in Plato's dialogues; he dies only for another life. His final death is linked to the birth of Theaetetus as a young philosopher.

The inseparable theme of birth and death is further elaborated by the frame story of the dialogue. In this story, Euclides of Megara says to his guest Terpsion that he has himself made and preserved the text of the dialogue. He presents the text to his guest, after telling him the story of Theaetetus's painful death from his battle wounds. This story should remind us of another story—the Megarians provided a refuge for the followers of Socrates after his execution. In both cases, the Megarians perform the vital function of saving what is left after a painful death. In the *Theaetetus*, the pain of death sets the stage for the pain of birth. In fact, these two pains are inseparable in Plato's theory of immortality. In the dialogue, Theaetetus the interlocutor goes through the dual process of birth and death. He has to experience the pain of death as a Heraclitean for his rebirth as a philosopher. The record of this experience is kept by Euclides, who belongs to the Eleatic school of philosophy.

The text of the dialogue is the certificate of his initiation into the Eleatic school. After his exposure to the Heraclitean Cratylus, according to Diogenes Laertius, the young Plato withdrew to Megara at the age of twenty-eight to study with Euclides.[24] What was his philosophical ambition at that stage? Perhaps it is portrayed by the struggle of the young Theaetetus in labor pain. It was not simply to abandon the bankrupt legacy of Heraclitus and switch his allegiance to the Eleatic legacy. The *Theaetetus* stresses the fact that the Heracliteans and the Parmenideans have fallen into the same malady of not being able to talk, because their radical positions have rendered *logos* equally impossible. Hence, the most urgent task is to recover the possibility of discourse not only for the Heraclitean world of flux but also for the Parmenidean world of permanence. By using Theaetetus as his persona, Plato initiates this momentous task in the *Theaetetus*, and continues it in the *Sophist* and the *Statesman*. This is his birth as a philosopher in his own right, and it is reflected in the birth pain of the young Theaetetus.

The young Theaetetus is never alone, however; the young Socrates is his inseparable companion. They appear together in the *Theaetetus* (147d). They show up again together in the *Sophist* and the *Statesman*, and divide up their chore of responding to the Eleatic Stranger. Theaetetus takes on the chore in the *Sophist* and the young Socrates in the *Statesman*. They behave like a pair of twins. Both of them have exceptional talents, and have strong resemblance to the old Socrates. The young and the old Socrates share the same name. With his snub nose and prominent eyes, Theaetetus looks like the old Socrates (143e). At the opening of the *Statesman* (275d), the old Socrates stresses the resemblance and kinship of the two young men to himself.

These two gifted young men are meant to represent the two sides of the young Plato. The young Theaetetus represents the talent and aspiration that were already in the young Plato when he came to the historical Socrates, while the young Socrates represents the influence and inspiration the young Plato came to have under the guidance of the historical

Socrates. By this dual mask, Plato is recognizing the two essential components in the constitution of his mature self as a philosopher. This is my theory of Plato's personae, which I hope to substantiate in the remainder of this chapter.

Authorial Identification

Why does Plato introduce his own persona for the first time in the *Theaetetus*? And what does he try to accomplish by this dialogical device? In facing these questions, let us grant that the *Republic* is the apex in the development of the Platonic Socrates. But Plato the philosopher does not seem to feel a complete identification with this work. Glaucon and Adeimantus, who are the chief respondents to Socrates in the *Republic*, are his two brothers. This is an unusual event; Plato rarely installs his own kin as participants in his dialogues. Before the *Republic*, he did only once; after the *Republic*, only once more. In the *Charmides*, he installed his cousins, Charmides and Critias, as Socrates' respondents. It has often been said that these two characters were picked because they were personally deficient in the virtue of temperance. But Plato the author takes special pains in talking about the pride of his family and ancestry when he presents these two characters.

Among the early dialogues, the *Charmides* is given the pride of place. It celebrates the role of temperance as the sovereign virtue, just as the *Republic* displays the role of justice as the most comprehensive virtue. If the *Republic* is the culmination of the middle dialogues, the *Charmides* is the apex of the early dialogues. Once we recognize the respective centrality of these two dialogues in the early and the middle periods, we may be able to see the reason why Plato restricts the presence of his kin to these dialogues. Their kinship may represent his intellectual kinship to those two works. He may feel much closer to the *Charmides* than to any of the other early dialogues, just as Charmides and Critias are much closer in kinship to him than any other characters in the early dialogues. Plato the author freely expresses his pride in his own distinguished ancestry that goes back to Solon, when he presents the young Charmides at the beginning of the dialogue. This young man is simply stunning for his beauty and talent; he is not only a philosopher but also a poet. These impressive genetic traits are said to have been in his family as far back as Solon (154a–155a).

When Plato installs Glaucon and Adeimantus as Socrates' interlocutors in the *Republic*, he again takes special care in expressing an extraordinary praise of not only his brothers but his whole ancestry. Socrates refers to them as "sons of Ariston, whose race from a glorious sire is god-like" (368a). In kinship, Glaucon and Adeimantus are closer to Plato than any other characters in all his dialogues. But they are not Plato himself. By this dialogical device, Plato seems to indicate his feeling of exceptional kinship to the central ideas of the *Republic* and at the same time his unwillingness to admit a total identification of himself with those ideas. He may be saying that the *Republic* is not completely his own but a joint product of Socrates and Plato, that is, it is the final product in the long chain of Platonic elaboration on Socratic ideas. But it has not yet been fully appropriated by Plato the philosopher as his own.

This is Plato's self-identification gap with the *Republic*, and this gap widens in the *Parmenides*. To indicate this point, Plato installs his half-brother Antiphon to recite the whole story from memory (*Parmenides* 126b–127a). A half-brother is clearly further removed from Plato than his two real brothers, Glaucon and Adeimantus. By the time he wrote the *Parmenides*, he must have felt a wider gap between himself and the theory of Forms than he felt at the time of writing the *Republic*. What reasons does Plato have for feeling this gap? In my view, the basic reason for this gap is the obvious theoretical weakness of the *Republic*: its central doctrines concerning the existence of Forms and the nature of the Good have only been suggested and not yet demonstrated. Socrates proposes these doctrines and explains them with poetic metaphors and allegories, but does not subject them to any rigorous critique. Such a critique will require the metaphysical phase in Plato's career, which begins with the *Parmenides* and the *Theaetetus*.

The young Theaetetus and the young Socrates are introduced with a praise that far surpasses the praise of Charmides, Glaucon, and Adeimantus. Beyond these three occasions, no other young man is presented with lavish praise of his character or his family. With the young

Theaetetus and the young Socrates, Plato the author finally overcomes the gap between himself and his dialogues. But these two new characters play their role as Plato's own personae not only in the Eleatic Tetrad, but also in the Pythagorean Tetrad. The young Theaetetus grows up and becomes the Athenian Stranger of the *Laws*. Many commentators have identified the Stranger with Plato himself. Glenn Morrow says of this character, "The anonymity of the Athenian means that there is no independent character to be sustained, as is true of the Socratic dialogues, even the *Republic*; and Plato is free as nowhere else to put forward his own doctrines."[25] What happens to the young Socrates? He also grows up and becomes the Socrates of the *Philebus*.

As some scholars noted, the Socrates of the *Philebus* behaves quite differently from the Socrates of the early and the middle dialogues.[26] Unlike the latter, the former does not take the discussion directly to the main topic of inquiry, namely, the competition between pleasure and knowledge for the pride of place in the ranking of the goods. Instead, he introduces a series of dialectical exercises, and articulates two versions of constructivism, eidetic and ontic. These two versions grow right out of the *Sophist* and the *Statesman*, where he received his dialectical training as the young Socrates. But he is liable to be mistaken for the other Socrates, because he is now fully grown, and has become older and wiser. At *Statesman* 258a, the old Socrates had indeed stressed the resemblance of the young Socrates to himself. But one is the master of construction; the other is the master of definition.

As a joint persona of Plato, the young Socrates and the young Theaetetus are interchangeable. In the Eleatic Tetrad, Theaetetus is assigned to the *Sophist*, and the young Socrates to the *Statesman*. This division of labor is the division between the theoretical and the practical domain; the *Sophist* is for theory, and the *Statesman* is for practice. This division of labor between the two young men is switched in the *Laws* and the *Philebus*. The *Laws* belongs to practical knowledge, and the *Philebus* to theoretical knowledge. The fully matured Theaetetus becomes the Athenian Stranger, and takes charge of the *Laws*, while the fully matured new Socrates takes charge of the *Philebus*. In Plato scholarship, the reappearance of the old Socrates in the *Philebus* has been a puzzle ("Why is Socrates back?"), because he never appears again in any other late dialogues. However, this puzzle can be neatly solved by connecting the Socrates of the *Philebus* with the young Socrates, the perpetual companion of the young Theaetetus.

Plato, however, does not assign his persona to the *Timaeus* and the *Critias*. Instead of Theaetetus and Socrates, he installs two Pythagoreans as the chief speakers. By this dialogical device, he appears to present those two ''likely'' stories as essentially Pythagorean, and thus indicates his unwillingness to identify them as his own. For example, Timaeus says that the souls of men who led cowardly and wicked lives are reborn as women (90e). This derogatory view of women is clearly incompatible with Socrates' claim in the *Republic* that women are equal to men. By installing no persona of his own in the *Timaeus*, Plato may be telling us that the derogatory view of women is not his own, and that he is only recounting Pythagorean doctrine. As James Arieti notes, the entire tone of the *Timaeus* is far from serious and is often comical.[27]

The selection of dramatic characters appears to be Plato's way of indicating the source of thematic ideas presented in the dialogues. Let us call it the thematic association. In some dialogues such as the *Republic* and the *Laws*, he associates those ideas with himself, and this authorial relationship may be quite close or relatively remote. In a number of dialogues, he associates the source of thematic ideas with someone other than himself, for example, the Pythagoreans in the *Timaeus* and Protagoras in the *Protagoras*. In another group of dialogues, he makes a joint association. In the *Sophist*, for example, Theaetetus and the Eleatic Stranger play equally important roles of thematic association. This dialogue shows the metaphysical development of the young Theaetetus as Plato's persona under the influence of Eleatic tradition.

The thematic association should be distinguished from the thematic function. In this volume, we have noted that the *Phaedo*, the *Symposium*, the *Republic*, and the *Laws* should be read as Plato's four different responses to the Calliclean challenge. This is their thematic function. The thematic ideas of other dialogues are neither independent nor self-contained. Their thematic function is ancillary; they prepare, support, criticize, or revise one of these four central dialogues. For example, the *Protagoras*, the *Meno*, and the *Euthydemus* prepare for the composition of the *Republic*. The *Phaedrus* revises the *Symposium*. The *Parmenides* is a critical assessment of the theory of Forms in preparation for the *Sophist*; the Eleatic Tetrad is the preparation for the Pythagorean Tetrad. Within the Pythagorean Tetrad, the *Philebus* prepares for the *Laws*, while the latter is supported by the *Timaeus* and the *Critias*.

The thematic function is closely related to the thematic direction, which indicates whether any given dialogue should be located in the Platonic ascent or descent. The ascent is a much shorter journey than the descent. Only the *Phaedo* and the *Symposium* belong to the Platonic ascent, and all the later dialogues to the Platonic descent. The descent is a highly complicated and extended journey, which begins with Socrates' encounter with Protagoras in the *Protagoras* and ends with his reappearance in the *Theaetetus*. In the *Protagoras*, Plato uses him to introduce the notion of civic virtue and political art, which later becomes the art of constructing the Kallipolis. By this dramatic device, he may be indicating that he has derived the notion of civic virtue and political art from Protagoras. In fact, there is an ancient legend to the effect that the *Republic* was a plagiarism of Protagoras's work.[28] In the *Theaetetus*, Plato uses him to introduce the problem of perceptual knowledge. Thus, Protagoras plays a special role in the journey of descent; his ideas set the stage for its beginning and its end. The construction of an ideal city is the ultimate end of Platonic descent, and it is derived from the Protagorean notion of social order. But this ultimate end cannot be realized without securing the knowledge of phenomena, because an ideal city has to be established in the world of phenomena.

The knowledge of phenomena is the necessary means for the realization of Plato's ultimate end, and the *Theaetetus* is a prolegomena for the science of phenomena. Hence, the Platonic journey of descent cannot be completed without the *Theaetetus*. However, the *Republic* was written before the *Theaetetus*, that is, before the journey of descent was completed, and that can explain Plato's later dissatisfaction with the *Republic* or its deficiency. The construction of the Kallipolis is based on the knowledge of Forms, that is, without the knowledge of phenomena, although it is supposed to be realized in this world. Navigation cannot be a true art or science, if the pilot has only an opinion but no knowledge of the route of his navigation. Likewise, the Kallipolis cannot be a work of true political art unless it is based on the knowledge of phenomena. To be sure, even the *Theaetetus* does not deliver the science of phenomena; it is only a prolegomena that has to be worked out in the later dialogues. After consolidating his theory of empirical knowledge in these dialogues, Plato revises his central ideas of the *Republic* and composes the *Laws*. One of the central premises for this revision is the empirical knowledge of human nature. The *Laws* replaces the absolute sovereignty of a philosopher-king by the sovereignty of the law, because no mortals can, by their empirical nature, stand above the law without becoming arrogant and corrupt.

Because Protagoras plays a special role in the journey of descent, Plato treats him with special care and respect in both dialogues. In the *Theaetetus*, Plato assigns to Socrates the singular role of propounding Protagoras's doctrine of perception and even defending it. On no other occasion does Socrates perform such a singular role. In the *Protagoras*, he puts on another unusual performance; his behavior toward Protagoras is inordinately merciless and ill-mannered, while the latter behaves in a highly urbane and civilized way. Socrates' impolite behavior is so out of line with the general standard of his behavior in the other dialogues that it has been a puzzle for Plato scholars.[29] In my view, the behavioral difference of the two men is Plato's way of showing his greater respect for Protagoras than for Socrates in the *Protagoras*. The dramatic encounter of these two men in Plato's dialogue represents the interaction of two sets of ideas in his mind, which are derived from these two men. In the *Protagoras*, the Protagorean notion of civic virtue and political art takes on a far greater significance than the Socratic notion of ethical virtue.

All in all, Plato's journey of ascent and descent is to meet the challenge of Callicles. What is the ultimate character of this challenge? Callicles is not only a spokesman for the principle of power politics, but also represents the world of phenomena and its vital force, which Plato identifies as *eros* in its broadest and deepest sense. It is the basic force of desire and appetite that moves not only human beings but all other living things. In short, it is the principle of life. Callicles maintains that the gratification of appetite is the ultimate good, and that the unbridled power is the best means for gratification. Only those who cannot have such absolute power advocate the doctrine of self-restraint and moderation.

What is the best way to fulfill *eros*? This is the critical question posed by the challenge of Callicles. Plato can meet this challenge only by devising a better way of coping with the problem of *eros* than Callicles'. For this reason, the problem of *eros* is far more important for Plato than any other problem. He first tried to resolve this problem by disowning *eros* and disdaining the world of the body altogether (the *Phaedo*), and then by presenting the world of Forms as the most beautiful object of *eros* (the *Symposium*). In Plato's world, beauty and love (*eros*) go together; only the beautiful can truly fulfill our love. When he realized that the flight to the world of Forms was only an escape from the world of phenomena, he began his journey of descent for the momentous task of building a beautiful city in this world. The beauty of the Kallipolis is meant to replace the beauty of Forms in Plato's final scheme of realizing *eros*. Hence, the art of constructing the Kallipolis is the art of love. In the *Symposium*, Socrates says that he learned this art from Diotima; in the *Republic*, he transforms it into political art.

The art of love is the art of realizing oneself, because love in its Platonic sense is the intense longing for completing one's incomplete self. The *Symposium* advocates the completion of oneself in its vision of the beautiful Forms; the *Republic* tries to secure it in the community of mutual love (*philia*). In the latter, the art of love becomes political art. Since political art is political wisdom, it is the final product of *philosophia* (love of wisdom). In the *Republic*, political art creates the Kallipolis as the most ideal social order. But it is too much of a philosopher's dream to be workable in the real world. In the construction of the Kallipolis, Plato assembles all his beautiful ideals without seriously considering whether they can be realized in the world of phenomena. Since the Kallipolis is not given a solid empirical foundation, it is still suspended somewhere between this world and Platonic Heaven. To bring the Kallipolis completely down to earth and to demonstrate its feasibility in the language (*logos*) of this world is Plato's project from the *Republic* to the *Laws*. This project completes his journey of descent and eventually enables him to meet the challenge of Callicles on his own terms.

Notes

1. Vlastos, "The Theory of Social Justice in the *Polis* in Plato's *Republic*," in *Interpretations of Plato*, Helen North, ed. (Lugduni Batavorum: E. J. Brill, 1977), 31.

2. For example, Eduard Zeller once took this view in his *Platonische Studien* (Tuebingen: Osiander, 1839; Reissued by Rodopi, Amsterdam, 1969), 19–23.

3. This point is fully discussed by Andre Laks, "Legislation and Demiurge: On the Relationship between Plato's *Republic* and *Laws*," *Classical Quarterly* 9 (1990):209–29.

4. G. M. A. Grube says that the divine ruler in the age of Cronus refers to the philosopher-king of the *Republic*, though he does not take the myth of Cronus as a repudiation of the Kallipolis. *Plato's Thought* (Indianapolis, Ind.: Hackett, 1980), 279.

5. Klosko, *The Development of Plato's Political Theory* (London: Methuen, 1986), 190.

6. *Plato's Cretan City* (Princeton, N.J.: Princeton University Press, 1960), 576–77.

7. Popper, *The Open Society and Its Enemies* (London: Routledge, 1945), 1:86–201.

8. Rousseau, *Social Contract* 1.6.

9. Rousseau, *Social Contract* 2.4.

10. For a fuller account, see my *Kant's Platonic Revolution in Moral and Political Philosophy* (Baltimore, Md.: Johns Hopkins University Press, 1994), 93–130.

11. This point is stressed by Glenn Morrow, *Plato's Cretan City*, 58, 539, and by Stalley, *Introduction to Plato's Laws* (Indianapolis, Ind.: Hackett, 1983), 185.

12. Barker, *Greek Political Theory*, 5th ed. (London: Methuen, 1960), 343.

13. Kennedy, "Form and Substance in Private Law Adjudication," *Harvard Law Review* 89 (1976):1685–1778.

14. Kennedy, "The Structure of Blackstone's Commentaries," *Buffalo Law Review* 28 (1979):211–21.

15. Rawls, *A Theory of Justice* (Cambridge, Mass.: Harvard University Press, 1971), 42–45.

16. For further discussion, see my *Intuition and Construction* (New Haven, Conn.: Yale University Press, 1993), 13–16.

17. *The Development of Plato's Political Theory*, 201.

18. *Plato's Cosmology: The Timaeus of Plato* (London: Routledge, 1937), 4–5.

19. Throughout his life, Plato was concerned with the problem of balancing these two opposite traits. This problem is also discussed as an important feature of the royal art in the *Statesman* 306b–307d.

20. Diogenes Laertius, *Lives of Eminent Philosophers* 3.6.

21. This point is well noted by Eugenio Benitez and Livia Guimaraes, "Philosophy as Performed in Plato's *Theaetetus,*" *Review of Metaphysics* 47 (1993):308.

22. "Philosophy as Performed in Plato's *Theaetetus,*" 309.

23. Benitez and Guimaraes say, "The magnitude of Theaetetus's prospect is staggering." "Philosophy as Performed in Plato's *Theaetetus,*" 301. The frame story of the dialogue records Socrates' prophetic recognition of Theaetetus' great future (142c).

24. Diogenes Laertius, *Lives of Eminent Philosophers* 3.6.

25. Morrow, *Plato's Cretan City*, 74.

26. Dorothea Frede, Plato, *Philebus* (Indianapolis, Ind.: Hackett, 1993), xiii.

27. Arieti, *Interpreting Plato: The Dialogues as Drama* (Lanham, Md.: Rowman and Littlefield, 1991), 21–22.

28. Diogenes Laertius says that nearly all of the *Republic* is copied from the *Antilogikoi* of Protagoras, according to Aristoxenus. *Lives of Eminent Philosophers* 3.37.

29. This puzzle is discussed by Gregory Vlastos in his introduction to Plato, *Protagoras* (New York: Macmillan, 1956), xxiv–xxv.

CHAPTER NINE
Platonic Legacy

I have tried to articulate the hidden half of Plato's philosophy, mostly hidden in his late dialogues. But it is by far the greater half. Its many features are not only important and relevant for our times, but extremely ingenious and resourceful. Plato has shown a remarkable sensitivity to the problem of language. He warns against the danger of overlooking the three-term relation of subject-word-object in semantics; such an oversight is bound to lead either to Hermogenes' radical subjectivist view of language, or to Cratylus's obscurantism and mystification. He articulates the distinction between the logic of identity and the logic of resemblance. The former is the classical logic of classes or discontinua; the latter is the logic of continuum that allows no clear boundaries between different classes. The latter is infected with semantic indeterminacy (slippery slope arguments and the sorites paradox); the former is blessed with semantic determinacy. Though the classical logic of classes is appropriate for natural science, it is not very useful for the humanities and social sciences. The logic of resemblances is the logic of human sciences, which do not permit precision and exactitude.

The Derrideans could not have made such a big issue out of semantic indeterminacy if they and their audience had been well acquainted with the logic of resemblance. In this controversy, the Derrideans and their critics alike have not made the distinction between total (unconstrained) and partial (constrained) indeterminacy. If the meaning of a word is totally indeterminate, it can mean anything and everything. If it is partially indeterminate, its indeterminacy is restricted to only borderline cases. When the Derrideans argue for semantic indeterminacy, they usually mean the total and unconstrained indeterminacy. But such an assertion is self-defeating for the Derrideans. It does not even allow them to make their case for semantic indeterminacy because the thesis of total indeterminacy eliminates the distinction between determinacy and indeterminacy. For the sake of self-coherence, they must modify their thesis to that of constrained indeterminacy. The semantic thesis of constrained indeterminacy is built into Plato's logic of continuum and resemblance.

The logic of continuum and resemblance is the logic of phenomena. This logic was developed together with Plato's one-world view that replaces his two-world view. In this transition, his old idea of separation is replaced by his new idea of union and combination. In the early and the middle dialogues, he was obsessed with the problem of liberating the soul from the body, and escaping from this world to the other world. It is no exaggeration to say that those dialogues are animated by Plato's pervasive fear and distrust of this world and its corrosive force. This negative attitude may have largely reflected Plato's hatred of Athenian power politics and its appetitive ethos. How to cope with this negative attitude was his existential problem, and he tried to resolve it by his project of ascent and descent. His project of ascent is propelled by the hatred of this world, and its separation from the other world consolidates his flight to Platonic Heaven.

Plato's journey of descent, however, is his project to overcome this negative attitude and reappropriate the world of phenomena. To this end, he replaces the theme of separation with the theme of union—the union of soul and body, reason and passion, the union of individual souls in a social bond, and the union of social order with the order of the universe. His new conception of unity is different from his old conception of autocratic unity advocated in the *Republic*. In his new conception, multiplicity is as important as unity. The new unity consists in the balance of opposite forces, the gentle and the violent, authority and liberty. The system of checks and balances is the basic framework for sustaining order not only in the individual soul, but also in the political community. The art of balancing generates the spirit of harmony from the microcosm of the individual soul to the macrocosm of the universe.

As remarkably refreshing and resourceful as these features are, they do not capture all of Plato's lasting contributions. His enterprise can best be understood as the invention of a completely new discipline, which may be called normative philosophy. For a proper appreciation of this enterprise, I will try to situate Plato's accomplishment in its proper historical perspective.

Normative Philosophy

In the West, although philosophy has been known under a single name, it has comprised two quite different disciplines, normative and descriptive. Descriptive philosophy is the inquiry into the nature of reality. It began with the natural philosophers of ancient Greece and still thrives in the natural sciences of our day. Normative philosophy is the inquiry into the nature of normative standards and principles, which began with the distinction between nature (*physis*) and culture (*nomos*) by the sophists. Whereas nature is invariant, they argued, culture varies from place to place. There is only one nature, but there are many cultures. Nature is governed by the same principles everywhere, but each culture has its own norms and rules.

The central question in normative philosophy is the question of normative standards and principles. By what standards and principles are we to guide our life and govern our society? How do we know that those standards and principles are right? Though there have been many answers to these questions, all of them belong to one of two positions: normative positivism and transcendentism.[1] Normative transcendentism asserts the existence of standards and principles that transcend all positive normative systems. This view is Plato's invention; it is Platonism. His theory of Forms is a theory of transcendent standards and principles. In contrast, normative positivism, which denies the existence of transcendent standards and principles, accepts only the norms and rules established by the positive laws and conventions of each society. There can be no normative standards and principles apart from, or prior to, the emergence of positive laws and conventions. All of them are products of social construction. Platonism does not reject positive norms, but claims that they can be justified only by transcendent principles.

Normative positivism is older than Platonism; its origin can be traced back to the Greek sophists and it has been firmly espoused even in our century by such reputable philosophers as Ludwig Wittgenstein and H. L. A. Hart.[2] In spite of its venerable history, normative positivism is well known to have one fatal defect. It inevitably leads to relativism and nihilism. The validity and invalidity of normative judgments are always relative to some positive normative standards and principles, which vary from one society to another. Every normative perspective has to be internal; it has to be situated within some particular normative system. Normative positivism allows no external perspective. If we want to compare Hitler's Third Reich with the Weimar Republic, we have to make the comparison from the perspective of either the Third Reich or the Weimar Republic, or of a third country such as imperial Japan. There is no perspective that can transcend all these particular normative systems. This is the distasteful consequence of normative positivism.

For normative positivism, the absence of a transcendent perspective presents the serious problem of justification. In any normative system, the lower norms can be justified by the higher ones. But how can the higher norms, especially the highest ones (for example, Hans Kelsen's *Grundnorm* or John Rawls's basic principles of society), be justified? There is no way to justify the highest norms in a positivist system. It makes no sense even to raise the question of justification for the highest norms, because they owe their existence to nothing higher than themselves. They stand on *nothing* but themselves; normative positivism turns out to be normative nihilism. To be sure, some positivists claim to give the internal justification of a normative system by demonstrating its internal coherence. Two salient examples are John Rawls's theory of reflective equilibrium and Ronald Dworkin's theory of law as integrity.[3] But the internal coherence of a normative system cannot tell whether the whole system is just or unjust. Even the legal system of the Third Reich can be as coherent internally as any liberal democratic system.

The only way to avoid the relativistic and nihilistic consequence of normative positivism is to accept transcendent normative standards. This was Plato's motive for advocating his theory of transcendent Forms. If Platonism is taken as a commitment to transcendent normative standards, it is much broader than Plato's theory of Forms. For example, it clearly covers the theory of natural law, and even utilitarianism, which asserts at least one transcendental principle, namely, the principle of utility. No doubt, this is a defective version of normative transcendentism, but all the same it cannot operate without the Platonic commitment to some transcendent principle. But Platonism has its own problem: How can we know that there are such metaphysical entities as transcendent normative standards and principles? This question has been the most serious obstacle to accepting Platonism, and many philosophers have rightly thought that to endorse Platonism is as problematic as to endorse normative positivism. Some of them have tried to avoid the choice between Platonism and positivism by finding some other position. Let us consider the outcome of these attempts.

One outcome may be called naturalism; it tries to secure the foundation of all norms in the world of nature. For example, Aristotle appeals to human nature in his moral and political philosophy. But the nature he appeals to is not brute but idealized nature, which he calls the second nature of humanity. Brute nature cannot deliver a theory of civic virtue and political order. If natural law ever exists in human nature, it can be not in the brute nature of humanity, but in its idealized nature. But the idealization of nature requires a set of ideals, and Aristotle often locates those ideals in Athenian practices. However, these ideals must reflect either only the positive norms localized in Aristotle's Athens, or the transcendent normative standards and principles that have global significance and relevance. In the former case, Aristotelian naturalism reduces to normative positivism; in the latter case, it is a special version of Platonism in disguise.

Hobbes indeed takes brute nature as the basis for his theory of natural law. He does not claim to derive his natural law from nature; instead he constructs it as the best way to secure peace and prosperity in the state of nature. Thus he began the grand tradition of normative constructivism. Since then it has been looked upon by many as another way to avoid the choice between positivism and Platonism, and it has been known by a few other names. For example, all social contract theories from Hobbes to Rawls belong to constructivism. So does Hare's prescriptivism. Their common essence lies in the claim that normative rules and standards are not given by nature, but are constructed by human beings. The different versions of constructivism can be divided into two programs: (1) the program of formal construction, and (2) the program of ideal construction.

The program of formal construction is Kant's invention; it solely relies on the formal principle of consistency. Although it has been followed by many, it is a futile project. Because a formal principle is substantively empty, it can never produce any substantive normative standards and principles. Any substantive results derived from a formal program of construction are achieved by a sleight of hand, which introduces substantive considerations under the guise of formal operation.[4] The program of ideal construction usually takes two stages, input and output. For example, John Rawls constructs the original position, and then derives his two principles of justice from it. The construction of the original position is the input stage; the derivation of the two principles is the output stage. This distinction also applies to Hobbes's constructivism. His input stage consists of the state of nature and the human beings rational enough to devise the best ways to preserve themselves. His output stage is the derivation of his natural laws.

The important stage is the input stage; it determines what sort of laws or principles will be derived in the output stage. The construction of the input stage is largely governed by some basic ideals, for example, the principle of liberty, equality, or utility. These basic ideals can be justified in terms of either positivism or Platonism. For example, John Rawls gives a positivistic justification to the Kantian ideals of liberty and equality, which provide the normative basis for the construction of his original position. He justifies the acceptance of those ideals by the simple assertion that they are embedded in our political culture of liberal democracy.[5] Hence, his constructivism belongs to positivism. On the other hand, if their justification can be made on some transcendent principles, his program should belong to Platonism.[6]

Jürgen Habermas's discourse ethics is another program of construction.[7] It is his program of ideal dialogue for discussing and determining all normative issues. Unlike the monologue that is supposed to take place in John Rawls's original position, this dialogue will not be a hypothetical but an actual event. Hence, it is impossible to tell what laws and principles will be reached by any ideal dialogue until it really takes place. Therefore, Habermas makes no claim to derive any particular norms and standards; his discourse ethics does not have the output stage. It is a truncated constructivism. But even this special form of constructivism cannot avoid the choice between positivism and Platonism, because the construction of an ideal speech is governed by a set of ideal conditions. Habermas says that these ideal conditions are derived from universal or transcendental pragmatics, and that they are further combined with a set of moral ideals governing ethical discourse. He has yet to face the question of whether these ideals are transcendent or only positive norms imbedded in our political culture. Depending on his answer to this question, his program of construction will also belong to either positivism or Platonism.[8]

Beyond this theoretical problem of normative ideals, Habermas's theory of ideal speech faces the problem that arises from the rule of unanimity that is embedded in his consensus theory of truth. Since this rule is perhaps the simplest form of constructivism, its adoption may appear to be innocuous and unproblematic. However, the rule of unanimous decision has presented insurmountable problems for political theorists. Just imagine that a political community cannot make its decisions about repairing old roads and opening new schools without everyone's consent. Such a decision procedure is not only impractical but tyrannical; it gives every voter the awesome power to paralyze the entire political community.[9] Political paralysis is clearly a serious case of injustice, and its recognition and avoidance requires an appeal to the transcendent principle of justice.

Instead of using the rule of unanimity and the ideal speech as rule of practical politics, let us imagine that we adopt it as a method of making normative judgment about the past events, for example, whether *Dred Scott v. Sandford* was a right or wrong decision. For almost a century and half, this historical case has been a topic of continuous discussion in our country, but this discussion cannot settle the question unless and until it fulfills two ideal conditions. First, it should have been conducted under specified ideal conditions; second, it should have produced a consensus. It is hard to say whether the first condition is fulfilled or not, but it is obvious that no consensus has been reached. It is highly unlikely for us to see the day when these two ideal conditions are fulfilled in the real world. Yet Habermas insists that his ideal speech is meant to be not an imaginary conversation conducted under ideal conditions, but a real historical event. In that case, the ideal speech does not have the remotest chance of becoming an instrument for deciding whether *Dred Scott* or any other controversial case has been rightly or wrongly decided. There is absolutely no prospect of consensus on such a controversial issue.

This critique of Habermas's program equally applies to pragmatism, if it is taken as another proposal for settling normative issues. In fact, Habermas constructed his program of ideal speech by adopting Charles Peirce's pragmatic theory of truth as consensus.[10] Let us distinguish this ideal version of pragmatism from the instrumental version, which has lately become fashionable in jurisprudence. Because the function of law is only instrumental, some legal pragmatists claim, the formalist conception of law as a body of immutable principles should be replaced by the pragmatic conception that the right judicial decision is the one that works well rather than the one that faithfully follows some immutable principle. The pragmatic criterion of working well is clearly different from the criterion of consensus; the former cannot be as crippling as the latter. But any legal decision or system can be justified by the pragmatic criterion of success. The *Dred Scott* case surely worked well for the slave owners; so did the Nazi law for the Third Reich.

The instrumental conception of law is not really a radical innovation by legal pragmatists, but an old truism that has been operative in all legal systems. We do not obey the law for its own sake; the law should be not our master but our servant. Even the highest law of our nation has been established as an instrument to achieve a set of specified ends, as prescribed by the Preamble to the Constitution. But the pragmatic criterion of success can only lead to a normative chaos, because it can be the success of injustice as well as of justice. We can avoid normative chaos by redefining the pragmatic criterion as working well for justice and not for injustice. But what sort of justice are we appealing to, the positive or the transcendent? Thus we come back to the choice between positivism and Platonism.

Besides constructivism and naturalism, there have been two other attempts to avoid the choice between positivism and Platonism: emotivism and moral realism. These two are designed to achieve the same goal of avoidance by disavowing the need for normative standards and principles. The emotivists flatly deny the existence of norms, Platonic or positivistic, and explain the function of normative assertions without any recourse to normative standards and principles. Normative judgments have no truth value; they are neither true nor false. Their function is not to assert any truth but to express our emotion, or attitude.[11] Emotivism is a corollary of logical positivism, which reduces all reality to physical reality. This reduction eliminates the ground for normative philosophy altogether, and restricts philosophy to its descriptive function. During the heyday of logical positivism, for this reason, philosophy of science was regarded as the first and sometimes the only true philosophy. But I suppose those days are behind us.

Moral realism is not an invention of our century. It is the common-sense view, which was officially championed by Francis Hutcheson and other British moral sense theorists in the eighteenth century. It has lately been resurrected as a reaction to the logical positivist reduction of all reality to a complex of purely physical entities. The moral realists claim that normative properties such as the moral property of being disloyal or the legal property of being culpable are as real as the physical properties of colors and sounds, size and weight. This claim is quite confusing because there are three different ways of recognizing the existence of moral properties and relations. First, we can recognize them by virtue of positive norms and rules. Second, we can do the same by virtue of transcendent standards and principles. Third, we can do it without appealing to any normative rules and standards, positive or transcendent.

The first of these three positions reduces moral realism to normative positivism, and I suppose no moral realist wants to advocate normative positivism. The second position reduces moral realism to Platonism, and this cannot be the real claim of moral realists, either, because they want to locate the object of their discourse in the world of phenomena.

The third position is indeed different from the first two; it claims the existence of moral properties and relations totally independent of all normative standards, positive or transcendental. This appears to be the real moral realism. So understood, moral realism is a product of naive moral consciousness, which precedes critical moral consciousness. Only critical consciousness recognizes the indispensability of normative rules and standards for the perception of moral properties and relations. These rules and standards are unnecessary for naive consciousness, because it believes that moral properties and relations are as real as physical properties and relations. This is the view of naive commonsense.

For a better understanding of the difference between naive and critical consciousness, let us consider the nature of athletic actions and properties. On the football field, the actions of players can be described in purely physical terms. But those actions also have athletic properties; for example, scoring a goal or getting fouled is an athletic property, which cannot be described in terms of purely physical properties. So every act on a football field has both physical and athletic properties. For naive consciousness, these two types of properties are on a par; both of them have independent existence. The touchdowns and fouls are the objects of direct observation just as much as the motion and speed of a running back are. For critical consciousness, however, the two types of properties are not on a par. Whereas physical properties have independent existence, the existence of athletic properties presupposes the acceptance of athletic norms and rules.

If we can return to the world of naive consciousness, we can accept moral realism and avoid the choice between normative positivism and Platonism, a choice made inevitable by the emergence of critical consciousness. However, we can return to naive consciousness only by extinguishing critical consciousness. Such a return is not easy for philosophical consciousness; it is just like the return to the land of lost innocence. Even if such a return is possible, there is no way to secure the durability of naive consciousness thus regained, because it is notoriously an easy prey to critical consciousness and normative nihilism. The moral realists can save their position from the menace of critical consciousness and normative nihilism by disowning their affiliation with the naive realists. They can reject the moral properties and relations that belong to naive consciousness, and recognize only the moral properties and relations that can be perceived by an ideal (or normal) observer under ideal (or normal) conditions.

So we can distinguish the ideal from the naive moral realism. One belongs to naive moral consciousness and the other does not. But an ideal observer and ideal conditions are not empirical objects and facts, but ideal constructions. The ideal moral realism turns out to be a special version of constructivism. How is its ideal observer going to be constructed? Is she going to be equipped with any normative standards and principles? If they are not, they will be useless for "observing" moral properties and relations. If they are so equipped, those standards and principles have to be either positivistic or Platonic. Thus the ideal moral realism cannot avoid the choice between Platonism and positivism, because it is a special form of constructivism.

Platonism vs. Positivism

The inevitable choice between positivism and Platonism, however, has had a peculiar history in our century. It has never been allowed to become a choice. In our normative discourse, the choice between Platonism and positivism has never been mentioned. Nor has Platonism ever been recognized as the dialectical counterpart of normative positivism. Platonism has curiously been ignored even in our discussion of normative relativism and nihilism, because it has been firmly consigned to the limbo of irrelevancy. By the end of this century, some philosophers have recently observed, not much can be said about Platonism except that it has finally become defunct and completely lost its following.[12] Even the impressive accomplishments in Plato scholarship have done little for demonstrating the relevance of Platonism for our normative discourse, because most of them have been conducted in the pedantic arena of logical analysis and textual exegesis.

To be sure, this century has produced a far more imposing series of commentaries on Plato's dialogues than any other century. But this endless series of commentaries has only confirmed the sneaking suspicion

that Plato's philosophy is finally fit only for the studio of classical studies. I do not know of a single scholar who has shown pride and confidence in talking about the power and truth of Plato's philosophy. Plato
scholars are highly contentious when they argue with each other. But
when they talk about the value of Plato's philosophy, their tone invariably becomes timid and apologetic. Even Whitehead's celebrated statement that the history of Western philosophy is a series of footnotes on
Plato has not been of much help for reinstating Platonism. When this
cryptic statement was made, the grand tradition of Western philosophy
itself was already falling apart, and the great Platonic legacy was only
becoming a relic of the remote past. All in all, the twentieth century has
enjoyed fabulous success in embalming Plato's works for the mauso-
leum of obsolete classical texts.

In the meantime, however, Plato's ideas have displayed their irre-
pressible force by haunting us in different guises. Beginning with John
Rawls, many have tried to find a way out of the relativistic and nihilistic
abyss of normative positivism by reviving the legacy of Aristotle,
Hobbes, Rousseau, Locke, and Kant. But most of these revival attempts
have turned out to be disguised appeals to some transcendent normative
standards and principles, although it has long been quite unfashionable
to claim their transcendent origin. It is indeed high time for us to settle
our account with Plato himself instead of flirting with his shadows. This
is what I have tried to do in this volume. But it has not been an easy
task because his dialogues are highly elusive and their interpretation
requires an extraordinary insight. At least, I have shown the impossibility of disregarding Platonism in normative discourse, by demonstrating
that it is the inevitable dialectical counterpart to positivism. This is
especially so in the two domains of justification and construction.

In the domain of justification, there is no way to avoid the choice
between Platonism and positivism for the following reason. First, it is
impossible for any moral or political system to operate without positive
norms. Second, the positive norms either have to be accepted without
justification, or have to be justified by transcendent principles. The former is normative positivism; the latter is Platonism. The same problem
arises in the domain of construction; there are only two ways of constructing positive norms, that is, either by accepting Platonism for its

foundation or by rejecting it. Thus, Platonism and positivism divide the entire universe of normative discourse into two opposing camps, and there can be no third camp although many have tried to find it. Hence all normative disputes fall into two types; they are either intermural or intramural. The intramural disputes are conducted within each of the two camps, and the intermural disputes are the disputes between the two camps.

The relationship between these two camps is not symmetrical. The Platonic camp does not reject the existence of positive norms, as the positivist camp denies the existence of transcendental norms. Whereas the latter accepts only positive norms, the former accepts both norms, positive and transcendent. The Platonic camp only denies the independent existence of positive norms, because their construction and justification presuppose the existence of transcendent standards and principles. Positivism is a single-dimension theory; it recognizes only the positive dimension of normative rules and standards. Platonism is a double-dimension theory; it recognizes both dimensions, positive and transcendent. This is perhaps the best way to characterize the difference between the two camps of Platonism and positivism. In most discussions, both Platonism and positivism are presented as theories of only one dimension, that is, positivism as a theory of positive norms and Platonism as a theory of transcendent norms. Though this may be true of the skyscraper version of Platonism, it mischaracterizes the nature of its bedrock version, which provides the normative basis for the construction of positive norms.

Normative Intuition

The dimensional difference between the two camps of positivism and Platonism can perhaps be shown in the operation of normative intuition. According to positivism, our normative intuition has only one dimension because it is shaped exclusively by positive norms. It is a product of acculturation and indoctrination. According to Platonism, our normative intuition has two dimensions, positive and transcendent. The positive dimension is shaped by positive norms, but the transcendent dimension transcends all positive norms because it is the intuition of transcendent standards and principles. The Platonic conception of normative intuition is much more complex than the positivist conception. Let us now see which of these two theories can give a better account of our normative experience.

Just imagine that we are going to live by only positive normative intuition and without any appeal to transcendent normative intuition. There may be nothing wrong with our life under positive norms, as long as they are decent and humane. But we cannot tell whether our positive norms are humane or inhumane without appealing to the transcendent dimension of our normative intuition. By its positive dimension, we can never find anything amiss with our positive norms, for every positive norm is just and good by its own standard. If our normative intuition is restricted to its positive dimension, we can never subject positive norms to external criticism because there are no external criteria for such a critique. A purely positive intuition never allows an external perspective; its perspective is always internal.

If our normative intuition has only one dimension, it can be only a single-edged sword. It can cut only by the edge of positive norms. But our normative judgment appears to be a double-edged sword; it can cut either with its positive edge or with its transcendent edge. Which of these two edges will be used largely depends on our purpose on each occasion, and it is sometimes hard to tell which of them is really being used. To be sure, we are more likely to use the positive edge more often and more readily than the transcendent edge, but we will do so only with the hope and belief that our positive intuitions are in accord with our transcendent intuitions. On the other hand, whenever we are unsure of our positive norms and standards, we feel the duty to subject them to careful scrutiny. But such a scrutiny can be made only by using the transcendent edge of our normative intuition.

Platonism entails not only that our normative intuition is a double-edged sword, but also that its positive dimension depends on its transcendent dimension. That is, there is asymmetry between the two edges of our normative intuition in their genesis. The existence of positive intuition depends on instruction; it can be developed by instilling positive norms in the human mind. The positivists generally assume that the human mind is a tabula rasa, on which we can inscribe any positive norm by instruction and indoctrination. It is impossible to inculcate positive norms in cows and donkeys because they do not have the basic intuition of right and wrong, which is transcendent. The mind would indeed be a tabula rasa, if it were devoid of such an intuition, and no positivistic instruction could ever make a dent on it. The transcendent intuition is the necessary precondition for the development of positive intuition; it is *transcendental* in the Kantian sense. Likewise, transcendent normative principles are transcendental; they are the necessary precondition for the construction of positive norms.

Even in mathematics, our intuition is double-edged; it is composed of positive and transcendent dimensions. The positive mathematical intuition is developed by mathematical training; the transcendent mathematical intuition is presupposed by such training. We cannot teach mathematics to cows and donkeys by simply exposing them to a frequent recitation of numbers or a repeated display of numerals, because they do not have basic mathematical sense. The same distinction obtains for our linguistic intuition. The positive linguistic intuition is developed by the acquisition of competence in a particular language; the transcendent linguistic intuition is presupposed by such acquisition. What Noam Chomsky calls linguistic competence belongs to transcendent intuition; it depends on the innate knowledge of universal grammar.[13] It is the transcendental condition for the development of positive linguistic intuition.

The grammar of each natural language is a positive norm; universal grammar is a transcendental norm. The question of whether the subject of a sentence comes before or after the predicate cannot be settled by our transcendent linguistic competence or intuition, because it can be answered differently for different languages and because different languages have different positive norms for governing the relative positions of subject and predicate. On the other hand, the concept or general formula of predication belongs to our transcendent linguistic competence or intuition, because it is a matter of universal grammar that transcends the boundary of natural languages. It is impossible for anyone to learn the positive rule of predication in any natural language without the intuitive understanding of the transcendent concept of predication.

We can make the same distinction for our musical intuition in particular and aesthetic intuition in general. Our positive musical intuition is shaped by training and exposure to a particular style of music (for example, the Romantic music of the nineteenth century, Baroque music, or rock music). Each style of music is defined and differentiated from other styles by its positive norms. Positive norms govern the most basic elements of musical composition, that is, what sort of scale is to be used, how many notes are to be contained in the scale, what is the size of the interval between two notes, what sort of rhythm, what sort of tonality and harmony, and so on. The different forms of composition such as the fugue, the sonata, and the tone poem also belong to positive norms. Our positive musical intuition is derived from positive norms, and our transcendent musical intuition from transcendent norms. However, the cultivation of positive intuition again presupposes the transcendent intuition, because we cannot learn a system of positive musical norms without using our native musical sense, our transcendent intuition.

Positive intuition is acquired; transcendent intuition is innate. The former grows only as a graft on the latter. This inseparable link between the positive and the transcendent intuitions can explain one important feature of Socratic definition. As we have repeatedly noted in this volume, there are two stages in the Socratic definition, the conventional and the transcendent. The conventional stage relies on positive intuition; it is the examination and articulation of the conventional understanding of positive norms. The transcendent stage relies on transcendent intuition; it appeals to the intuition of transcendent principles. Hence, the definitions delivered in the transcendent stage invariably turn out to be highly general and abstract. In the *Laches*, for example, the definition of courage in the transcendent stage was the knowledge of good and evil in general; in the *Charmides*, the definition of temperance was the knowledge of oneself. This general tendency is due to the fact that the intuition of transcendent Forms is highly general and indeterminate.

In the Socratic definition, the conventional stage is coextensive with the domain of positive intuition, and it has all the definiteness of positive norms. As the Socratic definition moves beyond the conventional stage, it becomes more and more indeterminate because it has to deal with the intuition of transcendent Forms. This transition, however, does not introduce any new cognitive devices or perspectives, because the initial intuition that is appealed to at the beginning of definition contains all the necessary intuitive elements for both the conventional and the transcendent stage. For the initial intuition contains both the positive and the transcendent dimensions. Because the transition from the conventional to the transcendent stage introduces no new epistemic devices, the demarcation between the two stages has seldom been noted by Plato scholars.

The two intuitions, positive and transcendent, constitute the beginning and the end of all education. Transcendent intuition provides the basis for all education; the cultivation of positive intuition is its end, which is none other than the construction of culture. Without education, there can be no world of culture. This is the basic difference between nature and culture. This is why Plato repeatedly stresses the importance of education in the *Protagoras*, the *Meno*, the *Republic*, and the *Laws*. But we cannot teach music to the tone deaf; the transcendent musical intuition must be presupposed for all musical education. The transcendent musical intuition is not sufficient for our musical life, because it is too primordial and too indeterminate. It can be made determinate by exposure to particular music and its positive norms. Here lies the function of musical training and education; it endows our transcendent intuition with its positive dimension or intuition.

The distinction between positive and transcendent intuitions may be useful even for unraveling the often confused and confusing arguments of the communitarians, which can take on many different dimensions. On the simplest level, their claim is more or less a truism: a community has its own integrity and its own goodness, which cannot be exhausted by the private interests of its members. Their claim becomes somewhat mysterious when they talk about the identity of the self. They denounce the Kantian concept of the self, or the concept of the unencumbered self, whose identity transcends its communal bonds. In their view, the Kantian concept is not only empty but false. It is simply impossible even to imagine the identity of oneself without embedding it in our community. The self would be nothing, a nonentity, without being defined by the values and standards of its community.[14]

The self that has nothing but positive intuitions is the encumbered self. It can never transcend the positive norms of its community, nor can it subject them to critical scrutiny. It is the encumbered self, whose identity is totally determined by the norms and values of its community. On the other hand, the self that is equipped with transcendental intuitions can transcend the positive norms of its community. It can subject the positive norms to critical scrutiny, and imagine itself as free of its bondage to the community. It is the unencumbered self, whose identity cannot be defined by the norms and values of its community. What the communitarians call the Kantian self is the Platonic self, and their rejection of it amounts to their rejection of transcendent intuitions. In that case, their vaunted communitarianism turns out to be just another label for normative positivism; it accepts the positive values of one's own community as "the authoritative horizons."[15]

Normative Intuition and Sociobiology

On the surface, a theory of intuition looks like a psychological theory of how the mind thinks and feels. If we can give a psychological theory of intuition, then we can avoid the difficult ontological question of whether there are such transcendent objects as Platonic Forms. Hence, there is always the temptation to reduce the theory of intuition to psychology or some other empirical science. Such a reduction is impossible for the following reasons. There are two components for the constitution of intuition: the act and the object. My intuition of natural numbers is composed of my mental act and its object. The mental act belongs to the human psyche, but the object does not. The theory of the act is psychological; the theory of the object is ontological.

Let us imagine that we are communicating with some extraterrestrial beings, whose brain structure and function are radically different from ours. Their conceptual act of thinking about natural numbers and their additions may be psychologically different from ours, but the mathematical objects of their thought should be the same as those of our thought if our communication is successful. These objects are not psychological but ontological entities. Intuitions can be identified or differentiated in terms of their objects. Even within the same domain of mathematics, our algebraic intuition is different from our geometric intuition, because they involve different objects. The positive geometric intuition is again different from the transcendent geometric intuition, because they are governed by different objects. The objects of positive intuition exist in a positive culture; the objects of transcendent intuition exist in the eternal realm.

In a theory of intuition, the ontological question of objects (What is the object of intuition?) is far more important than the psychological question of acts (Which faculty performs the act of intuition?). In the celebrated dispute between the British moral sense theorists and the rational intuitionists, ironically, the psychological question was the central one. Neither of the two camps ever questioned the existence of the objects of moral sense. Therefore their dispute was philosophically insignificant, although it may have been psychologically interesting. As long as a frog has the power of discriminating flies from leaves and grass, it does not matter whether the frog owes its power of cognition to sense or intellect.

Recently, there have been many attempts to revive the moral sense theory by grafting it upon sociobiology and evolutionary psychology.[16] Let us now see whether they can avoid the ontological question. James Wilson says that all of us are born with a set of moral sentiments such as sympathy for others, fairness, self-control, and duty. Since even children have moral sense, Wilson says that they are intuitive moralists.[17] Most of the moral sentiments he cites are natural instincts that have developed with the evolution of humankind, but there are some moral sentiments that he regards as cultural products. For example, he says that the Western sense of individual right and freedom has been a product of the peculiar Western European family system, which has enjoyed the right of private possessions.[18]

So there are two kinds of moral sentiment, natural and cultural. This distinction appears to correspond to our distinction between two kinds of normative intuition, positive and transcendent. In his lexicon, the two expressions, ''the moral sense'' and ''the moral intuition,'' are interchangeable. Wilson never makes the distinction between the two kinds of moral sense, because he never faces the ontological question. For him, the question of moral sense is purely psychological and sociological. But this empirical approach presents a serious problem for the justification of moral sentiments. On what ground can the sociobiologists justify our moral sentiments? This question divides into two parts, because there are two kinds of moral sentiments. For the justification of cultural moral sentiments, Wilson simply appeals to the cultural tradition. This is normative positivism.

The justification of natural moral sentiments can take two approaches. One of them is to say that the moral sentiments have been approved and appropriated by our culture. In that case, the justification of natural moral sentiments cannot be different from that of cultural moral sentiments. The other approach is the sociobiological argument; moral sentiments are conducive or sometimes indispensable for the survival of human species. Wilson espouses this familiar Darwinian argument, but this argument has to face the difficult problem of discriminating moral from immoral sentiments. The moral sentiments are not the only instincts that are given by nature; we are born with a host of other natural instincts such as love and hate, envy and jealousy, the impulses for violence and aggression. Many of these sentiments are branded as immoral. What is the criterion for the distinction between moral and immoral instincts? Since the instincts themselves cannot make this distinction, we have to appeal to our normative intuition. But our normative intuition has to be either positive or transcendent, and this distinction cannot be made by a psychological or biological criterion, because it presupposes the ontological distinction between positive and transcendent norms.

Let us now see how the Darwinian criterion works. The sentiments are moral when they serve the survival of our species, and immoral when they do not. But it is very hard to tell which of our instincts do indeed serve this vital function. Consider the role of sympathy for our survival. When the earth was sparsely populated by a few thousand human beings, the sentiment of sympathy was indeed important for the survival of Homo sapiens. But those ancestral conditions of ours have drastically changed during the past few millennia. Now that the earth is burdened with the population of over six billion human beings and her natural resources are rapidly getting depleted, the sentiment of sympathy may only increase the human population and eventually bring about the demise of the entire species. On the other hand, the sentiments of envy and aggression may be highly useful in reducing the size of the human population and secure the survival of our species.

As long as the survival of our species is the only criterion, it is impossible to tell which sentiments are moral and which sentiments are immoral. By the Darwinian criterion, even the so-called immoral sentiments such as envy and cruelty can never be branded as immoral, because the human species could not have survived so long without those instincts. Darwin himself was terrified to realize how brutal the design of natural selection was, and how contrary our natural instincts were to his own ethical principle of utilitarianism.[19] The principle of natural selection naturally leads to the Calliclean principle of power and greed, and Herbert Spencer's social Darwinism rather than to any moral principles. As we noted more than once, Callicles says that his principle of power politics is the basic principle of survival and conquest in the world of beasts. Darwin could not live with the principle of natural selection, however; he espoused the principle of utility. What morally counted for him was evidently not the mere survival of our species, but its greatest happiness.

As we have already noted, the principle of utility is a transcendent normative ideal, which goes beyond the domain of sociobiology. But the Darwinian criterion of survival is scientific and positive. If our moral sentiments are shaped and justified by this criterion, they are positive intuitions. On the other hand, if they are shaped and justified by some transcendent standards and principles, they are transcendent intuitions. Even sociobiology cannot avoid the choice between normative positivism and Platonism. These two provide different accounts of normative intuitions and their objects, which can never be reduced to positive sciences such as psychology or sociobiology.

Platonic Universalism

Platonic Forms are the universal normative principles that are presupposed for the construction of all positive norms. If so, we have to correct our earlier statement that transcendent standards and principles are external to positive normative systems. On the contrary, we should say, they are as internal to all positive normative systems as their own positive standards and principles are. By appealing to transcendent standards and principles, we do not take an external perspective. Though they are internal, they still provide a universal perspective because they form the common foundation of all positive normative systems. Only by virtue of this shared foundation can we meaningfully compare different normative systems, and even talk across their boundaries. In some extreme cases such as the Nazi law or the former American slavery law, to be sure, the common foundation of transcendent principles is so unrecognizably disfigured by the positive law that to appeal to those principles may look like adopting a totally external and alien perspective. However, that does not affect the universal presence of Platonic Forms.

Platonism does not reject all positive norms and intuitions. On the contrary, the transcendent standards and principles require the service of positive norms and intuitions, because they are too indeterminate to govern our decisions and behavior in the practical world. Just imagine that all of us are told to pay our fair shares of income tax by computing them in accordance with the transcendent principle of fairness. We would be totally at a loss. As we saw in chapter 7, the indeterminate standards and principles of Platonic Heaven have to be translated and articulated into positive norms and rules. This is the heart of Platonic construction: our transcendent intuition provides the common basis for the construction of all positive norms and rules. By virtue of this shared basis, we can meaningfully compare different normative systems, communicate across their boundaries, and even identify ourselves with the normative problems of alien cultures.

Normative construction need not be limited to the conscious act of individual agents; it can take place as a collective historical development over a long period of time as, for example, with the development of natural languages. In the *Cratylus*, as we saw in chapter 4, language is regarded as *nomos* par excellence, and the name givers are called the *nomos* givers. All of us collectively and unconsciously participate in the construction and reconstruction of our natural language. Such prominent social institutions as the medieval Catholic Church, the British common law, and the U.S. Constitution are not the conscious achievement of any single individual or group of individuals, but the product of collective construction. This cumulative process of construction is like the long journey that the Athenian Stranger undertakes with his Spartan and Cretan friends in the *Laws*. Although the Athenian Stranger is concerned with the stability of the laws, he also stresses the endless need of repairing and revising them from generation to generation whenever they are found inadequate (*Laws* 769a–771a). Probably, Plato stages the *Laws* as a dialogue on a journey in order to stress the nature of legal construction as an ongoing cumulative process.

This is the process of cumulative wisdom that goes together with the principle of collective wisdom embodied in the system of councils for the government of Magnesia. Even the work of construction in the *Laws* is not self-contained; it builds on the legal traditions of Athens, Sparta, and other Greek cities. Cleinias says that his legislative mission is to construct a legal code on the basis of existing laws, whether they are the laws of Crete or other states, provided that their quality is superior (*Laws* 702c). This cumulative process is described by Glenn Morrow as follows:

> Again and again we have seen Plato take in hand some familiar historical institution—for example, the popular courts, the music and gymnastics of Athenian education, the worship of the Olympians—or some deeply rooted tradition—such as respect for the rule of law, or the devotion of citizens to their polis—and, in the light of the larger end which it is adapted to serve, make it over into a form fitted for his model city. Outright invention plays almost no part at all in his work.[20]

The secret of collective and cumulative wisdom also underlies the Nocturnal Council. Because the composition and function of this Council are discussed well after the completion of legislation for Magnesia, some scholars have thought that it does not belong to the *Laws*, or even claimed that it was added on later by one of his editors. When the Athenian Stranger introduces this controversial institution, he describes its function as the preservation of the laws he has constructed for Magnesia (960bc). But its function is not only to preserve but also to improve upon the laws. For this purpose, the members of the Nocturnal Council will meet regularly to study their laws, by considering how well they serve their original purpose and function. The Council will also consult the citizens who have gone abroad and observed the laws of other states, and enlist the assistance of its junior members who function as the eyes and ears on the domestic affairs (961a, 965a). It is a permanent institute of research and inquiry for correcting the deficiencies of the laws and adjusting them to new situations.[21]

For Plato, the process of cumulative and collective wisdom is not anything unique for Magnesia. The same process produces most positive laws. But the cumulative and collective wisdom is derived from our shared experience, which presupposes our intuition of transcendent standards and principles. Hence transcendent intuitions are the necessary preconditions for all normative constructions and instructions. So we have to revise our earlier statement that the entire universe of discourse is divided into two opposing camps, Platonism and positivism. Platonic Forms are required for both camps, although only one of them recognizes it. Thus, normative positivism turns out to be only one special form of Platonism, and its specialty lies in its failure to see its own Platonic origin. Platonism is truly universal because Platonic Forms are the a priori conditions for all normative discourse and experience. Let us label this position as Platonic universalism.

From the perspective of Platonic universalism, no positive law can be exempt from the continuous process of critical review. Even our nation's supreme law, the Constitution, is no exception; it has to be critically reviewed in terms of our transcendent intuitions. This Platonic view of justification is the best way to appreciate the unique institution of judicial review in American politics. On what grounds do the nine justices of the Supreme Court have the right to overturn the majority decisions of Congress? This is the notorious problem of countermajoritarianism for judicial review, and it is an insoluble one on the supposition that majoritarian rule is always self-justifying. The Platonists cannot accept this supposition; for them, nothing is self-justifying except the Form of Justice. Majoritarian rule, like any other rule, can do injustice. If judicial review can be a practically effective constraint on the misbehavior of majoritarian rule, it can be justified on Platonic grounds.

Platonic universalism may bring some unexpected embarrassment for the Platonists; even bad normative systems such as Nazism should now be seen as different articulations and realizations of the same Platonic Forms. Indeed, this is the most serious problem for the bedrock version of Platonism. Given the fact that Platonic Forms are highly indeterminate, it is obvious that they can be articulated and realized in many different ways. From this we may have to conclude that all positive norms are just, but this conclusion is not Platonic but Neoplatonic. The basic difference between Platonism and Neoplatonism lies in the role of transcendent Forms. For the Neoplatonists, the One is the ultimate source and author; everything emanates from it. Hence, everything is justified. As Hegel says, whatever is real is rational; whatever is rational is real.[22] Even Hitler's Germany or Stalin's Russia is no exception to this Hegelian rule.

For Platonism, the transcendent Forms are indeed the source of all our positive norms, but they are not their authors. For example, the mathematical Forms are the sources for mathematical construction, but they are not its authors. It is not the Forms but human beings who construct mathematical models. But the fact that the mathematical Forms are the ultimate source for the construction of all mathematical models does not guarantee that all of them are equally good or that all of them are free of errors. We can compare different mathematical models and rank them, because all of them are based on the same transcendent mathematical intuitions. Our transcendent intuitions link the constructed mathematical models to the mathematical Forms. Without this common reference and measure, every mathematical system would be a self-contained formal system, which could not be meaningfully compared with any other system.

Platonic Forms play the same role for construction in music and poetry. The different musical styles are defined by their positive norms. Baroque music is different from the music of classicism, because they are governed by two different sets of positive norms. These two styles of music are again different from the Romantic music, because its positive norms are again different from theirs. All these positive norms are constructed from the common basic musical intuition that transcends all musical styles. From this it does not follow that they are equally good in the same respect, although it may be impossible to make a determinate ranking of these positive musical norms. Some positive norms can do violence to our transcendent musical intuition, just as some political and legal systems can do violence to our transcendent sense of justice. Such has been the case with many styles of avant-garde music (not to be confused with the new age music), and they have gone the way of oblivion.

Likewise, from the fact that Platonic Forms are the ultimate source for the construction of all positive normative systems, it does not follow that all of them are equally just or that none of them contains injustice. Some of them may be faithful to Platonic Forms; others may distort or degrade them for the promotion and protection of private interests. Unlike normative positivism, Platonism can provide the transcendent perspective for comparing different positive normative systems and for assessing their merit and demerit. The transcendent perspective can give us the objective distinction between the good and the bad realizations of Platonic Forms. Without this distinction, we would inevitably succumb to normative relativism and positivism. But Platonic Forms provide the universal perspective to contain relativism and positivism.

This universal perspective is crucial for understanding the importance of ethical and cultural pluralism. During the past few years, though relativism has been driven out of fashion, it has been replaced by the new vogue of pluralism. What is the difference between relativism and pluralism? Why is pluralism a respectable position, whereas relativism is a disgraceful one? Though these difficult questions have called forth many different responses from the pluralists, the plausible ones appeal to some universal or transcendent values and principles. For example, John Kekes appeals to the primary values, which are accepted by all reasonable human beings as the essential requirements for the realization of a good life. These values are context independent; they are the transcendent values that transcend all cultural contexts.[23] Though the primary values are universal, they can be realized in many different forms. This is the crux of his moral and cultural pluralism.

Likewise, Amy Gutmann recognizes normative universalism as the only way to avoid the evil of cultural and political relativism.[24] She proposes the distinction between comprehensive universalism and deliberative universalism. The former is the claim that there is a set of universal principles of justice that equally apply to all political communities, in spite of their cultural and geographical differences. These universal principles can dictate all political decisions at any stage of human history. Since the existence of such universal principles is highly unlikely, Gutmann favors deliberative universalism, which consists of (1) a set of substantive principles of justice that are unreasonable to reject or necessary for deliberation, and (2) a set of procedural principles that can support actual deliberation about fundamental moral conflicts.[25]

The important feature of deliberative universalism is its requirement of deliberation. Why is the procedure of deliberation required for it, but not for comprehensive universalism? In fact, most people would subscribe to the Aristotelian view that the application of any general principle requires some deliberation. Evidently, the deliberation required for deliberative universalism is different from the deliberation of application. So let us distinguish between the deliberation of application and the deliberation of construction. Unlike the deliberation of application, the deliberation of construction is not required for the application of general principles, but for their articulation and specification. In that case, the two different forms of universalism operate with two different kinds of general principles. Whereas the substantive principles of comprehensive universalism are determinate enough for their direct application to the practical world, the principles of deliberative universalism are so indeterminate that they have to be translated and articulated into a set of determinate norms and rules.

These two kinds of universal principles correspond to the two versions of Platonism, whose difference was explicated in chapter 7. In the skyscraper version, the Forms were conceived as concrete and determinate paradigms that can be directly applied to the world of phenomena. In the bedrock version, this doctrine of paradigmatic Forms was revised; they are now understood to be too abstract and too indeterminate for such a direct application. They can only provide the normative basis for constructing the positive norms and rules. The bedrock version of Platonism consists of two phases: the recognition of transcendent principles and their articulation into positive norms. These two phases are remarkably similar to the two phases of Amy Gutmann's deliberative universalism. But she does not locate her universal principles in Platonic Heaven; she characterizes them as those principles that are unreasonable to reject. What is unreasonable to reject or reasonable to accept? What is the criterion of rational acceptance and rejection? Thus Gutmann's version of universalism hinges on the notion of rational choice.

Elsewhere I showed how slippery the notion of rational choice is, because the same word *rationality* has been used for referring to three different conceptions: formal rationality, instrumental rationality, and ideal rationality.[26] Let us use these three conceptions to decide what sort of universal principles should be accepted for Amy Gutmann's deliberative universalism. The concept of formal rationality only requires formal consistency in the acceptance of universal principles. This formal requirement makes no significant difference for the choice of substantive principles, because it is the minimum requirement for any set of substantive principles. The concept of instrumental rationality means that the choice of all substantive principles only serves the instrumental function of fulfilling some given ultimate end. But what should be our ultimate end? Since this question cannot be settled by the instrumental reason, we have to appeal to the notion of ideal rationality.

The notion of ideal rationality is to make rational choices in terms of the ideals that we already intuitively accept, because they are inevitably in our transcendent normative intuitions. The concept of justice is one such intuitive ideal. Without presupposing such intuitive normative ideals, there is nothing reasonable to accept or unreasonable to reject except for instrumental reasons. The notion of ideal rationality is embedded in our intuitive normative consciousness. We cannot reject the concept of justice, not because it serves some instrumental function, but because we cannot preserve our normative rationality without accepting it. Just imagine someone telling us that she wants to be normatively rational, but at the same time that she totally disregards all the questions of justice. We would have to say that such a person is irrational or simply mad. The transcendent normative ideals constitute our normative rationality, which in turn provides the normative basis for the construction of all the different human cultures. This is the Platonic account of universalism and pluralism; it alone can clearly distinguish pluralism from relativism. It is really Plato's philosophy of culture.[27]

Notes

1. The two terms, *transcendent* and *transcendental*, should not be confused. *Transcendent* is a Platonic term, which means transcending the world of phenomena; *transcendental* is a Kantian term, which means being a necessary condition for something.

2. Wittgenstein, *Philosophical Investigations* (New York: Macmillan, 1953); Hart, *The Concept of Law* (Oxford: University Press, 1961).

3. Rawls, *A Theory of Justice* (Cambridge, Mass.: Harvard University Press, 1971), 48–51; Dworkin, *Law's Empire* (Cambridge, Mass.: Harvard University Press, 1986), 176–275. My extended discussion of Rawls's theory of reflective equilibrium is in my *Intuition and Construction* (New Haven, Conn.: Yale University Press, 1993), 46–70.

4. For further discussion of this point, see my *Intuition and Construction*, 144–74; *Kant's Platonic Revolution in Moral and Political Philosophy* (Baltimore, Md.: Johns Hopkins University Press), 95–129.

5. Rawls, "Kantian Constructivism in Moral Theory: The Dewey Lectures 1980," *Journal of Philosophy*, 77 (1980):515–72.

6. This point is explained in my *Intuition and Construction*, 63–70.

7. Habermas, *Moral Consciousness and Communicative Action*, trans. Christian Lenhardt and Shierry Nicholson (Cambridge, Mass.: MIT Press, 1991), 43–115.

8. For further discussion of this point, see my *Kant's Platonic Revolution*, 224–29.

9. This point is fully discussed by James Fishkin in his *Tyranny and Legitimacy* (Baltimore: Johns Hopkins University Press, 1979), 68–69.

10. Habermas, *Knowledge and Human Interests*, trans. Jeremy Shapiro (Boston: Beacon Press, 1971), 91–92.

11. Charles Stevenson, *Ethics and Language* (New Haven, Conn.: Yale University Press, 1944).

12. Stephen Darwall, Allan Gibbard, and Peter Railton, "Toward *Fin de siecle* Ethics: Some Trends," *Philosophical Review* 101 (1992):115, 187.

13. Chomsky, *Cartesian Linguistics* (New York: Harper and Row, 1966).

14. These views are expressed by Charles Taylor, *Hegel and Modern Society* (Cambridge: University Press, 1979); Alasdair MacIntyre, *After Virtue* (Notre

Dame: University Press, 1981); Michael Sandel, *Liberalism and the Limits of Justice* (Cambridge, Mass.: Harvard University Press, 1982).

15. Taylor, *Hegel and Modern Society*, 157–59.

16. A recent survey of these attempts is given by Robert Wright, *The Moral Animal* (New York: Random House, 1994), and James Wilson, *The Moral Sense* (New York: Free Press, 1993).

17. *Moral Sense*, 191.

18. *Moral Sense*, 200–207.

19. *Moral Animal*, 337.

20. Morrow, *Plato's Cretan City* (Princeton, N.J.: Princeton University Press, 1960), 591.

21. This point is stressed by Morrow, who compares the Nocturnal Council to Plato's Academy. *Plato's Cretan City*, 509.

22. For further discussion of this point, see my *Kant's Platonic Revolution*, 200–217.

23. John Kekes, *The Morality of Pluralism* (Princeton, N.J.: Princeton University Press, 1993), 17–37.

24. Amy Gutmann, "The Challenge of Multiculturalism in Political Ethics," *Philosophy and Public Affairs* 22 (1993), 171–206.

25. "The Challenge of Multiculturalism," 200.

26. *Intuition and Construction*, 1–118.

27. A Platonic view of culture is fully spelled out in Kant's philosophy of history. For details, see my *Kant's Platonic Revolution*, 79–94.

Index

Cornford, F. M., 129, 165–66, 215n1, 216n14, 216n15, 246n9
courage, 19–21, 46, 83, 96, 241, 260
Cratylus, the, 132–41, 146, 152, 181, 222, 249, 312
Critias, the, 250, 268–70, 272, 286
culture. *see* convention

Dancy, R. M., 162
Darwin, Charles, 310–11
definition, 17–19, 70, 86, 175–76, 219–23, 306–7
Demiurge, 236–40, 268, 270
Derrida, Jacques, 139, 291–92
desire, 37, 264
dialectic, 64, 110, 121–23, 140, 202–7. *see also* the method of collection and division
difference, 146, 152–60, 176, 178, 180–81, 192, 236
Diogenes Laertius, 290n20, 290n24, 290n28
Dionysus, 60, 66, 128
Diotima, 57, 72, 105
Dorter, Kenneth, 51–52
Dover, K. J., 33n23

education, 75–87, 91, 96–97, 254, 266, 275, 307
elenchus, 26–27, 174
emotivism, 299
equality, 235, 254–55, 296
ethics, 73, 94, 250–51
Euthydemus, the, x–xi, 84, 91–94, 97–98, 110, 126, 247
Euthyphro, the, 7–11, 14–19, 26, 71

Ferrari, G. R. F., 132
Fine, Gail, 148–51
Fishkin, James, 319n9
Fogelman, Brian, 182n11
Forms, xi–xii, 44, 47, 49–50, 70–73, 88, 104, 113–16, 119–25, 180, 185–214, 217–23, 231–32, 237,

242–43, 249–50, 274, 283, 288, 306, 311, 315–16
Fowler, D. H., 182n20
Frame, Douglas, 107n9
Frede, Dorothea, 246n4, 290n26
Friedlander, Paul, 84
friendship, 31–32, 35–42, 99–106, 111–16, 248, 253–55, 265–66, 268, 288

geometry, 117–19
Gettier paradox, 156–58
god, 240, 274
good, the, 37–38, 104–5, 122–23, 221, 260, 266
Gorgias, 29, 56, 61, 74, 86
Gorgias, the, x–xi, xv, 1–7, 26, 28–32, 50, 53, 64–65, 90–91, 95, 99, 104, 106, 110, 121, 247–48, 264–68, 271–72, 274, 280
Gosling, J. C. B., 246n3
government, forms of, 97, 256–57
greed, xvi, 6, 28, 30, 41, 53, 100
Green, Peter, 12, 33n19–22
Griswold, Charles, 124, 129, 244
Grote, George, 122
Grube, G. M. A., 289n4
Guimaraes, Livia, 290n21–23
Guthrie, W. K. C., 33n27, 67n12, 142n3, 142 note 16, 183n25, 246n6
Gutmann, Amy, 316–18

Habermas, J., 296–98
Hackforth, R., 67n13, 142n11, 246n4
happiness, 97, 274
harmonics, 117–19
hedonism, 83. *see also* pleasure *and* pain
Heraclitus (or Heraliteans), 211–12, 260, 277, 281
history, 62–66, 264–75
Hobbes, 101, 295–96, 302
Houston, Jean, 107n4, 107n10
Howland, Jacob, 98, 107n12, 107n13

About the Author

T. K. Seung was born in North Korea in 1930 and escaped to South Korea in 1947. In 1950, when the Korean War broke out, he was a freshman at Yonsei University in Seoul. He joined the ROK Army and spent the next three years in the combat zone. After the Korean War, he came to Yale and studied philosophy and law. He is now teaching at the University of Texas at Austin, where he is the Jesse H. Jones Regents Professor in Liberal Arts, Professor of Philosophy, Professor of Government, and Professor of Law.

He is the author of *The Fragile Leaves of the Sibyl: Dante's Master Plan* (1962), *Kant's Transcendental Logic* (1969), *Cultural Thematics: The Formation of the Faustian Ethos* (1976), *Structuralism and Hermeneutics* (1982), *Semiotics and Thematics* (1982), *Intuition and Construction: The Foundation of Normative Theory* (1993), and *Kant's Platonic Revolution in Moral and Political Philosophy* (1994).

In the last two of these publications, he has been trying to revive Platonism as the foundation of normative theory, and the present volume is a part of this continuing endeavor. In this volume, he employs a special technique of interpretation that he developed in his *Cultural Thematics* and *Semiotics and Thematics*. This is the method of thematic dialectic. By using this method, he explicates the thematic structure and progression of the entire Platonic corpus.